Kantian Nonconceptualism

Dennis Schulting
Editor

Kantian
Nonconceptualism

palgrave
macmillan

Editor
Dennis Schulting

ISBN 978-1-349-71022-5   ISBN 978-1-137-53517-7   (eBook)
DOI 10.1057/978-1-137-53517-7

Library of Congress Control Number: 2016950068

© The Editor(s) (if applicable) and The Author(s) 2016
Softcover reprint of the hardcover 1st edition 2016 978-1-137-53516-0

The author(s) has/have asserted their right(s) to be identified as the author(s) of this work in accordance with the Copyright, Designs and Patents Act 1988.
This work is subject to copyright. All rights are solely and exclusively licensed by the Publisher, whether the whole or part of the material is concerned, specifically the rights of translation, reprinting, reuse of illustrations, recitation, broadcasting, reproduction on microfilms or in any other physical way, and transmission or information storage and retrieval, electronic adaptation, computer software, or by similar or dissimilar methodology now known or hereafter developed.
The use of general descriptive names, registered names, trademarks, service marks, etc. in this publication does not imply, even in the absence of a specific statement, that such names are exempt from the relevant protective laws and regulations and therefore free for general use.
The publisher, the authors and the editors are safe to assume that the advice and information in this book are believed to be true and accurate at the date of publication. Neither the publisher nor the authors or the editors give a warranty, express or implied, with respect to the material contained herein or for any errors or omissions that may have been made.

Cover image © Interior of the Sint-Odulphuskerk in Assendelft, Pieter Jansz. Saenredam, 1649, reproduced by permission of the Rijksmuseum, Amsterdam

Printed on acid-free paper

This Palgrave Macmillan imprint is published by Springer Nature
The registered company is Macmillan Publishers Ltd. London

Introduction

One of the most frequently quoted statements from Immanuel Kant's *Critique of Pure Reason* is that "thoughts without content are empty, [and] intuitions without concepts are blind" (A51/B75). Ever since John McDowell's seminal book based on his Locke lectures, *Mind and World*, first published in 1994, this dictum, which can be taken as exemplifying the salient point of Kant's epistemological argument in the *Critique*, has been associated with a general Kantian approach to solving issues in the theory of knowledge that concern the justification of our beliefs about the world and the possibility of perceptual knowledge. In particular, McDowell referred to it as an apt metaphor for seeing a solution to bridging any supposed gap between our mental states or beliefs and the world of sensible objects to which our beliefs must be answerable. The intertwinement of sense content (Kant's "intuition") and conceptuality, of which this dictum appears to speak, gives us a sense of how objects constrain our judgements, thoughts and beliefs about them, without resorting to explanations that either succumb to the Myth of the Given or rest content with a form of coherentism.

McDowell interprets Kant's notion of "intuition" as an "experiential intake", which is not "a bare getting of an extra-conceptual Given, but ... a kind of occurrence or state *that already has conceptual content*" (emphasis added). What McDowell means by this is that an intuition

v

has representational *content* if (and only if) it expresses a relation to a mind-independent object, for which it must already show the *capacity* to judge that "*things are thus and so*" (McDowell 1996:9). Thus, "representational content cannot be dualistically set over against the conceptual" (1996:3); rather, the representational content of an intuition—that is, the content of a genuine experience, not just a sensation—and the conceptual are inextricably integrated. The content of the experience is that things are thus and so, and "it becomes the content of a judgment if the subject decides to take the experience at face value", to judge *that* things are thus and so. There is no discrepancy between the fact that things are thus and so and the judgement that they are thus and so (McDowell 1996:26). It means that the content in one's taking something to be the case, in an intuition, is amenable to rational assessment for the correctness or truth of one's experiential intake; our thinking must be answerable to the world, and at the same time empirical justifications for our beliefs cannot just consist in "impingements on the conceptual realm from outside" (1996:6). This, for McDowell, makes the representational content of an intuition already conceptual: intuitions, or sensible intakes of how the world is, are thus to be located *inside* what Wilfrid Sellars called the "space of reasons", so that they provide genuine justifications for our beliefs about objects to which they are, in a sense, *rationally* linked, rather than merely causally—a merely causal impact from objects would merely, as McDowell puts it, "operat[e] outside the control of our spontaneity" (1996:8). McDowell thinks—and this shows the truly Kantian spirit of his account—that the spontaneity of our thought must somehow *internally* be seen to be linked to our empirical experiences, as already operative in the deliverances of sensibility, for experiences to provide genuine justifications of our beliefs. Receptivity of sense content and spontaneity of thinking cooperate at the most fundamental level, already in sensibility, such that the "relevant conceptual capacities are drawn on *in* receptivity" (1996:9). Whereas this "expansive" spontaneity, which is not limited to the activity of thinking, is thus "subject to control from outside our thinking" (1996:11), at the same time the conceptual capacities that are operative in sensibility must be seen as *intimately* linked with the active exercise of the same capacities in judgements. In short: "thoughts and intuitions are rationally connected" (1996:17–18). For McDowell, it is thus that Kant teaches us that "the understanding is already inextricably implicated in the deliverances of sensibility themselves" (1996:46).

McDowell originally specifically positioned his explicitly conceptualist reading of Kant's dictum against Gareth Evans's (1982:227) idea of nonconceptual informational states, which Evans believed are located precisely "outside the sphere of the conceptual" (McDowell 1996:56). Evans argued that perceptual content must thus be considered nonconceptual:

> The informational states which a subject acquires through perception are *non-conceptual*, or *non-conceptualized*. Judgements *based upon* such states necessarily involve conceptualization: in moving from a perceptual experience to a judgement about the world (usually expressible in some verbal form), one will be exercising basic conceptual skills. But this formulation (in terms of moving from an experience to a judgement) must not be allowed to obscure the general picture. Although the subject's judgements are *based upon* his experiences (i.e. upon the unconceptualized information available to him), his judgements are not *about* the informational state. The process of conceptualization or judgement takes the subject from his being in one kind of informational state (with a content of a certain kind, namely, non-conceptual content) to his being in another kind of cognitive state (with a content of a different kind, namely, conceptual content). (Evans 1982:227)

As McDowell notes, for Evans perceptual experiences that are states through which the subject of experience gathers "information" about the world have content that is nonconceptual, and which is distinct from the content of a judgement when "conceptual capacities are first brought into operation" (1996:48). This point about perceptual experience is a salient issue in the current debate on nonconceptual content, also in the Kantian variant of this debate, which was instigated by an influential article published by Robert Hanna in 2005 (Hanna 2005). It is important to note that for Evans—and McDowell (1996:48–9) makes a point of this—it is not the case that perceptual informational states are *ipso facto experiences* (Evans 1982:157). For Evans, such states only count as "conscious perceptual experience" if its nonconceptual content also "serves as the input to a *thinking, concept-applying, and reasoning system*" (1982:158). The difference between Evans and McDowell is that whereas Evans sees experiences indeed as a rational basis for judgements, he sees those experiences

viii   Introduction

as outside the domain of the conceptual, where McDowell locates them explicitly inside it. It remains to be seen therefore to what extent the strong nonconceptualism endorsed by the likes of Hanna, who argue that it must be possible to have perceptual *experiences*, of some sort, that are not dependent on thought and do not necessarily form a basis for judgement, can be seen as of similar lineage as Evans's nonconceptualism. It seems that Evans's notion of "experience" is much closer to Kant's, who links experience strictly to an empirical cognition (B147), which thus involves, at least potentially, the capacities of the understanding and judgement. Hanna, by contrast, argues that

> Nonconceptualism holds that nonconceptual content exists and is *representationally significant* (i.e., *meaningful in the "semantic" sense of describing or referring to states-of-affairs, properties, or individuals of some sort*);

and at the same time

> (a) that there are cognitive capacities which *are not determined* (or at least not *fully* determined) *by conceptual capacities*, and (b) that the cognitive capacities which outstrip conceptual capacities can be possessed by rational and non-rational animals alike, whether human or non-human. (Hanna 2005:248; emphasis added)

Hanna asserts that contemporary nonconceptualism (e.g. Heck 2000; Speaks 2005; see the further references in Hanna 2005:248)[1] can be directly traced back to Evans, but it seems that what is emphasised in the above quotation from Hanna, namely that nonconceptual content is "representationally significant" in the sense of "describing or referring to states-of-affairs, properties, or individuals of some sort", might be taken as involving what Evans rather refers to as the "thinking, concept-applying, and reasoning system", or at least the necessary availability of such a system for perceptual states to become experiences that refer to objects. And as McDowell has said, the "very idea of representational content brings with it a notion of correctness and incorrectness: something with a certain content

---

[1] For an excellent discussion of contemporary nonconceptualism, see Brewer (2005) and Byrne (2005).

Introduction **ix**

is correct, in the relevant sense, just in case things are as it represents them to be" (1996:162), which McDowell at any rate sees as grounds for endorsing a view of conceptuality already thoroughly implicated in sensibility. Evans does not endorse the idea of conceptual capacities being endogenous to perceptual experiences, but at least he sees informational states as experiences only when they serve as input to thoughts and judgements. Hanna's nonconceptualism seems much stronger in its emphasis on nonconceptual content as completely independent of capacities that link it to thought.

Whatever the case may be as to Evans's position in relation to contemporary forms of nonconceptualism, it seems clear that McDowell's appeal to Kant as a chief ally of conceptualism that goes "all the way out to the impressions of sensibility themselves" (1996:69) should not be taken at face value. Hanna has made it at any rate clear in the aforementioned article, and in a series of follow-up papers (Hanna 2008, 2011a, b, 2013a, b),[2] that Kant can certainly be read as a nonconceptualist. Hanna has provided reasonable grounds for believing that, at the very least, Kant may *also* be regarded as a founder of nonconceptualism. Kant is of course manifestly a conceptualist insofar as the possibility of empirical cognition is concerned—in order for us to have objectively valid (read: cognitively significant) representations or experience of spatiotemporal objects, we need to presuppose a priori concepts, categories, which cannot be derived from empirical experience. These categories first secure a relation to an object, and in fact first enable us, by means of an a priori act of synthesis of representations, to conceive of what an object is. Apart from the categories, we do not have the means to secure a relation to an object. Any sensible content, "intuition" (*Anschauung*) in Kant's terminology, must be brought under the categories for it to be cognitively significant. Thus, representations that are not brought under the categories, and so are not "conceptualised", have no cognitive relevance, they are "less than a dream", as one prominent conceptualist in the post-Kantian tradition, Robert Pippin, says, referring to a well-known phrase of Kant's in the Transcendental Deduction of the categories (henceforth TD).[3]

---

[2] See also Hanna (2006, 2015).

[3] See Pippin (2015b:71). The passage in TD is at A112. Pippin's reading is discussed critically in Chap. 10 in this volume.

x   Introduction

But, while not denying that Kant is a conceptualist about the possibility of knowledge, Hanna has shown that such a picture of Kant the conceptualist as portrayed above downplays the clearly nonconceptualist tendencies in the theory of knowledge that Kant advances in the *Critique*, which can be supported by arguments from other parts of Kant's corpus. Some of the very central planks of Kant's Critical philosophy show these nonconceptualist tendencies. In stark contrast to the rationalist philosophers, who saw sensory perception as just a confused presentation of what conceptual thought or reasoning represents clearly and regarded the difference between sensibility and conceptual thinking as merely one of degree in terms of more or less conceptual distinctness, Kant fundamentally differentiates between a sensible uptake of the world, by means of what he calls "intuition", and category-governed acts of conceptualisation, which need to be based on intuitions. Kant speaks of the "two stems of human cognition" (A15/B29), which must not be confused (A50–1/B75–6) and have their distinctive roles to play in establishing cognition: in sensibility we are directly acquainted with objects by means of intuitions, whereas the understanding coordinates and subsumes already given representations under concepts. Intuition is the term that indicates the *immediate* and *singular* relation to an object and the way that an object is directly *given* to us (A19–20/B33–4; A320/B377; cf. A239/B298), in contrast to a concept, which is a *mediate* way of relating to the object, namely, mediately by way of an intuition (A19/B30; A68/B93), and first gives universality and determinacy to our relation to objects. Each thus has a distinctive and distinct role in the formation of knowledge of objects. Moreover, Kant holds that intuition and concept each have a pure form. Space and time are the necessary irreducible forms of sensibility, of any empirical intuition, the so-called "forms of intuition"; as Kant explicates in the Transcendental Aesthetic (TAe), they are pure and a priori, but they are specifically not concepts. By contrast, what, following Aristotle, Kant calls "categories" are a priori pure concepts which must be applied to given intuitions in order for conceptual cognition to arise; the categories first enable the *determinate* relation to a given object (B137).

The Kantian nonconceptualist emphasises that notwithstanding their necessary cooperation so as to enable empirical knowledge, first, sensibility and the understanding have *separate* roles to play (A50–1/B75–6), second, intuitions are *given* prior to thinking (B132) and, third, intuitions do not need the categories or the functions of understanding, acts of a priori synthesis, to *be* intuitions. The nonconceptualist often points out that Kant emphatically says that in case they were not found to be in accord with the categories, "appearances would nonetheless offer objects to our intuition, *for intuition by no means requires the functions of thinking*" (A90–1/B123; emphasis added).[4] The salient point in the debate on Kantian nonconceptualism is whether it is at all required that the functions of the understanding are applied to intuitions for the latter to be representationally significant, where of course a lot depends on how one interprets "representationally significant", which greatly influences one's position in the debate. Kantian nonconceptualists, or at least those who endorse what has been called *relative* nonconceptualism (Speaks 2005), do not deny that intuitions and categories are conjoined in the case of knowledge (Allais 2009:386); nonconceptualists are conceptualists about the possibility of *knowledge*, but not about the possibility of intuitions. For what they do deny is that even to *have* intuitions requires the categories or acts of a priori synthesis, a view that is often held by those who see Kant as, broadly speaking, a conceptualist about knowledge. Kantian conceptualists argue that, if not the categories as such, at least the synthesis of the imagination (or the threefold synthesis in the A-Deduction) is required to *generate* intuitions—though it is difficult to see how one can prise apart the categories and the acts of synthesis and not run into regress problems (see Schulting 2010/2012, 2015b).

There are various systematic reasons for denying that even to *have* intuitions requires the categories, or at least the a priori synthesis of the imagination. Prime among them are the arguments that Kant provides in TAe (and, *mutatis mutandis*, already earlier in his pre-Critical works, which first advance his new theory of space, such as *Directions in Space* and the "Inaugural Dissertation"), which would appear to indicate that the nature of space and time, the pure forms of intuition, is such that their characterising features are incompatible with holding the view that space and time themselves are in any way products of the synthesis of the imagination,

---

[4] For detailed discussion of the problems surrounding the interpretation of this passage, see Schulting (2015b).

Introduction

let alone the concepts of the understanding. Often it is held, by Kantian conceptualists, that the understanding, at least by virtue of the imagination, is responsible for the *unity* of space and time, and that as such the understanding, at least by virtue of the synthesis of the imagination, *generates* space and time itself. But Onof and Schulting (2015) have shown that the *sui generis* unity of space (and analogously that of time, though they do not argue for it), as delineated in TAe, is irreducible to the unity that is bestowed on it by the understanding by means of the synthesis of the imagination.[5] The synthesis of the imagination, or indeed the understanding, can thus not be regarded as that which is responsible for the *sui generis* unity of space (and time), even though it is true of course to say that they are responsible for the *determinate* unity of space (and time).

However, in response to the nonconceptualists, those Kantians who see Kant as a conceptualist have argued that to read his chief argument nonconceptualistically contradicts the primary goal of TD, namely to argue that *all* intuitions must be regarded as subject to the categories in order to refute the sceptic in showing that pure concepts are indeed objectively valid and necessarily applicable to our experience as well as the objects of our experience. There are many controversial issues involved with this claim, and it is not certain if the conceptualist has a point here, but it does seem problematic for the nonconceptualists to explain how essentially or even relatively nonconceptual representation by virtue of intuition is in fact a priori connected to conceptual content in cases of actual empirical knowledge expressible in actual judgements. Some of the problems facing Kantian nonconceptualists as well as conceptualists in view of the aims of TD are discussed in Schulting (2015b).[6]

The debate on Kantian nonconceptualism has meanwhile, in a very short period of time, become fairly sophisticated and factorised, and so cannot in fact be seen as simply a debate between "the nonconceptualists" and "the conceptualists". Among the nonconceptualists, there are those that espouse a *strong* nonconceptualism, which seems incompatible with Kant's conceptualist aims (as indeed Hanna acknowledges), and those

---

[5] See also McLear (2015) and, by contrast, Land (2014a) and Messina (2014).

[6] See also my account in Schulting (2010), which was translated from the Dutch and published in amended form as Schulting (2012b), and which forms the basis of Schulting (2017), Chap. 5.

that espouse a *relative* nonconceptualism, which is compatible with Kant's conceptualism about the possibility of knowledge (e.g. Allais), whereas the standard distinction in the philosophy of mind between state and content nonconceptualism appears to play a less significant role in the debate on Kant's nonconceptualism. Among the conceptualists, there are those that argue, or at least seem to argue, that there is no distinction between intuitional and conceptual contents, so that intuitional content must be regarded as thoroughly conceptually laden, although that does not mean that we must always explicitly formulate *judgements* to have experience; and there are those that argue that, if not the categories per se, then at least the synthesis of the imagination is required in order to *have* intuitions, or at least in order for intuition first to be a *unified* manifold of representations. And there are those that could be called "obscurist-conceptualists", who hold that categories are required in an "obscure" way (in the technical rationalist sense of the word) for the generation of intuitions (cf. Grüne 2009). These are all very complicated matters that obviously cannot be dealt with here in an introduction.

The publication of Hanna's first article on Kantian nonconceptualism in 2005, and Christian Wenzel's in the same year (Wenzel 2005), but especially Lucy Allais's paper from 2009, catalysed a veritable deluge of articles (and a handful of books) from both the nonconceptualist and conceptualist camps among Kant scholars. Let me list the ones that are directly connected with the debate that has been taking place in Kant studies over the last few years: Bauer (2012), Bowman (2011), Connolly (2014), Faggion (2015), Ginsborg (2008), Godlove (2011), Gomes (2014), Griffith (2012), Grüne (2008, 2009, 2011), Heidemann (2013b), Kreis (2015), Land (2011, 2015a), McLear (2014b), Newton (2016), Onof and Schulting (2015), Pereira (2013), Pippin (2013, 2015b), Schlicht (2011), Schulting (2010, 2012b, 2015b), Tolley (2013), Tomaszewska (2014) and Williams (2012).[7] In her contribution to this volume, Allais provides an excellent survey of some of the most important

---

[7] For other papers (and books) directly relevant to the topic of Kantian nonconceptualism, see also Gardner (2013), Haag (2007), Heidemann (2012), La Rocca (2013), McLear (2011), Pippin (1993, 2005, 2015a), Rohs (2001), Schulting (2012c, 2015a), Sedgwick (1993), Stephenson (2015b), Vanzo (2012, 2013) and Watkins (2008, 2012). Heidemann (2013a) collects Bowman (2011), Hanna (2011a, b), Ginsborg (2008), Godlove (2011), Grüne (2011) and Schlicht (2011).

xiv   Introduction

of these papers, while critically engaging with conceptualist construals of Kant's theory of cognition and answering objections to her own nonconceptualist reading. The most important recent monograph published on the topic by Stefanie Grüne (Grüne 2009) is extensively and critically discussed in Land (2014b), McLear (2014a) and Vanzo (2014).[8] A more detailed discussion of the views of the earlier and later McDowell (1996, 1998, 2009) as well as of Hanna and Allais can be found in Schulting (2010, 2012b, 2017). Lastly, Pippin's Hegelian-inspired conceptualist reading of Kant is critically addressed in Chap. 10 of this volume.

Prior, and parallel, to the debate on Kantian nonconceptualism strictly speaking, there has been extensive discussion of the nonconceptuality of intuition specifically in regard to Kant's philosophy of mathematics; besides the aforementioned paper by Onof and Schulting, the work by Carson (1997), Friedman (1992, 2000, 2012), Parsons (1992) and Patton (2011) should be especially mentioned in this regard.[9] In this volume, there are a further four papers by Stefanie Grüne, Robert Hanna, Thomas Land and Clinton Tolley, which expand on this topic from both broadly conceptualist (Grüne and Land) and broadly nonconceptualist (Hanna and Tolley) perspectives; among other things, they particularly deal with the notion of nonconceptuality in relation to the *unity* of space (see Chaps. 4, 5, 7 and 11).

For the present collection of essays, ten papers were especially commissioned from some of the most prominent participants in the debate, and I contributed a paper myself. Undoubtedly, discussions about whether Kant can or should be considered a nonconceptualist, in whatever sense, will continue unabated, but it is hoped that this volume will increase our understanding of Kant's position in the debate on nonconceptualism, and of his own overall views in, among other areas, the theory of knowledge, the philosophy of mathematics, the philosophy of mind and aesthetics. What follows is a brief summary of all the chapters.

---

[8] Cf. Grüne's responses to both Land and McLear (Grüne 2014a, b). For discussion of some of Grüne's views, see also Schulting (2017), Chap. 6, and Onof, Chap. 9 in this volume.
[9] See also the relevant articles by Land (2014a), McLear (2015), Messina (2014) and Onof and Schulting (2014).

As already mentioned, in Chap. 1 Lucy Allais provides a very helpful overview of the current debate on nonconceptualism in Kant scholarship, by drawing on those papers that represent what appear to be central argumentative possibilities. She also responds to certain objections from conceptualists, and in some respects makes concessions to the conceptualist, whilst holding on to her original claim that Kant is committed to a kind of nonconceptualism and that our approach to his central arguments such as in TD is best served by entertaining a nonconceptualist notion of intuition. She emphasises that her modestly nonconceptualist interpretation is entirely compatible with thinking that all intuitions *are* conceptualised, that conceptualisation radically transforms what is given in intuition, and that for what is given in intuition to play a role in cognition intuitions must be conceptualised.

In Chap. 2, Sacha Golob addresses the relation between the argument and goal of TD and nonconceptualism. It appears that one of the strongest motivations for conceptualist readings of Kant is the belief that TD is incompatible with nonconceptualism. But, Golob argues, this belief is simply false: TD and nonconceptualism are compatible both on an exegetical and a philosophical level. Placing particular emphasis on the case of non-human animals, Golob discusses in detail how and why his reading diverges from those of Ginsborg, Allais, Gomes and others. He suggests ultimately that it is only by embracing nonconceptualism that we can fully recognise the delicate calibration of the trap which the *Critique* sets for Hume.

In their essay "On the Relation of Intuition to Cognition", in Chap. 3, Anil Gomes and Andrew Stephenson zero in on how recent debates in the interpretation of Kant's theoretical philosophy have focused on the nature of Kantian intuition and, in particular, on the question of whether intuitions depend for their existence on the existence of their objects. Gomes and Stephenson show how opposing answers to this question determine different accounts of the nature of Kantian *cognition* and suggest that progress can be made on determining the nature of intuition by considering the implications different views have for the nature of cognition. They discuss the relation of cognition to our contemporary conception of knowledge, the role of real possibility and Kant's modal condition on cognition, and the structure and purpose of TD.

In Chap. 4, Stefanie Grüne considers a challenge to the standard interpretation of Kant's conception of the generation of intuitions, which

xvi   Introduction

says that, for intuitions to arise, sensibility and understanding have to cooperate, because sensations only form intuitions, if they are synthesised by the understanding. This challenge has been raised by Colin McLear, for example, who argues that it follows from the Metaphysical Exposition in TAe that intuitions cannot be the result of an intellectual synthesis. In her chapter, Grüne argues that, contrary to McLear's claim, the Metaphysical Exposition is compatible with the assumption that in order for intuitions to be produced sensations have to be synthesised by the understanding.

Robert Hanna aims to demonstrate, in Chap. 5, an essential connection between Kant's nonconceptualism and his transcendental idealism, by tracing this line of thinking in his work directly back to his pre-Critical essay of 1768, *Concerning the Ground of the Ultimate Differentiation of Directions in Space*. Hanna concludes that the most important implication of the central argument in *Directions in Space* is that Kant's nonconceptualism is foundational for any *philosophically defensible* version of his transcendental idealism, namely, transcendental idealism for sensibility.

Dietmar Heidemann takes a wholly novel approach, in Chap. 6, to the topic of Kant and nonconceptualism by looking at his *Critique of the Power of Judgement* for seeking confirmation of his nonconceptualism. Surprisingly, the current debate about Kantian conceptualism and nonconceptualism has completely overlooked the importance of Kant's aesthetics. Heidemann shows how this debate can be significantly advanced by exploring Kant's aesthetics, that is, the theory of judgements of taste and the doctrine of the aesthetic genius, as discussed in the Third *Critique*. The analysis of judgements of taste demonstrates that nonconceptual mental content is a condition of the possibility of aesthetic experience. The subsequent discussion of the doctrine of the aesthetic genius reveals that aesthetic ideas must also be conceived in terms of nonconceptual mental content. Heidemann finally restricts Kant's aesthetic nonconceptualism to the way aesthetic perceivers cognitively evaluate works of art, whereas the doctrine of the genius cannot count as a viable form of aesthetic nonconceptualism.

Thomas Land argues, in Chap. 7, that Kant's theory of spatial representation supports a moderately conceptualist view of his theory of intuition. In making the case for this, Land focus on three aspects of the theory of spatial representation: the distinction Kant draws between the original representation of space and the representations of determinate spaces, the doctrine of the productive imagination, and the doctrine of the a priori determination of sensibility by the understanding. Land explains why these three aspects support a moderately conceptualist view of intuition and considers a number of objections.

In Chap. 8, entitled "Getting Acquainted with Kant", Colin McLear focuses his attention on the central question whether Kant thinks that experience has nonconceptual content, or whether, on his view, experience is essentially conceptual. McLear argues that in a certain sense this question is ill-conceived. He presents an alternative means of framing what is at issue in terms of a debate about the dependence relations, if any, that exist between different cognitive capacities. According to McLear, we should distinguish between Intellectualism, according to which all objective representation (understood in a particular way) depends on acts of synthesis by the intellect, and Sensibilism, according to which at least some forms of objective representation are independent of any such acts (or the capacity for such acts). He also articulates a challenge to Intellectualist interpretations based on the role that Kant indicates alethic modal conditions play in achieving cognition.

By examining relevant texts and considering the systematic coherence of Kant's position, Christian Onof asks, in Chap. 9, whether there is at all a place for nonconceptual content in the Critical philosophy. Starting with representations with conceptual content, Onof successively examines (i) whether there is more to representations whose conceptual content is well established than is captured by means of concepts, and (ii) the possibility of representations with *merely* nonconceptual content. With these questions answered in the affirmative, Onof addresses the issue of the dependence of representations with *merely* nonconceptual content upon those with conceptual content. Onof thereby distances himself from standard nonconceptualist views. He concludes with some broader considerations about the functions of the limited notion of nonconceptual content that his chapter identifies.

In my own contribution, in Chap. 10, I am interested in how, following Hegel's critique of Kant, recent Hegelians have interpreted Kant's claims in TD, in particular. Hegelians such as Robert Pippin think that in TD Kant effectively compromises or wavers on the strict separability of concepts and intuitions he stipulates at A51/B75. For if the argument of TD, in particular in its B version, is that the categories are not only the necessary conditions under which I *think* objects, by virtue of applying concepts, but also the necessary conditions under which *anything is first given in sensibility*, the fixed separation of concepts and intuitions seems incompatible with the very aim and conclusion of TD. I want to examine these charges by looking more closely at Pippin's reading of TD and his more general approach to Kant's strategy. Pippin believes the orthodox Kant cannot be retained, if we want to extract something of philosophical value from TD. He defends a Kantian conceptualism shorn of the remaining nonconceptualist tendencies, which are in his view antithetical to the spirit of Kant's Critical revolution. I believe, however, that we must retain the orthodox Kant, including its nonconceptualist tendencies, in order not to succumb to an intemperate conceptualism.

Finally, in Chap. 11, Clinton Tolley argues, first, for a sharper distinction between three kinds of representation of the space of outer appearances: (i) the original intuition of this space; (ii) the metaphysical representation of this space via the a priori concept "expounded" in TAe; and (iii) the representation of this space in geometry, via the construction of concepts of spaces in intuition. Tolley then shows how more careful attention to this threefold distinction allows for a conservative, consistently nonconceptualist and non-intellectualist, interpretation of the handful of suggestive remarks Kant makes in TD about the dependence of various representations of space on the understanding—against recent interpretations which argue that TD's remarks require that Kant revise the impression given in TAe (and elsewhere) that intuition in general, and the original intuition of space in particular, enjoys a priority to, and independence from, all acts and representations of the understanding.[10]

Dennis Schulting
ds196901@gmail.com

---

[10] I should like to thank Christian Onof and Marcel Quarfood for providing "quality assurance" during the preparation of this volume, and Brendan George for his enthusiasm about the project. I also thank Christian and Marcel for their comments on an earlier version of this introduction.

Contents

1 Conceptualism and Nonconceptualism in Kant: A Survey of the Recent Debate 1
Lucy Allais

2 Why the Transcendental Deduction is Compatible with Nonconceptualism 27
Sacha Golob

3 On the Relation of Intuition to Cognition 53
Anil Gomes and Andrew Stephenson

4 Sensible Synthesis and the Intuition of Space 81
Stefanie Grüne

5 Directions in Space, Nonconceptual Form and the Foundations of Transcendental Idealism 99
Robert Hanna

6 Kant's Aesthetic Nonconceptualism 117
Dietmar H. Heidemann

xix

xx Contents

7 Moderate Conceptualism and Spatial Representation 145
Thomas Land

8 Getting Acquainted with Kant 171
Colin McLear

9 Is There Room for Nonconceptual Content
in Kant's Critical Philosophy? 199
Christian Onof

10 On an Older Dispute: Hegel, Pippin and the Separability
of Concept and Intuition in Kant 227
Dennis Schulting

11 The Difference Between Original, Metaphysical
and Geometrical Representations of Space 257
Clinton Tolley

Bibliography 287

Index 303

Note on the Contributors

Lucy Allais is Professor of Philosophy at the University of Witwatersrand, Johannesburg, and Henry E. Allison Endowed Chair in the History of Philosophy at the University of California, San Diego. Allais specialises in Kant's philosophy and issues in ethics. She has published in, among others, *British Journal for the History of Philosophy*, *Philosophy and Phenomenological Research*, *Journal of Moral Philosophy*, *Journal of the History of Philosophy* and *South African Journal of Philosophy*. She is the author of *Manifest Reality: Kant's Idealism and his Realism* (Oxford University Press, 2015).

Sacha Golob is Lecturer in Philosophy at King's College London, UK. His research focuses on the intersection between Kantian and post-Kantian philosophy and contemporary work on the philosophy of mind, aesthetics and philosophical methodology. As well as publications in *Kantian Review*, *European Journal of Philosophy* and *British Journal for the History of Philosophy*, he is the author of *Heidegger on Concepts, Freedom and Normativity* (Cambridge University Press, 2014) and the editor of the *Cambridge History of Moral Philosophy* (Cambridge University Press, forthcoming).

Anil Gomes is Fellow and Tutor in Philosophy at Trinity College, Oxford and CUF Lecturer (Associate Professor) in Philosophy at the University of Oxford. His main interests are in the philosophy of mind and Kant's theoretical philosophy and, in particular, in issues which arise at their intersection. Gomes has published in journals such as *Kantian Review*, *Kant-Studien*, *British Journal of Aesthetics*, *Dialectica*, *Erkenntnis*, *Inquiry* and *Philosophical Psychology*. Recent

xxii   **Note on the Contributors**

papers include "Kant on Perception: Naïve Realism, Nonconceptualism and the B-Deduction" (*Philosophical Quarterly*, 2014), "On the Particularity of Experience" (*Philosophical Studies*, 2016) and "Naïve Realism in Kantian Phrase" (*Mind*, forthcoming). Together with Andrew Stephenson, he is the editor of the collection of essays *Kant and the Philosophy of Mind* (Oxford University Press, forthcoming).

Stefanie Grüne is Assistant Professor of Philosophy at the University of Potsdam, Germany. She obtained her PhD degree in philosophy from the Humboldt Universität Berlin in 2007 and specialises in Kant, early modern philosophy and philosophy of mind. Grüne is the author of *Blinde Anschauung. Die Rolle von Begriffen in Kants Theorie sinnlicher Synthesis* (Klostermann, 2009), has published in *International Journal of Philosophical Studies, European Journal of Philosophy* and *Hegel-Studien* and has contributed to various edited volumes.

Robert Hanna is an independent philosopher and co-director of *Critique & Contemporary Kantian Philosophy*. He obtained his PhD from Yale University, and he has held research or teaching positions at the University of Cambridge, the University of Colorado at Boulder, the University of Luxembourg, PUC-PR Brazil, Yale University and York University, Canada. He is a philosophical generalist, with a broadly Kantian orientation, and has authored or co-authored six books, the most recent of which is *Cognition, Content, and the A Priori: A Study in the Philosophy of Mind and Knowledge* (Oxford University Press, 2015). He is currently working on a four-book series on the nature of human rationality, entitled *The Rational Human Condition*.

Dietmar H. Heidemann is Professor of Philosophy and Chair of Department at the University of Luxembourg. Heidemann specialises in Kant and German Idealism, epistemology, philosophy of mind and subjectivity, and metaphysics. He has published numerous journal articles and contributions to edited volumes, and is the author of *Kant und das Problem des metaphysischen Idealismus* (de Gruyter, 1998) and *Der Begriff des Skeptizismus. Seine systematischen Formen, die pyrrhonische Skepsis und Hegels Herausforderung* (de Gruyter, 2007). He is also the editor of *Kant and Nonconceptual Content* (Routledge, 2013) and co-editor of *Warum Kant heute? Systematische Bedeutung und Rezeption seiner Philosophie in der Gegenwart* (de Gruyter, 2004). Heidemann is publisher and editor of the *Kant Yearbook* (2009–) and is a member of the board of the Internationale Kant-Gesellschaft.

Note on the Contributors   xxiii

Thomas Land is Assistant Professor of Philosophy at Ryerson University, Toronto. His research focuses on Kant and the development of Kantian ideas in both German idealism and contemporary philosophy of mind and epistemology. Publications include "Kant's Spontaneity Thesis" (*Philosophical Topics*, 2006), "Spatial Representation, Magnitude and the Two Stems of Cognition" (*Canadian Journal of Philosophy*, 2014), "Nonconceptualist Readings of Kant and the Transcendental Deduction" (*Kantian Review*, 2015) and "No Other Use Than in Judgment? Kant on Concepts and Sensible Synthesis" (*Journal of the History of Philosophy*, 2015).

Colin McLear is Assistant Professor in the Philosophy Department at the University of Nebraska–Lincoln. He specialises in early modern philosophy, Kant and the philosophy of mind. Representative publications include "Kant on Animal Consciousness" (*Philosophers' Imprint*, 2011), "Two Kinds of Unity in the *Critique of Pure Reason*" (*Journal of the History of Philosophy*, 2015) and "Kant on Perceptual Content" (*Mind*, 2016).

Christian Onof is Honorary Research Fellow in Philosophy at Birkbeck College, University of London, and Reader at the Faculty of Engineering, Imperial College London. He has published on Kant's ethics and metaphysics, on Heidegger and Sartre, as well as on the nature of consciousness in the *Philosophical Review*, *Kantian Review*, *Kant-Studien*, *Kant Yearbook*, *Philosophy and Phenomenological Research*, and *Journal of Mind & Behavior*, as well as in various edited volumes. He is co-founder of the journal *Episteme*, and a member of the editorial board of *Kant Studies Online*.

Dennis Schulting is a former Assistant Professor of Metaphysics and its History at the University of Amsterdam and obtained his PhD in philosophy from the University of Warwick, UK, in 2004. He specialises in Kant and German idealism, with a focus on issues in philosophy of mind, epistemology, metaphysics and philosophy of religion. He has published in journals such as the *Philosophical Review*, *Kant-Studien*, *Kantian Review*, *Kant Yearbook*, *Studi kantiani*, *Hegel Bulletin*, *Algemeen Nederlands Tijdschrift voor Wijsbegeerte* and *Tijdschrift voor Filosofie*, and has contributed to multiple edited volumes. He is the author of two books on Kant's Transcendental Deduction: *Kant's Deduction and Apperception: Explaining the Categories* (Palgrave Macmillan, 2012) and *Kant's Radical Subjectivism: Perspectives on the Transcendental Deduction* (Palgrave Macmillan, 2017). Schulting is also the editor of *The Bloomsbury Companion to Kant* (2nd edn; Bloomsbury, 2015) and is co-editor, together with Jacco

xxiv Note on the Contributors

Verburgt, of *Kant's Idealism: New Interpretations of a Controversial Doctrine* (Springer, 2011). Current research is focused on Kant's theory of teleology in the Third *Critique* and on his moral theology. Future projects include an introductory book on Hegel's *Science of Logic* and a third monograph on *Original Apperception: Self-Consciousness in Kant and German Idealism.*

Andrew Stephenson is a Leverhulme Visiting Researcher at the Humboldt Universität in Berlin. He obtained his PhD in philosophy from Oxford University. Stephenson works on Kant's theoretical philosophy, in particular his theory of experience and its relation to concerns in contemporary philosophy of mind and epistemology. His recent publications include "Kant, the Paradox of Knowability, and the Meaning of 'Experience'" (*Philosophers' Imprint*, 2015) and "Kant on the Object-Dependence of Intuition and Hallucination" (*Philosophical Quarterly*, 2015). He is also the co-editor, with Anil Gomes, of the collection of essays *Kant and the Philosophy of Mind* (Oxford University Press, forthcoming).

Clinton Tolley is Associate Professor of Philosophy at the University of California, San Diego. He has held Mellon and Ford Fellowships, and received his PhD from the University of Chicago in 2007. His work focuses on the influence of Kant's idealism on later developments in theoretical philosophy in the nineteenth and twentieth centuries, with a special interest in philosophy of logic and mathematics, theories of concepts, and accounts of intentionality. He has published in journals such as *Journal of the History of Philosophy*, *European Journal of Philosophy*, *History of Philosophy of Logic* and *Kantian Review*, and is the co-editor and co-translator (with Sandra Lapointe) of *New Anti-Kant* (Palgrave Macmillan, 2014). Tolley is currently working on a book about Kant's account of the role of appearances in the constitution of experience.

Key to Abbreviations of Cited Primary Works

Throughout this collection of essays the abbreviations listed below are used for reference, followed by the volume and page numbers of the respective volume in the Akademie edition (AA) of Kant's work (*Kant's Gesammelte Schriften*, Berlin: de Gruyter, 1900–), in which the cited work appears. However, for the *Critique of Pure Reason* the standard way of citation by means of reference to the pagination of the A and B edition is adhered to. Works by Hegel are cited, by volume and page numbers, from the critical Akademie edition (GW = *Gesammelte Werke*) of Hegel's works (Hamburg: Meiner, 1968–). Works by Fichte are cited, by volume and page numbers, from the Akademie edition (GA = *Gesamtausgabe*) of Fichte's works (Stuttgart-Bad Canstatt: Frommann-Holzboog, 1962–).

All English language quotations from Kant's works in this book are from *The Cambridge Edition of the Works of Immanuel Kant*, ed. P. Guyer and A. Wood (Cambridge: Cambridge University Press, 1992–), except for *On Kästner's Treatises*, which is cited from the translation by C. Onof and D. Schulting, which appeared in Kant (2014). Translations from Hegel's *Glauben und Wissen* are from G.W.F. Hegel, *Faith & Knowledge*, trans. and ed. W. Cerf and H.S. Harris (Albany, NY: SUNY Press, 1977).

xxvi   **Key to Abbreviations of Cited Primary Works**

A/B	*Critique of Pure Reason*, 1st (1781) and 2nd (1787) edition
Anth	*Anthropology from a Pragmatic Point of View* (AA 7)
BDG	*The Only Possible Argument in Support of a Demonstration of the Existence of God* (AA 2)
Br	*Correspondence* (AA 10–11)
DfS	*The False Subtlety of the Four Syllogistic Figures* (AA 2)
FM	*What Real Progress Has Metaphysics Made in Germany Since the Time of Leibniz and Wolff?* (Prize Essay) (AA 20)
GMS	*Groundwork of Metaphysics of Morals* (AA 4)
GUGR	*Concerning the Ultimate Ground of the Differentiation of Directions in Space* (AA 2)
GuW	G.W.F. Hegel: *Glauben und Wissen* (GW 4)
KpV	*Critique of Practical Reason* (AA 5)
KU	*Critique of the Power of Judgement* (AA 5)
Log	Jäsche Logic (AA 9)
MAN	*Metaphysical Foundations of Natural Science* (AA 4)
MSI	*De mundi sensibilis atque intelligibilis forma et principiis* ("Inaugural Dissertation") (AA 2)
NG	*Attempt to Introduce the Concept of Negative Magnitudes into Philosophy* (AA 2)
NTH	*Universal Natural History and Theory of the Heavens* (AA 1)
OKT	*On Kästner's Treatises* (AA 20)
Prol	*Prolegomena to Any Future Metaphysics* (AA 4)
Refl	*Reflexionen* (AA 14–19)
RGV	*Religion Within the Boundaries of Mere Reason* (AA 6)
ÜE	*On a Discovery Whereby Any New Critique of Pure Reason is to be Made Superfluous by an Older One* (AA 8)
V-Lo/Busolt	Busolt Logic Lectures (AA 24)
V-Lo/Wiener	Vienna Logic Lectures (AA 24)
V-Met-K2/Heinze	Metaphysics Lectures K2 (AA 28)
V-Met-L2/Pölitz	Pölitz Metaphysics Lectures II (AA 28)
V-Met/Mron	Mrongovius Metaphysics Lectures (AA 29)
W	J.G. Fichte: *Versuch einer neuen Darstellung der Wissenschaftslehre* (1797/98) (GA I,4)
WDO	*What Does It Mean to Orient Oneself in Thinking?* (AA 8)
WL	G.W.F. Hegel: *Wissenschaft der Logik. Zweiter Band. Die subjektive Logik* (GW 12)

1

Conceptualism and Nonconceptualism in Kant: A Survey of the Recent Debate

Lucy Allais

1.1 Introduction

As this volume attests, a lively debate has been taking place among Kant interpreters as to whether Kant's position in the First *Critique* and other Critical works contains something like the contemporary notion of non-conceptual mental content. The aim of this chapter is to provide a survey of central moves in this debate. I do not claim to give an exhaustive account, or to refer to every paper on the topic, but rather to draw on papers that represent what seem to me to be central argumentative possibilities. It must be stated up front that I am far from a neutral surveyor of this debate: I have defended attributing a kind of nonconceptualism to Kant in a number of places.[1] And my conclusion in this chapter is still

---

[1] Allais (2009, 2010, 2012, 2015) and Allais (forthcoming a, b).

L. Allais (✉)
Department of Philosophy, Wits University, Gauteng, South Africa

Department of Philosophy, University of California San Diego, San Diego, CA, USA
e-mail: lucy.allais@wits.ac.za

© The Editor(s) (if applicable) and The Author(s) 2016
D. Schulting (ed.), *Kantian Nonconceptualism*,
DOI 10.1057/978-1-137-53517-7_1

both that Kant is committed to a kind of nonconceptualism and that a nonconceptualist reading of intuition must be our starting point in approaching central arguments such as the Transcendental Deduction of the categories (TD). However, conceptualists have put forward important arguments, which have changed my mind about some of the arguments and texts, and have made more precise (and perhaps more modest) exactly what I take Kant's nonconceptualism to be. I suggest that whether Kant is a conceptualist about *perception* (as opposed to intuition) remains unresolved in the literature and requires further clarification of what he means by "perception". Researching for this paper has again reminded me of what I take to be one of the major contributions to come out of this debate: lively dispute and clarification of key terms in Kant's philosophy, such as intuition, sensation, perception, cognition and synthesis. As I argue, the debate about nonconceptualism is crucial for understanding the key question of the role of synthesis in TD. Despite ongoing disagreements, it seems to me that a reasonable amount of helpful common ground has been reached with respect to this.

Two questions one might ask immediately on entering this debate are, first, what is nonconceptual content, and, second, does Kant say anything explicitly about the issue? Answering the first question precisely requires detailed argument, so I shall start by answering it roughly, and then, in Sect. 1.2, shall look at basic textual evidence invoked by both sides of the debate. This will also help clarify how contemporary terminology does (and does not) map onto Kant's terminology. The remainder of the chapter will look at the philosophical grounds for the various positions in the debate.

Most broadly, nonconceptual content is mental content that is independent of concepts. One crucial question here is whether being *independent* of concepts means content that actually is presented to us without any concepts being applied to it, or content that *could* be presented to us independently of whether or not we had the ability to apply concepts. As we shall see, some conceptualists argue that Kant thinks that there is not, in fact, any mental content presented to the consciousness of adult human beings that does not fall under concepts; this, however, does not show that all mental content is essentially conceptualised, since it does not show that there are no representations which *could not* be presented to us independently of conceptualising. I shall argue that debate about

1 A Survey of the Recent Debate 3

the question of whether Kant thinks there are mental representations that we do not in fact conceptualise is inconclusive, but that there are strong grounds for thinking that he holds there to be mental representations which do not depend on conceptualisation to play their role in cognition, and which could be presented to us independently of conceptualisation.

A further question is what is meant by "mental content". In the contemporary debate about nonconceptual content what is at issue is often perceptual content. As we shall see, however, what Kant means by "perception" is disputable and it has been argued that he uses the word in a technical sense that does not straightforwardly map onto the contemporary debate.[2] Further, much of the debate about nonconceptualism in Kant concerns his indisputably technical term "intuition". Some writers use this term interchangeably with perception,[3] but Kant, notably, does not (it is also importantly different from what he means by "sensation"). Kant introduces intuitions and concepts as two essentially distinct but mutually dependent ingredients of cognition. He holds that concepts are general and mediate representations that enable us to think objects, while intuitions are singular and immediate representations that give us objects (A320/B377; A19/B33; A50/B74; A713/B741; V-Lo/Wiener, 24:905; V-Met/Mron, 29:800, 888, 970–3). Concepts enable us to have general thoughts (A68/B93; A69/B94). Kant says repeatedly that the role intuitions play in cognition is that of *giving* us objects and that this is something thought can never do (A19/B33; A239/B298; A719/B747). The fact that Kant holds that intuitions are mental representations that are essentially distinct from concepts might seem to support attributing to him nonconceptual content. But, on the other hand, the fact that intuitions and concepts are together necessary for us to have cognition might seem to support denying that Kant has an account of nonconceptual content. Thus, in evaluating the attribution to Kant of nonconceptualism we need to consider how he understands intuitions and what their role in cognition is, how this relates to what he calls experience, perception, and cognition, and what the dependence relations are between the components of cognition.

---

[2] See McLear (2014b:771–2) and Tolley (MS b).

[3] For example, Griffith (2012) explicitly assimilates intuition to perception.

In the contemporary debate about nonconceptual content a distinction is drawn between the nonconceptualist idea that there is mental content that is essentially distinct from conceptually structured content and the different nonconceptualist idea that a subject could have representational content while lacking the concepts needed to describe that content. I shall argue that there are grounds for thinking that, for Kant, intuitions are mental representations that are completely different in structure from conceptual mental content and which could play their role in cognition independently of being conceptualised.

It seems to me impossible to dispute that Kant is a conceptualist about *cognition*; he does not think we have or could have cognition without the application of concepts (A51–2/B75–6; A320/B377). Similarly, I think that the overwhelming evidence is that Kant does not think we could have what he calls "experience" without concepts, but this is simply because what he means by "experience" is empirical cognition (and not, for example, phenomenological consciousness).[4] Whether or not Kant is a conceptualist about *perception* is less clear. As I shall show, conceptualists have clear texts to appeal to here. On the other hand, a few nonconceptualists have, it seems to me, given compelling reasons for caution here, based on seeing specifically what Kant means by "perception", and that he may be using the word technically.[5]

I shall argue, in agreement with Colin McLear (2014b:772), that the debate about whether Kant has some kind of nonconceptualism really turns on what I have called *conceptualism about intuition*: whether Kant holds that intuitions are mental representations that could be presented to us whether or not we had the capacity to apply concepts.[6] While preparing this chapter it struck me that if one were explaining the debate in Kant to a contemporary philosopher who was unfamiliar with it, he or she might expect the debate about nonconceptualism in Kant to concern whether the kind of representations intuitions are (singular, immediate representations that give us objects) is best understood as representations that present us with mental content. In fact, however, as we shall see, much of the

---

[4] See McLear (2014b:771).
[5] See Golob (2014), McLear (2014b:771–2) and Tolley (MS b).
[6] See Allais (2015) and Allais (forthcoming a).

debate concerns whether intuitions can in fact play their role of being singular and immediate representations that give us objects independently of their being conceptualised. The central debate, in other words, is not about whether intuitions have some kind of representational content but about whether intuitions are independent of concepts. My survey of the recent debate leaves me unconvinced by conceptualist arguments on this position. However, I shall argue that there are grounds for making significant concessions to the conceptualist. Conceptualists provide reasons for attributing to Kant the view that we are in fact presented with intuitions that are conceptualised; my argument is merely that he does not hold that intuitions are dependent on being conceptualised for their possibility—for their being intuitions. Further, some commentators on both sides of the debate have argued that it is unclear whether we should call what intuitions present us with "content".[7] Therefore, there is a sense in which the claim I hold to be indisputable—that intuitions do not depend on the application of concepts to be intuitions, and to play their role in cognition—might not be committed to nonconceptual *content*.

1.2 Things Kant Says Directly

If we ask whether there are any texts in which Kant explicitly expresses commitments with respect to this debate, we find a few which seem clear and indisputable, but that may seem to pull in different directions. In terms of claims made explicitly in the text, Kant asserts that *perception* depends on the application of concepts (in favour of conceptualism about perception) and that having objects presented to us in *intuition* does not (in favour of nonconceptualism about intuition). However, as we shall see, in both these cases opponents have responses as to why we should not read the texts as saying what appears to be explicitly asserted. I first discuss these texts and shall then go on to argue that most of the textual claims commentators have appealed to do not straightforwardly support either side of the debate independently of philosophical interpretation and context.

---

[7] See McLear (2016) and Stephenson (2015b).

6   L. Allais

Among the most apparently straightforward things Kant says in relation to this debate are:

> Consequently all synthesis, through which even perception itself becomes possible, stands under the categories. (B161)

> All possible perceptions, hence everything that can ever reach empirical consciousness, i.e., all appearances of nature, as far as their combination is concerned, stand under the categories. (B164–5)

These passages seem to give strong support to thinking that Kant is a conceptualist about perceptual content. A response made by nonconceptualists to this is to argue that Kant's use of the term "perception" is highly specific and technical, and does not map onto what is meant by perceptual content in the contemporary debate, but rather refers to having a certain kind of awareness of what one is perceiving (A120).[8] In this sense, I do not *perceive* the bricks of a house if I am not aware of myself as doing so, even though, in seeing the house, I am seeing the bricks.[9] Understanding whether Kant is a conceptualist about perceptual content in the contemporary sense therefore requires clarifying what Kant means by perception. This is too big a topic to be resolved here; I simply note that a positive off-shoot of the nonconceptualism debate is that it has contributed to detailed attention to this.

It is important to see that if we took these passages to show conclusively that Kant is a conceptualist about *perceptual content*, this would not resolve the question about whether he is a conceptualist about *intuition*. Both sides of the nonconceptualism debate have sometimes run together perception and intuition; but these are importantly different in Kant's account.[10] While the (apparently) straightforward textual evidence seems to support conceptualism about perception, in terms of things Kant (apparently) straightforwardly says, he very clearly denies that

---

[8] This is argued in detail by McLear (2014b) and Tolley (MS b). See McLear (2013) for a detailed account of Kant's view of perception and Matherne (2015) for an account of the role of imaginative synthesis in perception.

[9] See Golob (2014).

[10] On the nonconceptualist side, I think I did this in Allais (2009); on the other side, see Griffith (2012).

1 A Survey of the Recent Debate   7

having objects presented to us in intuition is dependent on the possibility of conceptualising. He says:

> Since an object can appear to us only by means of such pure forms of sensibility, i.e., be an object of empirical intuition, space and time are thus pure intuitions that contain *a priori* the conditions of the possibility of objects as appearances, and the synthesis in them has objective validity. [1] *The categories of the understanding, on the contrary, do not represent to us the conditions under which objects are given in intuition at all, hence objects can indeed appear to us without necessarily having to be related to functions of the understanding,* and therefore without the understanding containing their *a priori* conditions. ... For [2] *appearances could after all be so constituted that the understanding would not find them in accord with the conditions of its unity,* and everything would then lie in such confusion that, e.g., in the succession of appearances nothing would offer itself that would furnish a rule of synthesis and thus correspond to the concept of cause and effect, so that this concept would therefore be entirely empty, nugatory, and without significance. [3] *Appearances would nonetheless offer objects to our intuition, for intuition by no means requires the functions of thinking.* (A89–91/ B122–3; emphasis added)

The central conceptualist strategy for responding to this passage is to claim that, when Kant here says that objects can be presented to us in intuition independently of the categories, he is talking about an apparent possibility that he is in fact going to foreclose in the arguments in TD. As Thomas Land, for example, puts the point: "For dialectical purposes, Kant describes a scenario that he wants to show does not obtain" (Land 2015a:31). Brady Bowman (2011:422–3) argues that what Kant is talking about here is a merely formal or logical possibility that he is going to go on to show, in the argument of TD, is not a real possibility. Similarly, Anil Gomes (2014:6) argues that the passage expresses a mere epistemic possibility that will later be shown not to be a genuine metaphysical possibility at all, and Stefanie Grüne (2011:476) argues that Kant is here stating the opposite of what he believes, in order to motivate why there should be a transcendental deduction of the categories.

These readings simply do not fit with what Kant actually says in the passage. In the italicised section I have numbered [1], Kant states categorically, and not as a possibility he is going to foreclose, that the categories are not conditions of objects being given to us in intuition and that objects can appear to us without being related to the functions of the understanding. What Kant is in fact going to go on to deny is the possibility he mentions in the italicised part of the quotation numbered [2]: he is going to argue that appearances *are* so constituted that they are in accordance with the conditions of the unity of the understanding. However, Kant explicitly says that even in the case of the apparent possibility he is going to foreclose, appearances would still offer objects to our intuition (italicised sentence [3]), *for intuition by no means requires the functions of thinking*. The conceptualist reading of this passage is simply not what Kant actually says. Rather, he says that he is going to show that objects presented to our experience do fall under the categories, but that this is not a condition of their being presented to our intuition, that their being presented to us in intuition does not depend on the categories, and that even if they did not fall under the categories they could still be presented to us in intuition.

This is not decisive, because philosophical, argumentative considerations can override what seem to be straightforward claims, and, as we shall see, the details of the argument of TD do present the conceptualists with their strongest case. It seems clear, however, that we should start by looking for a way of reading the argument of TD that is consistent with the claims Kant very explicitly makes in this passage, in introducing TD, and if a reading is available that is consistent with what Kant says in this passage, that should count strongly in its favour. "Kant contradicts himself" should be an interpretation of last resort.

So far we have seen Kant explicitly saying that perception is dependent on concepts and explicitly denying that intuition is. There are two further groups of passages which, in my view, clearly support nonconceptualism. The first are the places where Kant discusses animal perception. As McLear (2011) shows, there is good evidence that Kant attributes the capacity for objective perceptual awareness to animals that lack concepts. Kant says that "animals are *acquainted* with objects too, but they do not *cognize* them" (Log, 9:65). While he denies that the ox can see a gate as a gate, he clearly says that it sees the gate (DfS, 2:59), and he says that

1 A Survey of the Recent Debate   9

> from the comparison of the similar behaviour in the animals (the ground for which we cannot immediately perceive) to that of humans (of which we are immediately aware) we can quite properly infer *in accordance with the analogy* that the animals also act in accordance with *representations* (and are not, as Descartes would have it, machines). (KU, 5:464n.; trans. amended)[11]

Conceptualists can respond to these passages by denying that they are consistent with the First *Critique*, or by arguing that our perception is transformed by conceptualisation, and is entirely different from animal perception. The version of nonconceptualism I hold is compatible with the latter, as it merely argues that intuitions do not depend on conceptualisation to play their role of presenting us with particulars, and not that our intuitions are not in fact conceptualised, or that this does not transform them.[12]

The final group of passages that speak explicitly for a form of nonconceptualism are those in which Kant discusses incongruent counterparts.[13] He says that

> we can ... make the difference between similar and equal but nonetheless incongruent things (e.g., oppositely spiralled snails) intelligible through no concept alone, but only through the relation to right-hand and left-hand, which refers immediately to intuition. (Prol, 4:286)

This clearly indicates that he thinks there is content in our perceptual experience that cannot be captured conceptually. However, it does not show that he thinks that we are presented with perceptions or intuitions that are not conceptualised, or even that we could be. While it unambiguously says that there is more to our experience than can be captured conceptually, it does not give reason to attribute to Kant the view that we ever have or can have perceptual experience that is not conceptualised.

I have presented a passage in which Kant explicitly denies that intuitions depend on concepts. Against this, conceptualists have appealed to a

---

[11] See also McLear (2014b).

[12] See Schulting (2015b:569) for a similar account of a moderate nonconceptualism.

[13] See Hanna (2005), and Hanna, Chap. 5, this volume.

10   L. Allais

passage in which Kant seems to say the opposite. In a notorious footnote to §26 of TD, Kant says that

> space, represented as *object* (as is really required in geometry), contains more than the mere form of intuition, namely the *comprehension* of the manifold given in accordance with the form of sensibility in an *intuitive* representation, so that the *form of intuition* merely gives the manifold, but the *formal intuition* gives unity of the representation. In the Aesthetic I ascribed this unity merely to sensibility, only in order to note that it precedes all concepts, though to be sure it presupposes a synthesis, which does not belong to the senses but through which all concepts of space and time first become possible. For since through it (as the understanding determines the sensibility) space or time are first *given* as intuitions, the unity of this *a priori* intuition belongs to space and time, and not to the concept of the understanding (§24). (B160n.)

I discuss this footnote in Sect. 1.5.2. For now I shall note a few points. Crucially, this footnote is notoriously complex and obscure, and requires much interpretation. (Indeed, Onof and Schulting [2015] have recently devoted a very long and very helpful paper just to this footnote!)[14] Since much of Kant's discussion here concerns different kinds of representation of space and time (including concepts of space and time), it is only the last sentence which seems to support nonconceptualism about intuition, since it says that space and time are first *given* as intuition through a synthesis of the understanding. Finally, the conceptualism that seems to be directly stated here is very moderate, involving the understanding but not concepts (since Kant says it is a synthesis that precedes all concepts).

In my view, all the other passages commentators have appealed to are far from explicit on their own, and require detailed philosophical interpretation to be shown to support one side or the other of this debate, so are definitely not decisive. I shall mention some passages that have been appealed to by conceptualists, before going on to assess these philosophical arguments. A very famous passage that has been thought to support conceptualism is Kant's saying that

---

[14] They quote Falkenstein as saying that this footnote is "so obscure that it can be made to serve the needs of any interpretation whatsoever" (Onof and Schulting 2015:4).

1 A Survey of the Recent Debate 11

without sensibility no object would be given to us, and without under-standing none would be thought. Thoughts without content are empty, intuitions without concepts are blind. ... The understanding is not capable of intuiting anything, and the senses are not capable of thinking anything. Only from their unification can cognition arise. (A51/B75–6)

Both conceptualists and nonconceptualists have noted, however, that this passage is inconclusive for our debate.[15] Kant is talking in the passage about the necessary dependence of concepts and intuitions for *cognition*, not about whether they have any independent representational content. And while "blind" may sound like something empty of representational content, both "blind" and "empty" are metaphorical. It is indisputable that Kant does not mean "empty" literally, since he thinks that there are many thoughts with respect to which we cannot be given intuitions but which are not empty of content: this is true, in his view, of all of transcendent metaphysics. There is therefore simply no reason, independently of further philosophical argument and the overall text, to take "blindness" to literally mean having no representational content.[16]

Other passages that conceptualists have appealed to include Kant's stating:

The same function that gives unity to the different representations *in a judgment* also gives unity to the mere synthesis of different representations *in an intuition*, which, expressed generally, is called the pure concept of understanding. (A79/B104–5)[17]

---

[15] See Allais (2009:392ff.) and Connolly (2014:319). Bauer (2012:223) argues that Kant makes it clear both that the blindness of intuition is total and that the blindness is the emptiness of cognitive content. He does not, however, provide strong evidence for this. He points out that Kant says that the understanding is necessary for objects to have relation to an object, and therefore for cognition to have the possibility of being true (A62–3/B87), and that the synthetic unity of apperception is necessary for anything "*to become an object for me*" (B133). These are important passages that the nonconceptualist must respond to (I discuss them in detail in Allais 2015 and Allais, forthcoming a), but whether Kant's notion of "relation to an object" and of something being possible as an object of cognition are the same as having any representational content at all is certainly not apparent simply from the texts quoted.

[16] There is even less reason to take it to mean something specific and technical, like intentional content, as Williams (2012:60) does, given that Kant says nothing to explain that this is how he is using the word.

[17] This is appealed to by Bauer (2012:217).

12   L. Allais

> All combination, whether we are conscious of it or not, whether it is a combination of the manifold of intuition or of several concepts, ... is an action of the understanding, which we would designate with the general title *synthesis*. (B130)[18]

> Thus all manifold of intuition has a necessary relation to the *I think* in the same subject in which this manifold is to be encountered. (B132)[19]

> The synthetic unity of consciousness is therefore an objective condition of all cognition, not merely something I myself need in order to cognize an object, but rather something under which every intuition must stand *in order to become an object for me*. (B138)[20]

As nonconceptualist interpreters have pointed out, these passages raise complex questions about the interpretation of TD, the notion of unity, the role of synthesis, the role of apperception, and the idea of cognising an object as an object. Systematic philosophical argument is therefore needed with respect to these texts. I discuss this in Sect. 1.5.

1.3   The Role of Intuition and the Nature of Intuition

Arguments on both sides of our debate appeal to the role of intuition in cognition. An argument made by conceptualists is based on the idea that intuition could not play a justificatory role in cognition if it were outside "the space of reasons", and that thinking that it could would be to fall prey to the so-called Myth of the Given. Following John McDowell's (1994, 1998) influential conceptualist position,[21] a common claim is that intuitions serve as a "constraint" on conceptual thought. For example,

---

[18] Ibid.

[19] This is appealed to by Bowman (2011:422).

[20] Bauer (2012:223) takes this passage as decisive.

[21] McDowell's reading is discussed in detail by Williams (2012).

Nathan Bauer (2012:218) claims that intuitions serve two roles in cognition: supplying sensible content that gives significance to our thoughts and makes knowledge of the world possible, and providing a constraint on conceptual activity. He argues that intuitions must have "the appropriate normative structure to serve as reasons in support of our beliefs", that this is why they must be conceptualised, and that if they were not conceptualised Kant's position would involve "a problematic appeal to the Given" (Bauer 2012:218). Land (2011:213) also argues for conceptualism in terms of rejecting the Myth of the Given, and says that the objective unity of intuition must be produced by the understanding for intuition to play a role in the space of reasons.

In response to these kinds of argument, Eric Watkins has pointed out that there are different versions of the Myth of the Given, with Sellars rejecting the empiricist idea of taking sense-data as knowledge that is primitively given (Watkins 2008:513), while for McDowell the problem is thinking that a natural fact could do what can in fact be achieved only by a normative fact (Watkins 2008:517). As Watkins (2008:518) points out, Kant is no empiricist, and rejects the idea that anything given could suffice for knowledge or cognition, so is not subject to the worry Sellars is concerned to reject. In his response to the version of the concern from McDowell, Watkins shows how the deliverances of sense (sensations) play a role in Kant's account of cognition, as input into conceptual functions. A further response is to emphasise the difference, in Kant's account, between intuition and sensation. Intuitions make an essential contribution to cognition but this is not, I argue, best understood either as their serving as reasons or as the constraint provided by sensation.[22]

In my view, projecting onto Kant the McDowellian concern with how perceptual states can serve as justifiers for beliefs—and therefore, the argument goes, must be conceptually structured—fails to pay attention to the role for which Kant actually invokes intuition. Kant does not speak of intuitions as justifiers or things that can serve as reasons for beliefs. Rather, he says that intuitions give us objects. As I understand his claim that intuitions

---

[22] See Allais (2010, 2015).

14   L. Allais

give us objects, Kant means that they directly present us with objects: they give us acquaintance with the objects of cognition.[23] Acquaintance is not justification: it is a relation of direct presentation. This explains the immediacy of intuitions (as opposed to the mediacy of concepts); it explains the singularity of intuitions (as opposed to the generality of concepts, which means that they do not uniquely individuate); and it explains how intuitions can make good what concepts fail to provide: a guarantee that there is an object corresponding to the concept. Intuitions guarantee the existence of their objects because they present their objects. On my reading, Kant holds that intuitions give us acquaintance with the objects about which we think (where acquaintance involves the presence of the object in consciousness) and that without the possibility of acquaintance with objects our conceptual thought would not constitute cognition.[24] It would simply be a free play of concepts, which would not succeed, on its own, in connecting to a world, so would not be a properly objective representation, or cognition.

It is important to see that this is compatible with the conceptualist claim that Kant thinks that intuitions also need to be structured in a way that makes them fit our concepts, and that this structuring is necessary for us to be in a position to take perceptual experiences as reasons or justifiers.[25] The disagreement concerns whether this structuring is necessary for intuitions to be intuitions: singular and immediate representations that give us acquaintance with objects. My view is that intuitions do not depend on conceptual structuring to give us objects, but that being given objects is insufficient for cognition, and what is given in intuition must be synthesised, in accordance with the categories, before it can constitute cognition. Thus, the version of nonconceptualism I argue for here is quite close to conceptualism in agreeing that an unsynthesised (unconceptualised) given could not constitute cognition. However, the disagreement

---

[23] See Allais (2015), Chap. 7, Allais (forthcoming a), and McLear (2016). See also McLear, Chap. 8 in this volume.

[24] This chapter is focused on the question of Kant's conceptualism. A further crucial question with respect to intuition, which I do not discuss here, is whether or not intuitions involve the presence of the objects they represent. Stephenson (2015b) argues against the idea that they do, and the options with respect to this question are helpfully summarised by Gomes and Stephenson in Chap. 3 in this volume. I argue that intuitions involve the presence of the objects they represent in Allais (2010, 2015).

[25] See Pendlebury (1995).

is still significant. As we shall see in Sect. 1.5, conceptualists argue that conceptually governed synthesis is needed for intuitions to be intuitions: to be singular (unified) representations that give us objects.[26]

1.4 The Transcendental Aesthetic

Nonconceptualists have found fertile ground in the Transcendental Aesthetic (TAe) and work on this debate has, it seems to me, resulted in attention to important but perhaps previously somewhat neglected aspects of Kant's position here. For example, Clinton Tolley's argument in Chap. 11 in this volume demonstrates the importance of paying detailed attention to the different ways in which Kant thinks we represent space, and McLear's work has crucially focused on the different kinds of unity Kant holds to be involved in intuition and concepts, which brings out their different structures.[27] As McLear shows, TAe clearly supports thinking that intuition has a fundamentally different structure from conceptual structure and that Kant's account includes both aesthetic and intellectual accounts of unity, namely, intuitional unity and conceptual unity, respectively. The former has a whole-part structure, in which something is given as a unity prior to its parts being cognised, while conceptual unity involves running through parts and synthesising them.[28]

This is significant for our debate in a number of respects. Crucially, it gives nonconceptualists important resources for responding to those passages in TD where Kant says that synthesis introduces unity to intuitions. Since Kant has two notions of unity, which he holds to have fundamentally different structures, these passages cannot be taken to show that all intuitional unity is dependent on conceptualising. On the contrary, in my view, conceptually governed synthesis introduces conceptual unity to intuitions which already have intuitional unity.

That intuition has this different structure is crucial to Kant's arguments in TAe. He argues that it is precisely *because* space and time present us with

---

[26] See, for example, Ginsborg (2008).
[27] See McLear (2015).
[28] I also argue this in Allais (2015) Chap. 7, and Allais (forthcoming a, b).

16   L. Allais

individuals that our primary representations of them are *not* conceptual; an argument for space and time being intuitions and *not* concepts could not turn on the claim that space and time present us with individuals if our representations of space and time needed to be organised conceptually to present us with individuals. Kant's third argument for the claim that our representation of space is an a priori intuition turns on the idea that there is a way of representing unity or singularity that is different from conceptual unity and that we are presented with space and time as unified in this way. Kant says that the way we represent the oneness of space is as a single given whole, rather than through first representing parts of space and putting them together to represent the whole of space, and he says that representing space in this way is prior to being able to represent its parts (A25/B39). He thinks that this is the opposite of the way in which we grasp a whole/unity/oneness conceptually, which requires running through parts and putting them together. As McLear argues,

> Kant's point in the third and fourth arguments of the Metaphysical Exposition of space (and similarly of time) is that no finite intellect could grasp the extent and nature of space as an infinite whole via a synthetic process moving from part to whole. (McLear 2014b:773)

Similarly, Onof and Schulting write:

> The content of a concept is characterized by Kant in terms of marks that are related to it as partial representations .... We would, however, not be able to complete a synthesis of an infinite number of such partial representations. Thus while concepts are generated by synthesis of a finite number of partial representations, this cannot be the case for space, given that space is an infinite given magnitude. (Onof and Schulting 2015:9)

These arguments from TAe provide very serious problems for conceptualists, because seeing intuition as dependent on concepts for having intuitional unity makes it almost impossible to make sense of Kant's arguments and claims in this section.

1.5 The Deduction

While TAe provides materials that seem to support nonconceptualism, conceptualists find their strongest argumentative grounds in TD. Indeed, a common conceptualist strategy is to argue that the apparent independence of intuitions from concepts in the way Kant presents his arguments in TAe has to be revised in the light of the arguments of TD.[29] There are two main features of the arguments in TD that I shall look at in this regard: (i) the role of synthesis in unifying intuition (Sect. 1.5.1) and (ii) the aim of TD in showing that all objects of experience fall under the categories (Sect. 1.5.2).

1.5.1 Synthesis

Synthesis is a central notion in TD. Kant states:

> By *synthesis* in the most general sense ... I understand the action of putting different representations together with each other and comprehending their manifoldness in one cognition. (A77/B103)

A central part of the argument in TD involves the idea that synthesis introduces unity to intuition. This plays a very strong role in motivating conceptualism about intuition. The idea is that although Kant presents intuitions as singular and immediate representations that give us objects they could not really be singular or give us objects unless they represent unified particulars, and if synthesis is needed to produce unified intuitions, then intuition is not independent of whatever is involved in synthesis. Kant sees concepts as rules of synthesis and the categories as rules governing a priori synthesis, and argues in TD that we synthesise the manifold of intuition and the manifold in intuitions according to these a priori rules of synthesis. This seems to lead to the conclusion that the categories are necessary for intuitions to play their role of being singular representations that give us objects.

---

[29] See, for example, Bauer (2012) and Ginsborg (2008).

18   L. Allais

A number of conceptualist interpreters present this argument. I cite a few examples. Gomes states that

> Kant takes intuitions to depend on acts of synthesis. And acts of synthesis are undertaken by the understanding: they take the manifold of intuition and combine it according to rules. (Gomes 2014:3)

Aaron Griffith argues that categories as rules for guiding synthesis in the generation of an intuition are required for perception (Griffith 2012:196) and that

> empirical intuition involves a synthesis that unites its distinct sensory impressions into a single representation of a determinate object (table) with determinate properties (brown). This synthesis, they [conceptualists] argue, is always directed by rules, and these rules are concepts (cf. A105). Since the understanding provides these concepts, it governs the synthesis that makes perception possible. Hence, the activity of the understanding is a necessary condition for perceptions of objects, according to their argument. (Griffith 2012:198)

Land holds that "sensible synthesis unifies sensible manifolds in such a way that they come to exhibit objective unity" (Land 2011:215–16).[30] Jessica Williams argues that "if, as Kant writes, synthesis 'stands under the categories', then it does not seem that intuition can have representational content apart from the categories" (Williams 2012:67). Hannah Ginsborg (2008:66) argues that synthesis of the imagination is needed to form images of objects, therefore for perception, therefore for intuition. Grüne states that

> in the A Deduction as well as in the B Deduction Kant proves the objective validity of the categories by showing that contrary to what one first might think it is *not* the case that the understanding does not play any role in the formation of an intuition. In both deductions Kant states two things: (i) sensible representations have to be processed or rather synthesized in order for intuitions to be formed, (ii) the synthesis of sensible representations

---

[30] See also Bauer (2012:227) and Land (2015a:25).

only results in the formation of intuitions if concepts function as rules for synthesis. (Grüne 2011:476)[31]

She holds that

> an intuition is not directly delivered by sensibility, but is the outcome of an activity of mental processing which Kant calls synthesis of the understanding. The manifold for intuition by contrast is the material that is delivered by sensibility and is not yet synthesized or processed by the understanding. This manifold, as long as it is not synthesized, is neither object-directed nor conscious. (Grüne 2011:476, also 480)

The crucial claim here is that categorially governed synthesis is the source of intuitional unity, and is necessary for us to be presented with an empirical intuition of a particular (Bauer 2012:227; Griffith 2012:200). On this view, unsynthesised intuition would merely give us a booming, buzzing confusion of sensation, "not individuated objects" (Bauer 2012:228; cf. Griffith 2012:201). There are two main nonconceptualist responses to these arguments. An argument put forward by Robert Hanna, and also considered by me in earlier work,[32] is to say that there are forms of synthesis that do not involve conceptualisation.[33] In support of this, it can be argued that Kant primarily attributes synthesis to the imagination, not to the understanding (A77–9/B103; A98–102; A115–16). This argument has not impressed conceptualists, as they argue that the syntheses with which Kant is concerned in TD *are* conceptually governed—indeed, governed by the categories.[34]

Another strategy, which I have pursued more recently,[35] is to argue that whether or not synthesis always involves the understanding, the unity that synthesis introduces to intuition in TD is not the unity that is necessary for intuitions to be singular and immediate representations that give us objects. In other words, the argument in TD is not concerned with

---

[31] See also Land (2015a:30) and Pippin (1993:294).
[32] Allais (2009).
[33] See Schulting (2015b) for discussion.
[34] See Schulting (2015b:575).
[35] Allais (2015) and Allais (forthcoming a).

20   L. Allais

what is necessary for intuitions to be intuitions (to be unified in the way that is necessary for them to be singular and immediate representations that give us objects), but for intuitions to be unified in the different way that is necessary for them to be cognised—for them to be grasped as objects using concepts and to have concepts applied to them.[36] As we saw in Sect. 1.4, there are good reasons for thinking that there is more than one kind of unity in Kant's account, and that intuitional unity involves something being presented as one all at once, *without* needing a synthesis of its parts. In TD, Kant talks about unifying a manifold of intuitions and the manifold in an intuition; this is most straightforwardly read as something that is done *to* intuition. But if it is something done to intuition, then it does not produce intuition. To say that we have a manifold of intuitions that must be synthesised does not mean that we do not have intuitions (that we have a mass of unorganised sensations). On the contrary, the most straightforward reading is that we have intuitions but that the appearances given in these intuitions are not ordered or classified, and we are not in a position to think about them as objects (and in this sense, nothing is "an object for me").

Similarly, the thought that there is a manifold *in* an intuition that needs to be synthesised does not mean that we do not have the intuition (singular, immediate representations that give us an object) without this synthesis. Again, the most straightforward reading is that we have the intuition but there is something we need to do (synthesise) to this intuition to grasp its complexity. Conceptualists think that Kant initially presents intuition as distinct from concepts but then shows that they are not really distinct, because they are dependent on conceptually governed synthesis. But at no point in his discussion of synthesis in TD does Kant note this supposed revision of view. Not only does he not say that intuitions depend on concepts in this section, as we have seen, he explicitly denies this.

On my view, rather than thinking that without conceptualisation we have a blooming buzzing confusion, Kant's view is that what intuition

---

[36] Thus we can read the claim that the same function that unifies concepts in a judgement also unifies intuition (A79/B104–5) not as a claim about what produces unified intuition but as about a function that (conceptually) unifies intuitions that already exist (so already have intuitional unity).

gives us without concepts is a manifold of particulars that are unclassified and that have within them a manifold that cannot be grasped as such—we cannot grasp the things given to us as complexes of properties or of parts. Kant says that without synthesis representations would not be connected and would rather be "unruly heaps", and "no cognition at all would arise" (A121). One way of reading "unruly heaps" could be to see it as a mass of entirely unorganised sensations that does not present outer particulars. But this is by no means compulsory, and would not fit the fact that Kant is talking about what gets us from *intuition* to *cognition*. (He discusses what gets us from sensation to intuition—the a priori forms of intuition—in TAe.) Particulars which have not been classified (are not represented as having properties), and which we are not able to classify, could certainly qualify as unruly heaps.

Williams states that

> the entire debate over whether Kantian intuitions are conceptual or non-conceptual hinges on how we understand the synthetic activity of the imagination. If synthesis is guided by the understanding, then it counts as a conceptual capacity, and McDowell is correct in claiming that the deliverances of sensibility already depend on the exercise of conceptual capacities in sensory consciousness. If, on the other hand, synthesis does not depend on the understanding (or at least not always), as Allais and Hanna have claimed, then intuitions would seem to be able to present us with concrete particulars to which we can be directed apart from any conceptual activity. (Williams 2012:69–70)

I agree with her that the most important and influential argument for conceptualism hinges on the role of synthesis with respect to intuition. However, as I have just argued, the question is not just whether the syntheses involved in TD involve the understanding but whether they are necessary for intuitions to give us objects—whether they are something that produces intuition (is responsible for intuitional unity) or something that is done to intuition (introduces intellectual unity). A number of conceptualist interpreters argue that categorial synthesis is needed for our representations to have objectivity, or objective "purport", or to be about anything (Bauer 2012:227; Griffith 2012:201). In my view, by contrast, intuition, independently of conceptualisation, plays a crucial and

22   L. Allais

independent role in giving thought objective validity through giving us acquaintance with the objects about which we think. Conceptualisation is needed for us to grasp (think, understand) the objects that are presented to us as objects, and so is needed for cognition. The advantage of this reading is that it can take seriously Kant's account of what intuitions are, their role in cognition, their essential distinctness from concepts, the arguments in TAe, and his denial that intuitions depend on concepts at the beginning of TD. At the same time, it can take seriously the role of synthesis in organising intuition, and the claim that this is necessary to bring what is given in intuition to concepts (A78/B103). The possibility of this move therefore, in my view, is a serious obstacle to attributing conceptualism about intuition to Kant.

1.5.2 The Aim of the Deduction and the Argument Concerning Space and Time (Including the Notorious Footnote)

A final conceptualist argument from TD that I shall consider is the claim that nonconceptualism would undermine what Kant aims to prove in TD: that all objects of our possible experience fall under the categories. Gomes, for example, argues that, unless the argument goes through by showing that the categories are necessary for objects of experience, all TD will show is that the categories are necessary for a certain kind of thought and not that they necessarily apply to all objects of experience. This is the difference between showing that we must apply (use, think with) the categories and showing that the categories must apply (that objects actually fall under them) (Gomes 2014:11). Clearly, showing that all objects in experience are subject to the categories is not the same as showing that their being subject to the categories is necessary for them to be given to us in intuition.[37] Thus, this conceptualist argument requires showing

---

[37] Griffith claims that "if he intends to show that 'everything that may ever come before the senses' stands under the categories, then even sense perception without judgment stands under the categories" (2012:207). We have already seen that there is an important distinction between a nonconceptualism which denies that the objects of our perception are brought under the categories, and one which denies that they need be brought under the categories in order to be given to us in intuition.

that the latter is a step in Kant's argument for the former. Ginsborg, for example, argues that

> part of the aim of the deduction is to show that the pure concepts have application to objects given to us in experience. And the idea that understanding is required for perceptual synthesis seems to be an essential part of achieving this aim. Kant says in §21 of the second edition Deduction that he will show "from the way in which empirical intuition is given in sensibility that its unity is none other than that which the category prescribes to the manifold of a given intuition in general". Only by thus explaining "the a priori validity of the category in regard to all objects of our senses", will "the aim of the deduction be fully attained". But his strategy for showing that the unity of empirical intuition is "none other than" the unity prescribed by the categories seems to depend on claiming that this unity is due precisely to the spontaneity of understanding. (Ginsborg 2008:69)[38]

The arguments for conceptualist readings of this part of TD tend to focus on §26, in which Kant argues for the categories through their role in enabling us to cognise space and time, and therefore all objects which are given to us in space and time. Kant here argues that space and time themselves, as intuitions which contain a manifold, require a "determination of the *unity* of this manifold in them" (B160). However, to say that our representations of space and time must be synthesised to be cognised as determinate is not the same as saying that they must be synthesised in order to be given to us in intuition; and since the latter would make nonsense of central arguments in TAe, there are strong grounds against seeing it as what Kant is saying here. In contrast to the conceptualist reading of this section, Onof and Schulting argue that the proof-structure of TD in fact makes sense

> only insofar as space is recognized as having a structure that is *independent of* the synthetic unity established by the categories, namely, as having its own unicity, so that the problem of the unification under the categories of any manifold given within such a structure arises as a further question for the second part of TD. (Onof and Schulting 2015:23)

---

[38] See also Land (2015a:33).

In my view, in this final stage of TD Kant argues that we need to synthesise space and time, in ways governed by the categories, in order to cognise them. He says that it follows that everything given in space and time is subject to this synthesis: everything given in space is subject to categorial synthesis. This enables him to conclude that what is given in intuition is not just limited to the conditions of intuition but also to those of the conceptual component of cognition, but the argument does not go by way of showing that categorial synthesis is needed for objects to be given to us in intuition.

As we saw in Sect. 1.2, Kant does say in a footnote to this section that it is through a synthesis of the understanding (which precedes all concepts) that space and time are first given as intuitions. However, as Tolley's chapter in this volume and Onof and Schulting's (2015) in-depth discussion of this footnote show, what kind of representation of space and what kind of unity are at issue in this passage is by no means obvious. Onof and Schulting argue that "what is at stake is *the grasp of the unicity of space by the faculty of the understanding*", and that "it is insofar as the unicity of space *is to be something for me*, and therefore to contribute to my experience of an objective world, that it requires a synthesis" (2015:27–8). While I think these arguments show the conceptualist strategy to be, at best, inconclusive, the discussion highlights the significance of the relation between our debate and the interpretation of TD, both in terms of the aims and the argumentative strategy of TD.

An alternative nonconceptualist response to TD is to argue that there are spatiotemporal objects of conscious perception to which the categories do not apply. Hanna argues this, and therefore holds that his nonconceptualist reading of Kant is inconsistent with an important part of TD. This is a very specific form of nonconceptualism, since the claim here is not that intuitions or perceptions in general are not conceptualised, but merely that some special objects within our experience do not fall under the categories (Bowman 2011:423), which again brings out that there are different versions of nonconceptualism. My nonconceptualist view of intuition does not require the actual or possible existence of what Hanna (2011b) calls "rogue objects"—objects which do not fall under the categories. Hanna argues that *we* are rogue objects, since he claims we are presented to ourselves as transcendentally free beings. However, as

Grüne (2011:479) points out, we do not have intuitional experience of ourselves as transcendentally free beings. It is also, in my view, disputable in what sense the categories are not applicable to our cognition of our freedom, since Kant holds it to be crucial to freedom that it is cognised as a *causality*.

1.6   Conclusion

I have suggested that whether Kant is a conceptualist about *perceptual* content (in our sense) is not an issue which the literature has conclusively resolved; resolving it requires detailed attention to just what he means by "perception". While Kant's views on incongruent counterparts support thinking that perceptual content outstrips our conceptual resources, this does not show that we are or could be presented with perceptions which have not been conceptualised. I have argued that TAe, as well as the things Kant says about intuition, provide strong grounds for thinking that intuitions are representations that present us with perceptual particulars, and that they do this independently of conceptualisation. Whether TD undermines this view of intuition depends on how the role of synthesis in TD should be understood—whether synthesis is needed to constitute intuitions or is something done to intuitions and whether this synthesis must involve concepts and/or the understanding—and how we should read the final stage in TD's argument about the need to synthesise our representations of space and time. This issue is therefore important for understanding one of the central arguments in the *Critique*. I have suggested ways of understanding the role of synthesis in TD that are compatible with nonconceptualism about intuition. This nonconceptualism, however, is relatively modest: it is entirely compatible with thinking that all our intuitions *are* conceptualised, that this process radically transforms what is given in intuition, and that this process is necessary for what is given in intuition to play a role in cognition.

2

Why the Transcendental Deduction is Compatible with Nonconceptualism

Sacha Golob

2.1 Introduction

The debate over Kantian nonconceptualism is primarily a debate about the ability of intuition to function independently of the understanding. More specifically, it is a debate about whether the capacity to intuit spatio-temporal particulars is dependent upon the capacity to deploy concepts. The dispute is often also presented in terms of perception: nonconceptualists hold that "the application of concepts is not necessary for our being perceptually presented with outer particulars" (Allais 2009:384), whilst conceptualists contend that at least some concepts "have an indispensable role" in even "the mere perceptual presentation of particulars" (Griffith 2012:199; similarly Falkenstein 2006:141). There are, however, complications in Kant's use of the terms *perceptio*, *Wahrnehmung* and *Perception*: whilst standard contemporary usage employs "perception" to

---

S. Golob (✉)
Department of Philosophy, King's College London, London, UK
e-mail: sacha.golob@kcl.ac.uk

© The Editor(s) (if applicable) and The Author(s) 2016　　　**27**
D. Schulting (ed.), *Kantian Nonconceptualism*,
DOI 10.1057/978-1-137-53517-7_2

mark intentionality in contrast with mere sensation (for example Burge 2010:7), Kant often uses these terms to mark conscious states, including sensation, in contrast to those states "of which we are not conscious" (Anth, 7:135; cf. A320/B376, A225/B271).[1] I shall therefore mainly frame matters in terms of intuition, but I shall speak of "perception", understood in the standard modern way, when discussing other commentators who do so.

Why does the question of Kantian nonconceptualism matter? There are three reasons. Most obviously, it is directly connected to many of the central exegetical puzzles raised by the First *Critique*: how, for example, should we understand Kant's theory of intentionality or the interdependence of the Aesthetic and the Analytic? Second, it bears on Kant's reception within the canon. The very different pictures of Kant's theoretical work found in Marburg neo-Kantianism and in phenomenology, for example, stem in large part from different readings of the relationship between intuition, imagination and thought (compare Natorp 1910:276 and Heidegger 1997:37–8). Third, the philosophical issues in play are still live ones in the current debate. Tyler Burge's criticisms of "compensatory individual representationalism", for example, echo many of the points made by the nonconceptualist Kant (e.g., Burge 2010:16, 155). By better understanding Kant's own views, we can simultaneously get clearer on the merits of those arguments, and on their implications for contemporary philosophy of mind.

The purpose of this chapter is to introduce and then to undermine one of the key reasons for construing Kant as a conceptualist, namely the widespread assumption that nonconceptualism is incompatible with the Transcendental Deduction (TD). I am not attempting here to demonstrate that Kant was a nonconceptualist. There are too many other issues in play—the multiple non-equivalent notions of intentionality, synthesis and objectivity involved for example—for that to be viable in a single chapter. Furthermore, space prohibits the type of detailed textual work needed to fully substantiate nonconceptualism at an exegetical level.

---

[1] I do not think the solution here is as simple as emphasising the distinction between *Wahrnehmung* and *Perception* that is clouded by the English "perception", although that is a good first step (see A225/B271, and compare Prol, 4:200 and A320/B376).

2 TD's Compatibility with Nonconceptualism   29

This is partly because doing so would involve line by line treatment of some of the most opaque and controversial passages in Kant's writings (A89–90/B122–3 or B160–1, for example). It is partly because I regard TD as a promissory note, a note which is actually cashed only as we move through each of the Principles. I have argued directly and in detail for nonconceptualism in two recent papers, appealing to Kant's treatment of perception and synthesis (Golob forthcoming a), and to his views on animals and on objectivity (Golob forthcoming b). But my aim here is both more programmatic and more strategic: I want to show how TD, qua transcendental argument, is entirely compatible with nonconceptualism in at least one good sense of that term. I thus aim to remove one of the major obstacles to the acceptance of such nonconceptualism. I say "nonconceptualism in at least one good sense of that term", and it is obviously important that the debate does not degenerate into a merely verbal dispute. As I discuss, there are multiple forms of "nonconceptualism", and I suspect that even some self-identified "conceptualists" may ultimately be happy to subscribe to my conclusions. But if those conclusions are right then at least some forms of Kantian conceptualism are mistaken, and some widespread worries about TD and nonconceptualism are misplaced—these results would be neither trivial nor merely terminological.

Before getting underway, we need to sharpen up the theses under discussion. There has been a great deal of discussion of the distinction introduced by Jeff Speaks between "relative" and "absolute" nonconceptualism (Speaks 2005:360; cf. Hanna 2011a). I shall follow Lucy Allais in arguing only for what Speaks labelled "relative nonconceptualism", that is, for the view that subjects might have intuitions of spatiotemporal particulars whilst lacking any corresponding conceptual capacities (Allais 2009:386; Speaks 2005:360).[2] But I think there is another issue which is often muddied when formulating the debate, namely, the relationship between humans and non-rational animals (henceforth "animals"). For example, Anil Gomes, in a recent article which I discuss in detail below, defines nonconceptualism as the view that "intuitions can present us with

---

[2] I follow Allais in borrowing "particulars" from P.F. Strawson as a broader alternative to something like "material object": "Material objects, people and their shadows are all particulars" (Strawson 1959:15).

30   S. Golob

empirical objects without any application of concepts" (Gomes 2014:2). My concern is that building a tacit reference to rational agents, "us", into the definition occludes several important issues.

First, suppose that nonconceptualists were right *about animals*, that is, that Kant believed that animals were indeed able to have intuitive representations of spatiotemporal particulars despite completely lacking conceptual capacities. Suppose further that these representations were intentional in the sense of possessing accuracy conditions (the dog tricked by an optical illusion would thus *mis*represent the world, in line with the standard representationalist move). In that case, one could not justify Kantian conceptualism in the human case by arguing that conceptual capacities were required merely for having intuitions as opposed to sensations, nor that they were required even for spatiotemporal perception in the modern sense of "perception", nor that they were necessary simply for intentionality. But these are moves often made by conceptualists (e.g. Ginsborg 2008:65 or Griffith 2012:198; I discuss the specifics of these articles below). So if nonconceptualism applies to the animal case, that would have significant implications for how one understands the role of concepts in the case of rational sensible agents like us.

Second, suppose that nonconceptualists were right *only about animals*, that is to say, that Kant believed that no rational agent had intuitions that were not in some sense conceptually determined. In that case Kantian nonconceptualism would be strikingly different from many contemporary forms of the view, which are driven by global considerations about perception. Thus Richard Heck, for example, motivates his brand of nonconceptualism by asking his (presumably) human readers to "consider your current perceptual state" (Heck 2000:489). So if Kantian nonconceptualism applies or only applies to the animal case, it would have substantial implications for how one sees both rational agents and the links between the *Critique* and contemporary philosophy of mind. The upshot is that it is vital to track the interaction between the human and animal cases; for simplicity, I shall deal only with adult humans.[3] Above all, it

---

[3] Infants can be naturally incorporated by treating their perceptions as similar to those of animals: at least up to a certain point, infants, like animals, lack any "online" faculty of understanding (Anth, 7:127).

is simply not good enough to say that Kant was just unconcerned with animals. Not only is this textually clearly untrue (consider KU, 5:464 or Log, 9:64–5 to name two of many passages), it is philosophically indefensible insofar as one's position on the animal case has direct consequences, as just sketched, for the human case: even if the historical Kant had never given animals a moment's thought, it would be radically unsatisfactory if his system had no way of accommodating such an obvious potential counter-example.

Bringing these points together with relative nonconceptualism, I thus distinguish:

Nonconceptualism about Animals (NCA) = The thesis that a non-rational animal can have an empirical intuition I of a spatiotemporal particular P without there being any conceptual capacity involved either in I or in any content which serves as the transcendental condition for I.

Nonconceptualism about Adult Humans (NCH) = The thesis that a rational sensible agent such as an adult human can have an empirical intuition I of a spatiotemporal particular P without there being any conceptual capacity involved either in I or in any content which serves as the transcendental condition for I.

In all cases, the relevant form of conceptualism is simply the denial of the corresponding nonconceptualist claim.

A few remarks on these definitions before proceeding. I shall take as given throughout the universally shared premise that animals lack understanding— so, for example, I take the conceptualist opponent of NCA to endorse the view that animals lack concepts and so lack intuitions rather than the textually unsustainable position that intuition requires concepts which animals do indeed possess (Anth, 7:127; A341/399). I have used "involved" in the definitions as an umbrella term for all the ways in which concepts might be employed—subsumption, determining imaginative or perceptual synthesis, and so on. "Involved" is also intended to allow for the looser, and exegetically more plausible, version of conceptualism whereby, whilst intuition makes a distinctive and irreducible contribution to intentionality, this contribution is necessarily dependent on some form of conceptual capacity (e.g. Engstrom 2006:17; for a harder line, see McDowell 1994:9). As for "particulars", I discuss this term and notions such as "object" in detail in Golob (forthcoming b). Here I want just to illustrate it by example. The supporter of NCA believes that a gazelle can see multiple particulars, for example approaching lions, arrayed in a three-dimensional egocentric space around it, particulars which are given as standing in at least primitive spatiotemporal relations, such as distance, and which can be tracked in at least a primitive way ("that one is moving closer").

I want also to say something about the role of modality here: a number of authors, for example Robert Hanna (2013a:5) and Dennis Schulting (2015b:569), present conceptualism in modal terms, framing the debate as one over whether intuitions are "conceptualisable"—in effect, this demands only the necessary possibility of conceptual involvement, as opposed to its actual occurrence. This tactic faces problems regarding the individuation of intuitions within the relevant counterfactuals. Suppose NCA is right and a dog and I both look at a ball. Is the dog's intuition "conceptualisable"? Well, it depends on how intuitions are individuated: that token mental state is not insofar as it is part of a system lacking any conceptual capacities, but its informational content might be in the sense that, when I look at the same view, the result is indeed conceptualisable. Fortunately, as will become clear, I think we can sidestep these issues altogether. As I argue in Sect. 2.3, within systems where concepts are available, some are in fact employed, and not simply employ*able*, in all but a handful of instances. So I shall operate with NCA and NCH as defined, rather than building in modal operators. In practice, many commentators do not mark the distinction between NCA and NCH: when setting up the debate and describing their views in Sect. 2.2, I shall thus talk loosely of "conceptualism" and "nonconceptualism". A final point before proceeding: as is common in the literature, I shall simply bracket the issue of transcendental idealism here. There are, of course, familiar and complex questions regarding the link between TD and Kant's idealism. But I think that the issue of nonconceptualism itself is largely independent of the precise answers we give to those questions: as I see it, nothing in what follows depends directly upon one's stance on transcendental idealism.[4]

2.2 The "Standard View": The Transcendental Deduction as Incompatible with Nonconceptualism

As Allais has put it, "probably the most obvious reason for reading Kant as a ... conceptualist is the Transcendental Deduction" (Allais 2009:401). The reason is that it is natural to see the second half of the B-Deduction, in particular, as arguing that the categories are necessary even for empirical intuition: Hannah Ginsborg thus views the falsity of nonconceptualism as necessary "if ... the Transcendental Deduction is to have any hope of success" (Ginsborg 2008:69). Her assumption is that only if the categories are necessary for intuitions can Kant answer the *quid juris*:

> The central line of thought ... is that the objective validity of the categories depends on their having a role to play, not just in explicit judgment, but also in our perceptual apprehension of the objects about which we judge. (Ginsborg 2008:70)

She takes this to flatly rule out nonconceptualism. Once one excludes any synthesis in which the understanding is involved, what remains is not intuitions, but merely sensations. She writes:

> The only candidates to be bearers of nonconceptual content are the sensible impressions belonging to "sheer receptivity", that is, sense-impressions or sensations. And while these clearly do not depend on concepts, it is implausible to view them as having representational content in the sense that is at issue in the debate over nonconceptual content. (Ginsborg 2008:68)

Brady Bowman likewise states that to allow nonconceptualised intuitions would be to "undermine the very purpose, not only of the

---

[4] In this, my approach is in line with the existing debate; see, for example, Allais (2009:385).

34   S. Golob

B-Deduction, but of the positive project of the First *Critique*" (Bowman 2011:421; similarly Grüne 2011:465–6). Such conceptualists clearly take Kant to deny NCH. Furthermore, whilst few devote much time to the case of animals, their reasoning naturally requires a denial of NCA as well, entailing that animals could not have either intuitions or perception (where that is read in the modern sense as implying intentionality), but instead rely merely on sensory awareness. Thus Ginsborg holds that the "strategy of the Deduction" requires that the understanding be necessary "for the intentionality of perceptual experience" (Ginsborg 2008:65); by extension, she restricts animals to a purely qualitative, sensory engagement with the world (Ginsborg 2006b:104n.43). Likewise, Aaron Griffith argues that TD requires that "understanding plays a role, not just in empirical thought or judgment, but also in empirical perception itself" (Griffith 2012:198); given the universally accepted premise that animals lack understanding, it follows that they are incapable of empirical perception too.

Whilst not solely motivated by TD—related views are found in John McDowell (1994:114) on somewhat different grounds—it is clear that for many TD is sufficient to render nonconceptualism untenable. In order to appreciate just how influential this line of thought is, note that *even* Hanna, a leading nonconceptualist, regards nonconceptualism as incompatible with the B-Deduction. Hanna is thus committed to the existence of what he calls "the Gap in the Deduction":

> The Gap in the B Deduction is that the B Deduction is sound only if Conceptualism is true, but Conceptualism is arguably false and Kant himself is a nonconceptualist. (Hanna 2011b:402)

In sum, there is widespread consensus that nonconceptualism require us to abandon TD. Call this consensus the *Standard View*. Unsurprisingly, once the Standard View is adopted, the rejection of nonconceptualism follows very rapidly. As Bowman observes, if nonconceptualism demands that we give up the central Kantian aim of validating the categories, "the principle of charity would seem to require that we reject the nonconceptualist interpretation" (Bowman 2011:422).

2 TD's Compatibility with Nonconceptualism   35

I am going to argue that the Standard View is false. But before getting into the details, I want to ensure that I am taking it on in its most persuasive form. So I am going to simply stipulate on two issues which benefit the defender of the Standard View. First, all commentators who identify a tension between TD and nonconceptualism read TD as centrally concerned with Humean worries about the justified application of the categories. Ginsborg, for example, states that the conceptualist "line of thought is … essential to the anti-Humean aspect of Kant's view in the *Critique*" (Ginsborg 2008:70). One might think that this assumption gave the nonconceptualist some room for escape. As Gomes, having himself argued for the Standard View, puts it:

> In raising this objection to nonconceptualist readings of Kant, I have assumed that the role of the Deduction is to respond to Humean worries about our *justified* application of a priori concepts to experience. And one may contest this claim. (Gomes 2014:14)

Gomes goes on to sketch some alternative readings of TD, framed in terms of the more traditionally rationalist debates which characterised the "Inaugural Dissertation". But I want simply to grant that the familiar "Hume-focused" reading is right, or is at least a key part of Kant's aim and so must be accommodated: the challenge for TD is to demonstrate the justified application of the categories to experience.

Second, commentators sometimes suggest that the nonconceptualist case rests principally on A89–90/B122. Griffith, for example, states that "the inspiration for the nonconceptualist reading comes primarily from a passage in §13 of the Transcendental Deduction" (Griffith 2012:196), whilst Schulting describes it as "the most important evidence for the nonconceptualist thesis" (Schulting 2015b:568). Conceptualists have usually responded by arguing that the text in question, which appears to allow explicitly for intuitions in the absence of conceptual capacities, is intended only to introduce a hypothetical scenario which Kant will then show is not in fact possible, or not in fact possible in any substantive or significant sense (e.g. Allison 1996:49–50). Now, I think Schulting (2015b) shows convincingly that the exegetical issues here are more complex than the conceptualist suggests. But for the purposes of this chapter,

36   S. Golob

I want again simply to stipulate: in rejecting the Standard View, I shall make no appeal to this text; given how disputed its meaning and purpose are, that would be too unsteady a foundation.

2.3   Allais's Attack on the Standard View

The Standard View has proved extremely influential. But it is not without dissenters. Before outlining my own position, it will be helpful to sketch as a counterpoint Allais's reading, one of the few who explicitly assert the compatibility of TD and nonconceptualism. Allais's view is that

> the Deduction is specifically concerned with one aspect of cognition: the conditions under which we can *apply concepts to objects in judgments*. ... In the Deduction, he wants to show that a priori concepts are necessary conditions of being able to *apply empirical concepts in empirical judgments*. (Allais 2011b:102; second emphasis added)

The key here is that the categories are conditions neither on intuition nor on perception, but instead on the application of empirical concepts. By extension, it is perfectly possible to have completely unconceptualised intuitions. Thus, NCA, for example, immediately follows:

> A non-concept-having creature, which can discriminate spatial boundaries, can perceive located particulars but it cannot think about them; it cannot attribute properties to them. (Allais 2011b:103)

NCH may also follow if there are passages of human experience where empirical concepts are not involved in any way.

I want now to highlight three problems which Allais faces; this will help frame the discussion to come.[5] First, on Allais's construal, TD premises category use on empirical concept use. This will create a problem when responding to Hume, who will argue, as Berkeley does, that there is no need to postulate anything like Kantian empirical concepts in the

---

[5] Whilst I disagree with her on these issues, I would like to stress that I am, like all writing on this topic, deeply indebted to Allais's groundbreaking work.

2 TD's Compatibility with Nonconceptualism   37

first place—all that is needed is a tendency to associate groups of particular images (Hume 1978:20–1 [1.1.7.7–8]). Of course, Hume might be wrong about that, but it means that TD falls some way short of the ideal of a transcendental argument which begins from some premise the sceptic must accept or can be easily brought to accept. Second, suppose one granted that we do use empirical concepts in the Kantian sense. It is not immediately clear why that would require us to employ the categories: could not far weaker regularities suffice in place of, say, causal laws?[6] Nor is it clear why the categories should be thought of as in any sense a function of our subjectivity or synthesis: could it not simply be a fact that we are in a world sufficiently stable to allow the formation and use of empirical concepts, just as we happen to be in a world sufficiently hospitable to allow the formation of life? Of course both of these issues—the exact strength of laws Kant can establish and the issue of idealism—have been the subject of much debate. My point, though, is that Allais's approach threatens to create a structural weakness by beginning from a premise that seems unlikely to deliver the type of radical conclusions Kant claims. Third, there is a natural concern over Allais's ability to answer the *quid juris*. Gomes provides an elegant formulation of the worry:

> [Allais] takes these passages in the second part of the B-Deduction to show only that there is a way of *thinking* about objects as spatial that requires the input of the understanding. ... But it is compatible with this conclusion that all the judgements we so make are false. And if this were the case, our thinking about the world would be subject to an unavoidable error: we would be compelled, of necessity, to think of the world as containing persisting substances, capable of existing unperceived and standing to each other in causal relations; but none of these judgements about the world

---

[6] One might respond that the categories are necessary for empirical concepts because without category application we would be unable even to perceive spatiotemporal objects and so be unable to form or apply empirical concepts. Everything then hangs, of course, on what is meant by "objects". I cannot treat this here, but I discuss it in detail in Golob (forthcoming b). For current purposes, we can simply note that, reframed in these terms, what is missing in Allais is an argument as to why empirical concept use should require objects in any sense which implies the categories: why cannot intuitions of what happens to be de facto a reasonably regular set of inputs plus the powers of abstraction and comparison suffice? One option, of course, would be to claim that without the categories we lack even the empirical intuitions from which we abstract empirical concepts—but this move is obviously unavailable to Allais as a nonconceptualist.

would be accurate. … Humean scepticism about the justified application of a priori concepts will not be answered by showing only that we must apply the categories to experience, for that is compatible with the falsity of any such application. Kant needs the stronger claim: that the categories must apply. (Gomes 2014:10–12; I have inverted the order of these passages)

Let us grant that the categories are necessary conditions on our thinking about the world. Gomes's point is that this leaves untouched the question of by what right this application is not just unavoidable but legitimate, that is, by what right we can assume that spatiotemporal intuition actually contains referents for them. Allais's proposal certainly avoids the type of crude subjective necessity which Kant explicitly criticised (B167–8). The problem, however, is that it fails to show why the necessity she has identified should speak to anything more than the relationship between one set of concepts and another. Why should it actually govern spatio-temporal intuition itself?

2.4 The Proposal: An Alternative to the Standard View

It is now time to introduce my proposal. Once that is done, I shall unpack its implications for TD and the nonconceptualism debate.

The basic proposal is very simple: categorial synthesis is a necessary condition on and only on the representation of a certain privileged class of spatial or temporal relations (contrast this with Allais's model, where the categories are necessary conditions on empirical concept use). Applied to some categories, this proposal has a familiar feel: for example, given the necessarily successive nature of apprehension, it is only in virtue of categorial synthesis that subjects can represent the distinction between a succession of perceptions and a perception of succession, between the house and ship cases of the Second Analogy (A189–90/B234–5).[7]

---

[7] I am not claiming that category application ensures we cannot be mistaken when drawing such a distinction. My claim is rather that Kant thinks that applying the category is a necessary condition on being able even to represent the relevant contrast.

2 TD's Compatibility with Nonconceptualism   39

But its extension to other cases is likely to be much more controversial. For example, it is only in virtue of categorial synthesis, in this case involving the categories of quantity, that subjects can represent various mereological relations—including the fact that the parts of something together constitute its whole (A142–3/B182). As Kant puts it in the Prize Essay:

> The representation of a composite, as such, is not a mere intuition, but requires the concept of a composition [*Zusammensetzung*] ... that is not abstracted from intuitions ... but is a basic concept, and *a priori* at that. (FM, 20:271; trans. amended)

I have defended this approach textually in detail elsewhere and I want here only to highlight two features that distinguish it from more familiar discussions of texts such as the Analogies (for more details, see Golob forthcoming a).

First, as I see it, what the categories make possible is a complex *mix* of spatial and temporal representational achievements. In every case the challenge is created by the fact that Kant's account of what makes a representation conscious, rather than its being part of the much larger class of unconscious content (Anth, 7:136), is apprehensive synthesis, a process which "is always successive" (A189/B234; see also A99 and B160). The result is that some mechanism, namely the categories, is needed to represent relations which that successive synthesis obscures. Some of these relations are straightforwardly temporal. Others are more complex. For example, the problem of the Axioms arises when the parts of something are seen one after another: given this successive experience, how can one represent them as together constituting a single, simultaneous whole?[8] Mere association could, of course, allow one part to call to mind another. Yet a synchronic awareness of multiple items is not equivalent to an awareness of those items as together constituting something larger: as the Prize Essay observes, the notion of "composition" would still be missing. To put the point another way, an associative mind operates at most at the level of consciousness, joining various first-order representations by

---

[8] As the mention of simultaneity suggests, I think that all of the Principles ultimately closely interact: the ability to establish the type of mereological representation discussed in the Axioms goes hand in hand with the ability to represent objective simultaneity discussed in the Analogies.

40   S. Golob

associative links. But it would lack *self*-consciousness, that is, it would lack any higher order way of integrating these first-order representations. Given the successive nature of apprehension, such integration is vital if we are to combine intuitions so as to yield anything more than the crudest view of the world; otherwise, as successive, they would be merely "dispersed and separate in the mind" (A120).

Second, in line with this, I think there is a single argument running through TD and the Principles: an argument from the problems posed by apprehension to the role of the categories in re-enabling the relevant relational contents. However, I also think that this dialectical unity is in tension with Kant's introduction of several, non-equivalent distinctions between the mathematical and dynamical categories. In particular, there are passages where that architectonic encourages him to seek a specifically "immediate" proof for the mathematical categories; this would indeed make the categories a condition on mere perception as texts like B161 suggest (I say more on this passage specifically in Sect. 2.5). Thus at A162–3/B203–4, he argues that intuition must be an extensive magnitude since

> I cannot represent to myself any line, no matter how small it may be, without drawing it in thought, i.e., successively generating all its parts from one point, and thereby first sketching this intuition. ... Every appearance as intuition is an extensive magnitude, as it can only be cognized through successive synthesis (from part to part) in apprehension. (A162–3/B203–4)

Note here the core role for apprehension and successive awareness which I flagged. But at a more specific level, this is a bad argument on many grounds. Phenomenologically, why can I not just see the whole line at a glance (Van Cleve 1999:86)? Furthermore, if I cannot see the whole line at a glance, how do I know if the parts which I am "successively generating ... from one point" should lie straight or if they instead form a curve? Yet, if I can simply see the whole, why would I need to "successively" generate it "from one point" in the first place? The argument's significance, however, is that *were* it to have succeeded, it would have made the categories necessary even for such a simple act as representing a line—so vindicating conceptualism. In other words, my suggestion is

2 TD's Compatibility with Nonconceptualism   41

that the prima facie "pro-conceptualist" passages which link perception and the categories are the products of a misguided attempt to sustain the mathematical/dynamical architectonic. Furthermore, I think these weak arguments were ultimately discarded by Kant in favour of better, quite different claims—for example, as sketched, arguments which allow that an animal can indeed see a line at a glance, but which contend that such a creature would be unable to represent various mereological relations between the whole and its parts, relations such as "composition".[9]

Undoubtedly, much of what I have just said will be controversial. I am not going to rely on the details of my view in what follows, although I shall use it for illustrative purposes. Instead, my concern will be only with the broad principle that underlies it: namely, that categorial synthesis is a necessary condition on and only on the representation of a certain privileged class of spatial or temporal relations. Specifically, I want to bring out that principle's implications for the conceptualism debate.

TD is a transcendental argument; indeed, it has a good claim to some kind of exemplary role in defining how such arguments should look. The role of these arguments in Kant's philosophy is of course open to debate, for example, over how they link to idealism. But it seems that when such arguments play an anti-sceptical role, they necessarily have a basic core: Kant identifies a priori some X which is a necessary condition on some Y, where X is something the sceptic doubts and Y is something that the sceptic either assumes or can be brought easily to accept.[10] Let us also add in the assumption, which I simply granted the conceptualist in Sect. 2.2, that TD aims to justify the categories in the face of Humean fears. Now consider my proposal: within TD and the Principles, X is the categories and Y is the ability to represent the distinction between subjective and

---

[9] In order to avoid attributing such a weak argument to Kant, one might defend an alternative reading of this passage on which it concerns conditions only on some form of conceptual or discursive representation of the line. Textually this seems hard to sustain given the apparently unqualified scope of the passage ("I cannot represent to myself any line"). But were such a reading adopted, the passage would become immediately compatible with nonconceptualism—in accordance with the nonconceptualist strategy employed by both Allais and me, it would present categorial synthesis as a condition not on perception itself, but only on some more sophisticated achievement. So whilst I find this alternative reading questionable exegetically, its accuracy would only bolster the nonconceptualism I ultimately defend.

[10] This claim is compatible with the fact that there may be other transcendental arguments which do not play an anti-sceptical role (for example, the argument from geometry).

objective succession (the house and ship cases of the Analogies), or the ability to represent the successively seen parts of something as constituting its whole. Five points can then be made.

First, TD will be effective against Humean scepticism given the plausible assumption that such sceptics recognise our ability at least to *represent* such distinctions as that between an event (the ship case) and a successive perception of two unchanged, simultaneously existing, objects (the house case where my eye successively sweeps the façade). It seems likely that Hume would grant this—after all, debates between positivistic, projectivist and sceptical realist accounts of the *Treatise* are debates over what must be *added to* events in order to generate causality. Similarly, consider this remark from the *Treatise*:

> There is another very decisive argument, which establishes the present doctrine concerning our ideas of space and time, and is founded only on that simple principle, *that our ideas of them are <u>compounded of parts</u>, which are indivisible.* (Hume 1978:38 [1.2.3.12]; my underlining).

"Compounding" here is precisely the ability to represent multiple subparts as constituting a larger spatial whole, that is, exactly that ability which the Axioms claims is dependent upon the categories of quantity. So again, it seems that Hume does assume the abilities which I claim serve as TD's premise.

Second, even if you disagree with my reading of Hume, and think that he personally would not concede the abilities in question, any non-dogmatic empiricism must do so. Kant himself marks this clearly when he writes that "certainly no one will concede" that the manifold of the house is also successive—in other words, everyone must assume and draw the distinctions in question (A190/B235). Again, let me stress that the abilities in question concern a capacity to *represent* the relevant relations, not to always get them right. There will be many contexts—parallel moving trains, magic shows, etc.—in which I might mistake my successive perception of an enduring object for a change in that object. What matters is that it is a datum of any recognisably human experience that we can and do employ the relevant distinction: the Analogies' claim is that such a representational capacity assumes the categories. There is, of

2 TD's Compatibility with Nonconceptualism   43

course, a further question as to whether Kant was right about that, which I cannot address here; my aim here is to show that such a view is perfectly compatible with TD.

Third, at a textual level, the proposal is typically expressed by Kant in terms of "objectivity". So, for example, he summarises TD as a proof of the application of the categories to "whatever objects *may come before our senses*, not as far as the form of their intuition but rather as far as the laws of their combination are concerned" (B159). The issue here is clearly how we should understand the relevant notion of objectivity. I think the answer is as follows. Kant's overarching definition of objectivity in terms of the unity of the manifold (B137) is a placeholder—his aim is to argue from one such notion of unity or combination to another. Specifically, the Principles attempts to argue from (i) a definition of objects in terms of relations such as objective succession to (ii) the conclusion that such a datum requires categorial synthesis. So, for example, the Second Analogy attempts to move *from* this notion of objectivity:

> If … all sequence of perception would be determined solely in apprehension, i.e., merely subjectively, … it would not thereby be objectively determined which of the perceptions must really be the preceding one and which the succeeding one. In this way we would have only a play of representations that would not be related to any object at all. (A194/B239)

To this one:

> If we investigate what new characteristic is given to our representations by the *relation to an object*, and what is the dignity that they thereby receive, we find that it does nothing beyond making the combination of representations necessary in a certain way, and subjecting them to a rule. (A197/B242)

In other words, the objectivity argument is from the datum I discussed to the categories as conditions for it.

Fourth, unlike in Allais's account, we now have a clear explanation as to why categorial *synthesis* is involved. The problem I raised for her is that, even if the existence of causal laws were a necessary condition on empirical concept formation, it is unclear why the subject forming those concepts should need to think about causality—any more than the subject breathing needs to think about oxygen. There are, as Quassim Cassam (1987:369) has noted, possible explanations, for example, that Kant wanted to *guarantee* the possibility of empirical concept use by giving us the capacity to induce its conditions. But this leaves Kant in a weak position, for why, the empiricist may well ask, should we demand such a guarantee, any more than it makes sense to demand a guarantee that the atmosphere on earth had to be breathable (Cassam 1987:371)? On my account, in contrast, synthesis is naturally involved, irrespective of one's stand on idealism, because the categories are necessary conditions on our being able to *draw certain distinctions*—something that is essentially a mental exercise.

Fifth, and most importantly, it is a direct consequence of my approach that the categories are not necessary for empirical intuition. Rather, they are necessary *only* for representing certain complex relations among such intuitions. Indeed, one needs to grant this to even get to the point at which the Principles start: it is only because the cat does indeed intuit the mouse running along, or the parts of the house one after another, that the problem can arise as to the relation of those intuitions. So, on my proposal NCA follows directly. What about NCH? Well, the issue is whether adult humans might have an intuitive experience E where the relevant relations and distinctions were not in play either in E itself or in any of its transcendental conditions. The last clause is important here, and matters will depend on how one understands the role of larger space-times as conditions on smaller ones. Suppose a rational agent suffering from some momentary illness that puts all his categorial capacities "offline" for five minutes. During this time he perceives some series of images, and yet, due to his illness, lacks whatever ability is needed to represent that given series as either merely subjectively successive, as in Kant's house scenario, or objectively successive as in the ship scenario. Suppose, later recovered, he locates the strange experience in a larger spatiotemporal whole where the relevant distinctions do apply: "whatever I saw, it was after lunch". The categories might then be a necessary condition on placing the unknown occurrence within a larger spatiotemporal whole even if they were "offline" during it. Whatever one thinks about such a case, though, I think the basic points are clear enough. On the one hand, it

2 TD's Compatibility with Nonconceptualism   45

seems one might well have passages of experience in adult humans where the relevant relations and distinctions are not present, and thus where the categories are not needed. On the other hand, however, such distinctions are so basic a part of any recognisably adult human experience, that they typically will be present—and by extension so will the categories which sustain them. This is why, in Sect. 2.1, I did not place great weight on modal treatments of NCH. When the categories are available to a creature they will almost always be actually applied, although this will of course not normally be done explicitly, since they are conditions on comparatively basic feats.

At this juncture, some conceptualists might be happy to embrace these results: after all, if conceptualism is largely preserved at the human level, why do animals matter? I do not think it is fruitful to argue over the title "nonconceptualism", and elsewhere I have described the view as offering a picture of Kant as both conceptualist and nonconceptualist (Golob forthcoming a). But what *is* vital is that we be clear on the warrant for whatever "conceptualism" is in play; given NCA for example, one can no longer sustain readings, such as those of Ginsborg or Griffith, that make the categories a condition on mere intuition or perception.[11]

2.5   Assessing the Proposal

As I stated in Sect. 2.1, my purpose here is programmatic: I have not attempted to undertake the kind of detailed textual work needed to back the proposal fully. Instead, my aim is to provide a bird's-eye view of the dialectic, a view which shows how TD might be compatible with

---

[11] One option open to these authors at this point would be to follow Ginsborg's lead and emphasise the role of intentionality: perhaps the categories are a necessary condition for that. Given the wide variety of views on what constitutes intentionality, I cannot deal with that move here, unfortunately. I have addressed it in detail in Golob (forthcoming b). Another option would be to accept that, whilst the categories are not necessary for "perception" as we standardly use the term, they are necessary for some technical sense of "perception" which by definition involves apperception or other sophisticated capacities. This type of move is merely terminological and effectively concedes the case to nonconceptualism: exactly as the nonconceptualist claims, the mere intuition of spatio-temporal particulars itself, and thus perception in the usual sense, would be possible in the complete absence of conceptual abilities.

nonconceptualism in at least one significant sense. The basic point is this: if TD is read as suggested, the categories are necessary for and only for the representation of certain specific relations among empirical intuitions. By extension, they are not necessary simply for having empirical intuitions, nor for the representation of spatiotemporal particulars, nor for the representation of simple relations between them: the gazelle, for example, can represent the fact that one lion is closer than another.[12]

I want now to develop these results by returning to Allais's view, and to Gomes's criticisms of it. The difference between Allais and me concerns what the categories are necessary for. Gomes's worry was that Allais failed to respond adequately to the *quid juris*: by making category application a condition for a certain way of thought, the danger arose that, whilst we might need to think this way, there might nevertheless be no referents at the intuitive level for those concepts. But how does my own view fare with the *quid juris*? Kant's characterisation of the necessity required by the categories is well illustrated here:

> For, e.g., the concept of cause, which asserts the necessity of a consequent under a presupposed condition, would be false if it rested only on a subjective necessity, arbitrarily implanted in us, of combining certain empirical representations according to such a rule of relation. I would not be able to say that *the effect is combined with the cause in the object* (*i.e., necessarily*), but only that I am so constituted that I cannot think of this representation as otherwise than as so connected; which is precisely what the sceptic wishes most. (B168; emphasis added)

Gomes's point was effectively that, as far as intuition was concerned, Allais's story only establishes a subjective necessity: there is nothing at the intuitive level that mandates category application. On my story, in contrast, the categories are necessary precisely for the representation of "objects" where, as in texts such as A194/B238, "object" is a blanket term for the various distinctive spatiotemporal relations I have discussed. TD thus shows precisely that "the effect is combined with the cause in the

---

[12] For full discussion of the animal case, including the significance attached to the term "particular" and the distinction between the egocentric spatial awareness characteristic of animals and our own self-consciousness, see Golob (forthcoming b).

2 TD's Compatibility with Nonconceptualism   47

object (i.e., necessarily)"—since the categories are a transcendental condition under which such objects must be represented. In laying out his own position, Gomes argues that the categories must be necessary not simply for thought, but for the "unity of space and time". Very plausibly, he links this requirement to the proof structure of the B-Deduction:

> The first part of the proof, §§15–19, argues for the claim that we must apply the categories, whilst §§22–26 complete the argument by showing that the categories must apply. Kant's claim is that since the unity of space and time arises from a process of transcendental synthesis, that which is given in space and time stands under the unity of apperception. (Gomes 2014:12)

The key, though, is what "unity" means here. It might mean that awareness of pure space and time, which Kant takes to ground individual empirical intuitions (A24–5/B38–9). I think that this reading of Kant is deeply unappealing. It would entail that animals could not possess empirical intuitions and, by extension, that they could not perceive simple relations such as distance between the referents of such intuitions. I think the reading is also deeply mysterious. As Allais (2009:405–6) rightly emphasises, why should the ability to see a predator up ahead and track at least simple movement by that predator ("left a bit, coming closer …") depend on anything as sophisticated as the categories? So it seems to me the right way to approach Kant is to read "unity" as referring precisely to the type of sophisticated connection between representations which only the categories allow: for example, representing the distinction between an objective and a merely subjective time order. If this is right, one can grant much that conceptualists would want. So, for example, Gomes writes that

> we must read the process of synthesis offered in the first part of the B-Deduction as originating in the understanding and proceeding according to the categories. The synthesis of the manifold of intuition takes place according to the categories, contrary to the nonconceptualist suggestion. (Gomes 2014:13)

48   S. Golob

Whilst Gomes is right that some forms of nonconceptualism cannot accommodate his reading, it is fully compatible with my proposal provided "the synthesis of the manifold of intuition" is read as I just read "unity". Similarly, suppose one is concerned to limit talk of "figurative synthesis" only to the categorially determined transcendental synthesis of the imagination (Schulting 2015b:575ff.). Again, this is no problem: as I see it, animals are capable of various types of synthesis, notably apprehension, which marks the boundary between conscious and unconscious content, and also association (e.g. Br, 11:52). But there are clearly more advanced forms of synthesis which they lack, and it seems perfectly reasonable exegetically to reserve "figurative synthesis" solely for the imagination under the determination of the categories.

On my picture, then, the categories are indeed necessary for something that is in an important sense a spatiotemporal achievement; it is also an achievement that Kant's opponents typically take for granted, and one which they cannot reasonably deny. Of course, one might seek an even stronger position on which the categories are necessary simply for intuition in any form. As noted, I think this would bring with it many problems—particularly with respect to animals. But it is also unclear that this stronger view would deal any better with Gomes's original worry about the *quid juris*. After all, on the stronger view there would really be no such thing as a solely intuitive phenomenon—any intuitive representation would necessarily contain a disguised conceptual component.[13] By extension, the most this stronger proof could achieve would be to show that something pre-theoretically intuitive was actually interwoven with the understanding. Yet this is already accomplished by my reading: it shows, for example, that the capacity to draw what seem straightforward temporal distinctions rests on category use.[14]

In presenting my account, I have dealt with several objections. I want to close by addressing three final worries one might have about it. First,

---

[13] I do not think this line of thought is enough to absolve Allais's account from Gomes's original worry since her premise for the categories is not even pre-theoretically an intuitive matter, but rather explicitly appeals to empirical concepts. In any case, even if Allais is able to escape that problem in this way, I think the other concerns raised regarding her account in Sect. 2.3 stand.

[14] The case of the Axioms is a little more complex in this regard. For details see Golob (forthcoming a).

2 TD's Compatibility with Nonconceptualism   49

one might worry that my solution to the *quid juris* simply pushes the problem back a step. Suppose it is the case that the categories are necessary for representing the parts of something as constituting its whole or drawing the subjective/objective succession distinction. But then by what right do we do *those* things—do we not need simply to answer another *quid juris* there? I think the answer is no. Kant is clear that space and time do not require a corresponding proof, since they are in an important sense simply given (A89/B121–2). I would suggest that a similar warrant can be extended to what I above called any "basic datum of human experience", where such data can be identified, for example, by the fact that even Kant's empiricist opponents assume them. In this sense, I see Kant as combining phenomenological and transcendental approaches: he begins with a descriptive phenomenology, starting from points that "no one" can in fact deny (A190/B235) and regresses from that to substantive, transcendental conditions (I discuss this further below).

Next, one might feel that my view, by distinguishing intuitions which do not require concepts from a subset of specific relations among intuitions which do, compromises the goal of establishing "the strictly universal, i.e., exceptionless, validity of the categories" (Bowman 2011:423). This, Bowman warns, "is not a point on which Kant could compromise: it has to be all or nothing" (Bowman 2011:423). But why must it be all or nothing? Bowman is not explicit, but his thought is at least partly that compromising on this "would put us right back in the universe of Humean contingency from which the transcendental deduction is designed to release us" (Bowman 2011:421).

Yet TD can serve its anti-sceptical purpose perfectly well provided that it starts from a premise which Hume accepts—there is no need for that to be something as thin as "having intuitions" or "having perceptions". Perhaps, though, my approach only works if one treats TD in isolation from Kant's broader metaphysics. Taken in such isolation, it may seem reasonable to allow that human experience will involve the categories, but animal experience will not. However, the challenge runs, once you consider Kant's broader commitments the following problem arises: the phenomenal world is constituted by the synthetic acts of its perceivers, and so by allowing nonconceptual intuitions, you allow objects into that world which are not governed by causal laws, and thus not governed by, or amenable to, natural

50   S. Golob

science. Following Hanna, we might call these "rogue objects", that is, "spatiotemporal objects of conscious perception to which the categories either *do not necessarily apply* or *necessarily do not apply*" (Hanna 2011a:407). I agree that the thought of animals going round constituting non-lawlike bits of the world with every perception sounds problematic. But I think the worry can be assuaged—even if one subscribes to a strong reading of Kant's idealism. Suppose, for example, one reads Kant along Van Cleve's (1999:11) lines as a phenomenalist. The result would be that animals and rational sensible agents had, in an important sense, two distinct phenomenal worlds—their world would not be governed by causal laws since it would lack the sophisticated relations for which the categories serve as necessary conditions. Why should this be troubling? Note that anything that is experienced by us, including the animal itself, will, insofar as *we* locate it within a space-time where the relevant distinctions apply, be subject to causal laws. So there is no sense in which this other phenomenal world might disorder our own. Furthermore any minimally sophisticated system of experience, for example any system sophisticated enough to sustain natural science, will include the relevant distinctions and so the categories—so there is no threat to the primacy of, for example, Newtonian physics. Finally, it is of course central to Kant's system that space and time are in an important sense not ontologically ultimate: his interest, as he makes explicit, is in "*our*" mode of experience (B148–9; emphasis in original). In this sense, to borrow Jonathan Lear's (1984:233) phrasing, the "we" can never disappear—this marks an important difference between Kant's emphasis on our finitude, at least in the theoretical realm, and systems such as Hegel's. Given these points, I do not think that the possibility of an alternative, non-categorial, mode of sensible experience should be problematic.

Finally, one might object that there are texts which create problems for my reading, and which I simply have not dealt with. I agree with this; as I said, I cannot attempt a full exegetical defence here. But I can give some indication of why I am hopeful that it can be done. Consider, for example, B161. Summarising TD, Kant writes:

> Consequently all synthesis, through which even perception itself becomes possible, stands under the categories, and since experience is cognition through connected perceptions, the categories are conditions of the possibility of experience. (B161)

2 TD's Compatibility with Nonconceptualism 51

The final part of this, with its emphasis on connected perceptions, is amenable to my reading. But it may seem as if the other half shows that I am simply wrong: it states quite clearly that the categories are a necessary condition on "even perception [*Wahrnehmung*] itself". Yet things are more complex than this first glance suggests. First, as mentioned in Sect. 2.4, I fully accept that Kant occasionally says very conceptualist-sounding things. I have elsewhere tried to explain this as a by-product of a misguided attempt to maintain the mathematical/dynamical category distinction (Golob forthcoming a). Second, as noted in Sect. 2.1, it is deeply unclear what "perception" amounts to, an issue rooted in the interaction between the various terms Kant uses for it. There are texts which align it with phenomenological consciousness, as opposed to unconsciousness, a gloss which B160–1 appears to support (A225/B273; Prol., 4:200, read in conjunction with A320/B376). Yet, taken literally, that would entail that animals lacking the categories also lacked such consciousness, something Kant explicitly denies (Anth, 7:136), and surely a deeply unappealing result philosophically. So for B161 to be plausible, whatever else happens, "perception" there must mean something comparatively substantive—and that at least complicates the simple reading which seemed to provide a problem for me. Third, I think much of TD operates within a tacit scope modifier: its concern as Kant puts it at B149 is "*our* sensible and empirical intuition". It is thus open to me to claim that talk of "perception" here is what really means "adult human perception"—which I agree is categorial. Thus Kant himself immediately continues:

> Thus if, e.g., I make the empirical intuition of a house into perception through apprehension of its manifold [*Wenn ich also z. B. die empirische Anschauung eines Hauses durch Apprehension des Mannigfaltigen derselben zur Wahrnehmung mache*], my ground … is the category of *quantity*. (B162)

I read this with a strong emphasis on the pronoun and the possessive: he is describing the phenomenology of *his* adult human experience, and marking its transcendental conditions.

I have argued that Kant is, in at least some significant sense, a nonconceptualist: in particular NCA is true. Furthermore, insofar as the categories are brought into play by and only by the need to represent certain relations, even adult humans may in at least some cases have intuitive experiences which are entirely nonconceptual. Most importantly, even when the categories do apply, as in the overwhelming majority of our experience, this is not because they are a condition merely on having intuitions or on perceiving. These conclusions are not merely compatible with TD; they illuminate the delicate calibration of the trap which the *Critique* sets for Hume.[15]

---

[15] I would like to thank Lucy Allais, John Callanan, Anil Gomes, Robert Hanna, Dennis Schulting, Andrew Stephenson and Clinton Tolley for extremely helpful discussion of these issues. I am also very grateful to Dennis and to an anonymous referee for their comments on an earlier draft.

3

On the Relation of Intuition to Cognition

Anil Gomes and Andrew Stephenson

3.1 Introduction

> In whatever way and through whatever means a cognition may relate to objects, that through which it relates immediately to them, and at which all thought as a means is directed as an end, is *intuition*. This, however, takes place only insofar as the object is given to us; but this in turn, at least for us humans, is possible only if it affects the mind in a certain way. (B33)

It is has been said that the amount of attention paid to any given section of the *Critique of Pure Reason* is inversely proportional to its distance from the beginning of the book (Moore 2012:310). The above-quoted

---

A. Gomes (✉)
Department of Philosophy, Oxford University, Oxford, UK
e-mail: anil.gomes@trinity.ox.ac.uk

A. Stephenson
Department of Philosophy, Humboldt University, Berlin, Germany
e-mail: andrew.stephenson@philosophy.ox.ac.uk

© The Editor(s) (if applicable) and The Author(s) 2016
D. Schulting (ed.), *Kantian Nonconceptualism*,
DOI 10.1057/978-1-137-53517-7_3

54 A. Gomes and A. Stephenson

two sentences which open the Transcendental Aesthetic (TAe) illustrate the phenomenon. What is intuition? What is its role in cognition? How does intuition give us objects and in what sense is it immediate? The answers to these questions are fundamental to our understanding of Kant's project in the First *Critique*.

Our aim in this essay is largely procedural. We shall suggest that debates about the nature of intuition can be informed by more clearly recognising the implications that the various views have for our understanding of what Kant means by "cognition" (*Erkenntnis*). This gives us a way of making tractable the debates about intuition. For our assessment of views about intuition may depend on our assessment of their implications for cognition.

We proceed as follows. In Sect. 3.2, we characterise two opposing views on the nature of intuition which have dominated recent critical study. In Sect. 3.3, we show how those views determine two opposing views about the nature of cognition. In Sect. 3.4, we set out some implications of adopting each of the views about the nature of cognition. First, regarding real possibility and Kant's modal condition on cognition. Second, regarding the structure and purpose of the Transcendental Deduction of the categories (TD). This allows us to make explicit the commitments of adopting a particular view about the nature of intuition.

Our aim in this chapter is not to show that one account or other of intuition is to be preferred. None of the implications are obviously untenable and there is much to be said in their favour on both sides. Instead we hope to show how to make progress in debates about the nature of intuition by turning instead to the nature of cognition. It is the implications for cognition, we suggest, that will determine which account of intuition we should endorse.

3.2 Intuition

There are a variety of views one might take about the nature of intuition. One important division concerns the question of whether intuitions depend for their existence on the existence of their objects. Call views on which intuitions do so depend *Object-Dependent* views; call views on which they do not *Object-Independent* views.

We need not worry too much about vagaries in the terms "object" and "existence" here. Different kinds of intuition may have different kinds of object, and different kinds of object may enjoy different kinds of existence. Let the object of intuition be whatever is intuited. Then so long as there is some distinction to be had between such objects existing and not existing, we can allow that what this distinction amounts to might vary with the kind of intuition under consideration. *Mutatis mutandis* for the host of related issues that arise in the context of transcendental idealism. What objects are and what it is for them to exist will vary with one's favoured interpretation of transcendental idealism. We can safely abstract from these controversies in asking whether some given interpretation qualifies as an Object-Dependent view or an Object-Independent view *on its own construal of what the difference amounts to*. The same goes for the existence of intuitions themselves. What intuitions are and what it is for them to exist will vary with one's favoured interpretation of intuition. We can safely abstract from these controversies in asking whether some given interpretation qualifies as an Object-Dependent view or an Object-Independent view on its own construal of what the difference amounts to.

As for what it means for intuitions to "depend" for their existence on the existence of their objects, we have in mind any relation that yields a strict implication. Object-Dependent views say that, necessarily, if there exists an intuition i of some object o, then o exists. Object-Independent views deny this. Note that this way of drawing the distinction means that accounts on which certain kinds of intuition depend for their existence on the existence of their objects while certain other kinds of intuition do not, would count as Object-Independent views. For some purposes it might be useful to be more fine-grained than this, indexing the distinction to different kinds of intuition. This need not concern us here. The considerations that follow hold generally. Note also that this way of drawing the distinction means that accounts that are silent on whether intuitions depend for their existence on the existence of their objects count as neither Object-Dependent nor Object-Independent views. There may be many purposes for which it is legitimate to remain neutral on this matter. But a full account of intuition ought not and many accounts do not.

Object-Dependent views come in a variety of forms. Interpreters who agree that intuitions depend for their own existence on the existence of their objects might disagree over whether intuitions involve relations of perceptual acquaintance or merely causal relations to objects. They might disagree over whether or not intuitions have representational content, and even where there is agreement that intuitions do have such content, there might be disagreement as to its nature, preconditions or role.

Lucy Allais (2015), for instance, has argued that the intuition of an object is the "presence to consciousness" of that object.[1] Her model here is the contemporary relationalist or naïve realist theory of perceptual experience, according to which perceiving an object essentially involves standing in a primitive relation of perceptual acquaintance to it. Such relations are conceived of as requiring the existence of their relata. Thus Allais's view is a form of Object-Dependent view. Similarly for Colin McLear's (2016) reading of intuition. Intuition, according to McLear, is a state in which the intuiting subject is directly acquainted with "mind-independent tracts of [her] environment" (2016:96). These might be called *constitutional* forms of the Object-Dependent view. Intuitions depend for their existence on the existence of their objects because they are partly constituted by their objects.

Eric Watkins and Marcus Willaschek (forthcoming) prefer to cash out the relation between an intuition and its object in causal rather than constitutional terms, at least when it comes to empirical intuitions. They also give a fundamental explanatory role to representational content. For Watkins and Willaschek, "intuitions and concepts relate to their objects both *by representing them*, i.e., having an objective representational content, and *by referring to them*". Nevertheless, they think that "intuition establishes an immediate awareness of the existence of the object". Similarly for Clinton Tolley (2013:116). According to Tolley, intuitions have a nonconceptual representational content and are object-dependent in the sense that "they entail the *existence* of their objects", although they are not "object-involving" in the sense of containing the object to which the subject is related in intuition. Consider finally John McDowell (1998), who combines an Object-Dependent view with the claim that

---

[1] See also Allais (2009, 2010, 2011).

intuitions have exclusively conceptual content. For McDowell, "enjoying intuitions—having objects in view—is to be understood in terms of the same logical togetherness in actualizations of conceptual capacities that makes sense of the unity of a judgeable content" (1998:439–40). Having objects in view is to be understood here as a success state. If one intuits an object, then there really is an object that one has in view. Thus "Kant's conception of intuitions embodies a version of Evans's thesis that perceptual demonstrative content is object-dependent" (McDowell 1998:475).[2]

Object-Independent views also come in a variety of forms. Interpreters who agree that intuitions do *not* depend for their own existence on that of their objects might disagree over whether or not they have representational content, and even where there is agreement that intuitions do have such content, there might be disagreement as to its nature, preconditions or role. Stefanie Grüne (2009), for instance, argues that intuitions represent their objects by means of intuitive marks, or tropes. Such a means of representation, she emphasises, is independent of the existence of the represented object (Grüne 2009:42–3). Yet it is fundamentally different in kind to the way in which concepts represent their objects via discursive marks. According to Grüne, intuitions have an essentially nonconceptual content while at the same time being object-independent.

However—and perhaps unlike Object-Dependent views—Object-Independent views can plausibly be regarded as having a *locus classicus*: conceptualist intentionalist readings of Kant. Versions of this reading can be found in Richard Aquila (1983), Derk Pereboom (1988), Gerold Prauss (1971), Wilfrid Sellars (1968) (McDowell's conceptualist but Object-Dependent appropriation notwithstanding) and Hans Vaihinger (1892). The connection between the intentionalist reading of Kant and the Object-Independent view of intuition should not be surprising. It is a characteristic mark of intentional relations that they can hold between subject and object even when the latter fails to exist. According to Pereboom, for instance, intuitions manifest intentional relations that are

---

[2] Others who defend or express an Object-Dependent view include Abela (2002:35–6), Buroker (2006:37), Cassam (1993:117), Gomes (2014), Gomes (forthcoming), Hanna (2001:210; 2005:259), Setiya (2004:66), Thompson (1972:331), Warren (1998:221) and Willaschek (1997:547).

"concept-dependent" but "existence-independent". Elaborating on the latter, he says:

> For Kant, what we are immediately aware of in typical intentional relations are the contents of intuitions, some of which are real or, we might say, exist, and others of which are not real, or do not exist. (Pereboom 1988:325)[3]

Both the Object-Dependent view of intuition and the Object-Independent view of intuition have had their supporters. And debate about the merits of the two views has surfaced in the recent attention paid to the question of whether intuition depends on the conceptual activity of the understanding.[4] How, then, are we to decide between the two views? There are a number of exegetical questions and the debate continues in Grüne (2014a, b), Grüne (forthcoming), McLear (2014a), McLear (forthcoming b), Stephenson (2015b) and Stephenson (forthcoming). We shall not address these here. We believe that, alongside the exegetical issues, there are systematic structural considerations which bear on the decision. This is the line we pursue.

All the parties to this debate should accept the following characterisation of the relation between intuition and cognition:

(I): The role of intuition is to give objects for cognition.

This is stated in the opening sentences of TAe. It is repeated in a number of key passages.[5] For example, in the Introduction to the Transcendental Logic:

> Our cognition arises from two fundamental sources in the mind, the first of which is the reception of representations (the receptivity of impressions), the second the faculty for cognizing an object by means of these representations

---

[3] Others who defend or express an Object-Independent view include: Grüne (2014a), Grüne (forthcoming), Hintikka (1969), Howell (1973:217), Parsons (1992), Roche (2011:361, 370), Stephenson (2011, 2015b), Stephenson (forthcoming) and Wilson (1975:262).

[4] See Allais (2010:60), Hanna (2005:259) and Roche (2011:361).

[5] See also A95; B165; A155–6/B194–5; A239/B298; A719/B747.

3 On the Relation of Intuition to Cognition   59

(spontaneity of concepts); through the former an object is *given* to us, through the latter it is *thought* in relation to that representation (as a mere determination of the mind). Intuition and concepts therefore constitute the elements of all our cognition, so that neither concepts without intuition corresponding to them in some way nor intuition without concepts can yield a cognition. (A50/B74)

The use of this pure cognition, however, depends on this as its condition: that objects are given to us in intuition, to which it can be applied. For without intuition all of our cognition would lack objects, and therefore remain completely empty. (A62/B87)

And in TD:

There are two conditions under which alone the cognition of an object is possible: first, *intuition*, through which it is given, but only as appearance; second, *concept*, through which an object is thought that corresponds to this intuition. (A92–3/B125)

Two components belong to cognition: first, the concept, through which an object is thought at all (the category), and second, the intuition, through which it is given. (B146; cf. A95)

Furthermore, the characteristics of intuition—singularity and immediacy (A320/B376–7; Log, 9:91)—flow from this functional characterisation of intuition. Kant thinks that it is only if intuitions are singular and immediate that they can play the role of giving objects for cognition (A19/B33, B48; Prol, 4:282).[6] So there are grounds for taking (I) to be the most basic characterisation of intuition.

With this in mind, we can make tractable the question of which account of intuition to endorse by considering the following question: What must intuition be like if it is to play the role of giving objects

---

[6] This is further confirmed by the fact that Kant still talks about objects being given in intuition for the divine, intuitive kind of intellect, one that properly speaking lacks a discursive or general and mediate faculty (e.g. at B72; B138–9).

60   A. Gomes and A. Stephenson

for cognition? Answering this question can help us fix upon the correct account of intuition. Unfortunately, that task is made difficult by the fact that there is no agreement in the literature on how to understand the notion of cognition. We shall suggest in the next section that differing views on the nature of intuition determine differing views on the nature of cognition.

3.3   Cognition

The notion of *Erkenntnis* is central to the project of the First *Critique*. Kemp Smith renders the German term as "knowledge", as do Meiklejohn and Müller. Recent translations—most notably Guyer/Wood and Pluhar—prefer the term "cognition". We shall stick with the latter. But it is important to be clear that the acceptance of this usage does not settle the substantive interpretative issues concerning the nature of cognition.

To many, Kant seems to use the term in different ways. In the notorious *Stufenleiter* passage, for example, cognition is characterised as objective perception. Intuitions and concepts then seem to be both classed separately as cognitions in this sense, and as such are contrasted only with sensations, subjective representations which "refer to the subject as a modification of its state" (A320/B376).[7] But there is also a more restricted use of the term according to which cognition is the output of being given something in intuition *and* applying a concept or concepts to it. This is the sense of "cognition" in play in the passages quoted in the previous section, as well as in the infamous dictum:

> Thoughts without content are empty, intuitions without concepts blind. … Only from their unification [i.e., that of the understanding and the senses] can cognition arise. (A51–2/B75–6)

---

[7] Though see Tolley (MS a) for an alternative reading of this passage on which Kant's intention is not to classify intuitions and concepts as separate species of cognition but rather to unpack what is involved in cognition—this is especially amenable to what follows.

3 On the Relation of Intuition to Cognition 61

Kant goes on to call this "cognition in the proper sense" (A78/B103) and we take it that this restricted notion of cognition is the dominant one in the *Critique*. For one thing, cognition in the *Stufenleiter* sense, on the traditional reading of this passage, would seem to include mere "ideas", concepts "of reason" for which no object can be given in intuition, such as that of God. Yet Kant is often at pains to distinguish the mere *thought* we can have of such things from the *cognition* we can have of objects that *can* be given in intuition (e.g. at Bxxvi, B146, B165).

It is clear, then, that intuitions and concepts are each independently necessary for cognition "in the proper sense". We take it, further, that they are jointly sufficient: bringing an intuition under a concept *suffices* for cognition. This is crucial for arguments we present below. It is probably our most controversial assumption and we have no knock-down argument for it. Our motivations are largely negative. It is simply not clear what other, distinct conditions might be necessary for cognition. No other conditions have anything like the status that intuitions and concepts enjoy. Certainly, Kant does not seem to think that any further kind of *representation* is required. He says that "*two* components belong to cognition" (B146; emphasis added), that "intuition and concepts therefore *constitute the elements* of all our cognition" (A50/B74; emphasis added). No mention is made of any third element. Note that, to trouble our claim, any such additional element would have to be genuinely *distinct*. It is no problem if non-distinct representations are also involved in cognition, such as, in empirical cases, the sensations that constitute the manifold of empirical intuition. Similarly for additional conditions that are not additional representations.[8] According to the Object-Dependent view of intuition, for instance, the object of intuition must exist if there is to be an intuition of it. On such a view, it will be a condition on cognition that the object of cognition exist. More on this and other examples below. Such conditions are not conditions above and beyond those

---

[8] In some ways the example that follows is not optimal given this distinction between the requirement for some additional representation and the requirement for some other additional condition, since on some views the object of intuition will itself count as a representation. If this is your view, a better idea of the distinction will be given below when we come to some other potential conditions, like truth and justification. Consciousness is another potential condition that does not fit especially neatly into the distinction. But either way it again seems plausible that it would not constitute a genuinely distinct condition—that it would be involved in cognition simply in virtue of being involved in bringing intuitions under concepts.

that come for free with bringing an intuition under a concept. They are not really *additional* conditions on cognition at all.

What are the candidates for genuinely additional conditions on cognition? There might, for instance, be restrictions on *the way* in which an intuition must be brought under a concept if it is to amount to cognition. Again, it is just not clear what such restrictions might be. Kant does not explicitly say that there are any. But consider the following option. Suppose a subject intuits a painted horse and her intuition is brought under the concept of a zebra. Horses are not zebras; to judge of a horse that it is a zebra would be to judge falsely. So one might argue that this is not cognition because the intuition has not been brought under a concept in such a way as to produce or ground *knowledge*. On this account, cognition requires more than the subsumption of an intuition under a concept. It requires, further, that the subsumption be (or enable or produce something that is) true and, perhaps, justified.

This brings us to a second motivation for our view that cognition *just is* the bringing of an intuition under a concept. No doubt there is a close connection between cognition and knowledge. Intuiting a zebra and bringing this intuition under the concept of a zebra is surely a paradigmatic way of coming to know various things, such as that there are zebras. But there is increasing recognition that the *identification* of cognition with knowledge is incautious, at least if knowledge is understood as anything like the kind of propositional knowledge that has been the focus of much contemporary epistemology.[9] And if cognition cannot be identified with knowledge, then we have not been given reason to impose additional conditions on cognition beyond the bringing of intuitions under concepts.

Why is it a mistake to identify cognition and knowledge? Consider the traditional conception of knowledge as justified true belief. The most obvious problem with equating cognition and justified true belief might plausibly be regarded as a red herring. Kant occasionally talks about false cognitions (A55/B83; cf. A59/B84, A709/B737; Log, 9:50–1, 54). So too do we occasionally talk about false banknotes. What we really mean is pieces of paper that purport to be banknotes but aren't. There is nothing infelicitous in talking this way and perhaps it is how we should read Kant. His talk

---

[9] See, for example, Schafer (forthcoming).

3 On the Relation of Intuition to Cognition 63

of false cognitions is properly understood as talk about representations that purport to be cognitions but aren't, because they are false.

Two further problems are much more difficult to deal with. First, Kant does not seem to think of cognition as a species of assent, or holding-for-true (A820/B848ff.; Log, 9:66ff.). Cognition, unlike knowledge, does not entail belief. In this respect, the Kantian term that seems closer to knowledge is rather *Wissen*, and Kant keeps the terms *Wissen* and *Erkenntnis* apart with notable—one might even say uncharacteristic—consistency. Second, the same goes for justification. The closest Kantian analogue of justification is something involved in what he calls "objective sufficiency". And objective sufficiency is a feature of assents, not cognitions.[10]

To this last point it might be objected that all cognitions are either a priori or a posteriori, and these are surely justificatory notions, so there is after all a connection between cognition and justification. This might be true. Suppose for the sake of argument that cognitions are indeed the kind of things that can themselves be justified and that each is either a priori or a posteriori. This on its own is not enough to save the knowledge account of cognition. As Frege (1960:3–4) notices, whether or not some given cognition is to be classed as a priori, say, is a matter of how it *could in principle* be justified. This says nothing about how *or even whether* it is, as a matter of fact, justified.

None of the three traditional marks of knowledge fare well. This suggests that motivations for adding further conditions on cognition which arise from an identification of cognition and knowledge are to be resisted. There is of course much more to say and different aspects of this issue will arise again shortly. For the moment we hope to have said enough to have at least shifted the burden of proof onto those who think that further conditions are required for cognition, so as to allow us to continue working with the view that cognition arises from bringing an intuition under a concept without further conditions.

The opposing views on the nature of intuition have implications for how we should think of cognition. As already noted, the translation of

---

[10] Very different grounds for rejecting the cognition = knowledge thesis are developed in Stephenson (2015a).

64   A. Gomes and A. Stephenson

Erkenntnis as "knowledge" has been largely rejected.[11] But there are weaker and stronger ways of rejecting this translation. According to one weaker view—which nevertheless avoids the problems that dog the knowledge account—cognition is a certain kind of object-directed representation in which one picks out an actual object and predicates some property of it. This view understands cognition to be an objective representation in the sense that it concerns some particular object or objects. Call this the *Object-Dependent* view of *cognition*.

The Object-Dependent view is a step away from the equation of cognition with a kind of knowledge, since there can be thoughts that are object-directed but false. I can think of a man holding the martini glass that he is drinking martini, when in fact he is drinking water. This allows the view to make sense of the passages in which Kant talks of false cognitions, and in a less deflationary way than the knowledge view. But it is close to the knowledge view in an important sense: cognition, on the Object-Dependent view, is a kind of acquaintance with objects, one in which the subject is in touch with objects and able to think thoughts about them.[12] The Object-Dependent view is in this sense a generalisation of one core aspect of the traditional knowledge view. Otherwise put, the identification of cognition with a kind of knowledge entails but is not entailed by the Object-Dependent view.

An alternative view of cognition involves a stronger rejection of the traditional picture. According to what we shall call the *Object-Independent* view of *cognition*, cognition is a representation which has objective purport. What it is for a representation to have objective purport is for it to represent a state of affairs as obtaining. There are many ways one might cash out the details of this notion but we take it that it will involve the possession of truth-conditions.[13] Typically—though not always, as in certain cases of inner cognition—these truth-conditions will concern objects distinct in some way from the subject. What is important, for the Object-

---

[11] We acknowledge that this may well have been as much for linguistic reasons as for the reasons we just outlined—"cognition", unlike "knowledge" and like *Erkenntnis*, can take the plural, and it is closer to the Latinate *cognitio*, which Kant occasionally parenthetically appends.

[12] For discussion, including the connection of this view to those of Russell and Evans, see Allais (2010:60), McLear (2016:127ff.) and Schafer (forthcoming).

[13] See Burge (2010) for a recent discussion of these issues.

3 On the Relation of Intuition to Cognition 65

Independent view, is that representations can have objective purport even in cases in which there is in fact no actual object that one is representing. Thus the Object-Independent view allows that one can cognise without there being any actual object to which one is related in so cognising.

These two views come apart in one direction. Consider imaginings. In certain episodes of imagining, for instance hallucination, there is no really existing object to which one's imaginational representations are directed. So a subject cannot have cognition in the first sense. But one's imaginings may still represent objective states of affairs, perhaps by purporting to represent genuine objects. So there are representations which count as cognitions on the second view but not on the first. The converse does not hold: any cognition which is directed at objects will also purport to be objective. Just as any case of cognition according to the knowledge view will also be a case of cognition according to the Object-Dependent view but not conversely, any case of cognition according to the Object-Dependent view will also be a case of cognition according to the Object-Independent view but not conversely. The conditions the views place on cognition reduce in stricture from left to right—the knowledge view, the Object-Dependent view, the Object-Independent view.

Note that the intended sense of "purport" has nothing to do with whether or not the subject would be willing to assert that things really are as they are presented to her. In Kantian terms, for a representation to be objective does not require an act of assent. In the good case, where the subject's representation with objective purport is also an object-directed representation, the subject may falsely believe that she is imagining. In the bad case, where the subject's representation with objective purport is not also an object-directed representation, she might be fully aware of this fact. In both cases, she has a representation with objective purport but would not base an assertion upon her representation in the normal way, for she does not believe her eyes. Kant was clearly alive to such possibilities, and thus to the distinction between purport and assent. He refers to them in drawing out a shared feature of transcendental and optical illusion at the beginning of the Dialectic (A297–8/B353–4). Transcendental illusion does not cease to be an illusion once one has shown that it is an illusion any more than "the astronomer can prevent the rising moon from appearing larger to him, even when he is not deceived by this illusion"

(A297/B354). In these terms, the objective purport of a cognition is how things appear to the subject in having the cognition, independently of what she makes of how things appear to her when forming assents.

How do these two views of cognition relate to our two accounts of intuition? Given our chosen nomenclature, our answer should not be surprising. Assume that intuitions are object-dependent. Then one cannot have an intuition of an object o without o existing. So whenever one brings one's intuitions under a concept and makes a judgement about o to the effect that it is F, there will be some object o about which one is making a judgement. And since bringing intuitions under concepts is necessary for cognition, there cannot be cases of cognition in which one's cognitions have objective purport without there being some object to which one's cognition is directed. So the Object-Dependent view of intuition entails the Object-Dependent view of cognition.

Conversely, assume that intuitions are not object-dependent. Then one can have an intuition of an object o without there being any such o to which one is related. If one brings this intuition under a concept, then one has made a judgement that o is F without there being any o about which one has made a judgement. But bringing intuitions under concepts suffices for cognition, so one can cognise that o is F without there being some o at which one's cognition is directed. So the Object-Independent view of intuition is incompatible with the Object-Dependent view of cognition (and a fortiori the knowledge view). If we now assume further that the Object-Dependent and Object-Independent views of cognition partition the logical space, then the Object-Independent view of intuition entails the Object-Independent view of cognition. This last assumption might be controversial. Even so, the two views certainly fit very naturally together. For if one does not think that cognition requires there being actual objects to which one is related, then one is committed to thinking of cognition as extending beyond object-directed representations. And the natural way to do that is to take cognition to be any representation with objective purport, of which object-directed representations form merely a proper subset.

To summarise: one's view on whether or not intuitions are object-dependent has implications for one's views on the nature of cognition. On the view that intuitions are object-dependent, cognition must be thought of as a form of object-directed representation, whereas the view that intuitions are not object-dependent goes together most naturally with, and plausibly entails, the view that cognitions are representations with mere objective purport.

3.4 Implications

In this section we draw out two implications of adopting one or other view about the nature of intuition which result from their implications for the nature of cognition: first, regarding real possibility (Sect. 3.4.1); second, regarding the structure and purpose of TD (Sect. 3.4.2). These topics are closely connected.

3.4.1 The Modal Condition on Cognition

Kant endorses a link between cognition and what he calls "real" possibility. This is stated clearly in a footnote to the B Preface, which is worth quoting in full:

> To *cognize* an object, it is required that I be able to prove its possibility (whether by the testimony of experience from its actuality or *a priori* through reason). But I can *think* whatever I like, as long as I do not contradict myself, i.e., as long as my concept is a possible thought, even if I cannot give any assurance whether or not there is a corresponding object somewhere within the sum total of all possibilities. But in order to ascribe objective validity to such a concept (real possibility, for the first sort of possibility was merely logical) something more is required. This "more", however, need not be sought in theoretical sources of cognition; it may also lie in practical ones. (Bxxvi)

More specifically, then, Kant thinks it a necessary condition on cognition that the cognising subject be able to prove the real possibility of the object of her cognition. The opposing views of intuition yield different accounts of how we should understand this claim.

68   A. Gomes and A. Stephenson

The nature of real possibility is a complex and controversial issue that we cannot hope to cover fully here.[14] It suffices for present purposes to note that, whereas freedom from contradiction is necessary *and sufficient* for logical possibility, real possibility is stricter than this. "Something more is required", Kant says in the above-quoted footnote, later issuing "a warning not to infer immediately from the possibility of the concept (logical possibility) to the possibility of the thing (real possibility)" (A596/B624; cf. V-Met-L2/Pölitz, 28:1016). According to Kant, there are logical possibilities that are not real possibilities, but not conversely. He gives various examples of the logically possible but really impossible: thinking matter, or an extended subject which possesses a mind (BDG 2:85; cf. NTH, 1:355, RGV, 6:128–9); matter that has attractive forces but no repulsive forces (MAN, 4:511); a figure that is enclosed between two straight lines (A220–1/B268); and the being with all realities (A274/B330; cf. V-Met-L2/Pölitz, 28:1025–6). What matters here is not the really impossible and what makes it so. Our concern is with the really possible and how it is that cognition puts us in a position to prove it. In particular, our concern is with theoretical cognition. The last sentence of the B Preface footnote makes it clear that Kant's modal condition is also meant to hold for practical cognition, but let us put that to one side. What is it about the theoretical cognition of an object that distinguishes it from the mere thought of an object and provides the "something more"?

The natural answer, of course, is intuition. Unlike the mere thought of an object, the cognition of an object puts the subject in a position to prove the object's real possibility because cognition, unlike mere thought, involves intuition, and only really possible objects can be intuited. This also gives us an explanation for (I): the role of intuitions is to give objects for cognition because intuitions provide the kind of singular and immediate relation to objects that secures, and thereby puts us in a position to prove, their real possibility. Hence the fact that the opposing views of intuition yield different accounts of this connection.

Recall from Sect. 3.3 that all cases of cognition on the Object-Dependent view are cases of cognition on the Object-Independent view,

---

[14] See Stang (2016) for the most comprehensive account to date.

3 On the Relation of Intuition to Cognition 69

but not conversely. Otherwise put, the set of objects that one can cognise on the Object-Independent view is larger than the set of objects that one can cognise on the Object-Dependent view. Given the link between cognition and real possibility, it follows that the set of objects that cognition puts us in a position to prove really possible is larger on the Object-Independent view than it is on the Object-Dependent view. In particular, only the Object-Independent view and not the Object-Dependent view allows that cognition can put us in a position to prove the real possibility of non-actual objects. This initial difference has repercussions.

Take the Object-Independent view first. Why would it follow, as it does on the Object-Independent view, that cognition of non-actual objects puts us in a position to prove their real possibility? The most straightforward explanation would be that this is because real possibility is equivalent to—or at least is already entailed by—the kind of possibility Kant defines in the Postulates:

> Whatever agrees with the formal conditions of experience (in accordance with intuition and concepts) is *possible*. (A218/B266)

Call this *formal* possibility. Cognition through intuition puts us in a position to prove the real possibility of objects by showing that they are formally possible, which is to say compatible with our sensible and intellectual forms of space and time and the categories.

An example will illustrate the proposal. Consider the hallucination of a pink elephant. This is not a case of illusion. One is not seeing a grey elephant under unusual lighting conditions—there is in fact no elephant to which one is related. On the Object-Independent view, this is nevertheless a cognition of a pink elephant. Since being in a position to prove is a factive state—one is in a position to prove p, only if p—the modal condition on cognition entails that this suffices to show that a pink elephant is a really possible object. How can it do this when there is no pink elephant in existence? By showing that a pink elephant is in accordance with the formal conditions on experience, for formal possibility entails real possibility.

By contrast, the Object-Dependent view has it that one cannot have a cognition of an object without the object existing. Thus, it is not committed to cognition putting us in a position to prove the real possibility of non-actual objects, nor therefore is it committed to formal possibility being sufficient for real possibility. This is already an interesting result, but with a few additional assumptions we can say something stronger. Suppose that the Object-Dependent view takes formal possibility to be sufficient for real possibility. Then the Object-Dependent view has a similar explanation of how cognition puts us in a position to prove real possibility to that offered by the Object-Independent view above. All cognised objects are actual on this view, and presumably actuality entails formal possibility, so if this in turn entails real possibility, it is easy to see how cognition puts us in a position to prove real possibility.

But the supplementation of the Object-Dependent view with the claim that formal possibility is sufficient for real possibility raises questions. First, note that there is something superfluous about the middle step here. It is just as evident that actuality entails real possibility as it is that actuality entails formal possibility. So why go via formal possibility at all? Second, relatedly, there is also something superfluous about cognition here. Various other processes which do not count as cognition by the standards of the Object-Dependent view, such as hallucination and certain kinds of imagination, would also be sufficient for showing formal possibility, and thus real possibility if the entailment in question is allowed to stand. The thought, then, is that Kant seems to think there is something special about the relation between cognition and (our ability to prove) real possibility. The modal condition on cognition is not likewise a condition on any old state, nor even just on those with objective purport.

A defender of the Object-Dependent view who finds these questions pressing may instead opt to deny that formal possibility entails real possibility. What might ground such a denial? Suppose we strengthened the modal condition on cognition to a biconditional, so that cognition is not only sufficient but also *necessary* for us to be able to prove real possibility—it is not just one way but *the* way to get in a position to prove real possibility. Then it would follow, on the Object-Dependent view, that there are objects we can prove formally possible but not really possible, for instance the non-existent objects of hallucinations. And the most straightforward explanation would be that this is because formal

3 On the Relation of Intuition to Cognition   71

possibility does not suffice for real possibility—just the relationship we were looking for.

Indeed, we could go even further. If we now also assumed that all really possible objects are provably really possible, then it would follow, on the Object-Dependent view, that the only really possible objects are actual objects. For in effect what these assumptions together achieve is a restriction of what is really possible to what is cognisable, and the Object-Dependent view has it that only actual objects can be cognised. And since, as mentioned above, it is presumably the case that all actual objects are really possible, what we have here, on the Object-Dependent view, is a collapse of any (extensional) distinction between the really possible and the actual.

Recall from Sect. 3.1 that none of these potential implications is supposed to act as a *reductio* of the views in question. This holds for the current proposal too. Kant certainly recognises and considers extremely important a notion of possibility on which the possible coincides exactly with the actual (and indeed with the necessary). This notion of possibility is one on which what is possible is constrained not only by the formal conditions of experience but also by the empirical laws of nature along with its prior states (A230–2/B282–4).

In any case, several assumptions have been made and the issues that surround them are complex. For instance, the assumption that all real possibilities are provably really possible looks highly plausible in an idealist context. But here is not the place to conduct an investigation into the nature of Kant's idealism. We focus instead on saying a little more about the other key assumption in the preceding chain of reasoning, namely that cognition is not just one way but the *only* way to prove real possibility.

As a *general* thesis, the claim looks somewhat dubious. In the *Critique of Pure Reason* Kant denies that we can have cognition of God or immortality. He retains this doctrine in the *Critique of Practical Reason* but now he appears to argue that their real possibility is established through our knowledge (*Wissen*) of the moral law and freedom as its condition (KpV, 5:3–5). If so, and if establishing real possibility in this way suffices for proving it in the sense employed in the modal condition on cognition, then there are objects that we can prove really possible though not cognise. Perhaps Kant has some special notion of proof in mind in the modal condition. And even if not, it is not wholly implausible that these

72   A. Gomes and A. Stephenson

particular "practical" objects, presupposed in the practical use of pure reason, are the only exceptions. But in any case, recall that our primary interest is in theoretical cognition. The claim should be understood as restricted accordingly. The question is this: Is *theoretical* cognition, via intuition, necessary for us to be able to prove the real possibility of *theoretical* objects?

Kant slides easily and often between talking about the real possibility of objects and about the real possibility of concepts. It is evident that he takes the two ways of talking to be inter-translatable. This is an extremely widespread feature of his writings and is to be expected given his logic (see especially Log, 9:91ff.). Moreover, when he does start talking about the real possibility of concepts, Kant tends to equate it with objective validity. One such passage is the B Preface footnote quoted above. This suggests that proving the real possibility of an object and proving the objective validity of a concept are one and the same. In particular, being in a position to prove the real possibility of an object entails being in a position to prove the objective validity of the concept of that object. If this is right, then the prospects of finding evidence for our claim start to look quite good. For it seems to amount to the claim that a connection to intuition through cognition is a requirement of any concept having objective validity, which is a staple Kantian doctrine. Here is a passage from the Phenomena and Noumena chapter, for example:

> For every concept there is requisite, first, the logical form of a concept (of thinking) in general, and then, second, the possibility of giving it an object to which it is to be related. Without this latter it has no sense, and is entirely empty of content .... Now the object cannot be given to a concept otherwise than in intuition .... Without this they have no objective validity at all. (A239/B298; cf. KU, 5:351)

There is, however, a notable qualification in this doctrine. Establishing the objective validity of a concept requires the mere *possibility* of giving it an object in intuition. We were looking for evidence to support (a suitably restricted version of) the claim that cognition is necessary, and not only sufficient, for us to be able to prove real possibility. All we have so far is that the *possibility* of cognition plays such a role.

3 On the Relation of Intuition to Cognition   73

Nevertheless, it is far from obvious how we ought to analyse this qualification. One option might be to appeal again to the notion of formal possibility. In this case the claim would simply be that formal possibility is necessary for us to be able to prove real possibility, so far something ruled out by neither of our candidate views. But there are several other plausible analyses that would secure the required result that, for this form of the Object-Dependent view, only actual objects can be proved really possible. For instance, we have already seen that Kant countenances a notion of possibility on which nothing is possible that is not actual. Perhaps this is the notion of possibility involved in Kant's talk of possible cognition. And significantly weaker notions are available that would also suffice. In particular, it is quite natural to read "*o* is an object of possible cognition" as saying something like the following: it would be humanly feasible, given how things are with us now in the current state of information, for someone to get themselves into a position to cognise *o*.

The technical details of such an analysis are complex and not at all easy to fill out in the standard contemporary framework of possible worlds,[15] but the basic idea is simple. The objects of possible cognition do not include any old objects that happen to be cognised in some world structurally similar enough to our own. Assuming the Object-Dependent view, they include only the objects that exist in this world—the world where we are. Of course they need not actually be cognised by us now. But they do have to exist (have existed, etc.) if we are *to be able*, in the relevant sense, to cognise them. Possible cognition does not outstrip actual objects (though it is important to be clear that this is *not* to say that it does not outstrip actual cognition). The following well-known passage provides some support for such an interpretation of the notion of possibility at work in Kant's doctrine:

> That there could be inhabitants of the moon, even though no human being has ever perceived them, must of course be admitted; but this means only

---

[15] Anti-realists have done the most to articulate this notion. See Dummett (1993:45–6), Tennant (2000:829)—the best formal treatment—and Wright (2001:60). The commonly recognised connections between Kant and anti-realism could well provide a good source for more systematic support for the current proposal. For an application of the notion in the Kantian context, see Stephenson (MS).

> that in the possible progress of experience we could encounter them; for everything is actual that stands in one context with a perception in accordance with the laws of the empirical progression. (A493/B521)

Just as the possible progress of experience does not cover objects that do not actually exist, nor does possible cognition more generally.

There is of course much more to be said here. For our present, procedural purposes, it is enough to have set up some conditionals and to have highlighted some salient issues. It is natural for the Object-Independent view to take real possibility as already entailed by formal possibility, perhaps because it thinks formal possibility is just one particular species of real possibility. The Object-Dependent view can likewise take real possibility as already entailed by formal possibility, but only at the cost of making the relation to something actual superfluous in proving the real possibility of objects, and only at the cost of making the connection to intuition in cognition superfluous for proving the real possibility of objects. The alternative is for the Object-Dependent view to deny that real possibility is already entailed by formal possibility. And if it does not want to go further and collapse real possibility into actuality, then it must also deny either that all real possibilities are provably really possible or that only actual objects can be the objects of possible cognition in the relevant Kantian sense. Doing either would involve investigations that would likely take us to the very heart of Kant's Critical system.

3.4.2 The Transcendental Deduction of the Categories

Kant's aim in TD is to show that "without [the categories'] presupposition nothing is possible as *object of experience*" (A93/B126). For "the objective validity of the categories, as *a priori* concepts, rests on the fact that through them alone is experience possible" (A93/B126). As we have seen, showing the objective validity of a concept amounts to showing the real possibility of the objects that fall under that concept. So showing the objective validity of the categories requires showing the real possibility of objects that instantiate the categories.

What is involved in showing the objective validity of the pure concepts of the understanding, and thereby the real possibility of objects that instantiate them? Kant's solution involves the claim that "the manifold

3 On the Relation of Intuition to Cognition   75

in a given intuition also necessarily stands under categories" (B143), and that "from the way in which the empirical intuition is given in sensibility … its unity can be none other than the one the category prescribes to the manifold of a given intuition" (B144–5). The opposing views of intuition suggest different accounts of how to understand these claims.

Let us start with the Object-Independent view of intuition. On this view, intuitions need not have actual objects in order to give objects for cognition. Since bringing an intuition under a concept suffices for cognition, there are cognitions which do not represent actual objects. And since cognition involves showing the real possibility of objects that instantiate the concepts involved in one's cognition, doing so does not involve showing that there is an actual object which instantiates the concept in question. We suggested above that the best way to make sense of this claim is for the Object-Independent view to hold that real possibility is equivalent to, or at least already entailed by, formal possibility, which is to say compatibility with our sensible and intellectual forms.

The implication for TD is that showing the objective validity of the categories involves showing only that the categories accord with the formal conditions of intuition. Thus the claims that "the manifold in a given intuition also necessarily stands under categories" and that "from the way in which the empirical intuition is given in sensibility … its unity can be none other than the one the category prescribes to the manifold of a given intuition" are to be understood as claims about states which seem to present us with objects—*objective* representations in the sense, articulated in Sect. 3.3, of representations with objective *purport*. It is a condition on seeming to be presented with an object that such an object be presented as falling under the pure concepts. If showing that "the manifold in a given intuition also necessarily stands under the categories" is sufficient to show that "without [the categories'] presupposition nothing is possible as object of experience", then TD is completed when we see that all representations which purport to represent objects necessarily present objects as falling under the categories.

It is compatible with this conclusion that there are no objects which *actually* fall under the categories—or, at least, we need a further step to ensure that this is not so. So the Object-Independent view is committed to thinking that Kant's project in TD, as characterised above, can be secured without

76   A. Gomes and A. Stephenson

showing that there are objects which actually fall under the categories. And if the theorist rejects the above characterisation of Kant's project in TD, then they are at least committed to any further conclusion requiring extra work.

Consider next the Object-Dependent view. On this view, intuitions depend for their existence on the presence of the objects. Since the application of concepts to intuition is sufficient for cognition, cognitions are object-directed representations: representations which concern an actual object or objects. We noted above two options for the Object-Dependent view. The first combines the view with the claim that formal possibility is sufficient to prove real possibility. The second combines the view with the claim that formal possibility is insufficient to prove real possibility. We suggested that the first commitment threatens to make the connection to actuality superfluous in the case in which intuition of an object proves its real possibility. And we suggested that the second commitment can be supported by those who hold that cognition is not only sufficient for proving the real possibility of objects but, in the theoretical sphere, also necessary. These are quite different approaches and we treat them separately.

Consider the first form of the Object-Dependent view. This is the combination of the views that intuitions depend for their existence on the presence of their objects and that formal possibility suffices for real possibility. On the face of it, this view incurs no more commitments than the Object-Independent view, since it allows that there are ways to prove the real possibility of objects which do not require being related to something actual in intuition. But if the view is to take account of Kant's claim that TD shows "from the way in which the empirical intuition is given in sensibility that its unity can be none other than the one the category prescribes to the manifold of a given intuition", it must hold that showing the objective validity of the categories requires showing that all intuitions are presented as falling under the categories. And since intuitions depend for their existence on the presence of their objects, this amounts to the claim that TD, as characterised above, is secured when it is shown that there are actual objects to which we are related and which are presented to us as instantiating the categories. This is stronger than the reading given by the Object-Independent theorist, though it does not entail that there are objects which actually fall under the categories.

3 On the Relation of Intuition to Cognition 77

What about the second form of the Object-Dependent view? This is the combination of the Object-Dependent view with the claim that formal possibility is insufficient to prove real possibility. We noted above that this supplementation looks plausible if one holds that cognition is both sufficient and necessary for proving the real possibility of objects, which is to say if one holds that the modal condition on cognition is not intended simply as a one-way condition but also to draw attention to some very special connection between cognition via intuition and proofs of real possibility.[16] Let showing the objective validity of a concept be equivalent to showing the real possibility that an object falls under that concept. Let cognition be necessary to prove the real possibility of an object falling under a concept. And let cognitions be representations which concern only actual objects. Then showing the objective validity of a concept requires showing that there are actual objects to which one can be related which instantiate the concept. Thus showing the objective validity of the categories involves showing that there are objects which instantiate the categories. The Object-Dependent view, when supplemented with the claim that cognition is necessary for proving real possibility, takes Kant's project in TD to require showing that there are actual objects which instantiate the categories.

Actually, this is too quick. For although the Object-Dependent view is committed to intuitions depending for their existence on the presence of their objects, and thus to all cognitions picking out some actual object and predicating a property of it, it is not committed to any such predication being true. So it follows only that TD is secured when it is shown that there are actual objects to which we are related and which are presented to us as instantiating the categories, as on the first form of the Object-Dependent view. This is weaker than the claim that we are related to actual objects which do instantiate the categories. And it is stronger than the claim that all objective representations which purport to represent objects necessarily present objects as falling under the categories since this claim is compatible with there being no actual objects to which we are related.

---

[16] Remember that our focus is on theoretical cognition; see above.

78   A. Gomes and A. Stephenson

Can the Object-Dependent view be supplemented so as to entail the stronger conclusion? Well, any form of the Object-Dependent view which entails the existence of both the object of the intuition and its properties will entail the stronger conclusion. Those views which take *Erkenntnis* to be a form of knowledge are such. But note also that the form of the Object-Dependent view we are considering is one which takes cognition to be necessary for proving the real possibility of objects. And we suggested above that this view draws support from Kant's claim that establishing the objective validity of a concept requires the possibility of giving it an object in intuition—but only if the notion of possibility at play here is one on which possible cognition does not outstrip what is actual. If cognition requires that the attributes predicated of objects be true at least some of the time, then we do indeed have the result that the objective validity of the categories is shown only if we are (sometimes) related to actual objects which do instantiate the categories.[17]

This gives us three ways of understanding TD's aim of showing the objective validity of the categories. According to the Object-Independent view, this task is secured when we are shown that all objective representations which purport to represent objects necessarily present objects as falling under the categories. According to the first version of the Object-Dependent view, the task is secured when we are shown that there are actual objects to which we are related and which are presented to us as instantiating the categories. And according to the second version of the Object-Dependent view, the task is secured when we are shown that we are sometimes related to actual objects which do instantiate the categories. Only the last of these claims is incompatible with there being no actual objects which instantiate the categories.

The three readings have different implications for how we should understand TD's relation to "Hume's Problem" (Prol, 4:259–61) and its place and role in the *Critique* as a whole, in particular its relation to the Refutation of Idealism. We shall just say something brief about the first. On one reading of Hume's Problem, a satisfactory response to Humean scepticism involves showing not just that we are able to apply pure

---

[17] See Beck (1978) and Strawson (1966) for versions of this move. One source of support for the antecedent are Kant's claims about the dependency of inner intuitions on outer intuitions, e.g. at Bxli; see McLear (forthcoming b).

concepts to the objects given to us in intuition, but that the categories really do so apply.[18] Only the second form of the Object-Dependent view has TD, as characterised above, provide such a response. On another reading, Hume's Problem is already solved when it has been shown that we are able to apply the pure concepts to the objects given to us in intuition. That they may not be so applicable is the worry raised by Lambert and Herz in response to the "Inaugural Dissertation" and one can read TD as attempting to explain how a priori representations can apply to external things at all.[19] The Object-Independent view and the first form of the Object-Dependent view have TD, as characterised above, provide responses to this problem. This does not preclude these views from also taking Kant to want to show that the categories really do apply to the objects given to us in intuition, for they may hold that answering this version of Hume's problem requires a further step in a differently characterised TD, or else that we must draw on material beyond that of TD. Nevertheless, the different views on the nature of intuition imply differing interpretations of the structure of TD and its relation to Humean scepticism.

3.5   Conclusion

One important issue which divides accounts of Kantian intuition is the question of whether intuitions depend for their existence on the existence of their objects. We have suggested in this chapter that one's stance on this question will determine a stance on the nature of Kantian cognition. And one's stance on the nature of Kantian cognition will likewise shape a stance on the nature of real possibility, its relation to formal possibility and actuality, and an account of the purpose and structure of TD. It is on this ground, we suggest, that debates about the nature of Kantian intuition are to be decided.[20]

---

[18] See Gomes (2010, 2014) and Van Cleve (1999) for readings of TD in this vein.

[19] See Lambert's letter to Kant of 13 October 1770, in Br, 10:105, and Herz's *Observations on Speculative Philosophy*, in Watkins (2009:299). See Laywine (2001) for an account of the role Lambert's letter plays in Kant's intellectual development.

[20] For comments on earlier drafts, our thanks to Thomas Land, Colin McLear, Dennis Schulting, Clinton Tolley, an anonymous referee and especially to Daniel Sumner Smyth. Andrew Stephenson gratefully acknowledges the support of the Leverhulme Trust.

4

Sensible Synthesis and the Intuition of Space

Stefanie Grüne

4.1 Introduction

According to Kant, human beings have two different cognitive capacities, namely sensibility and understanding. At first glance, he seems to claim that these two capacities furnish the mind with two different kinds of representation. Whereas sensibility delivers intuitions, understanding delivers concepts. Still, there are many passages in the *Critique of Pure Reason* which suggest that the relation between sensibility and understanding is more complicated than this and that Kant rejects such a straightforward division of cognitive labour. He seems to think that in order for intuitions to arise, sensibility and understanding must cooperate. When acted upon by objects, sensibility delivers sensations, but not intuitions. In order for intuitions to be produced, these sensations

---

S. Grüne (✉)
Department of Philosophy, University of Potsdam, Potsdam, Brandenburg, Germany
e-mail: stefanie.gruene@uni-potsdam.de

© The Editor(s) (if applicable) and The Author(s) 2016
D. Schulting (ed.), *Kantian Nonconceptualism*,
DOI 10.1057/978-1-137-53517-7_4

82   S. Grüne

have to be processed or, as Kant says, "synthesised" by the understanding through the use of concepts. This, at least, is the standard interpretation of Kant's conception of the relation between sensibility and understanding. In recent years, however, the standard interpretation has been challenged. Lucy Allais (2009), Robert Hanna (2001, 2005) and Colin McLear (2015), for example, all claim that sensibility, independently of any assistance by the understanding, and therefore independently of any use of concepts, delivers intuitions. In a recent article, McLear argues that it follows from the third and fourth argument in the Metaphysical Exposition of the Transcendental Aesthetic (TAe) that intuitions have a kind of unity that cannot be the product of a synthesis of the understanding. He calls the position he argues against "Intellectualism" and the position he argues for "Sensibilism" and characterises the two positions in the following way:

> According to Intellectualism, all objective representation depends, at least in part, on the unifying synthetic activity of the mind. In contrast, Sensibilism argues that at least some forms of objective representation, specifically intuitions, do not require synthesis. (McLear 2015:79)

In this chapter, I shall argue for the claim, contrary to McLear, that the Metaphysical Exposition of TAe

(1) does not imply Sensibilism

and

(2) is not incompatible with a slightly modified version of Intellectualism.

In order to distinguish synthesis of concepts from synthesis of sensible representations, I shall call the second "sensible synthesis". The reason why McLear believes that the unity of intuitions cannot be the product of sensible synthesis is that according to him intuitions exhibit a part-to-whole structure that cannot be brought about by synthesis. Obviously, every representation that is produced by synthesising or combining several representations is a representation whose parts are prior to the whole

4 Sensible Synthesis and the Intuition of Space   83

representation. Yet, according to McLear, it follows from the third and fourth space (and time)[1] arguments that "the unity of aesthetic representation—characterized by the forms of space and time—has a structure in which the representational parts depend on the whole" (2015:91).

As I see it, one might reconstruct McLear's argument for the claim that the unity of intuition is not brought about by sensible synthesis or intellectual activity in the following way:

> **P1**: "If a representation has a structure in which the parts depend on the whole rather than a structure in which the whole is dependent on its parts, that representation cannot be a product of intellectual activity, but must rather be given in sensibility independently of such activity" (McLear 2015:90).
>
> **P2**: Pure intuitions of space and time have a structure in which the parts depend on the whole rather than a structure in which the whole is dependent on its parts.
>
> **C**: Pure intuitions of space and time cannot be a product of intellectual activity, but must rather be given in sensibility independently of such activity.

In order to evaluate this argument, it is important to note that Kant distinguishes between two different kinds of pure intuition, namely, between the intuition of a single infinitely large space (or time) and intuitions of finite spatial regions (or temporal intervals) (as for example the pure intuition of a line or a triangle). Accordingly, one should also distinguish between two versions of the argument I have just reconstructed, since its second premise and its conclusion can be understood in two different ways, depending on how one interprets the term "pure intuition of space and time".

> *First version of the second premise and the conclusion*:
> **P2***: The pure intuition of a single and infinite spatial (or temporal) whole has a structure in which the parts depend on the whole rather than a structure in which the whole is dependent on its parts.

---

[1] Like McLear himself, I concentrate on the pure intuition of space. Parallel considerations apply to the pure intuition of time.

C*: The pure intuition of a single and infinite spatial (or temporal) whole cannot be a product of intellectual activity, but must rather be given in sensibility independently of such activity.

Second version of the second premise and the conclusion:
P2**: Pure intuitions of finite spatial regions (or temporal intervals) have a structure in which the parts depend on the whole rather than a structure in which the whole is dependent on its parts.
C**: Pure intuitions of finite spatial regions (or temporal intervals) cannot be a product of intellectual activity, but must rather be given in sensibility independently of such activity.

McLear himself does not distinguish between these two versions of the argument. However, I think that in order to evaluate the argument it is essential to make this distinction. In Sect. 4.2, I examine the two versions of the argument and discuss how they relate to the truth or falsity of Sensibilism and Intellectualism. In Sect. 4.3, I shall make a proposal for how best to modify Intellectualism in such a way that it is compatible with the Metaphysical Exposition. In Sect. 4.4, I briefly discuss a second feature of pure intuitions concerning which one might think that intuitions that have it cannot be the product of sensible synthesis.

4.2 Two Versions of McLear's Argument

In the third argument from the Metaphysical Exposition Kant writes:

> Space is not a discursive or, as is said, general concept of relations of things in general, but a pure intuition. For, first, one can only represent a single space, and if one speaks of many spaces, one understands by that only parts of one and the same unique space. And these parts cannot as it were precede the single all-encompassing space as its components (from which its composition would be possible), but rather are only thought *in it*. It is essentially single; the manifold in it, thus also the general concept of spaces in general, rests merely on limitations. (A24–5/B39)

McLear is certainly right to claim that according to the Metaphysical Exposition the representation of a single and infinite spatial whole is prior

4 Sensible Synthesis and the Intuition of Space   85

to the representation of its parts.[2] In the third argument Kant points out that our representation of space is the representation of a single entity and that the representations of many spaces are representations of parts of this single space, where these parts "cannot as it were precede the single all-encompassing space as its components (from which its composition would be possible), but rather are only thought *in it*" (A25/B39). Thus, the pure intuition of a single and all-encompassing space has a structure in which the parts depend on the whole rather than a structure in which the whole is dependent on its parts. Furthermore, at the beginning of the fourth argument of the Metaphysical Exposition Kant characterises space not only as all-encompassing (which is compatible with the assumption that the single space is finite), but as infinite. He writes:

Space is represented as an infinite *given* magnitude. (A25/B39)

Thus, McLear is justified in holding **P2***. Since, as I see it, the first premise is uncontroversial as well, the first version of McLear's argument goes through and the intuition of a single and infinite spatial whole is shown not to be a product of intellectual activity, but to be given in sensibility independently of such activity. If one accepts—as McLear and I both do—that a necessary condition for having an intuition is that the representations that are contained in the intuition form a unity, one furthermore gets the result that the unity of the intuition of the single and infinite space is not the product of an intellectual activity. Thus, I completely agree with McLear that there are pure intuitions which are not the product of sensible synthesis and which have a unity that is not the product of sensible synthesis. Yet I disagree with him concerning the implications of this claim. As I see it, the first version of McLear's argument does not prove the truth of Sensibilism. Furthermore, even though it does prove that Intellectualism, as McLear characterises it, is indeed wrong, it does not prove the falsity of a slightly modified version of Intellectualism. As I have already said, McLear characterises Sensibilism as the claim that "at least some forms of objective representation, specifically intuitions, do not require synthesis" (McLear 2015:79). Even though, according to this characterisation, Sensibilism is compatible with the assumption that there are *objective representations* that

---

[2] See McLear (2015:89–90).

require synthesis (say, judgements), Sensibilism is not compatible with the assumption that there are *intuitions* that require synthesis. Yet the first version of McLear's argument only shows that there are two intuitions that are not the product of sensible synthesis, namely the intuition of infinite space and the intuition of infinite time. It does not show that pure intuitions of finite spatial regions or temporal intervals and empirical intuitions do not require sensible synthesis. Likewise, the argument only shows that the unity of the intuition of infinite space and time is not the product of sensible synthesis. It does not show that the unity of pure intuitions of finite spatial regions or temporal intervals and the unity of empirical intuitions is independent of intellectual activity. Thus, the first version of McLear's argument does not prove Sensibilism.

What about Intellectualism? Since McLear characterises Intellectualism as claiming that *all* objective representations depend on synthesis, the first version of his argument shows that Intellectualism, formulated in this way, is wrong. Yet it is possible to defend a modified version of Intellectualism, according to which all objective representations with the exception of the intuition of infinite space and time are the product of synthesis. Such a modified version of Intellectualism is not ruled out by the first version of McLear's argument. In Sect. 4.3, I shall argue that this way of modifying Intellectualism does not amount to a weak ad hoc solution, but is due to the fact that for Kant there is an important difference between, on the one hand, the pure intuition of infinite space and infinite time, and, on the other hand, all other intuitions. However, before I do that, I shall examine whether the second version of McLear's argument leads to a stronger conclusion than the first one. The second version of McLear's argument runs as follows:

> **P1**: "If a representation has a structure in which the parts depend on the whole rather than a structure in which the whole is dependent on its parts, that representation cannot be a product of intellectual activity, but must rather be given in sensibility independently of such activity" (McLear 2015:90).
>
> **P2****: Pure intuitions of finite spatial regions (or temporal intervals) have a structure in which the parts depend on the whole rather than a structure in which the whole is dependent on its parts.
>
> **C****: Pure intuitions of finite spatial regions (or temporal intervals) cannot be a product of intellectual activity, but must rather be given in sensibility independently of such activity.

4 Sensible Synthesis and the Intuition of Space 87

It is important to note that, in contrast to the first version of McLear's argument, it does not follow from what Kant says in the third and fourth arguments of the Metaphysical Exposition that the second premise is true. In the third argument, where the whole–part relation is treated, Kant only writes about the relation between the infinite spatial whole and its finite parts. He does not say anything concerning the relation between *finite* spaces and their parts. From the third argument we only learn that every finite space has to be represented as a limitation of infinite space, but we do not learn that the spatial parts of a finite space have to be represented as parts of this space. Thus, it does not follow from the third argument of the Metaphysical Exposition that pure intuitions of finite spaces have a structure in which the parts depend on the whole. Since the second premise is not supported by the Metaphysical Exposition, the argument as it is stated is not sound.[3]

To sum up. Since the first version of McLear's argument only shows that the pure intuition of infinite space and time cannot be the product of sensible synthesis and the second version is not sound, he does not manage to prove that the Metaphysical Exposition is incompatible with the assumption that there are intuitions the formation of which requires sensible synthesis. Quite the contrary, the third and fourth arguments of the Metaphysical Exposition are compatible with assuming that the formation of pure intuitions of finite spatial regions and temporal intervals as well as the formation of empirical intuitions require sensible synthesis. Thus, the Metaphysical Exposition does not imply the truth of Sensibilism.

4.3 A Modified Version of Intellectualism

I now turn to the question of whether the claim that for Kant the intuitions of infinite space and of infinite time are the only ones that do not presuppose sensible synthesis is an ad hoc reaction to the observation that the Metaphysical Exposition is not compatible with the assumption that these intuitions are the product of sensible synthesis or whether

---

[3] Of course, since the spatial parts p_1–p_n of a finite space s are finite spaces as well, they too have to be represented as limitations of an infinite space. But this does not imply that they have to be represented as limitations of s. Thus, even though p_1–p_n have to be represented as limitations of an infinite space, this does not imply that the intuitions of p_1–p_n are dependent on the intuition of s.

there might be an explanation for why Kant treats empirical intuitions and intuitions of finite spaces and times differently from the intuitions of infinite space and of infinite time. I shall argue that there is a crucial difference between, on the one hand, the intuition of infinite space and time, and, on the other hand, all other intuitions, and that it is because of this difference that for Kant the claim that the formation of an intuition presupposes sensible synthesis is not valid for the intuition of infinite space and time. More precisely I argue for the following claim:

(i) The intuitions of infinite space and of infinite time are the only ones for which it is true that the object of the intuition is not phenomenally present to the subject of the intuition.

If one accepts this claim and furthermore believes—as I do—that

(ii) the function of sensible synthesis is to make the object of a complex sensible representation phenomenally present to the subject and thereby to generate an intuition,[4]

then it is easy to understand why the intuitions of infinite space and of infinite time are the only ones that do not require sensible synthesis. If sensible synthesis is required for making the object of a complex sensible representation phenomenally present, but the objects of the intuition of infinite space and of infinite time are not phenomenally present, then the coming into being of these intuitions does not require sensible synthesis. I therefore suggest that Intellectualism be modified in the following way:

Intellectualism*: All representations of objects that are phenomenally present to the subject depend on sensible synthesis.

---

[4] I have chosen this way of formulating the function of sensible synthesis for reasons of simplicity. According to my interpretation of the function of sensible synthesis, a more accurate characterisation of this function would be the following. Sensible synthesis is required for relating the qualitative and the spatiotemporal content of complex sensible representations to an object and making it phenomenally present to the subject. In other words, sensible synthesis is required for transforming the qualitative and the spatiotemporal content of complex sensible representations into intentional content and making this content phenomenally present to the subject.

4 Sensible Synthesis and the Intuition of Space 89

In this part of my essay I only argue for claim (i). I do not argue for claim (ii) because the question concerning the function of sensible synthesis is a very complicated matter and McLear's argument is supposed to show that, regardless of how exactly one characterises the function of sensible synthesis, any characterisation according to which the function of sensible synthesis is to *generate* intuitions has to be wrong, because it is inconsistent with Kant's claims in the Metaphysical Exposition of the Concept of Space. Since the goal of this chapter is not the positive goal of proving that the function of sensible synthesis *indeed is* to produce intuitions, but only the more modest negative goal of showing that Kant's arguments in the Metaphysical Exposition do not imply that the function of sensible synthesis cannot be characterised in this way, I shall only argue for claim (i). Should I be successful in persuading the reader of the truth of (i), the way is then open to accept the modified version of Intellectualism (Intellectualism*) I have proposed above. This is because, given the truth of (i), that is, the truth of the claim that the intuitions of infinite space and time differ from all other intuitions in that for the former it is not true that the object of the intuition is phenomenally present to the subject, and given the assumption that the function of sensible synthesis is to make the objects of intuitions phenomenally present, one can explain why Kant believed that all intuitions except for the intuitions of infinite space and of infinite time are produced by sensible synthesis.

Before I start arguing for (i) let me make a short remark about how I understand the term "phenomenally present". As I use the term, an object is phenomenally present to a subject if and only if there is something it is like for the subject to have a representation of the object. In other words, to say that an object is phenomenally present is to say that the representation of the object has a distinctive subjective or phenomenal character. It is not to say that the object seems to be really there or seems to exist. I take it that it is uncontroversial that the objects of empirical intuitions and the objects of intuitions of finite spatial regions and temporal intervals *are* phenomenally present in this sense. So in arguing for (i) I only argue for the claim that the objects of the intuitions of infinite space and of infinite time are *not* phenomenally present, whilst I do not argue for the claim that these are the *only* objects of intuition that are not phenomenally present.

90   S. Grüne

Let me first note that, phenomenologically, the claim that the objects of the intuitions of infinite space and of infinite time are phenomenally present is extremely implausible. To me at least, it is utterly unclear how an object that is unbounded in extent could be phenomenally present to a human being. It does not help to point out that to have an a priori intuition of space does not consist in having a *perception* of space. I completely agree that an a priori intuition of infinite space is not a perception. I take it that to have an a priori intuition of space, instead, is to have an imagination. Yet, in my view, the assumption that the object of an *imagination* of infinitely large space is phenomenally present to the subject of the imagination does not fare any better than the assumption that the object of a perception of infinite space is phenomenally present. Since it makes sense to speak of a visual field not only in the case of perception, but also in the case of imagination, and since the visual field in both cases is finite, the claim that an infinitely large object can be phenomenally present seems equally wrong in the case of the perception of an infinitely large object and in the case of the imagination of an infinitely large object.[5] Thus, the first reason not to ascribe the claim to Kant that the objects of the intuition of infinite space and of infinite time are phenomenally present is that one should not ascribe a very implausible claim to Kant, if one is not forced to do so. I shall now discuss several passages which speak in favour of assuming that Kant indeed did not believe that the objects of the intuitions of infinite space and of infinite time are phenomenally present. The first is a passage from *On Kästner's Treatises*, where Kant writes:

> That a line can be extended to infinity means so much as: the space in which I describe the line, is greater than every one line which I may describe in it; and thus the geometer grounds the possibility of his task of increasing a space (of which there are many) to infinity on the original representation of a unitary, infinite, *subjectively given* space. Now that the geometrically and objectively given space is always *finite* agrees completely with this; for it is only given through its being *constructed* [*gemacht*]. ... With this also agrees entirely what Raphson, according to Councillor Kästner's quotation

---

[5] McLear seems to agree on this point. Cf. McLear (2015:95).

4 Sensible Synthesis and the Intuition of Space 91

on p. 418, says, [namely] that the mathematician is always only concerned with an *infinito potentiali* [a potential infinite], and [that] *actu infinitum* (the metaphysically given [infinite]) *non datur a parte rei, sed a parte cogitantis* [an infinite in actuality is not given on the side of the thing, but on the side of the thinker]. (OKT, 20:420–1)

In this passage, Kant distinguishes between geometrical space, which is finite, and metaphysical space, which is infinite, and claims that only the first is objectively given, whereas the second is subjectively given. Here, the distinction between objective and subjective givenness has to be another distinction than the distinction between objective and subjective validity or reality, since for Kant both the representation of metaphysical space and the representation of geometrical space are objectively real. As I see it, it is most plausible to interpret "objectively given" as "given as an object". This interpretation is substantiated by the Latin quote at the end of the passage, where Kant takes himself to agree with the mathematician Joseph Raphson that the actual infinite is not given on the side of the thing or object.[6] That the actual infinite space is not given on the side of the thing cannot mean that space is not a thing in itself. If it meant this, then Kant would also have to deny that finite spaces are given on the side of the thing. Still, as we have seen, instead of denying this, he explicitly claims that finite spaces are given objectively or as an object. As far as I can see, the only alternative to understanding Kant's claim that the actual infinite space is not given on the side of the thing is to understand it as meaning that the actual infinite is not an object of intuition. Of course, it is not at all clear what it might mean to say that the infinite is not given as an object or that it is not an object of intuition. This is because Kant seems to understand the terms "object" and "relation to an object" in very different ways. Since Kant defines intuitions as singular representations that have an immediate relation to an object,[7] in some sense it must also be true for the intuitions of infinite space and infinite time that they have an object. Thus, there is a sense in which infinite space and time are

---

[6] Kant seems to misread *actu infinitum* as meaning "actual infinity", whereas it should be translated as "infinite in act" or "infinite in actuality". Cf. Kant (2014:312n.16).

[7] Cf. A320/B376–7.

92   S. Grüne

the objects of pure intuitions, and there is a sense in which they are not objects of intuition or given as an object.

In the present context, I do not want to say anything concerning the sense in which infinite space and time are objects of intuition. I only want to suggest that the sense in which they are not objects of intuition is that they are not objects that are phenomenally present to us. So far, of course, this is only a suggestion. Therefore, in the remainder of this section I shall discuss two passages which support my interpretation of the passage from *On Kästner's Treatises* as the correct one. The first is a passage from the Metaphysical Exposition of the Concept of Time where Kant writes:

> The infinitude of time signifies nothing more than that every determinate magnitude of time is only possible through limitations of a single time grounding it. (A32/B47–8)

According to this passage, in characterising time as being infinite, Kant only wants to say something about a property of finite periods of time, namely the property of being possible only as a limitation of a single (unlimited) time. As I see it, for Kant to claim that finite periods of time are only possible as limitations of a single time is the same as to claim that it is possible to have an intuition of a finite period of time only if one represents or experiences this period of time as part or limitation of a single time. In other words, it is possible to have an intuition of a finite period of time only if its property of being a limitation of a single time is phenomenally present to the subject of the intuition. Thus, when Kant writes that the infinitude of time signifies nothing more than a property of finite periods of time, he denies that time as an infinitely large object is phenomenally present to us. Instead what is phenomenally present to us is a property of finite periods of time, namely the property of being a part or limitation of a single time. I take it that for the property of being a part or a limitation of a single time to be phenomenally present amounts to experiencing a finite temporal interval as being surrounded by a larger period of time, which, regardless of how large it is, is always expected to be experienced as being surrounded by an even larger temporal

4 Sensible Synthesis and the Intuition of Space   93

period, and so on. Something like that at least is suggested by a sentence from the first-edition version of the fourth argument of the Metaphysical Exposition of the Concept of Space, in which Kant seems to equate the claim that space is represented as an infinite given magnitude with the claim that there is "boundlessness in the progress of intuition" (A25). Thus, according to my interpretation, even though for Kant we have an intuition of infinite space and time, what is phenomenally present in such an intuition is not a single infinitely large object, but a property of finite spatial regions or temporal intervals.

This interpretation is further substantiated by the way in which Kant explains how the a priori intuition of space is formed or acquired. In *On a Discovery*, Kant claims that all representations, including the pure intuitions of space and time, are acquired. Yet, when he explains how the a priori intuition of space is acquired, he only explains how such a priori intuitions are formed for which it is true that finite spaces are phenomenally present. He does not give two explanations, one for how we form a priori intuitions in which finite spaces are phenomenally present to us, and one for how we form an intuition in which infinite space is phenomenally present to us. As I see it, Kant's explanation of how the a priori intuition of space is acquired consists of two steps. First, he describes how representations with spatial content are formed. Second, he explicates how this content is isolated from empirical content.

Let me elaborate. In *On a Discovery*, Kant points out that the reason why our intuitions have *spatial* content is that there is an *innate ground* of this content in us. That the *spatial* content of our intuitions does not depend on external things in the world, but on an innate ground in us, is the reason why he characterises the intuition of space as *originally* acquired. Still, we would not have an intuition with spatial content if objects did not affect our senses. This is why he characterises the intuition of space as originally *acquired*. In *On a Discovery*, Kant writes:

> The ground of the possibility of sensory intuition is … the mere *receptivity* peculiar to the mind, when it is affected by something (in sensation), to receive a representation in accordance with its subjective constitution. Only this first formal ground, e.g., of the possibility of an intuition of

94   S. Grüne

space, is innate, not the spatial representation itself. For impressions would always be required in order to determine the cognitive faculty to the representation of an object (which is always a specific act) in the first place. Thus arises the formal *intuition* called space, as an originally acquired representation (the form of outer objects in general), the ground of which (as mere receptivity) is nevertheless innate. (ÜE, 8:222)

According to this passage, the innate ground of the content of the intuition of space is "the mere *receptivity* peculiar to the mind ... to receive a representation in accordance with its subjective constitution". The subjective constitution of our receptivity consists in delivering representations whose content has a certain formal structure, namely a spatial structure. Thus, the innate ground of our intuition of space is the innate disposition or capacity to deliver representations whose content is spatially structured. The reason why Kant denies that the pure intuition of space is innate is that, in order for this disposition or capacity to be activated and thus for representations with spatial content to be produced, objects have to affect receptivity so that there *are* any representations (namely sensations) that can be spatially structured. Clearly, this characterisation of the original acquisition of the pure intuitions of space and time is not complete. The representations that are formed when objects affect our receptivity are not a priori, but empirical intuitions. They are empirical intuitions the content of which also contains an a priori element, namely spatial structure. Thus, in a second step Kant has to explain how an intuition is formed that contains nothing but spatial structure. We find this explanation at the beginning of TAe in the *Critique of Pure Reason*. There, Kant writes:

This pure form of sensibility is also called *pure intuition*. So if I separate from the representation of a body that which the understanding thinks about it, such as substance, force, divisibility, etc., as well as that which belongs to sensation, such as impenetrability, hardness, color, etc., something from this empirical intuition is still left for me, namely extension and form. These belong to the pure intuition, which occurs *a priori*. (A20–1/B34–5)[8]

---

[8] See also A27/B43.

4 Sensible Synthesis and the Intuition of Space 95

From this passage we learn that, in order to form an intuition that contains nothing but spatial structure, we have to abstract from all empirical aspects of the content of an empirical intuition. In this way, we arrive at a pure intuition of space. Thus, since what is phenomenally present to a subject, when she has the empirical intuition with which she starts in order to form the pure intuition of space, is a finite spatial region, what is phenomenally present to the subject, when she has abstracted from all empirical aspects of the intuition and thus has formed a pure intuition of space, is still a finite spatial region.

Interestingly, Kant nowhere gives an additional or alternative explanation of how we form the intuition of space. Thus, his account from *On a Discovery* and from TAe is supposed to explain both how we form a priori intuitions of finite spatial regions and how we form the a priori intuition of infinite space. If what I have said so far is right, it turns out that, in having an intuition in which a finite spatial region is phenomenally present, one has an intuition of such a finite spatial region as well as an intuition of infinite space. And we can explain how this can be the case, if we assume—as I have suggested—that what is phenomenally present when one has an intuition of infinite space is a property of finite spaces, namely the property of being part of the all-encompassing space. Thus, the fact that an infinitely large object that is phenomenally present to subjects does not feature in Kant's account of the original acquisition of the pure intuition of space speaks in favour of my claim that the a priori intuition of infinite space is not an intuition in which the object of the intuition, namely infinite space, is phenomenally present to us.

I take it that my interpretation of the above passage makes plausible my claim that for Kant infinite space and time are not phenomenally present to the subject of the intuition of infinite space and time. Since the objects of all other intuitions are phenomenally present to the subject of the intuition we have found a central distinction between the intuition of infinite space and time, on the one hand, and all other intuitions, on the other. If one furthermore accepts the claim that the function of sensible synthesis is to make the objects of intuitions phenomenally present, then one can see why according to Kant the formation of the intuition of infinite space and infinite time does not presuppose sensible synthesis even though the formation of all other intuitions presupposes

96   S. Grüne

such a synthesis. Thus, we now have an explanation for why the fact that Intellectualism, as McLear formulates it, is false is compatible with the assumption that in the case of empirical intuitions and a priori intuitions of finite spaces and times the formation of such intuitions presupposes sensible synthesis.

4.4   The Argument from the Infinite Divisibility of Space

In the last part of this chapter, I briefly discuss another reason for the assumption that intuitions of finite spaces cannot be the product of sensible synthesis. In the argument I have discussed so far, the property that was supposed to make it impossible that the pure intuition of space could be the product of sensible synthesis was the property of having a structure in which the parts depend on the whole. However, there is another property of the intuition of space, the possession of which might be supposed to speak against assuming that pure intuitions of space depend on sensible synthesis. This is the property of being a continuous magnitude, that is, "the property of magnitudes on account of which no part of them is the smallest (no part is simple)" (A169/B211). Because finite spaces are continuous magnitudes, they contain infinitely many parts. Still, our understanding being a capacity of finite beings cannot synthesise infinitely many parts. Thus, we get the following argument, which is supposed to show that intuitions of finite spaces cannot be the product of sensible synthesis:

> *Argument from the infinite divisibility of space:*
> **P1**: Intuitions of finite spaces are intuitions of continuous magnitudes.
> **P2**: If intuitions of continuous magnitudes were the product of sensible synthesis performed by the understanding, then the understanding would have to synthesise infinitely many parts.
> **C1**: If intuitions of finite spaces were the product of sensible synthesis performed by the understanding, then the understanding would have to synthesise infinitely many parts.
> **P3**: The understanding cannot synthesise infinitely many parts.

4 Sensible Synthesis and the Intuition of Space   97

C2: Intuitions of finite spaces cannot be the product of sensible synthesis performed by the understanding.[9]

This argument is formally valid. Furthermore, the first premise is uncontestedly true. Thus the soundness of the argument depends on the truth of the second and third premises. Even though both premises might seem to be plausible, from what Kant says in the Axioms of Intuitions and in the Anticipations of Perceptions it follows that he could not accept both. Here are the relevant passages:

> I call an extensive magnitude that in which the representation of the parts makes possible the representation of the whole (and therefore necessarily precedes the latter). (A162/B203)

> Since the mere intuition in all appearances is either space or time, every appearance as intuition is an extensive magnitude, as it can only be cognized through successive synthesis (from part to part) in apprehension. All appearances are accordingly already intuited as aggregates (multitudes of antecedently given parts). (A163/B203–4)

> The property of magnitudes on account of which no part of them is the smallest (no part is simple) is called their continuity. Space and time are *quanta continua* .... All appearances whatsoever are accordingly continuous magnitudes, either in their intuition, as extensive magnitudes, or in their mere perception (sensation and thus reality), as intensive ones. (A169–70/B211–12)

---

[9] I am not sure whether McLear wants to attribute the argument from the infinite divisibility of space to Kant. On the one hand, he nowhere mentions an argument of this form and only claims that it is the property of having a structure in which the parts are dependent on the whole, which makes it impossible to assume that the pure intuition of space is the product of sensible synthesis. On the other hand, he not only discusses the third argument of the Metaphysical Exposition, in which Kant claims that the all-encompassing space is prior to its parts, but also the fourth argument, in which Kant claims that the representation of space contains infinitely many representations, and he claims that both arguments show that the pure intuition of space cannot be a product of sensible synthesis. Furthermore, there is at least one passage in which McLear seems to imply that the reason why the pure intuition of space cannot be dependent on sensible synthesis is that our understanding is finite: "Kant's point in the third and fourth arguments of the Metaphysical Exposition is that no finite intellect could grasp the extent and nature of space and time as infinite wholes via a movement from part to whole" (McLear 2015:91).

From these passages we learn two things that are relevant for evaluating the argument from the infinite divisibility of space. The first is that Kant defines extensive magnitudes as entities for which it is true that the representation of the whole entity depends on the representation of its parts. Furthermore, it turns out that for Kant a representation which has a structure in which the whole is dependent on its parts is the result of a successive synthesis. Thus, for Kant all (intuitive) representations of extensive magnitudes are the result of sensible synthesis. The second thing to note is that for Kant being an extensive magnitude is compatible with being a continuous magnitude. This follows from the last quote where he explicitly claims that *as extensive magnitudes* appearances are continuous magnitudes. Since for Kant an appearance is the "undetermined object of an empirical intuition" (A20/B34), it turns out that having an intuition of an extensive magnitude is compatible with having an intuition of a continuous magnitude. If we take the claim that all representations of extensive magnitudes are the result of synthesis together with the claim that being a representation of an extensive magnitude is compatible with being a representation of a continuous magnitude, we get the result that being a representation that is generated by sensible synthesis is compatible with being a representation of a continuous magnitude. Thus, by pointing out that intuitions are representations of continuous magnitudes one cannot show that they cannot be the result of sensible synthesis.

If, as I have shown, Kant accepts that representations of continuous magnitudes can be generated by sensible synthesis, then he has two options. Either he assumes that the understanding can synthesise infinitely many parts, or he assumes that by synthesising finitely many parts the understanding can produce the intuition of something that is infinitely divisible. In other words, Kant has to reject either the second or the third premise. Regardless of which one he rejects, the fact that he is willing to allow that one and the same object can be intuited as a continuous as well as an extensive magnitude shows that he would not accept the argument from the infinite divisibility of space.

5

Directions in Space, Nonconceptual Form and the Foundations of Transcendental Idealism

Robert Hanna

5.1 Introduction

The central aim of this chapter is to demonstrate an essential connection between Kant's nonconceptualism and his transcendental idealism by tracing this line of thinking in Kant's work directly back to his pre-Critical essay of 1768, *Concerning the Ground of the Ultimate Differentiation of Directions in Space* (*Directions in Space*, for short). What I shall argue is that Kant's nonconceptualism about the human mind goes all the way down into his metaphysics; that the apparent world fundamentally conforms to human sensibility even if it does not fundamentally conform to the human understanding; and that the basic source of all this is Kant's (pre-Critical but later also Critical) theory of space and how we represent it.

R. Hanna (✉)
Independent Scholar, USA
e-mail: bobhannahbob1@gmail.com

© The Editor(s) (if applicable) and The Author(s) 2016   **99**
D. Schulting (ed.), *Kantian Nonconceptualism*,
DOI 10.1057/978-1-137-53517-7_5

5.2 Transcendental Idealism, Conceptualism, Nonconceptualism, Kantian Conceptualism and Kantian Nonconceptualism

In a nutshell, Kant's thesis of transcendental idealism states that the basic structure of the apparent or phenomenal world necessarily conforms to the pure or non-empirical (hence a priori) structure of human cognition, and not the converse (Bxvi–xviii). Or in other words, Kant is saying that the phenomenal world fundamentally conforms to the a priori structure of the human mind, and it is not the case that the human mind fundamentally conforms to the phenomenal world, or indeed to any non-apparent or *noumenal* world.

And here is Kant's primary argument for transcendental idealism. If the human mind fundamentally conformed to the world, whether phenomenal or noumenal, then since human knowledge of the world would be contingent on the existence and specific character of that world, then a priori human knowledge of the world would be impossible (Br, 10:130–1). But a priori human knowledge of the phenomenal world, for example, in mathematics, is already actual and therefore really possible. So the phenomenal world necessarily conforms to the a priori structure of the human mind. And in particular, the phenomenal world fundamentally conforms to our a priori representations of *space* and *time*, because that is the only acceptable philosophical explanation of the real possibility of mathematical knowledge (MSI, 2:398–406; A19–49/B33–73).

So if Kant is correct, then he is saying that the world in which we live, move and have our being (by which I mean the phenomenal, natural and social world of our ordinary human existence) is fundamentally dependent on *our* minded nature, and not the converse. Correct or incorrect, transcendental idealism seems to me to be a deeply important philosophical thesis. For one thing, if transcendental idealism is true, then we cannot be inherently alienated from the world we are trying to know, as global epistemic sceptics claim, and human knowledge—not only a priori knowledge, but also a posteriori knowledge—is therefore really possible.[1]

---

[1] Hanna (2015), esp. Chaps. 3 and 6–8.

5 Directions in Space 101

In general, the thesis of conceptualism[2] states that the representational content of human cognition is essentially conceptual and necessarily determined by our conceptual capacities. *Strong* conceptualism states that our conceptual capacities are not only necessary but also sufficient for determining the content of human cognition, and *weak* conceptualism states that our conceptual capacities are not alone sufficient but also require a contribution from some or another nonconceptual capacity (e.g. the capacity for sense perception) in order to determine the (ultimately conceptual) content of human cognition. Correspondingly, the thesis of (essentialist content) nonconceptualism[3] states that at least some of the representational contents of human cognition are not essentially conceptual, and not necessarily determined by our conceptual capacities, and also that these contents, on the contrary, are essentially nonconceptual and necessarily determined by our nonconceptual capacities (e.g. the capacity for sense perception).

Although these distinctions might initially seem rather Scholastic or even trivial, the opposition between conceptualism and (essentialist content) nonconceptualism is a philosophically important one. This is because what is at issue is nothing more and nothing less than the nature of the human mind, and whether it is basically intellectual or non-intellectual. According to conceptualism, human minds are basically *intellectual* in character, having nothing inherently to do with the embodied, sense-perceiving, affective, desiring, animal side of human nature. By contrast, according to (essentialist content) nonconceptualism, human minds are basically bound up with the embodied, sense-perceiving, affective, desiring, animal side of human nature, and are *not* basically intellectual in character: on the contrary, the intellectual capacities of

---

[2] See e.g. McDowell (1994) and Sellars (1963, 1968).

[3] See e.g. Evans (1982). In the contemporary debate about conceptualism vs nonconceptualism, it is now standard to draw a distinction between *state* (or possession-theoretic) nonconceptualism and *content* nonconceptualism. State nonconceptualism says that there are mental states such that the subject of those states fails to possess concepts for the specification of those states. Content nonconceptualism, by contrast, says that some mental states have content that is of a different *kind* from that of conceptual content. In turn, *essentialist* content nonconceptualism says that the content of such states is of a categorically or essentially different kind from that of conceptual content. For a general survey of nonconceptualism, see Bermúdez and Cahen (2015). For the distinction between state and content nonconceptualism, see Heck (2009). And for the distinction between non-essentialist and essentialist content nonconceptualism, see Hanna (2008, 2011, 2015, Chap. 2).

the human being constitutively presuppose, and are thereby grounded on and built on top of, the non-intellectual capacities.[4] Hence the philosophical debate about conceptualism vs nonconceptualism is really a debate about whether an *intellectualist* or a *non-intellectualist* conception of the human mind is the correct one. This has far-reaching implications not only for other parts of the philosophy of mind, but also for epistemology, metaphysics, ethics and even political philosophy, to the extent that it depends on ethics and philosophical anthropology.

Although both conceptualism and (essentialist content) nonconceptualism are competing theses/doctrines in contemporary philosophy of mind, their philosophical origins both go back to Kant.[5] Hence it is possible to defend either *Kantian* conceptualism or *Kantian* (essentialist content) nonconceptualism as competing interpretations of Kant's theory of human cognition in particular and of his philosophy of mind more generally.

Now according to Kant, our conceptual capacities are located in the *understanding* (*Verstand*), whose operations yield concepts, judgements/propositions and inferences, when those operations are also supplemented by our further intellectual capacities for apperception or self-consciousness, for judgement and belief, and for logical reason or inference. By contrast, according to Kant, our nonconceptual capacities are located in *sensibility* (*Sinnlichkeit*), which contains both a non-intellectual sub-capacity for sense perception and also a non-intellectual sub-capacity for imagination, and whose operations yield material or formal intuitions, material images, and formal images or schemata. Human sensibility for Kant, it must also be noted, *further* contains non-intellectual sub-capacities for feeling, desiring and sensible willing or "the power of choice" (*Willkür*). In other words, sensibility for Kant is as much non-cognitive or practical, as it is cognitive or theoretical. Since Kant believes that the understanding and sensibility, as capacities, are essentially distinct from and irreducible to one another, and also that both are required for ratio-

---

[4] The inherent connections between intellectualism and conceptualism, on the one hand, and between non-intellectualism and nonconceptualism, on the other, are developed in detail in Hanna (2015), esp. Chaps. 2–3, and Hanna (MS), Chap. 5.

[5] See e.g. Hanna (2005) and McDowell (1994).

5 Directions in Space 103

nal human cognition (and in the case of human practical reason, a.k.a. "the faculty of desire", both are required for rational human action and agency), Kant is also a *cognitive capacity dualist.*

But is Kant a conceptualist or a nonconceptualist? Or in other words, is Kant a cognitive *content* dualist as well as a cognitive *capacity* dualist? Or in still other words, is Kant an *intellectualist* about the nature of the human mind, or a *non-intellectualist*? The intellectualist thesis of Kantian conceptualism states that for Kant the representational content of human cognition is essentially conceptual and necessarily determined by the understanding. And just as there are strong and weak versions of conceptualism in general, so too there are strong and weak versions of Kantian conceptualism.[6] By contrast, the nonintellectualist thesis of Kantian (essentialist content) nonconceptualism states that for Kant at least some of the representational contents of human cognition are not essentially conceptual, and not necessarily determined by the understanding, and also that these contents, on the contrary, are essentially nonconceptual and necessarily determined by our sensibility.[7]

The classical or standard line of Kant interpretation in twentieth-century Anglo-American philosophy simply took it as obvious that Kant is a conceptualist and also an intellectualist. So the nonconceptualist interpretation of Kant is importantly revolutionary and unorthodox, and even if it were not correct (although I do think it *is* correct), nevertheless it has forced conceptualist, intellectualist Kantians to rethink, re-argue and rework their previously unchallenged view.[8]

Now I can reformulate the main aim of this chapter more precisely, in four sub-claims:

---

[6] See e.g. Bauer (2012), Bowman (2011), Ginsborg (2006a, 2008), Golob (2014), Griffith (2012), Grüne (2009), Land (2011), McDowell (2009, 2013), Pippin (2013), Wenzel (2005), and Williams (2012).

[7] See e.g. Hanna (2008, 2011), Hanna and Chadha (2011), Laiho (2012), and Tolley (2013). Weaker versions of Kantian nonconceptualism are defended by e.g. Allais (2009), McLear (2015), Onof and Schulting (2015), and Rohs (2001).

[8] See e.g. McLear (2014b).

(i) That Kant is an (essentialist content) nonconceptualist.

(ii) That there is a specifically non-intellectualist version of Kant's transcendental idealism that depends inherently on the nature of human sensibility.

(iii) That Kant's (essentialist content) nonconceptualism is foundational for any philosophically defensible version of his transcendental idealism.

(iv) That this line of thinking in Kant can be traced directly back to his pre-Critical *Directions in Space* essay.

Or in other words, what I want to claim is that Kant's non-intellectualism about the human mind goes all the way down into his *metaphysics*; that it is defensibly arguable that the apparent world fundamentally conforms to human *sensibility* even if it does not fundamentally conform to the human *understanding*; and that the basic source of all this is Kant's (initially pre-Critical but later also Critical) theory of *space* and how we represent it.

5.3 Directions in Space and the Essentially Nonconceptual Form of Our Representation of It

Kant's *Directions in Space* essay contains an argument against the *relational* or Leibnizian view of space and in favour of the *absolute* or Newtonian view of space, but this merely scratches the surface of Kant's argument. The relational theory of space states that the nature of space is necessarily determined by extrinsic relations between objects in space. By contrast, the absolute theory of space, as Kant understands it, states that the nature of space is necessarily determined by a single universal framework—a *global space-frame*—in which physical objects are inherently embedded or located as filling up and realising proper parts of the global space-frame, whose structure necessarily includes certain special intrinsic relational topological properties that allow for fundamental *asymmetries*, in addition to the familiar Euclidean relational topological properties and relations, which are symmetrical.

5 Directions in Space 105

According to Leibniz, who was a relationist about space, the objects standing in extrinsic relations are monads. So space is actually a "well-founded phenomenon" for Leibniz, and strongly supervenient on the intrinsic non-relational properties of noumenal monads. Nevertheless, other relationists about space, including Kant himself in the *Physical Monadology*, hold that these objects are actually material point-sources of causal forces in real physical space. So the version of relationism that Kant was working with in *Directions in Space* is not an orthodox Leibnizian theory.

According to Newton, who was an absolutist about space, the single universal framework in which physical objects are embedded is itself a noumenal entity. But Newton was unaware (as far as I know) of the idea that the structure of absolute space contains special asymmetry-allowing intrinsic relational topological properties. Hence the version of absolutism that Kant was working with in *Directions in Space* is also not an orthodox Newtonian theory.

According to Kant in *Directions in Space*, space does indeed constitute a global frame for embedding or locating physical objects, like Newtonian space, but also and much more importantly it is an *egocentrically centred, orientable space* with inherent structural asymmetries such as mirror-reflected incongruence or "handedness" in qualitatively identical objects (enantiomorphy),which Kant also calls "incongruent counterparts" (see GUGR, 2:378–83). "Orientable spaces" are spaces with intrinsic directions, and "egocentric centring" means that the specific characteristics of an orientable space is fixed indexically and locally by conscious embodied perceivers who are themselves actually embedded or located within the total global space-frame.

In *Directions in Space*, Kant discovered that structural asymmetries such as handedness can be detected and differentiated only by the essentially non-intellectual, nonconceptual, outer sensibility of living, embodied, conscious, cognising subjects like us, who are actually embedded or located in such a global space, and therefore that there is a necessary isomorphism between the representational form of the outer sensibility of such subjects, the abstract structure of that global space, and the material structure of perceivable objects also embedded or located in that global space. Kant writes:

Because of its three dimensions, physical space can be thought of as having three planes, which all intersect each other at right angles. *Concerning the things which exist outside ourselves: it is only in so far as they stand in relation to ourselves that we have any cognition of them by means of the senses at all. It is, therefore, not surprising that the ultimate ground, on the basis of which we form our representation*[9] *of directions in space, derives from the relation of these intersecting planes to our bodies.* The plane upon which the length of our body stands vertically is called, with respect to ourselves, horizontal. This horizontal plane gives rise to the difference between the directions which we designate by the terms *above* and *below*. On this plane it is possible for two other planes to stand vertically and also to intersect each other at right angles, so that the length of the human body is thought of as lying along the axis of the intersection. One of these two vertical planes divides the body into two externally similar halves, and furnishes the ground of the difference between the *right* and *left* side. The other vertical plane, which also stands perpendicularly on the horizontal plane, makes possible the representation of the side *in front* and the side *behind*. (GUGR, 2:378–9; trans. amended and emphasis added)

Since the distinct feeling of the right and left side is of such great necessity for judging directions, *nature has established an immediate connection*

---

[9] I have substituted "representation" (*Vorstellung*) here and further below for Kant's "concept" (*Begriff*). My rationale is this. In Hanna (2006), Chap. 5, while working out a rationally charitable step-by-step argument-reconstruction of the Transcendental Aesthetic (TAe), I argued for Kant's shifting from a general, loose sense of "concept" in the pre-Critical and proto-Critical writings, where it basically means the same as "representation", to a narrower, technical sense of "concept", which means an essentially general, descriptive or "attributive" representation, in TAe and the rest of the First *Critique* and other Critical and post-Critical writings (including the *Jäsche Logic*), where it sharply contrasts with his use of "intuition", which means an essentially singular or "directly referential" representation. This sharp contrast between the meanings of "concept" and "intuition" begins to emerge in the "Inaugural Dissertation", but unfortunately they are not made fully terminologically explicit there. Moreover, and to make things even worse for interpreters, in TAe Kant *still* does not fully terminologically update the material he took from the "Inaugural Dissertation", and occasionally uses "concept" of space (or time) when he really means "representation of space (or time)" or "pure intuition of space (or time)". This causes not only significant interpretive confusion, it also gives the false appearance of occasionally making Kant seem blatantly self-contradictory—e.g. when he says explicitly that the "concept" of space (or time) is *not* a concept but instead a pure intuition, etc. Assuming all this is true, and again applying rational charity in philosophical interpretation, we can avoid equal confusion in the retrospective, proto-Critical direction only by substituting "representation" for "concept" in *Directions in Space*, when Kant would, with philosophical hindsight, clearly intend to be talking either neutrally about representations that are either "concepts" or "intuitions" in the later, narrower, technical senses of those terms, or else specifically about "intuitions" in the later, narrower, technical sense.

5 Directions in Space 107

between this feeling and the mechanical organisation of the human body. (GUGR, 2:380; emphasis added)

In short, the apparent or phenomenal world must conform to the form of our embodied outer sensibility, that is, the apparent or phenomenal world must conform to the form of human outer intuition.

Now for Kant the form of human outer sensibility or intuition is *essentially nonconceptual* for three reasons. First, Kant says explicitly in the *Critique of Pure Reason* that intuitions of outer sense or inner sense, which pick out appearances—the undetermined objects of empirical intuitions (A20/B34)—are possible for us independently of the functions of our understanding, that is, independently of our concepts:

Since an object can appear to *us only by means of … pure forms of sensibility, i.e., be an object of empirical intuition,* space and time are thus pure intuitions that contain *a priori* the conditions of the possibility of objects as appearances, and the synthesis in them has objective validity. (A89/B121–2; emphasis added)

Objects can indeed appear to us *without necessarily having to be related to functions of the understanding.* (A89/B122; emphasis added)

Appearances can certainly be given in intuition *without functions of the understanding.* (A90/B122; emphasis added)

Appearances could after all be so constituted that the understanding would not find them in accord with the conditions of its unity, and … in the succession of appearances nothing would offer itself that would furnish a rule of synthesis and thus correspond to the concept of cause and effect, so that this concept would therefore be entirely empty, nugatory, and without significance. *Appearances would nonetheless offer objects to our intuition, for intuition by no means requires the functions of thinking.* (A90–1/B123; emphasis added)

That representation that can be given prior to all thinking is called *intuition.* (B132)

The manifold for intuition must already be *given prior to the synthesis of understanding and independently from it.* (B145; emphasis added)

108   R. Hanna

Second, Kant explicitly claims in some pre-Critical writings and also Critical writings alike that at least some non-human animals (e.g. oxen) and some non-rational human animals (e.g. ordinary human infants) are capable of sense perception and thus capable of inner and outer sensory intuition, but do not possess conceptual capacities.[10]

Third, and most importantly for our purposes, our pure or non-empirical representation of space picks out egocentrically centred, orientable, asymmetric structural topological properties of space that *cannot* be represented by the understanding and concepts. This is shown by the "incongruent counterparts" argument, which, in a nutshell, says:

> **P1**: Incongruent counterparts, like our right and left hands, by hypothesis, are such that they possess all their *conceptually* representable qualities in common, yet they still are essentially different because they are incongruent.
>
> **P2**: This incongruence and the essential difference between our right and left hands is immediately and veridically represented by human cognisers, but only by means of our empirical *intuition* of real objects in physical space and also our pure sensory *intuition* of the structure of space, as necessarily conforming to the form of our outer sensibility or intuition.
>
> **C**: Therefore, our pure or non-empirical (hence a priori) representation of space is necessarily underdetermined by concepts.[11]

When the conclusion of the "incongruent counterparts" argument is conjoined with the first two reasons, then it follows that the form of our outer sensibility or intuition is essentially nonconceptual and also a priori. Therefore, in *Directions in Space*, at least implicitly, Kant is saying that the basic structure of the apparent or phenomenal world necessarily conforms to the essentially nonconceptual a priori form of human embodied outer sensibility or intuition.

---

[10] See e.g. McLear (2011).

[11] For more fully spelled out versions of this argument, see Hanna (2008, 2011).

5 Directions in Space 109

This line of argument is made even more explicit in, and furthermore is strongly supported by, Kant's doctrine of the nature of space in the "Inaugural Dissertation", *On the Form and Principles of the Sensible and the Intelligible World* (1770), by his argument for the transcendental ideality of space in the *Prolegomena to Any Future Metaphysics* (1783), and by his later discussion of geographical spatial orientation in the essay "What Does It Mean to Orient Oneself in Thinking?" (1786):

> *The representation*[12] *of space is … a pure intuition,* for it is a singular concept, not one which has been compounded from sensations, although it is the fundamental form of all outer sensation. Indeed, this pure intuition can easily be seen in the axioms of geometry, and in any mental construction of postulates, even of problems. That space does not have more than three dimensions, that between two points there is only one straight line, that from a given point on a plane surface a circle can be described with a given straight line, *etc.*—none of these things can be derived from some universal concept of space; they can only be *apprehended* concretely, so to speak, in space itself. *Which things in a given space lie in one direction and which things incline in the opposite direction cannot be described discursively nor reduced to characteristic marks of the understanding by any astuteness of the mind. Thus, between solid bodies which are perfectly similar and equal but incongruent, such as the left and right hands (in so far as they are conceived only according to their extension), or spherical triangles from two opposite hemispheres, there is a difference, in virtue of which it is impossible that the limits of their extension should coincide—and that, in spite of the fact that, in respect of everything which may be expressed by means of characteristic marks intelligible to the mind through speech, they could be substituted for one another. It is, therefore, clear that in these cases the difference, namely, the incongruity, can only be apprehended by a certain pure intuition.* (MSI, 2:402–3; emphasis added)

What … can be more similar to, and in all parts more equal to, my hand or my ear than its image in the mirror? And yet I cannot put such a hand

---

[12] See note 9 above, and also Hanna (2001), Chaps. 4 and 5.

as is seen in the mirror in the place of its original; for if the one was a right hand, then the other in the mirror is a left, and the image of the right ear is a left one, which can never take the place of the former. Now there are no inner differences here that any understanding could merely think; and yet the differences are inner as far as the senses teach, for the left hand cannot, after all, be enclosed within the same boundaries as the right (they cannot be made congruent), despite all reciprocal equality and similarity; one hand's glove cannot be used on the other. What then is the solution? These objects are surely not representations of things as they are in themselves, and as the pure understanding would cognize them, rather, they are sensory intuitions, i.e., appearances, whose possibility rests on the relation of certain things, unknown in themselves, to something else, namely our sensibility. Now, space is the form of outer intuition of this sensibility, and the inner determination of space is possible only through the determination of the outer relation to the whole space of which the space is a part (the relation to outer sense); that is, the part is possible only through the whole, which never occurs with things in themselves as objects of the understanding alone, but well occurs with mere appearances. *We can therefore make the difference between similar and equal but nonetheless incongruent things (e.g., oppositely spiralled snails) intelligible through no concept alone, but only through the relation to right-hand and left-hand, which refers immediately to intuition.* (Prol, 4:286)

In the proper meaning of the word, to *orient* oneself means to use a given direction (when we divide the horizon into four of them) in order to find the others—literally, to find the *sunrise*. Now if I see the sun in the sky and know it is now midday, then I know how to find south, west, north and east. *For this, however, I also need the feeling of a difference in my own subject, namely, the difference between my right and left hands. I call this a* feeling *because these two sides outwardly display no [conceptual] characteristic difference in intuition.* If I did not have this faculty of distinguishing without the need of any difference in the objects, between moving from left to right and moving in the opposite direction and thereby determining *a priori* a difference in the position of the objects, then in describing a circle I would not know whether west was right or left of the southernmost point of the horizon, or whether I should complete the circle by moving north and east and thus back to south. Thus even with all the objective data of the sky, I orient myself *geographically* only through a *subjective* ground of differentiation. (WDO, 8:134–5; trans. amended and emphasis added)

5 Directions in Space   111

This way of reading *Directions in Space*, however, is confusingly concealed by the way that Kant formulates his main thesis in the essay:

> My purpose in this chapter is to see whether there is not to be found in the intuitive judgements about extension, such as are to be found in geometry, clear proof that: *absolute space, independently of the existence of all matter and as itself the ultimate foundation of the possibility of the compound character of matter, has a reality of its own.* (GUGR, 2:378)

In other words, the notion of *absolute* space, as Kant is using it in *Directions in Space*, is ambiguous between

(i) a *global space-frame* with orientability, egocentric centring and structural asymmetries that fundamentally conforms to the essentially nonconceptual representational structure of human outer sensibility or intuition,

and

(ii) *noumenal* space, as in Newton.

But by the time of the "Inaugural Dissertation", however, and then later in TAe in the *Critique* and throughout the Critical period, it is perfectly clear that for Kant the global space-frame must be transcendentally ideal, and cannot be noumenal.

5.4 The Essentially Nonconceptual Form of Our Representation of Space and Transcendental Idealism for Sensibility

So for all these reasons I want to claim that the central argument in *Directions in Space* is almost certainly the major philosophical breakthrough that Kant famously reports when he says in one of the *Reflexionen* that "the year '69 gave me a great light" (Refl 5037, 18:69).

112   R. Hanna

To be more precise, what Kant had discovered between 1769 and 1772 is what I call *transcendental idealism for sensibility*. In 1772, Kant told Marcus Herz that if the human mind conformed to the world, whether phenomenal or noumenal, then a priori knowledge would be impossible (Br, 10:130–1). But by 1770 Kant already also held that a priori knowledge of the phenomenal world is actual and therefore really possible in mathematics, hence the phenomenal world must conform to the non-empirical sensible structure of the human mind, and more specifically must conform to our a priori representations of space and time, since that is what makes mathematics really possible (MSI, 2:398–406). In other words, then, transcendental idealism for sensibility says that the apparent or phenomenal world fundamentally conforms to the essentially nonconceptual a priori forms of human sensibility, our representations of space and time.

In turn, this line of thinking is so important to Kant's later philosophical development during the fully Critical period from 1781 to 1787, spanning the A and B editions of the First *Critique*, and also during what I like to call his *post*-Critical period after 1787, that I think we should explicitly isolate the period from 1768 to 1772, and call it Kant's *proto*-Critical period, in order to distinguish it sharply from his dogmatic slumber-filled Leibnizian-Wolffian *pre*-Critical period.

In any case, Kant worked out explicit proofs for transcendental idealism for sensibility in the "Inaugural Dissertation" and again in TAe in the First *Critique*. The simplest version of the proof, provided in TAe, goes like this:

P1: Space and time are either (i) things in themselves, (ii) properties of/relations between things in themselves, or (iii) transcendentally ideal.
P2: If space and time were either things in themselves or properties of/relations between things in themselves, then a priori mathematical knowledge would be impossible.
P3: But mathematical knowledge is actual, via our pure intuitions of space and time, and therefore really possible.
C: Therefore, space and time are transcendentally ideal. (A23/B37–8; A38–41/B55–8)

There is, of course, much more that can and should be said about this highly controversial argument. What is most crucial for our purposes here, however, is that this version of transcendental idealism relies *only* on essentially nonconceptual content and the nature of human sensibility, and *neither* relies on concepts and the nature of human understanding, *nor* does it entail that the phenomenal world necessarily conforms to our concepts and the nature of human understanding.

5.5 Transcendental Idealism for the Understanding and the Gap in the B-Deduction

Indeed, after his major philosophical breakthrough between 1768 and 1772, it took Kant another *15 to 17 years* to work out what he regarded as a fully cogent argument for what I call *transcendental idealism for the understanding*. More precisely, transcendental idealism for the understanding says that the apparent or phenomenal world necessarily conforms to the essentially conceptual a priori forms of human understanding, namely the pure concepts of the understanding or categories. Kant's argument for this thesis is of course contained in the A (1781) and B (1787) edition versions of the Transcendental Deduction of the Pure Concepts of the Understanding (TD). But given what Kant says in the B-Preface to the First *Critique*, we must take the B-Deduction to be the *definitive* version of the argument. In turn, the explicit conclusion of the B-Deduction is that the pure concepts of the understanding or categories are necessarily applicable to "all objects of the senses in general", that is, to all actual and possible appearances (B150–61).

It is also to be particularly noted that if the B-Deduction is sound and transcendental idealism for the understanding is true, then at the very least weak Kantian conceptualism is true. But contrapositively, if Kantian non-conceptualism is true, then all forms of Kantian conceptualism are false, transcendental idealism for the understanding is false, and the B-Deduction is unsound. Moreover there are strong Kantian nonconceptualist reasons for thinking that TD, in *either* version, but particularly the B-Deduction, is unsound. Elsewhere, I have called the Kantian nonconceptualist argument for the unsoundness of the B-Deduction "The Gap in the B-Deduction" (Hanna 2011, 2016). The Gap argument, in a nutshell, goes like this:

P1: If the B-Deduction is sound, then the pure concepts of the understanding or categories are necessarily applicable to all appearances.

P2: But if Kantian nonconceptualism is true, then there are actually, and therefore also really possibly, at least some appearances, veridically cognised by empirical and pure intuition, that necessarily fall outside the categories, which I call "essentially rogue objects". The most obvious example of this would be a conscious but non-rational animal's veridical intuition of the difference between the right and left sides of its body.[13] More precisely, incongruent counterparts, as cognised by animal perceivers without conceptual capacities, are essentially rogue objects.

C: Therefore, the B-Deduction is unsound.

Correspondingly, it also follows that transcendental idealism for the understanding is false: not all appearances necessarily conform to the categories and concepts more generally; indeed, at least some appearances *cannot* conform to the categories or to any concepts whatsoever.[14]

5.6   Conclusion

If the arguments I have briefly summarised here are sound, then (i) transcendental idealism for sensibility and transcendental idealism for the understanding are logically independent, (ii) transcendental idealism for sensibility—based in particular on Kant's arguments in *Directions in Space* and more generally on his philosophical breakthrough between 1768 and 1772—is true, and (iii) transcendental idealism for the understanding is false.

Correspondingly, then, the most important implication of the central argument in *Directions in Space* is that Kant's nonconceptualism is foundational for any *philosophically defensible* version of his transcendental idealism, namely, transcendental idealism for sensibility. Hence it is impossible to put forward a philosophically defensible but also recognisably Critical-period Kantian metaphysics or theory of cognition without also being a

---

[13] There are also several more exciting but also less obvious examples, all of which have to do with the real possibility of human freedom. See Hanna (2011, 2016).

[14] See also Schulting (2015b).

Kantian nonconceptualist and thereby necessarily relying on some arguments from Kant's proto-Critical period.

This in turn implies, as I mentioned above, the philosophically important claims that Kant's non-intellectualism about the human mind goes all the way down into his metaphysics; that the apparent world fundamentally conforms to human sensibility even if it does not fundamentally conform to the human understanding; and that the basic source of all this is Kant's (proto-Critical but later also Critical) theory of space and how we represent it.

6

Kant's Aesthetic Nonconceptualism

Dietmar H. Heidemann

6.1 Introduction

The literature that has been produced to date on the question of whether or not Kant is a nonconceptualist is overwhelming in quantity and quality. The debate is far from coming to an end, not least because there is still disagreement even about how to understand the most fundamental make-up of Kant's theory of knowledge and mind in regard to conceptualism and nonconceptualism. Among others, a major point of difference concerns the nature of Kantian sensibility and intuition, that is, whether an intuition is a singular representation, directly referential, phenomenal, subjective or objective, and whether or not it plays an independent role in cognition. Analogously, a second point of difference concerns the nature of concepts in Kant, that is, in what sense they are to be conceived as general, indirectly referential representations, how they are formed and how

---

D.H. Heidemann (✉)
Institute of Philosophy, University of Luxembourg, Luxembourg
e-mail: dietmar.heidemann@uni.lu

© The Editor(s) (if applicable) and The Author(s) 2016
D. Schulting (ed.), *Kantian Nonconceptualism*,
DOI 10.1057/978-1-137-53517-7_6

they relate to intuition. The main difficulty in this context is that in his published work Kant himself does not clearly indicate if his theory is to be construed along the lines of what nowadays is called "conceptualism" or "nonconceptualism". Even worse, prima facie his work seems to provide support for both conceptualist and nonconceptualist interpretations.[1]

Besides the general disagreement among interpreters of Kant's theory of knowledge and mind, there is a second reason why the debate has not yet been settled. So far the discussion has almost exclusively focused on transcendental idealism, that is, on Kant's writings on theoretical philosophy in the more narrow sense. Interpreters usually just concentrate on the First *Critique*, the *Prolegomena* and corresponding publications in order to show that Kant is a conceptualist or a nonconceptualist.[2] The Third *Critique*, that is, Kant's aesthetics, has been completely neglected in the debate. This is very surprising all the more because it is in his aesthetics that Kant explicitly addresses the problem of nonconceptualism. In what follows I shall show that in the Third *Critique* Kant puts forward arguments that help to make significant progress concerning the question of whether or not his theory of knowledge and mind is to be construed as a version of nonconceptualism. The Third *Critique* seems to be an important source for providing evidence in support of a nonconceptualist reading of Kant. For according to Kant aesthetic experience is cognition of a special kind that does not bear on conceptual activities. This is because the cognitive appreciation of the beautiful is not derived from rule-governed procedures of the mind, although aesthetic evaluation is expressed in *judgements* of taste. As Kant himself puts it, what is "beautiful" "pleases universally without a concept" (KU, 5:219), and "without concepts, is represented as the object of a *universal* satisfaction" (KU, 5:211).

---

[1] For such diverging interpretations see, for instance, the articles collected in Heidemann (2013a). A further difficulty is that some of those who argue for a conceptualist reading of Kant do so explicitly from a Hegelian point of view, most notably McDowell (cf. e.g. McDowell 2009). Hegelian readings are, of course, not immanent interpretations of Kant and make assumptions Kant does not share. On such assumptions see Engelhard (2007). See also Schulting, Chap. 10 in this volume.

[2] Kant's writings on practical philosophy do not play any significant role in the debate, since ethics is not informative about the way humans cognise.

6 Kant's Aesthetic Nonconceptualism 119

The debate on Kantian conceptualism and nonconceptualism has completely overlooked the importance of Kant's aesthetics.[3] That is not to say that the role of cognition and hence of concepts in Kant's aesthetics has been ignored in the literature. In recent years the relation between theory of knowledge and aesthetics in Kant's Critical philosophy has even been examined in great detail, although without taking into account the debate on nonconceptual content. The volume *Aesthetics and Cognition in Kant's Critical Philosophy* (Kukla 2006),[4] for example, is a collection of articles that explicitly relate Kant's aesthetics to the Critical theory of knowledge. Although the contributions cover important topics from Kant's theory of cognition, such as the cognitive function of sensible particulars, discursive judgement, the cognitive structure of aesthetic judgement and the role of reflective judgement, they do not engage with the issue of contemporary nonconceptualism. Nonconceptuality is merely mentioned by Richard Manning (2006:66–7) in his discussion of Wilfrid Sellars and John McDowell in connection with the cognitive status of "nonconceptual impressions" and the possibility of conceptually informed intuitions. Rudolf Makkreel (2006:243) makes the rather ambivalent observation "that whereas Kant defined a pure aesthetic judgment to be nonconceptual, most aesthetic judgments are at least in part conceptual".[5]

---

[3] To some degree Ginsborg (2006c) is an exception. Although she is not so much interested in the principal question of whether or not Kant is a nonconceptualist, which she covers in Ginsborg (2008), she interprets Kant's theory of judgement of taste as a theory of perceptual truth-independent normativity. That is to say, perceptual normativity as expressed in judgements of taste is a condition of experience "making concepts available to us", i.e. of "bringing the objects of experience under empirical concepts" (Ginsborg 2006c:406). Thus, Ginsborg (2006c:407–14, in particular) makes use of Kant's theory in order to elaborate her own systematic account of experience and normativity. Her discussion of nonconceptualism is therefore not so much focused on Kant's aesthetics itself. But this is what I shall do in this chapter.

[4] Other recent examples of publications that emphasise the cognitive dimension of Kant's aesthetics are Hughes (2007), Kalar (2006), and Kirwan (2004). An earlier example is Ginsborg (1990).

[5] Makkreel continues that judgements of taste "may presuppose already familiar empirical concepts, as when we refer back to prejudices of taste, or more general concepts, as when we orient our judgment to exemplary models" (2006:243). He writes further: "Moreover, they may project aesthetic ideas that disclose affinities with rational ideas and can in turn suggest new concepts. Since we grow up with logical as well as aesthetic prejudices, it is unlikely that we ever confront the world without any concepts. They may be inadequate concepts, or mere representational concepts as found through the logical reflection .... This means that the so-called nonconceptual judgment of taste, 'This rose is beautiful', and the more generic judgment, 'This flower is beautiful', use vague representational concepts rather than determining concepts with the defining marks of things" (Makkreel

In what follows it will become clear that, as in the discussion of Kant's theory of aesthetic judgement in general, Makkreel's use of "nonconceptual" is in many respects different from its use in the contemporary debate on nonconceptualism. That is not to say that, regarding nonconceptualism, the discussion of the role of concepts in Kant's aesthetics is unhelpful. On the contrary, Sect. 6.2 starts off from that discussion in order to illuminate that judgements of taste are cognitive judgements of a special kind, that is, they are not just expressions of aesthetic feeling. As I shall argue, the cognitive quality of judgements is a necessary precondition of nonconceptuality, which Kant's judgements of taste clearly meet. After having shown, in Sect. 6.2, that Kantian judgements of taste have cognitive quality, Sect. 6.3 proceeds by an analysis of the nonconceptual character of judgements of taste in Kant's aesthetics. I explicate that nonconceptuality is a crucial feature of judgements of taste and explain what this means.

Nonconceptuality is not only present in Kant's theory of aesthetic evaluation. It is also a systematic element of his theory of the creation of art. In Sect. 6.4, I demonstrate in what sense the art-creating "genius" is "a *talent* for producing that for which no determinate rule can be given" (KU, 5:307), hence, that art production does not imply conceptual activity either and therefore counts as a second systematic instance of Kantian nonconceptualism.

If my argument is correct, then Kant's aesthetics implies nonconceptualism, that is, it proves that Kant is a nonconceptualist. However, my argument faces a serious objection. From the fact that Kant advocates nonconceptualism in aesthetics it does not follow, one might contend, that he is a nonconceptualist in the straightforward cognitive sense of nonconceptualism. For Kant might be a nonconceptualist in aesthetics but a conceptualist in the theory of cognition and mind. In Sect. 6.5, I shall conclude that the kind of aesthetic nonconceptualism Kant advocates is incompatible with being a conceptualist in purely cognitive terms.

2006:243). For a view similar to Makreel's, see Ameriks (2003b:336). In general, Ameriks defends a "conceptualist" or "objectivist" interpretation of judgements of taste. Cf. Ameriks (2003b:338–43).

6.2 The Cognitive Character of Judgements of Taste

The aim of this section is to illustrate that judgements of taste are cognitive judgements of a special kind and that the *cognitive* quality of judgements is a necessary precondition for judgements exhibiting nonconceptual content. The initial question to be asked, then, is whether or not Kantian judgements of taste meet this precondition. For if they did not, it would be hard to see why Kant's aesthetics should be at all relevant for the debate on nonconceptualism.

Many philosophers agree that conceptualism can be defined as the view that cognisers can have mental representations of objects only if they possess the adequate concepts by means of which they can specify what they represent. By contrast, nonconceptualists hold that mental representations of objects do not necessarily presuppose concepts by means of which the content of these representations can be specified. Whereas conceptualists deny the possibility of nonconceptual mental representations of objects, nonconceptualists do not contest that mental representations of objects can in principle involve concepts. However, according to nonconceptualism, cognisers do not have any conceptual mental representations of objects such that these representations bear phenomenality and intentionality.[6]

What should be clear from the beginning is that nonconceptual content cannot be cognitively relevant independently of judging. That is to say, nonconceptual content as some kind of causally effected unstructured sensory given is not the issue in the controversy over nonconceptual content. For even most conceptualists do not deny that, for example, in sense-perception the human sensory apparatus is confronted with such

---

[6] Cf. Heidemann (2013b:1). Different definitions can of course be given. However, for the purpose of this chapter I take the above-mentioned definitions to be uncontroversial. In what follows, the somewhat standard division of nonconceptualism into state and content nonconceptualism will turn out to be useful. According to state nonconceptualism, mental states have nonconceptual content if the cogniser does not possess adequate concepts in order to specify this content. According to content nonconceptualism, the representational content in question is fundamentally different from conceptual content. I shall get back to that distinction in the following two sections. For a discussion of alternative definitions of (state and content) nonconceptualism, see Bermúdez and Cahen (2015).

a sensory given. What they dispute is rather that a sensory given as such can at all be cognitively relevant. For in order, for example, to fulfil the function of justifying (perceptual) beliefs, a sensory given must bear phenomenality and intentionality, and therefore be representationally efficacious. However, a pure sensory given does not seem to have this capacity. It is only on the level of judgement (belief) that perceptual content is *cognitively* relevant, that is, in moving from sensory given to conceptual or propositional structure in judgements. This is clearly the case in Kant's theory of cognition and, as we shall see, in his aesthetics too.

According to the transcendental doctrine of judgements, we can "trace all actions of the understanding back to judgments, so that the *understanding* in general can be represented as a *faculty for judging*. ... it is a faculty for thinking". And: "Thinking is cognition through concepts" (A69/B94). Now Kant maintains that "the understanding can make no other use of ... concepts than that of judging by means of them", that is, by organising concepts according to a logical "function" that is "the unity of the action of ordering different representations under a common one" (A68/B93). The well-formed product of such a cognitive operation is a "judgment" as "the mediate cognition of an object" (A68/B93). Judgements are "mediate" because concepts are discursive and do not directly refer to objects.[7] For concepts as general representations cannot individuate singular objects by themselves but only with the help of intuition or perceptual reference:

> Since no representation pertains to the object immediately except intuition alone, a concept is thus never immediately related to an object, but is always related to some other representation of it (whether that be an intuition or itself already a concept). Judgment is therefore the mediate cognition of an object, hence the representation of a representation of it. In every judgment there is a concept that holds of many, and that among this many also comprehends a given representation, which is then related immediately to the object. (A68/B93)

It is crucial that the connection between judgement and intuition is not self-explaining but needs to be argued for. Kant claims that the

---

[7] Cf. Heidemann (2002).

6 Kant's Aesthetic Nonconceptualism   123

same function that gives unity to the different representations *in a judgment* also gives unity to the mere synthesis of different representations *in an intuition*, which, expressed generally, is called the pure concept of the understanding. (A79/B104–5)[8]

The argument here is that the pure concepts of the understanding, that is, the categories, parallel the logical functions in that the latter are simply to be conceived as determinations of intuition. It is by means of conceptual, categorial determination that a sensible given of intuition is subject to judgemental structure. However, the conceptual determination in judgement does not make intuition per se conceptual all the way down since the sensible manifold given in intuition retains its nonconceptual nature in terms of a singular representation while being part of the judgemental structure. For Kant, the cooperation of concept and intuition in judging is a minimal condition of cognition in terms of objective representation. That is to say, nothing can count as (objective) cognition except a judgement.

Although Kant makes it clear at the beginning of the Analytic of the Beautiful, in the *Critique of Judgement*, that the "judgment of taste" is not to be conflated with a "logical", "cognitive judgment" (KU, 5:203), aesthetic cognition cannot be conceived just as some kind of feeling, of which a perceiver is conscious, for it, too, depends on judgement: "What is required for calling an object beautiful must be discovered by the analysis of judgments of taste" (KU, 5:203n.). The reason why a "judgement of taste" is not a logical "cognitive judgment" is that

> in order to decide whether or not something is beautiful, we do not relate the representation by means of understanding to the object for cognition, but rather relate it by means of the imagination (perhaps combined with the understanding) to the subject and its feeling of pleasure or displeasure. (KU, 5:203)

---

[8] In the *Prolegomena* Kant formulates this as follows: "The given intuition must be subsumed under a concept that determines the form of judging in general with respect to the intuition …; a concept of this kind is a pure *a priori* concept of the understanding, which does nothing but simply determine for an intuition the mode in general in which it can serve for judging" (Prol, 4:300).

The feeling of pleasure or displeasure, however, cannot be objective in the same sense as a logical cognitive judgement. For an aesthetic feeling is about the subjective state the perceiver is in, given the affection through the representation she has, rather than about the logical determination of a sensible given through concepts such as in a cognitive judgement.

On the other hand, judgements of taste share several features that logical cognitive judgements have. First, Kant's analysis of the judgements of taste in the Third *Critique* follows the order of the "logical functions" of cognitive judgements in the First *Critique* because judgements of taste always contain "a relation to the understanding" (KU, 5:203n.). As the Third Moment of the judgement of taste (KU, 5:219ff.) in particular emphasises, aesthetic cognition involves the activity of understanding and imagination, that is, of *faculties of cognition*, just as in logical cognition. Now since judgements of taste are determined through logical functions and since they refer to something given in intuition, that is, an object of aesthetic evaluation, categories must be operative in judgements of taste as they are in logical judgements. To be sure, in terms of aesthetic cognition judgements of taste are not based on determining judgement such that in aesthetic cognition, that is, in "calling an object beautiful" (KU, 5:203n.), an object of intuition is determined according to concepts. Judgements of taste rather originate in reflective judgement according to the purposive relation of the faculties of cognition involved, that is, understanding and imagination, and their "free play" or "harmony" (KU, 5:217–18).[9] Nevertheless, categories are operative in judgements of taste in two respects:

(i) We can regard judgements of taste as ordinary judgements of perception. In stating, "This flower is beautiful" (KU 5:281), to take Kant's standard example, we can focus on the flower as an ordinary physical object and determine it according to the categories whilst abstracting from aesthetic evaluation. In this case, the emphasis is on the given object in intuition and its properties.

---

[9]On the free and harmonious play of the faculties of cognition, see Sect. 6.3. Cf. Allison (2001:98–118).

6 Kant's Aesthetic Nonconceptualism 125

(ii) We may consider the aesthetic predicate "beautiful" that arises from contemplation by abstracting from the "existence of an object" and merely relying on the "feeling of pleasure and displeasure" (KU, 5:209). As much as this "feeling" belongs to intuition and justifies[10] the judgement, albeit in the peculiar aesthetic way, categories must be in play here, too. For the aesthetic feeling is not to be seen as an unspecified one but as a feeling that can be conceived according to categorial ordering, although "without a concept of the object" (KU, 5:217).[11]

Second, according to Kant "universal communicability of our cognition" is to be "assumed in every logic and every principle of cognitions that is not skeptical" (KU, 5:239). "Universal communicability" is not a surprising constraint for logical cognition and stands in close connection with objectivity and universality. It is a feature of cognition that Kant does not address in the First or Second *Critique*. However, it coheres well with his overall conception of enlightenment and his emphasis on the publicity of reason after 1788.[12] In the *Critique of Judgement* Kant explicitly mentions "universal communicability" as a "requisite" not only "for a *cognition in general*" but also for "a judgment of taste", although "without presupposing a determinate concept" (KU, 5:217–18). The reason Kant gives seems uncontroversial: if "cognitions and judgments" would not "be able to be universally communicated", "they would have no correspondence with the object" and hence could be nothing over and above "a merely subjective play of the powers of representation, just as skepticism insists" (KU, 5:238). Logical and aesthetic cognition alike thus share the feature of universal communicability since cognitive judgements and judgements of taste equally refer to objects they make claims about.

Third, the fact that logical cognitive judgements and judgements of taste must be universally communicable already implies the claim that they must be universally valid judgements. With respect to judgements

---

[10] Kant states that the judgement of taste is "one whose determining ground *cannot* be *other than subjective*", i.e. a "feeling" (KU, 5:203).

[11] In what sense aesthetic evaluation implies categorial determination in a different way than as in logical cognitive judgements will be discussed in Sect. 6.3.

[12] Cf. Gunkel (2015).

126   D.H. Heidemann

of taste this might come as a surprise since all judgements of taste are singular judgements. As we shall see further below, Kant attributes universal validity to judgements of taste, not because we can generalise over aesthetic predicates according to conceptual rules, but because aesthetic cognition originates in universally valid cognitive faculties, the understanding and imagination, whilst it is determined through subjective aesthetic feeling. Hence, both logical cognitive judgements and judgements of taste lay claim to universality, the former in the objective sense, the latter in the subjective sense.[13]

In this section, I have argued that according to Kant the *cognitive* quality of judgements is a necessary condition for nonconceptual content. Although judgements of taste cannot count as logical cognitive judgements, they are cognitive in several respects and are therefore in principle capable of exhibiting nonconceptual content. From the fact that judgements of taste have this capability it does not necessarily follow that they really do exhibit nonconceptual content. In Sect. 6.3, I show in what respect nonconceptual content can in fact be attributed to judgements of taste.

6.3   Nonconceptual Content and Judgements of Taste

As already mentioned in the introduction to this chapter, there are two candidates for nonconceptuality in Kant's aesthetics. First, nonconceptual content plays a crucial role in aesthetic evaluation, that is, in judgements of taste as expressions of such evaluation. Second, nonconceptual content has a systematic explanatory function in the theory of aesthetic creation of the genius of art in that the genius conceives of aesthetic ideas in terms of rules bearing upon nonconceptual content. In the present section, I analyse the role of nonconceptual content in

---

[13] One might think that subjective and objective universality of cognition are two fundamentally distinct claims in kind. As we shall see in Sect. 6.3, subjective universality should not be conceived as "private" universality but as universality according to universally valid subjective cognitive faculties. Here, I do not address "universality" as it has been discussed in the literature on Kant's aesthetics. For a critical discussion of various interpretations see Allison (2001:98–118).

aesthetic evaluation. In the following section (Sect. 6.4) I shall look at the role of nonconceptual content in the genius's creation of artwork.

That nonconceptual content is operative in judgements of taste seems to be obvious from what Kant maintains about the nature of those judgements at two prominent places in the Analytic of the Beautiful. In the Second Moment of the judgement of taste it reads:

> The beautiful is that which, without concepts, is represented as the object of a *universal* satisfaction. (KU, 5:211; heading)

The Fourth Moment involves a similar claim:

> That is *beautiful* which is cognized without a concept as the object of a *necessary* satisfaction. (KU, 5:240; heading)

In both cases the expression indicating nonconceptuality, namely "without concepts" and "without a concept", is used adverbially. In the first case, the way in which we represent the beautiful is nonconceptual, in the second case the cognition of the beautiful is nonconceptual. From this observation the question arises whether, in Kant's aesthetics, the adverbial use of "nonconceptual" is the same as the more standard adnominal use of "nonconceptual", as in "nonconceptual content" or "nonconceptual perception".[14] This question can only be answered by means of a more comprehensive discussion of judgements of taste, since the argument for aesthetic nonconceptuality is composed of different lines of thought in the Analytic of the Beautiful.

---

[14] At first glance, representing or cognising something without concepts, i.e. representing or cognising it nonconceptually, on the one hand, and representing or cognising nonconceptual content, on the other, does not amount to the same thing. Representing or cognising something without concepts is a state of mind that by definition does not involve concepts, while representing or cognising nonconceptual content can. For instance, assuming the fine-grainedness argument (cf. e.g. Evans 1982:229; for a discussion of the argument see Bermúdez and Cahen 2015) is correct, my perception of a fine-grained colour shade is intrinsically nonconceptual such that my corresponding state of mind is intrinsically nonconceptual too. However, I can give a conceptual description of the criteria by means of which nonconceptual as opposed to conceptual content can be identified, that is, cognised.

128   **D.H. Heidemann**

The First Moment of the judgement of taste, resulting in the "explication of the beautiful":[15] "that is *beautiful* which pleases universally without a concept" (KU, 5:219), already lays the ground for Kant's aesthetic non-conceptualism. In aesthetic cognition, Kant states that

> we do not relate the representation by means of understanding to the object for cognition, but rather relate it by means of the imagination (perhaps combined with the understanding) to the subject and its feeling of pleasure or displeasure. (KU, 5:203)

The different modes of relation of representations in a judgement explain why a judgement of taste is not a logical cognitive judgement. In a logical cognitive judgement the subject relates representations to an object as something distinct from its own state of mind. By contrast, in an aesthetic judgement the subject relates representations to the "feeling of pleasure and displeasure", that is, as Kant puts it, that "in which the subject feels itself as it is affected by the representation" (KU, 5:204). The reason why the "determining ground" of a judgement of taste is "subjective" (KU, 5:203) must not be seen in the fact that it is the subject as such that is relating representations, for this is also the case in cognitive, that is, objective judgements, where the understanding relates representations to objects. Relating representations to objects might imply relating them to external physical bodies. But this is not the primary meaning. In the first place, relating representations rather refers to the synthetic unity among them, made possible through the "*synthetic* unity of apperception" (B137). This is so because for Kant a (logical) judgement "is nothing other than the way to bring given cognitions to the *objective* unity of apperception" (B141), that is, the objective unity of the understanding.[16]

Judgements of taste work differently. The "determining ground" of a judgement of taste is "subjective" because here the cognitive faculty of pleasure and displeasure is affected with the result that the subject is in a

---

[15] The German reads *Erklärung des Schönen*. I have amended the translation from "definition of the beautiful" to "explication of the beautiful" because "definition" suggests that there is a clear-cut conceptual determination of the beautiful, which, according to Kant, is not the case.

[16] Cf. Heidemann (2012:50–6).

state of mind that Kant describes as "feeling", which the subject refers to itself. A "feeling", however, does not contribute anything to (objective) cognition. It rather results from a specific cognitive, conscious relation between the understanding and imagination in the subject. (The coming about and structure of that relation will be discussed below in more detail.) Kant clarifies the difference between the objective character of a cognitive judgement and the subjective character of a judgement of taste in the following way. A judgement is a cognitive or "logical" judgement if the understanding relates given empirical representations to the object. But in the case where the subject in terms of imagination relates given "rational" representations to its own inner cognitive state, that is, "its feeling", these representations would be "aesthetic" (KU, 5:204) and hence amount to a judgement of taste instead of a logical cognitive judgement. This seems to imply that the understanding is not capable of accessing feelings as objects of inner sense, although the understanding can bring them to consciousness by means of self-affection (cf. B150–6). By contrast, the imagination can access (aesthetic) feelings since it is capable of relating a representation "to the subject and its feeling of pleasure or displeasure" (KU, 5:203), which is the case only in a judgement of taste.

In Kant's aesthetic nonconceptualism the key term is "feeling" since "feeling of pleasure and displeasure" is the "determining ground" (KU, 5:203) of a judgement of taste. Like logical judgements that are objective because they are justified or determined through the objective relation of representations, judgements of taste are justified or determined through the relation of representations to the inner mental state the subject is in, to its "feeling". It is only because the subject is conscious of this feeling that it brings about judgements of taste. This is why the feeling of pleasure and displeasure is to be regarded as nonconceptual content in aesthetic cognition. As we have seen in Sect. 6.2, in order for mental content to count as nonconceptual content, this content must be phenomenal, intentional and representational. Aesthetic nonconceptual content (feeling) is phenomenal since in the mental state of aesthetic feeling it is somehow for the subject to be in that state; it is intentional since in that state the subject feels itself, that is, is directed toward itself; and it is representational since in that state the subject is representing the harmonious

130   D.H. Heidemann

relation of understanding and imagination.[17] It is for these reasons that the "feeling of pleasure and displeasure" justifies or determines judgements of taste, although in a merely subjective way.

Since judgements of taste are based on feeling they cannot have correctness conditions like logical cognitive judgements, it seems. For feelings can neither be correct nor incorrect, we just have them or not. By contrast, in order to believe that a person's perceptual judgement "This is a house" is correct, one must assume that the person's perceptual capacities are well-functioning, that there really is a house in the person's visual field, that the person is telling the truth, and so forth. Although in the case of aesthetic cognition there are no correctness conditions as in cognitive perceptual judgements, it is possible to describe the cognitive presuppositions of the coming about of aesthetic feeling. These presuppositions, as Kant outlines them in the Second Moment of the judgement of taste in particular, explain why the aesthetic feeling is to be seen as nonconceptual, whilst justifying mental content.

The Second Moment, including its nonconceptuality claim, is, as Kant emphasises, a logical conclusion from the First Moment. In the First Moment, Kant argues not only that the judgement of taste is not a logical cognitive judgement and that its determining ground is feeling, but also that this feeling conceived as aesthetic "satisfaction" is "without any interest" (KU, 5:204; heading) because in aesthetic cognition "satisfaction" does not have any interest in the existence of the evaluated object. This is not the case with satisfaction in the "agreeable" and the "good" (see KU, §§3–5), which is dependent on the existence of their respective objects. It is in this context that Kant for the first time in the Third *Critique* addresses the issue of nonconceptuality. Contrary to judgements about the agreeable and the good, the judgement of taste is "merely *contemplative*, i.e., a judgment that, indifferent with regard to the existence of an object, merely connects its constitution together with

---

[17] One might object that the intentional and represented object of an aesthetic state is the object of aesthetic predication. Hence, in the judgement "This flower is beautiful" the evaluating subject refers the predicate "beautiful" to the flower it perceives. In a sense this is true, since a judgement of taste is a (singular) judgement of perception. As we shall see, however, in his aesthetics Kant takes the perceiving, evaluating subject and the aesthetic state it is in as basis instead of the perceived, evaluated object.

6 Kant's Aesthetic Nonconceptualism   131

the feeling of pleasure and displeasure" (KU, 5:209). By contemplation Kant means the merely inward mental reflection and consideration of given representations in association with disinterested satisfaction. This specifically aesthetic cognitive processing is "not directed to concepts" and "neither *grounded* on concepts nor *aimed* at them" (KU, 5:209). It is nonconceptual in the first place because given reflective judgement there can be no concept under which the aesthetic feeling is to be subsumed. On the contrary, reflective judgement is first looking for such a concept, that is, the predicate "beautiful".

The rather uninformative reason that Kant provides in the First Moment for why judgements of taste do not involve concepts is that they are not logical cognitive judgements. The crucial argument for the nonconceptuality of aesthetic cognition is to be drawn from the Second Moment concerning the quantity of a judgement of taste. According to Kant, judgements of taste do not rest on "private conditions" (KU, 5:211) since they are expressions of a *disinterested* satisfaction. For that reason the subject of aesthetic evaluation is entitled to claim that the satisfaction is universal and "consequently he must believe himself to have grounds for expecting a similar pleasure of everyone" (KU, 5:211). Thus judgements of taste are supposed to be universally valid. The kind of universality in play here cannot count as objective universality because aesthetic universality "cannot originate from concepts", "for there is no transition from concepts to the feeling of pleasure or displeasure" (KU, 5:211–12). Although it is not a *private* judgement and hence is valid only for the author of that judgement, a judgement of taste cannot lay claim to objective but only to "subjective universality" (KU, 5:212).

"Subjective universality" is not a hybrid or even contradictory term, as one might think, because it sets limits to something that is in itself unrestricted. Kant clarifies this expression by contrasting it with objective universality. A cognition to which pertains objective universality is made possible through concepts of the object. According to the Kantian theory, a concept is a universal (abstract) representation that must be conceived of as a composite of marks. The concept "house", for instance, comprises those marks that are characteristic of houses such that a person *possesses* the concept "house" if she apprehends that composite of marks in the correct way. The concept "house" then allows for the subsumption of a given

132   D.H. Heidemann

intuition under it, which can be expressed in the singular judgement "This is a house". This perceptual cognition is made possible through the apprehension of the concept "house" and its correct application, and not by referring representations to the subject's state of mind. It therefore has objective and not just subjective universality.[18]

Cognition to which pertains subjective universality, that is, aesthetic cognition, does not allow for subsumption of an intuition under a concept. The aesthetic predicate "beautiful" in a judgement of taste must not be apprehended as a composite of characteristic marks such that what logically falls under that predicate must be called "beautiful". This would imply that by logical subsumption something could be deduced with objective universality as being "beautiful", which is impossible since a judgement of taste "does not pertain to the object at all" (KU, 5:215). That is to say, in subjectively universal judgements "the predicate of beauty is not connected with the concept of the *object* considered in its entire logical sphere, and yet it extends it over the whole sphere of *those who judge*" (KU, 5:215).[19] If "the predicate of beauty" were "connected with the concept of the object", that is, if objects were judged on the basis of concepts, "then all representation of beauty is lost" (KU, 5:215). Why aesthetic cognition cannot be concept driven is more than obvious for Kant:

> Whether a garment, a house, a flower is beautiful: no one allows himself to be talked into his judgment about that by means of any grounds or fundamental principles. One wants to submit the object to his own eyes, just as if his satisfaction depended on sensation; and yet, if one then calls the object beautiful, one believes oneself to have a universal voice, and lays

---

[18] Cf. KU, 5:214. Objective universality in terms of theoretical cognition, of course, implies the conception of the transcendental unity of apperception as developed in the Transcendental Deduction of the First *Critique*. See Heidemann (forthcoming).

[19] Cf. the Jäsche Logic: "Every concept, *as partial concept*, is contained in the representation of things; as *ground of cognition, i.e., as mark*, these things are contained *under* it. In the former respect every concept has a *content*, in the other an *extension*." In the note to this passage Kant adds that the "universality or universal validity of a concept does not rest on the fact that the concept is a *partial concept*, but rather on the fact that it is a *ground of cognition*" (Log, 9:95). Thus if we cognise *x* because we are in possession of the concept of *x*, this cognition is (logically) universal. As we have seen, this is not the case with aesthetic cognition.

6 Kant's Aesthetic Nonconceptualism   133

claim to the consent of everyone, whereas any private sensation would be decisive only for him alone and his satisfaction. (KU, 5:216)[20]

Consequently, in a judgement of taste the predication "is beautiful" is taken to be universally valid, hence as if it were an objectively true judgement, because the aesthetic satisfaction it tacitly expresses is a claim that everyone is called upon to endorse. The judgement "This flower is beautiful" (KU, 5:281) therefore seems to ascribe the predicate "beautiful" to the flower as if it were an objective quality of the flower. But this is clearly not the case in Kant's aesthetics,

> for the judgment of taste consists precisely in the fact that it calls a thing beautiful only in accordance with that quality in it by means of which it corresponds with our way of receiving it. (KU, 5:282)

It is for this reason that Kant's aesthetics reflects his enlightenment thought in general and can be termed "autonomous aesthetics". In this context "autonomous" does not refer to some kind of aesthetic self-legislation, for judgements of taste cannot operate by means of conceptual rules or norms. The term "autonomous" rather indicates that aesthetic cognition is based on first-person experience and cannot rely on heteronomous sources:

> Taste makes claim merely to autonomy. To make the judgments of others into the determining ground of one's own would be heteronomy. (KU, 5:282)

The autonomy of aesthetics rules out that a judgement of taste is "determinable by grounds of proof" because

---

[20] In the Deduction of the Judgement of Taste Kant makes basically the same point in his claim that "no objective principle of taste is possible": "By a principle of taste would be understood a fundamental proposition under the condition of which one could subsume the concept of an object and then by means of an inference conclude that it is beautiful. But that is absolutely impossible. For I must be sensitive of the pleasure immediately in the representation of it, and I cannot be talked into it by means of any proofs. Thus although critics, as Hume says, can reason more plausibly than cooks, they still suffer the same fate as them. They cannot expect a determining ground for their judgment from proofs, but only from the reflection of the subject on his own state (of pleasure or displeasure), rejecting all precepts and rules" (KU, 5:285–6).

134 D.H. Heidemann

that the approval of others provides no valid proof for the judging of beauty, that others may perhaps see and observe for him, and that what many have seen in one way what he believes himself to have seen otherwise, may serve him as a sufficient ground of proof for a theoretical, hence a logical judgment, but that what has pleased others can never serve as the ground of an aesthetic judgment. (KU, 5:284)

That there is no empirical ground of proof of a judgement of taste does not mean that there is an *a priori* one. For even if a piece of art meets all criteria that art critics have identified for something to be beautiful, my experience of that piece can still be without "favour" (*Gunst*) and no expert can convince me of the opposite by means of rationalising about that piece (cf. KU, 5:284, 210). Aesthetic cognition essentially presupposes first-person experience of the object of aesthetic evaluation. The experience a person has in aesthetic cognition is nonconceptual for the reasons just given. From the fact that aesthetic experience does not involve concepts nothing follows with respect to the very nature of nonconceptual experience. I have already mentioned that in aesthetic cognition representations qualify as nonconceptual because they are intentional, phenomenal and representational. Aesthetic nonconceptual content can now be characterised more precisely in the following way. Since aesthetic nonconceptual content is subjectively phenomenal, judgements of taste are determined through first-person experience. Kant illustrates this with the help of the following example:

Someone may list all the ingredients of a dish for me, and remark about each one that it is otherwise agreeable to me, and moreover even rightly praise the healthiness of this food; yet I am deaf to all these grounds, I try the dish with *my* tongue and my palate, and on that basis (not on the basis of general principles) do I make my judgment. (KU, 5:285; Kant's emphasis)

Kant's point here comes close to Thomas Nagel's argument in his article "What is it like to be a bat?" (Nagel 1991). Conscious experience is attached to a subjective, individual perspective from which this experience is made, and there are no conceptual means that could possibly detach it from that perspective in order to make the experience comprehensible from a third-person perspective, that is, by conceptually explaining to

6 Kant's Aesthetic Nonconceptualism 135

others what it is like to be in a particular mental state. This is the case with Kantian aesthetic cognition too. We cannot judge "This flower is beautiful" by way of conceptual inferences, because in a judgement of taste representations are not related to the object of aesthetic evaluation but to the state of mind of the evaluating subject. Kant obviously believes that since a judgement of taste is a (singular) judgement of perception the content of perception immediately justifies that judgement, which, as many conceptualists argue, seems to be problematic since perceptual mental content as such cannot constitute reasons as the justifying grounds of beliefs. This point will be taken up again in the conclusion below.

So far the question had to remain open as to what the aesthetic state of mind is in terms of content, or to put it differently, what we are conscious of in nonconceptual aesthetic experience that counts as the determining ground of judgements of taste. As it turns out, aesthetic nonconceptual content as the subjective determining ground of judgements of taste reveals itself as "the state of mind that is encountered in the relation of the powers of representation to each other insofar as they relate a given representation to *cognition in general*", that is, in the cognitive relation of "*imagination*" and "*understanding*" (KU, 5:217). Against the backdrop of what Kant has said with respect to the more formal side of the non-conceptuality requirement of judgements of taste this is substantiated. Because they are nonconceptual, judgements of taste must meet two conditions in particular. They cannot be grounded in the agreeable, that is, in pleasure, since in this case a judgement of taste would be merely private and hence pointless in view of an aesthetic *theory*. On the other hand, a judgement of taste cannot be objectively universal either, since objective universality only pertains to logical cognitive judgements. However, it must be possible to understand them as if they were objective. It is for this reason that Kant recognises "the universal capacity for the communication of the state of mind in the given representation ... as the subjective condition of the judgment of taste", such that aesthetic "pleasure in the object" is the "consequence" and not the presupposition of the judging (KU, 5:217).

Note that the "universal capacity for ... communication" is the condition of a judgement of taste rather than its determining ground or content. The "universal capacity for ... communication" is supposed to make sure that a judgement of taste can be the object of intersubjective assent that allows for subjective universality. If a judgement of taste is conditional upon universal communicability, what then is its universally communicable content? According to Kant, it is "the state of mind that is encountered in the relation of the powers of representation to each other insofar as they relate a given representation to *cognition in general*" (KU, 5:217). The aesthetic state of mind determines the "powers of cognition" in such a way that they are "set into play" by the "representation" (KU, 5:217). The "play" amounts to an unrestricted "free play", since it is not directed by concepts or any "particular rule of cognition" (KU, 5:217). A state of mind of this specific kind is, Kant says, a "feeling".[21] The aesthetic feeling is not entirely unexplainable, though. The "powers of cognition" in "free play" are "*imagination*" and "*understanding*". While the imagination engages with the "composition of the manifold of intuition", the understanding is directed towards the "unity of the concept that unifies the representations" (KU, 5:217). But the involvement of the understanding does not make the state of mind as such conceptual. The relation between imagination and understanding is not conceptually determined and does not generate a logical cognition. However, imagination and understanding are cognitive faculties in general and as such they represent the reason why a judgement of taste as being determined through the feeling of pleasure can be called (subjectively) universal:

> When we call something beautiful, the pleasure that we feel is expected of everyone else in the judgment of taste as necessary, just as if it were to be regarded as a property of the object that is determined in it in accordance with concepts; but beauty is nothing by itself, without relation to the feeling of the subject. (KU, 5:218).

Since the relation between imagination and understanding is not conceptually determined it cannot be termed "intellectual" (KU, 5:218).

---

[21] "There can be no objective rule of taste that would determine what is beautiful through concepts. For every judgment from this source is aesthetic, i.e., its determining ground is the feeling of the subject and not a concept of an object" (KU, 5:231). I cannot discuss here the "free play" of "imagination" and "understanding" in detail. On this issue, see Guyer (2009), who provides a critical overview of recent publications on this point.

6 Kant's Aesthetic Nonconceptualism 137

Rather, the *intellectual* relation between these two cognitive faculties is established in the doctrine of transcendental judgement of the First *Critique*. Accordingly, intuitions are subsumed under concepts (categories) with the help of schemata. Although (transcendental) schemata are heterogeneous in that they comply with both conditions of sensibility and understanding, they cannot be conceived as feelings or sentiments because they are rule-governed. For instance, the (transcendental) schema of substance is "the persistence of the real in time" (A144/B183). This transcendental determination does not allow for a *free* relating of imagination and understanding but formulates the (conceptual) rule according to which the category of substance can only be (objectively) applied to something that is persisting in time. The aesthetic relation between imagination and understanding is different. Here imagination and understanding are related without concepts in such a way that the mind *feels* it as "sensation" (KU, 5:219). The relation itself is characterised as a harmonious interplay to the effect that it is sensed as "mutual agreement". Kant also describes this relation as a "well-proportioned disposition", a relation that is specific in aesthetic experience but required for human cognition in general (KU, 5:219).

The nonconceptuality of judgements of taste, more precisely, of aesthetic experience as expressed in those judgements, has a direct impact on the central theme of the Third *Critique*, namely, the idea of purposiveness. It is because of their nonconceptuality that judgements of taste are *subjectively* purposive, since in aesthetic experience imagination and understanding stand in a particular purposive relation. Purposiveness becomes the linchpin of the argumentation because of the function that pleasure has in Kant's aesthetics:

> The consciousness of the causality of a representation with respect to the state of the subject, *for maintaining* it in that state, can here designate in general what is called pleasure. (KU, 5:220)

Kant conceives of an end as the representation of the effect that figures as the determining ground of its cause. The standard model of the representation of such an end is practical final causality such that the will as the faculty of desire represents an end before it causes itself to act.

138 D.H. Heidemann

In this case the end is represented by means of concepts. On the other hand, it is also possible to conceive of a state of mind as purposive without presupposing an end by assuming that the possibility of that state can be explained as if it were the product of a will. Kant calls this kind of purposiveness "purposiveness concerning form" (KU, 5:220), which is purposiveness that does not presuppose the (conceptual) representation of an end. Kant writes:

> Thus nothing other than the subjective purposiveness in the representation of an object without any end (objective or subjective), consequently the mere form of purposiveness in the representation through which an object is *given* to us, insofar as we are conscious of it, can constitute the satisfaction that we judge, without a concept, to be universally communicable, and hence the determining ground of the judgment of taste. (KU, 5:221)[22]

That which is subjectively purposive and complies with formal purposiveness in the aesthetic state of mind is the relation between imagination and understanding in their interplay and mutual animation. Their interplay is occasioned through pleasure as the determining ground of their aesthetic interactivity. However, there is no representation of an end involved here as the motivating purpose of that activity. The relation is purposive when, in experiencing the beautiful, the merely formal relation of imagination and understanding is such that pleasure is felt. Aesthetic feeling, being the product of cognitive faculties and the determining ground of judgements of taste, is a phenomenal, intentional and representational state of mind, but it is not conceptual.[23]

---

[22] In the Fourth Moment Kant argues that the beautiful is *necessarily* connected with satisfaction. The kind of necessity he has in mind here is not "objective necessity" but "exemplary" necessity: "Since an aesthetic judgment is not an objective and cognitive judgment, this necessity cannot be derived from determinate concepts, and is therefore not apodictic", it is "subjective necessity". In that sense, "the judgment of taste ascribes assent to everyone, and whoever declares something to be beautiful wishes that everyone *should* approve of the object in question and similarly declare it to be beautiful". The presupposition of this ascription is for Kant the "common sense" (cf. KU, 5:237–8).

[23] "The judgment is also called aesthetic precisely because its determining ground is not a concept but the feeling (of inner sense) of that union in the play of the powers of the mind, insofar as they can only be sensed" (KU, 5:228; cf. KU, 5:229–31).

6   Kant's Aesthetic Nonconceptualism   139

From what has been argued so far, it follows that in terms of his theory of aesthetic evaluation Kant is a nonconceptualist because the determining ground of judgements of taste is nonconceptual. The question now is whether with respect to his theory of creation of artwork he is a non-conceptualist, too.

6.4   Nonconceptualism and Aesthetic Genius

In the contemporary debate about nonconceptual content the *knowing that/knowing how* distinction is among the most debated. Accordingly, human beings know *how* to do certain things, although they are not capable of knowing *that* they do them, that is, they cannot conceptually grasp in a sufficiently precise way *what* they are doing. In his aesthetics, Kant already anticipates an argument along these lines. Accordingly, we must distinguish between "*art* as a skill" and "*science*", that is, between "*to be able*" and "*to know*" (KU, 5:303). Now Kant insists that someone who knows something (practical) completely (*auf das vollständigste kennt*) does not immediately know how to do it, that is, is not skilled to do it. For example, from the fact that someone is able to "describe quite precisely how the best shoe must be made" it does not follow that she is also "able to make one" (KU, 5:303–4). Therefore, practical skills can outstrip our conceptual capacities to the effect that, although we do not conceptually know, or describe, what we do, we can nonconceptually know how to do it.

The difference between *conceptually knowing that* and *nonconceptually knowing how* plays an important role in Kant's aesthetics of the genius. While the analysis of the judgement of taste represents the evaluative side of his aesthetics, the doctrine of the genius signifies its productive side. Thus the aesthetics of the genius is not about the cognition of the beautiful as such but reflects the possibility of artwork. It does not deal with the ontology of artwork, though, because Kant's answer to the question "How is a piece of art possible?" draws on the cognitive capacities of the aesthetic genius who is skilled to make art according to aesthetic ideas.[24] As we shall see, aesthetic ideas are to be conceived not as *discursive* representations, that is, concepts, but as intellectual intuitions. Kant's

---

[24] This does not imply that, for Kant, every artist is a genius since there are artists who imitate or copy the work of the aesthetic genius.

claim is that, on the basis of finite "mental powers", that is, "imagination and understanding" (KU, 5:316), the aesthetic genius originates aesthetic ideas that function as nonconceptual aesthetic norms. Aesthetic ideas cannot count as cognitions because finite human cognisers are not capable of having intellectual intuitions. However, the artwork in its exemplary aesthetic singularity figures as the representative of a nonconceptual aesthetic idea the genius has. Here the difficulty arises that the cognitive constraint of the First *Critique*, which implies that human cognisers are incapable of having intellectual intuitions, seems to be incompatible with the claim that the aesthetic genius, likewise a finite cogniser, can have such nonconceptual aesthetic ideas.

Kant presents the aesthetic genius as someone who has *exemplary* authority in the making of art. The genius, he writes, "is the talent (natural gift) that gives the rule to art" (KU, 5:307). These rules are special in that they are nonconceptual. As we already know from the discussion above, aesthetic evaluation cannot "be derived from any sort of rule that has a *concept* for its determining ground"; but, on the other hand, "without a preceding rule a product can never be called art" (KU, 5:307). For without this it would be an accidental product. For Kant, it is the aesthetics of the genius that makes it possible to explain how beautiful art is in accordance with rules whilst not being determined through concepts. There are at least four character traits he attributes to the aesthetic genius: first and foremost, "*originality*" and uniqueness in the making of art, that is, independently of conceptual rules; second, exemplarity, since the aesthetic genius's products are aesthetic "models"; third, cognitive nontransparency of her own making of art and incapacity to communicate the corresponding aesthetic "precepts"; and fourth, the normative capacity concerning beautiful art alone (KU, 5:307–8).

The sum of these attributes demonstrates that there cannot be a "science of the beautiful" (KU, 5:304). For science essentially relies on conceptually determined, communicable methods and rules that allow for proof or disproof of claims and their repeatability, for example, by way of experiments. This is not the case with beautiful art as created by the genius, for the "rule" the genius applies "cannot be couched in a formula to serve as a precept". It would have to "be abstracted from the deed, i.e., from the product", which for Kant is "difficult to explain", although the "*imitation*"

6 Kant's Aesthetic Nonconceptualism 141

of the genius's artwork is possible to a certain extent (KU, 5:309). The particular cognitive capacity belonging to the genius is the reason why beautiful art relies essentially on a nonconceptual representation of aesthetic creation. In aesthetic terms, Kant calls this capacity "*spirit*" (*Geist*), which functions as "the animating principle in the mind". It "purposively sets the mental powers into motion, i.e., into a play that is self-maintaining and even strengthens the powers to that end" (KU, 5:313). More precisely, this "principle" is "the faculty for the presentation of aesthetic ideas". Kant defines an "*aesthetic idea*" as

> that representation of the imagination that occasions much thinking though without it being possible for any determinate thought, i.e., *concept*, to be adequate to it, which, consequently, no language fully attains or can make intelligible. One readily sees that it is the counterpart (pendant) of an *idea of reason*, which is, conversely, a concept to which no *intuition* (representation of the imagination) can be adequate. (KU, 5:314)

Thus an aesthetic idea is an intuition that cannot be brought under concepts. Since it is to be conceived as a representation of how a piece of art is to be realised, an aesthetic idea is a nonconceptual mental representation. In contemporary terms, an aesthetic idea represents mental content that is fundamentally different from conceptual content such that Kant's aesthetics of the genius amounts to a kind of content nonconceptualism. Further, an aesthetic idea is not a *sensible* intuition, for it figures as a *rule* according to which the genius makes artwork in exemplary, original aesthetic creation. This constitutes the major difficulty in Kant's nonconceptualist aesthetics of the genius, namely, how to conceive of an aesthetic idea as a rule that is neither sensible nor conceptual but represents a product of the imagination, that is, of a finite cognitive faculty. As Kant himself puts it, aesthetic ideas are at the boundary of the possibility of cognition "because they at least strive toward something lying beyond the bounds of experience, and thus seek to approximate a presentation of concepts of reason (of intellectual ideas), which gives them the appearance of an objective reality; on the other hand, and indeed principally, because no concept can be fully adequate to them, as inner intuitions" (KU, 5:314).

The conceptual inadequacy of aesthetic ideas is due to their material overdetermination, for as representations of the productive (aesthetic) imagination they exceed any conceptual grasping. Although as such they pertain to the aesthetic genius who originates them, the perceiver of a piece of art can be indirectly affected by them in that the perception of a piece of art animates the imagination "to think more, although in an undeveloped way, than can be comprehended in a concept, and hence in a determinate linguistic expression" (KU, 5:315). The kind of proportionate relation between imagination and understanding that characterises aesthetic experience is present in the aesthetic genius's cognitive processing too. For the genius not only represents the concept of a piece of art as an "end" but conceives also the "material" "for the presentation of this concept". This is only possible by relating imagination and understanding in a purposive manner such that the genius nonconceptually knows how to achieve the aesthetic "end". The knowledge *how* to do it is represented by means of "*aesthetic ideas*, which contain rich material for that aim, hence the imagination, in its freedom from all guidance by rules, is nevertheless represented as purposive for the presentation of the given concept". Analogously to what is the case in aesthetic evaluation, the genius's creation of art occasions the "unintentional subjective purposiveness in the free correspondence of the imagination to the lawfulness of the understanding" (KU, 5:317–18).

By the look of it, then, Kant's aesthetics of the genius clearly implies nonconceptualism, more precisely, aesthetic content nonconceptualism, because aesthetic ideas are intellectual intuitions that count as nonconceptual rules and give rise to aesthetic norms. They are mental content that is fundamentally different from conceptual mental content. Although one might concede that aesthetic ideas are phenomenal, since it is somehow for the genius to have them, and also that they are intentional, since they are purposefully directed towards the realisation of an end, they cannot be conceived as representational. For aesthetic ideas are not discursive but intuitive intellectual representations that holistically combine the activity of productive imagination and understanding. However, any non-discursive working together of cognitive faculties is impossible for the human mind, because intuitions can only be subsumed under discursive concepts and cannot merge with them as is the case with aesthetic ideas.[25] For this reason the human mind, including the genius herself, cannot even understand how an aesthetic idea is capable of representing something, since this is beyond the scope of possible human cognition. The conclusion to be drawn, then, is that the aesthetics of the genius provides evidence for Kant's nonconceptualism, because Kant regards aesthetic ideas at least as logically possible representations, although the human mind cannot have them. For exactly that reason, however, the aesthetics of the genius cannot account for Kant's nonconceptualism in any positive sense.

6.5 Conclusion

The aim of this chapter was to argue that in his aesthetics Kant develops arguments that clearly present him as a nonconceptualist. His aesthetics offers two candidates for nonconceptuality: the doctrine of the judgement of taste, and the theory of the aesthetic genius. Judgements of taste can only prove to be nonconceptual, I have argued, if they are cognitive (although not logical) judgements. Since their content is phenomenal, intentional and representational, they meet the preconditions for nonconceptuality. As it turned out, Kant identifies the aesthetic feeling, as a subjective state of mind, to be the determining nonconceptual ground of a judgement of taste. That is to say, the aesthetic feeling represents the kind of nonconceptual mental content on the basis of which a perceiver attributes the predicate "beautiful" to an object in a singular judgement in order to form a perceptual belief such as "This flower is beautiful". The theory of the judgement of taste therefore strongly supports the view that Kant is a nonconceptualist. This is not the case with his theory of the aesthetic genius. Although an aesthetic idea as originated by the genius in creating art is a nonconceptual intuitional representation that figures as a nonconceptual rule of art, it cannot account for Kantian

---

[25] Kantian nonconceptualism is therefore not independent of transcendental idealism since the latter theory determines what kind of nonconceptual mental content cognisers such as ourselves can at all represent. Concerning the intrinsic connection between nonconceptualism and transcendental idealism, compare Tomaszewska (2014:104–25).

144   **D.H. Heidemann**

nonconceptualism, because human cognisers are incapable of cognitively accessing intellectual intuitions.

The remaining positive outcome, then, is that in his theory of the judgement of taste Kant proves to be a nonconceptualist. The natural objection to this finding would be that although Kant endorses non-conceptualism in aesthetics, he might be a conceptualist in his theory of cognition and mind. I do not think that this objection holds because, as has been shown, judgements of taste are cognitive judgements of a special kind and therefore count as beliefs that are legitimately informative about the world, albeit only on the aesthetic level of subjective universality. The bigger problem is that it is not clear how the nonconceptual content in a judgement of taste can in fact justify a perceptual aesthetic belief. A promising solution to this problem could be that judgements of taste are perceptual (singular) judgements that directly connect a nonconceptual mental content to a propositional state of mind, that is, a belief. This seems to imply that intuition, or perception, respectively, refers directly to objects.[26] Such a solution of course has still to be spelled out in general terms, and not only with respect to judgements of taste in Kant's aesthetic nonconceptualism.

---

[26] Elsewhere I have shown that this is clearly Kant's view and why this view includes *direct* (empirical) realism (cf. Heidemann 1998:56–85). However, as Schulting (2015b:575–80) points out, nonconceptual intuition must not be conceived merely as a product of *synthesis speciosa*, since *all synthesis* is conceptually informed.

7

Moderate Conceptualism and Spatial Representation

Thomas Land

7.1 Introduction

In this chapter, I approach the debate between conceptualist and nonconceptualist readings of Kant's doctrine of intuition through the lens of his theory of spatial representation. This theory is of great significance for the debate, but so far has not received the attention it deserves.[1] One indication of the need for further discussion is the fact that the theory of spatial representation has been invoked on opposing sides of the debate as providing support for one side and presenting a serious problem for the other (for the nonconceptualist side see, for instance, Allais 2009 and McLear 2015; for the conceptualist side see, for instance, Ginsborg 2008 and Griffith 2012). My aim here is to show that the theory of spatial representation supports a certain kind of conceptualist reading, namely

---

[1] For two notable exceptions see Onof and Schulting (2015) and Tolley, Chap. 11 in this volume.

T. Land (✉)
Department of Philosophy, Ryerson University, Toronto, ON, Canada
e-mail: tland@philosophy.ryerson.ca

© The Editor(s) (if applicable) and The Author(s) 2016   **145**
D. Schulting (ed.), *Kantian Nonconceptualism*,
DOI 10.1057/978-1-137-53517-7_7

146   T. Land

a moderately conceptualist reading. I begin by giving an account of this reading (Sect. 7.2). I then discuss the aspect of Kant's theory of spatial representation that speaks in favour of this reading. This concerns the distinction Kant draws between what he calls the original representation of space, on the one hand, and the representations of determinate spaces, on the other, together with the claim that the latter depend on a particular kind of synthesis (Sect. 7.3). Next, I address three objections that have been raised by proponents of nonconceptualist readings to the conceptualist reading of this aspect of Kant's theory (Sects. 7.4 and 7.5). Finally, I consider a further objection that has been raised by nonconceptualists and that is based on a different aspect of Kant's theory, namely the holistic character of spatial representation, and explain why this objection is unsuccessful (Sect. 7.6).

7.2   Moderate Conceptualism

For the purposes of this chapter, a nonconceptualist reading of Kant is one according to which intuition does not depend for its objective purport on any exercise of spontaneity.[2] Intuitions are the representations of sensibility, and on a nonconceptualist reading sensibility is self-standing in the sense that it is a capacity whose actualisations are in principle independent of any acts of spontaneity.[3] Intuitions are characterised by Kant as singular representations of objects, which in contrast to concepts stand in immediate relation to objects (A50/B74; A320/B377), and the

---

[2] For instances of such a reading, see Allais (2009, 2015), Golob (2014), Hanna (2005, 2008, 2011b), McLear (2014b, 2015) and Tolley (2013). The position is usually defined in terms of a dependence on the possession of concepts. While this is not incorrect, I believe it is more fruitful to frame the issue in terms of the dependence (or otherwise) on exercises of spontaneity, as the focus on concepts can lead to a distorted picture of the doctrine of sensible synthesis, to be introduced below. See Land (2015b) for discussion. Note that my claims in this chapter are limited to the kinds of intuitions that mature human beings enjoy. Non-human animal intuitions, for instance, do not exhibit the kind of spontaneity-dependence I claim here for mature human intuitions. I discuss this issue in Land (forthcoming).

[3] A note on terminology: I take it that the notion of a capacity (power) and its exercise or actualisations is fundamental to Kant's discussion. Thus, sensibility and understanding are capacities, and the representations Kant attributes to them (intuitions, concepts, etc.) are their actualisations, exercise or acts. Talk of "act" in this connection carries no implication of being active as opposed to passive; a passive (receptive) power can be in act just as much as an active (spontaneous) power.

7 Moderate Conceptualism and Spatial Representation 147

nonconceptualist takes the upshot of this to be that there is a kind of cognitive relation to an object for which sensibility on its own can fully account. According to the nonconceptualist, then, intuitions stand in a cognitive relation to objects—they possess objective purport—yet do so in a way that does not depend, in principle, on any actualisations of spontaneity.[4]

By contrast, conceptualist readings of Kant hold that intuition does depend on actualisations of spontaneity for its objective purport.[5] On this kind of view, sensibility does not deliver representations that stand in cognitive relations to objects off its own bat—either because the representations it delivers off its own bat do not stand in a cognitive relation to objects or because it does not deliver the relevant representations off its own bat.

Some conceptualists hold that spontaneity can be exercised in two distinct ways. One of these is judgement, the other is the act of the productive imagination, sometimes referred to as sensible synthesis.[6] I shall offer an account of the difference between these two ways of exercising spontaneity shortly. But first I wish to use this distinction to characterise two different versions of conceptualism, which, following widespread usage, I call strong and moderate conceptualism, respectively.[7] Strong conceptualists hold that intuition depends for its objective purport on the exercise of spontaneity in a certain kind of judgement. Specifically, they hold that an intuition of an object o has objective purport only if it is "taken up" into a judgement concerning, specifically, object o. That is, on this view, an intuition has objective purport only to the extent that a singular judgement about the object of that very intuition occurs.

By contrast, moderate conceptualists hold that the objective purport of intuitions depends on the act of the productive imagination, hence

---

[4] On this definition of nonconceptualism, the view can allow for the possibility of actualisations of sensibility that, as a matter of fact, do involve acts of spontaneity. The point is that this is not necessary for intuition to represent objects in the relevant sense.

[5] See e.g. Ginsborg (2008), Griffith (2012), Grüne (2009), Land (2015a), Longuenesse (1998a), McDowell (1998, 2009), Pippin (1982) and Sellars (1967, 1978).

[6] It should be noted that this term is not Kant's. I use it as a generic label for any act of synthesis (among which Kant appears to distinguish different species) that is distinct from synthesis in judgement in the way I explicate below.

[7] Note that these labels are used in different ways. See Schulting (2015b) for an alternative usage.

on the exercise of spontaneity in sensible synthesis, which they take to be distinct in kind from the exercise of spontaneity in judgement. Depending on exactly what one takes sensible synthesis to be, there can be different versions of this view.[8] On the version to be defended here the act of the productive imagination itself depends (for its "unity", as Kant likes to say) on judgements of a certain kind. So it would be false to characterise moderate conceptualism generically as the view that intuition depends only on sensible synthesis, not on judgement (even though there are versions of moderate conceptualism that take this view; see Ginsborg 2008 and Grüne 2009). Generically, moderate conceptualism should be characterised as the view that, for any empirical intuition, no singular judgement concerning the object of that particular intuition need occur for that intuition to have objective purport. This serves to distinguish moderate conceptualist from strong conceptualist views. So all versions of moderate conceptualism share the commitment that the spontaneity-dependence of the objective purport of an intuition does not consist in the fact that a particular intuition must be "taken up" into a judgement concerning, specifically, the object of this very intuition.

For the moderate conceptualist (in my sense of that term), sensible synthesis constitutes a distinct kind of exercise of spontaneity from judgement because the act of sensible synthesis differs from the act of judgement in crucial respects. In my own view, the two most salient respects are the following: first, sensible synthesis is extended in time, while judgemental synthesis is not.[9] As Kant says repeatedly, sensible synthesis is "successive".[10] Judgement, on the other hand, is not extended in time; it is not successive.[11] Second, sensible synthesis pertains to a type

---

[8] Thus, the versions of Ginsborg (2008), Grüne (2009), Longuenesse (1998a) and Sellars (1967, 1978) all differ from my own.

[9] It might be thought that being extended in time makes sensible synthesis empirical, since time for Kant is a form of empirical intuition. But this is not Kant's view; see e.g. B155n.: "Motion, as *description* of a space, is a *pure* act of the *successive* synthesis of the manifold in outer intuition in general through productive imagination" (emphasis added).

[10] See A103; B154; B155n.; A145/B184; A163/B203–4; A167–8/B209–10; A170/B211–12.

[11] Judging is an act of the intellect, that is, an act of the subject's "self-activity" or "spontaneity" (B130). It is not a sensible representing. As a consequence, it is not subject to the form of inner sense, time. Nor, therefore, is it extended in time. This is not to deny that we can have sensible representations of our own mental states. For helpful discussion see Geach (1969).

7 Moderate Conceptualism and Spatial Representation 149

of representing that has one kind of structure; judgemental synthesis pertains to a type of representing that exhibits a different kind of structure. The structure of sensible representing is spatiotemporal; its matter is a spatiotemporal manifold. It is not predicative. The structure of judgement is predicative; its matter consists in concepts rather than a spatiotemporal manifold.[12]

Both sensible synthesis and judgemental synthesis, however, are acts of spontaneity. The hallmark of spontaneity for Kant is self-consciousness. So both sensible synthesis and judgemental synthesis are self-conscious. The sense in which they are self-conscious can, very roughly, be explained by means of the following analogy. It is plausible to think that one can have beliefs only if one has some kind of grasp of the nature of belief. For instance, if one understands that beliefs require justification, that being presented with countervailing evidence may require one to modify a belief, that beliefs stand in inferential relations, and so on. Precisely how detailed and explicit this understanding must be is difficult to say. Thus, it seems plausible to think that one need not be able to articulate this understanding in order to count as possessing it. It would be sufficient if one manifests it behaviourally (perhaps especially in linguistic behaviour). Again, precisely what counts as doing that may not be easy to determine. But the general idea seems plausible enough.

If the same is true of judgement, as Kant understands this term, then judgement is self-conscious in the sense intended here. To say that judgemental synthesis is self-conscious, then, is to say that a creature capable of such synthesis possesses an understanding of the nature of this act. Specifically, she possesses an understanding of the kind of unity that is characteristic of judgement, for Kant. She understands, for instance, that the concepts making up the matter of a given judgement are claimed by this judgement to belong together, not in virtue of an associative mechanism she happens to have, but rather in virtue of "being combined in the object" (B142). She also understands that any given judgement will form part of a worldview and thus stand in certain relations to other judgements, with which it must not, for example, be inconsistent. Again,

---

[12] This is compatible with holding that the content of some concepts is, or includes, a spatiotemporal manifold.

this understanding need not be very explicit. But it must be present in some form or other for an activity to count as judging.

According to moderate conceptualism in the version considered here, sensible synthesis also exhibits self-consciousness, and this amounts to roughly the following. A creature capable of sensible synthesis has an understanding of the kind of unity that is characteristic of this act, for Kant. She understands, for instance, that a prior phase of an act of sensible synthesising is a phase of the very same act as the current phase, and is therefore a distinct part of the same complex representational whole (see especially A103). This, in outline, is what it means to say that both judgement and sensible synthesis are acts of spontaneity.

Support for moderate conceptualism comes from four principal (and interconnected) sources. First, in a number of passages Kant appears to be saying that there is a kind of synthesis that is (i) an act of spontaneity which is (ii) distinct from judgemental synthesis and (iii) required for intuitions to have the kind of unity on account of which they are representations of objects.[13]

Second, proponents of moderate conceptualism contend that their view is required by Kant's argument in the Transcendental Deduction. More precisely, they contend that Kant is in a position to show that the categories are objectively valid only if he can show that the categories are necessary not just for objectively valid judgement, but also for the perceptual apprehension of objects in empirical intuition. Furthermore, in contrast to strong conceptualism, they hold that what Kant's argument requires (and what he actually seeks to show) is that the application of the categories in the perceptual apprehension of objects takes a form that is specifically distinct from their application in judgement, in that it concerns the act of intuiting itself.[14]

---

[13] See A99–102; B151–2; B153–4; B160n.; B162n.; A141–2/B180–1; B202–3; A163/B204; A170/B211–12; A723/B751.

[14] For detailed discussion see Land (2015a). Thanks to Dennis Schulting for requesting clarification of this point.

7 Moderate Conceptualism and Spatial Representation 151

Third, moderate conceptualism seems to be required by the doctrine of apperception. This doctrine appears to entail that an intuition is cognitively significant only if it has the kind of objective purport to which it is essential that it is understood as objective purport by the creature enjoying the intuition.[15]

Finally, moderate conceptualism seems to be implied by Kant's theory of spatial representation. This theory appears to say that it is possible to represent a determinate spatial extent only by means of sensible synthesis. But outer intuitions represent their objects as taking up determinate extents of space. Therefore, outer intuitions are possible only by means of sensible synthesis.[16]

Critics of moderate conceptualism deny that any of these four sources support the position. My concern in this chapter is with those critics who advocate nonconceptualism.[17] In what follows I wish to focus specifically on the fourth source of support for moderate conceptualism, that is, Kant's theory of spatial representation. Proponents of nonconceptualism tend to argue that this theory in fact provides evidence *against* moderate conceptualism and instead supports their own position. In what follows, I shall first spell out in more detail why proponents of moderate conceptualism take their position to be supported by Kant's theory of spatial representation. I then consider three objections to this claim that have been raised by proponents of nonconceptualism and argue that these misfire. Finally, I briefly consider the holistic character of intuitions and argue that, contrary to what proponents of nonconceptualism have claimed, this aspect of Kant's theory too supports moderate conceptualism.

---

[15] This point is central to the work of John McDowell (see e.g. McDowell 1998, 2009). See also Engstrom (2006).

[16] An analogous point applies to inner intuitions and time.

[17] So I shall not engage with strong conceptualism here. I do so in Land (2015b). Note, however, that the discussion below in Sect. 7.4 provides reasons for rejecting strong conceptualism.

7.3 Representing Determinate Spaces

In a number of important passages (some of which will be discussed below) Kant employs a distinction between (what he sometimes calls) the original representation of space, on the one hand, and the representation of a determinate space, on the other. The original representation of space is that which constitutes the form of sensibility, that is, that which constitutes the form of the capacity to have intuitive representations in virtue of being affected (see B40 in combination with A26/B42). By contrast, by the representation of a determinate space Kant seems to mean the representation of, for example, the volume of space occupied by a particular object or the representation, in pure intuition, of a particular geometrical figure. Since the Transcendental Aesthetic (TAe) is primarily concerned with the original representation of space, what this suggests is that we should not take the teaching of TAe as constituting Kant's full account of spatial representation.[18] Instead, we should think of this account as comprising both the doctrine concerning the original representation of space and the doctrine concerning the actualisation of sensibility in determinate acts of spatial representing.

One important passage in which this distinction is in play is found in the Axioms of Intuition. It contains the bulk of Kant's argument for the synthetic a priori judgement that all appearances are, as regards their intuition, extensive magnitudes. Here is the passage:

> All appearances contain, as regards their form, an intuition in space and time, which grounds all of them *a priori*. They cannot be apprehended, therefore, i.e., taken up into empirical consciousness, except through the synthesis of the manifold through which the representations of a determinate space or time are generated, i.e., through the composition of that which is homogeneous and the consciousness of the synthetic unity of this manifold (of the homogeneous). Now the consciousness of the homogeneous manifold in intuition in general, insofar as through it the representation of an object first becomes possible, is the concept of a magnitude (*Quanti*). Thus even the perception of an object, as appearance, is possible

---

[18] For discussion of this point, see Longuenesse (1998a:214–27) and Sutherland (2005a).

7 Moderate Conceptualism and Spatial Representation 153

only through the same synthetic unity of the manifold of the given sensible intuition through which the unity of the composition of the homogeneous manifold is thought in the concept of a *magnitude*. (B202–3)

In the first sentence of the passage, Kant reiterates the thesis of TAe that the representations of space and time function as forms of intuition, which is to say that anything apprehended in empirical intuition (that is, all appearances) is represented as being in space and time; more precisely, as located at, and taking up, a particular position in space and time. He then claims that it follows from this that appearances can only be apprehended by means of the same kind of synthesis through which a determinate space is represented. This synthesis is subsequently characterised as an act of composition of a homogeneous manifold. Moreover, this synthesis involves what Kant calls the consciousness of the synthetic unity of a manifold of homogeneous parts. But this consciousness just *is* the concept of a magnitude. It follows, Kant argues, that the perception of an object requires a synthesis in accordance with the concept of a magnitude. Accordingly, the representation of objects in space, though crucially dependent on sensibility, is equally dependent on spontaneous synthesis, which is just what the moderate conceptualist claims.

Another passage is the following well-known passage from the end of the B-Deduction:

If, e.g., I make the empirical intuition of a house into a perception through apprehension of its manifold, my ground is the *necessary unity* of space and of outer sensible intuition in general, and I as it were draw its shape in agreement with this synthetic unity of the manifold in space. This very same synthetic unity, however, if I abstract from the form of space, has its seat in the understanding, and is the category of the synthesis of the homogeneous in an intuition in general, i.e., the category of *quantity*, with which that synthesis of apprehension, i.e., the perception, must therefore be in thoroughgoing agreement. (B162)

The passage concerns the perception of objects in space and Kant's point is that perceiving an object in space requires application of the category of quantity because spatial representation in general requires the representation of the "synthetic unity of the manifold in space". More specifically, perception of an object requires representing the particular shape the object has. That is, in terms of the passage from the Axioms, it requires the representation of a determinate space. The determinate space in question, however, is represented by "as it were draw[ing] [the] shape". As other passages make clear, "drawing" is a term that Kant frequently uses to refer to sensible synthesis.[19]

Assuming that we can treat "perception" here as equivalent to "empirical intuition" in the sense of "intuiting" (as opposed to "intuited"), these two passages, and the doctrine expressed in them, offer prima facie support for a moderately conceptualist view.[20] Indeed, since proponents of a nonconceptualist reading of Kant tend to hold that outer empirical intuition constitutively involves what it seems natural to characterise as the representation of determinate spaces, these passages provide reasons for doubting that nonconceptualist readings can be sustained once Kant's full theory of spatial representation is taken into account. Thus, according to Allais, Kant "thinks that representing objects spatially involves representing them with some degree of determinateness (as located, as having size, shape, and spatial relations to each other)" (2009:399; see also Allais 2015:166n.40). According to McLear, empirical intuition involves "a presentation of something in a spatially and temporally contiguous manner—e.g. the perceptual presentation of shape and coextensive color" (2015:105).

Nonconceptualists, however, are aware that prima facie passages such as these pose a problem for their position and argue that in fact these passages do not support moderate conceptualism; that, on the contrary, they are fully compatible with nonconceptualism. To make the case for this, nonconceptualists offer the following three considerations. First, they argue that there is a terminological distinction between empirical intuition and perception and, further, that the passages exclusively concern perception and therefore have no bearing on the question whether *empirical intuition* depends on sensible synthesis. Perception, according to this

---

[19] See B154; A162–3/B203–4; A170/B211.

[20] For the claim that Kant uses terms like "intuition" in both of these senses, see Sellars (1976:405, 413–16) and Allison (2004:82).

7 Moderate Conceptualism and Spatial Representation   155

line of thought, is a form of cognition and like any form of cognition requires the cooperation of sensibility and understanding, hence synthesis. But again, since perception is distinct from empirical intuition nothing follows from this point regarding the synthesis-dependence of the latter.[21]

The second consideration is that when Kant talks about the representation of determinate spaces, and of the kind of synthesis required for this, he is talking about a certain kind of judgement. In particular, he is talking about judgements in which spatial properties are ascribed, as one might do as part of a geometrical inquiry or in measuring the size of some object. This consideration also relies in part on the claim that cognition, for Kant, requires the application of concepts in judgement. Here is how Allais puts the point:

> In the Axioms Kant talks about what it takes to *apprehend* appearances and about cognizing determinate spaces and times. He argues that appearances can be *cognized* only through successive synthesis in apprehension which corresponds to representing them as extensive magnitudes. ... What this synthesis is a condition of is cognizing and apprehending appearances, not being given them [in intuition]. (Allais 2015:172; second emphasis added)

The third consideration brought forth by nonconceptualists is that a view on which spontaneous synthesis is required for the representation of determinate spaces in empirical intuition is committed to sense atomism. Sense atomism is the view that what is given in intuition are mere sensations, which are atomistic in the sense that one could, in principle, have a sensation that does not stand in determinate relations to other possible (or actual) sensations and which, therefore, must first be synthesised to stand in such relations and thereby yield empirical intuitions of objects. But, the argument is, sense atomism is incompatible with Kant's conception of the part–whole structure of space, according to which space is such that any part of it presupposes the whole. Since space is the form of intuition, the argument continues, Kant does not hold sense atomism. He holds, rather,

---

[21] See McLear (2014b:771–2, 779–80) and Tolley (2013:123–25).

156   T. Land

that what is given in intuition itself exhibits a priority of whole over part. So empirical intuition does not depend on spontaneous synthesis.[22]

In response, I address the first two considerations jointly, in the following section (Sect. 7.4), before discussing the third consideration at greater length, in Sect. 7.5. The rationale for doing so is that the issue under discussion concerns Kant's claim that representing a particular material object requires representing it as occupying a determinate space and that this in turn requires a certain kind of synthesis. The terminological move nonconceptualists make here (i.e. the first consideration) is intended to support the claim that this synthesis concerns judgemental representing, as opposed to sensible representing (i.e. the second consideration).[23]

7.4   The Synthesis of the Productive Imagination

I now wish to argue that there is strong evidence that Kant does not conceive of the synthesis in question as a judgemental synthesis. As a consequence, he does not conceive of what he calls representing a determinate space as a matter of making a certain kind of judgement. On the contrary, he appears to think of representing a determinate space as something one does in having an outer intuition (of either the pure or empirical variety). This evidence comes from three sources, which are closely connected:

---

[22] See Allais (2015:171–2) and McLear (2015:88, 93–4).

[23] It should be noted that the textual evidence for the terminological claim is ambiguous. Besides passages that seem to suggest it (see, in addition to B162 and B202–3, Prol, 4:304), there are also passages suggesting the opposite (e.g. B422n.; Anth, 7:134n.). What seems clear is that Kant uses "perception" (*Wahrnehmung*) to refer to what, without begging the question, can be described as the combination of empirical intuition and consciousness (see e.g. ÜE, 8:217). It is less clear what this implies regarding the meaning of "empirical intuition". Addressing this issue fully would exceed the scope of this chapter. However, following Allison (2004:193) I wish to note that locutions like "making an empirical intuition into a perception" (cf. B162) can equally well be explained by noting that terms like "intuition" and *Anschauung* are ambiguous between the -*ing* and -*ed* senses and that Kant often appears to employ them in the latter sense (for a clear instance see B278). See also note 20 above. With regard to B202–3 it should also be noted that Kant appears to take the claim that *perception* is possible only through synthesis in accordance with the concept of a magnitude to entail the claim that all *intuitions* are magnitudes (which is, after all, what the principle of the Axioms of Intuition states).

7 Moderate Conceptualism and Spatial Representation 157

first, the context of the passage from the Axioms of Intuition quoted above; second, the doctrine of the productive imagination; and third, various passages in which Kant talks about representing a line. I shall discuss these in turn.

The context of the passage from the Axioms makes it clear that the synthesis Kant is talking about is the synthesis of the productive imagination.[24] But when Kant first introduces the doctrine of the productive imagination (and its synthesis), his explanation for this choice of label is that imagination is, generally, the power to have a *sensible intuitive* representation even in the absence of an object affecting one.[25] So the synthesis of the productive imagination is not (or not merely) an act of judging; it is, rather, an act that generates intuitive representations. Indeed, for this very reason Kant is at pains to distinguish the synthesis of the productive imagination from the bare synthesis of the understanding, unaided by imagination. The latter generates judgements (or, rather, consists in judging), the former generates intuitions.[26]

In a number of passages, Kant presents the act of representing a line as an example of the synthesis of the productive imagination. In each of these, this act is described as an act of "drawing".[27] Specifically, it is an act of "motion, as *description* of a space" (B155n.), which in the case of a line amounts to the motion of a point. The act is further characterised as successive. Both of these characterisations strongly suggest that this act is not an act of judging: first, it is difficult to see what it could be for a judgement to be an instance of the activity of drawing; second, judging is not extended in time, and so is not successive. Furthermore, in one of these passages Kant says explicitly that the synthesis of the productive imagination does not concern the ascription of properties to an object that is anyway given in intuition. On the contrary, it concerns the "generation of shapes" (A163/B204). Thus,

---

[24] See e.g. A163/B204: "On this successive synthesis of the productive imagination, in the generation of shapes, is grounded the mathematics of extension (geometry)"; see also A164–5/B205.

[25] Cf. B151; see also B154, where Kant says that the synthesis of the productive imagination is what is necessary for having a "*determinate* intuition" (emphasis in original).

[26] "As figurative, it [i.e. the synthesis of the productive imagination] is distinct from the intellectual synthesis without any imagination merely through the understanding" (B152).

[27] See note 19 for a list of these.

I cannot *represent* to myself any line, no matter how small it may be, without drawing it in thought, i.e., successively generating all its parts from one point, *and thereby first sketching* [*verzeichnen*][28] *this intuition.* (A162–3/B203; emphasis added)

This passage appears to say that the synthesis of the productive imagination concerns the generation of a sensible representation (by means of the successive generation of representations of its parts).[29] By implication, if by "cognition" is meant a kind of mental act that is distinct from the mere having of an intuition and consists in the application, in judgement, of concepts to what is given in intuition, the synthesis of the productive imagination does not concern cognition, *pace* Allais's claim in the passage quoted above. Accordingly, in the continuation of this passage Kant says that "all appearances are ... *intuited* as aggregates" (A163/B204; emphasis added), and the context makes it clear that to represent something as an aggregate is to represent it by means of a successive synthesis in accordance with the categories of quantity.

At this point, the nonconceptualist might concede that the passages I have cited do not concern judgement, but might insist that it does not follow from this that they concern empirical intuition. For it is plausible, the nonconceptualist might say, that they concern a very specific kind of act, namely, the construction of a mathematical concept in pure intuition. Constructing a concept in pure intuition, however, is something very different from being given an object in empirical intuition. This manoeuvre, however, would not succeed. For Kant is explicit—for instance, in the passage from the Axioms quoted above—that the *same* synthesis that is responsible for the representation of a determinate space in pure intuition is also responsible for the representation of a determinate space in empirical intuition. As far as representing a determinate space is concerned, therefore, pure intuition does not differ from empirical intuition.

---

[28] *Verzeichnen* might be better translated as "noting", "exhibiting" or "registering". See Grimm 1854/1961, vol. 25, cols 2494–503; see also Bxxii, where Guyer/Wood render *verzeichnen* as "catalog".

[29] The preceding sentence makes clear that Kant's topic is *representation*; specifically, the particular way in which extensive magnitudes are represented: "I call an extensive magnitude that in which the representation of the parts makes possible the representation of the whole (and therefore necessarily precedes the latter)" (A162/B203).

7 Moderate Conceptualism and Spatial Representation   159

There is, then, strong evidence that the nonconceptualist reading of the passages in which Kant appears to be saying that intuition is dependent on the synthesis of apprehension, such as those from B162 and B202–3 discussed above, fails. In particular, the claim that these passages do not concern intuition as such, but rather a distinct act of cognising what is anyway given in intuition, is incompatible with the doctrine of the productive imagination, which appears to be central to Kant's theory of spatial representation in general.

7.5 Sense Atomism and the A Priori Determination of Sensibility by the Understanding

What I have said so far does not yet address the third consideration that proponents of nonconceptualism have raised in response to the passages from B202–3 and B162, that is, the claim that the moderately conceptualist position is committed to sense atomism and that this is incompatible with Kant's conception of the distinctive part–whole structure of sensible intuitive representations. I shall now turn to this consideration and argue that it cuts no ice because it overlooks an important aspect of Kant's theory of intuition. This is the doctrine of the a priori determination of sensibility by the understanding. When this doctrine is taken into account, it becomes clear that the moderately conceptualist reading is not committed to ascribing sense atomism to Kant.

I wish to argue that any cognitively significant empirical affection of sensibility exhibits synthetic unity partly in virtue of the fact that the understanding determines sensibility a priori to be in accord with its unity.[30] More precisely, the claim is that any *material, empirical* determination of sensibility "from the outside" (by objects) presupposes a *formal, a priori* determination of sensibility "from the inside" (by spontaneity).[31] For this

---

[30] The qualification is needed to make room for the contribution of empirical synthesis, such as the synthesis of apprehension.

[31] See Engstrom (2006:18–9). Longuenesse (1998a:199–242) also holds that the affection of sensibility by the understanding is a necessary condition of an empirical intuition's having objective purport, but her articulation of this position differs from the one presented here.

160   T. Land

reason, it is not the case that a moderately conceptualist view of Kant's theory of intuition is committed to sense atomism. A sensation, for Kant, is an actualisation of sensibility brought about by an object's affecting the senses. It is necessarily empirical and we might call it a material actualisation of sensibility. It must be distinguished from what we might call a formal actualisation of sensibility. This is the affection of sensibility by the understanding, which pertains only to the form of sensibility, not to any sensible matter. If, however, any material actualisation of sensibility presupposes its formal actualisation and if, moreover, the formal actualisation imparts consciousness of spatiotemporal unity to sensibility (that is, if on account of the formal actualisation a sensible manifold is apprehended as a unity), then Kant is not a sense atomist. On the contrary, any sensation will have spatial or temporal properties and because of this will stand in determinate relations to other possible (or actual) sensations.[32]

Does Kant hold that material actualisations of sensibility presuppose its formal actualisation? To argue that he does, I shall first discuss a number of passages supporting the claim that there is a formal actualisation of sensibility and then present a number of passages that make it clear that this actualisation is presupposed by any actualisation of sensibility in empirical intuition.

The most prominent discussion of the a priori determination of sensibility by understanding occurs in §24 of the B-Deduction. Kant argues that because there is a pure manifold of sensibility, there is an

---

[32] It might be thought that this claim commits me to the view that, for Kant, there can be no sensations that are not intuitions; and, therefore, no sensible representations that are merely "modification[s] of [the subject's] state" (A320/B376) without at the same time being representations of objects. My response is that, when Kant distinguishes sensations from intuitions and speaks of the former as the matter of intuition, he is not *thereby* committing himself to the view that there could be mere sensation without any spatiotemporal properties; mere matter without form, that is. His view might well be the following. Any sensible representation exhibits the formal properties of sensible representations, namely, spatiotemporal properties. But among sensible representations we can distinguish two species: mere sensations, on the one hand, and intuitions, on the other. The former are merely subjectively valid, the latter, objectively. The latter have sensations as their matter. So talk of sensation *simpliciter* is indeterminate with regard to the representational species to which it refers: a sensation is either a mere sensation or it is an intuition. For helpful discussion see McDowell (2009:108–26). Note also that the view articulated in the text is compatible with the claim at B208 that sensation *an sich* is neither spatially nor temporally extended. For the context of the passage makes clear that sensation in *this* sense is a mere abstraction. So the claim does not imply that qua matter of empirical intuition sensations are not in time or space.

7 Moderate Conceptualism and Spatial Representation 161

exercise of spontaneity in synthesis that is not dependent (at least not immediately) on anything's being given in empirical intuition:

> Since in us a certain form of sensible intuition *a priori* is fundamental, which rests on the receptivity of the capacity for representation (sensibility), the understanding, as spontaneity, can determine inner sense by means of the manifold of given representations in accord with the synthetic unity of apperception, and thus think *a priori* synthetic unity of the apperception of the manifold *of sensible intuition*. (B150; trans. corrected)

Kant goes on to clarify that this exercise is not merely an act of judging. It is, rather, an act of the productive imagination, and this entails that it is an act that generates a sensible representation. Since sensibility is a receptive capacity, sensible representations depend for their actuality on sensibility's being affected. Sensibility can be affected by objects in space, in which case its affection produces sensations (though not necessarily *mere* sensations). But it can also be affected "from the inside", that is, by the spontaneous stem of the cognitive capacity. Such affection need not produce sensation and so need not be empirical. As Kant argues in §24, it can be an affection of sensibility merely with regard to its form and be a priori. Still, like any affection of sensibility, the a priori affection of sensibility is an actualisation of sensibility, that is, the bringing about of a sensible representation (albeit a special kind of sensible representation, namely, a formal intuition). Accordingly, Kant speaks of spontaneity's "determining" sensibility, where, in the sense intended here, to determine something is in general to bring about the actualisation of a potentiality and, more specifically, for x to determine y is for y to be actualised in virtue of being affected by x. See, for instance, the following two passages:[33]

---

[33] In this sense of "determine", a receptive capacity is one that is determined from without, while a spontaneous capacity is one that is self-determining. Compare Kant's claim, at B151–2, that spontaneity is "determining", whereas sense is "merely determinable"; see also A373, where Kant speaks of an object's determining sense by way of sensation, and B277n. Note that it is clear that the sense of "determine" here cannot be the "epistemic" sense, according to which an object is determined with respect to some predicate just in case a thinker represents the object as having that predicate (see Stang 2012:1128). For there would be no point in characterising the *senses*—as opposed to, say, objects sensed—as determinable if this was meant in the epistemic sense.

[The exercise of the understanding in figurative synthesis, i.e. in the guise of the productive imagination, is one] through which it [i.e. the understanding] is capable of itself determining sensibility internally with regard to the manifold that may be given to it [i.e. the understanding] in accordance with the form of its [i.e. sensibility's] intuition. (B153)

The understanding therefore does not *find* some sort of combination of the manifold already in inner sense, but *produces* it, by *affecting* inner sense. (B155)

The a priori determination of sensibility by the understanding yields unity in the manifold that belongs to sensibility originally, that is, in virtue of its pure form. With regard to inner sense and its form, time, the determination of sensibility by the understanding thus yields the representation Kant sometimes refers to as the "formal intuition" of time.[34]

These passages, then, provide evidence that Kant recognises an exercise of spontaneity in a synthesis that is a priori, that pertains to the forms of sensibility, space and time, and that brings about—indeed, partly *constitutes*—a representation that is an intuition. Now, to show that, contrary to the objection raised by Allais, the moderate conceptualist is not committed to seeing Kant as a sense atomist, I also need to argue that the a priori determination of sensibility by understanding is a condition of empirical actualisations of sensibility, that is, of empirical intuition. If this is the case, then the claim that empirical intuition depends on synthesis is fully compatible with the idea that sensations for Kant are not atomistic in the sense defined above. On the contrary, sensations will be just as holistic as the spatiotemporal form of the capacity whose actualisations they are.

In support of this contention I wish to cite three passages. The first is from §26 of the B-Deduction. At B160–1 Kant argues that the apprehension of the manifold in an empirical intuition must be in accordance

---

[34] See B160 and A268/B324. So what Onof and Schulting (2015:6) refer to as "the standard interpretation" of the notion of formal intuition, according to which a formal intuition is distinguished from the mere form of intuition by being "determined" in a judgement (that is, brought under some concept in a judgement), is false. It rests on ignoring the doctrine of the a priori determination of sensibility by the understanding.

7 Moderate Conceptualism and Spatial Representation 163

with the forms of intuition, space and time. These forms, however, are themselves intuitions and this entails that they are represented as exhibiting synthetic unity. In a notorious footnote he adds the following clarification: to say that space and time are themselves intuitions is to say that they exhibit a kind of unity that presupposes a synthesis, the synthesis, namely, by means of which "the understanding determines the sensibility" (B161n.). Clearly, the implication is that the synthesis by means of which the understanding determines sensibility is a condition of the synthesis of apprehension in empirical intuition. Consequently, the determination of sensibility by the understanding is a condition of empirical intuition.[35]

The second passage comes from the Axioms of Intuition. Here Kant writes that "empirical intuition is possible only through the pure intuition (of space and time)" (A165/B206). And he goes on:

> The synthesis of spaces and times, as the essential form of all intuition, is that which at the same time makes possible the apprehension of the appearance. (A165–6/B206)

As the passage specifies, the "synthesis of spaces and times" concerns the formal aspect of intuition. It is precisely the synthesis that accounts for the difference between the *mere* form of intuition, which exhibits mere manifoldness, and a *determinate* spatial or temporal intuition, which exhibits unity of the manifold. So it is the synthesis by means of which the understanding a priori determines sensibility.[36] Kant's point, then, is that this synthesis is a condition of the possibility of empirical intuition.

---

[35] The nonconceptualist will of course insist that this last inference is not warranted because the synthesis of apprehension concerns, not empirical intuition, but rather perception, which is a distinct act of the mind from empirical intuition. But at this juncture in the dialectic the issue is whether or not the moderate conceptualist position is committed to seeing Kant as a sense atomist. To rebut this charge it is not necessary to provide independent grounds for the falsity of nonconceptualism. We are entitled to assume the moderately conceptualist reading.

[36] See B154: "Inner sense, on the contrary, contains the mere *form* of intuition, but without combination of the manifold in it, and thus it does not yet contain any *determinate* intuition at all, which is possible only through the consciousness of the determination of the manifold through the transcendental action of the imagination (synthetic influence of the understanding on the inner sense), which I have named the figurative synthesis".

164   **T. Land**

The third passage is found in the A-Deduction and will require a slightly longer discussion.[37] At A99 Kant writes:

> Every intuition contains a manifold in itself, which however would not be represented as such if the mind did not distinguish the time in the succession of impressions on one another [...].

This passage appears to be saying the following. (i) Every intuition is internally complex, in the sense that it "contains a manifold *in* itself" (emphasis added). (ii) This manifold is represented as a manifold. (iii) There is a condition that must be satisfied for (ii) to be the case, namely the condition that "the mind ... distinguish the time in the succession of impressions on one another". (iv) This condition is satisfied. Of course, (ii) and (iv) are not stated in so many words in the passage; but the combination of subjunctive mood in the subordinate clause and indicative mood in the main clause clearly implicates (ii) and (iv). The passage continues as follows:

> [...] for *as contained in one instant* no representation can ever be anything other than absolute unity. (A99; trans. amended)[38]

Here, we are given a reason for one or more of the claims contained in the first half of the passage. What this reason is becomes clear if we consider that by "instant" Kant means a boundary or "place of limitation".[39] This means that an instant is not temporally extended, just like a point

---

[37] For a different reading of this passage than the one that follows, see Tolley (2013:122–3).

[38] Guyer/Wood have "moment" where I have "instant". The German is *Augenblick*. This is significant because *Augenblick* is also the word used in the passage from A169/B211 quoted in the footnote below, which offers an explanation of Kant's usage of the term. In that passage Guyer/Wood have "instant", so for the sake of consistency I have opted for "instant" in both passages.

[39] This is made explicit in the following passage: "The property of magnitudes on account of which no part of them is the smallest (no part is simple) is called their continuity. Space and time are *quanta continua*, because no part of them can be given except as enclosed between boundaries (*points* and *instants*), thus only in such a way that this part itself is in turn a space or a time. Space therefore consists only of spaces, time of times. *Points* and *instants* are only boundaries, i.e., mere places of their limitation; but places always presuppose those intuitions that they are supposed to limit or determine" (A169/B211; trans. amended, emphasis added). Guyer/Wood translate "that limit or determine them" where I have "that they are supposed to limit or determine". The original is "*die sie beschränken oder bestimmen sollen*". Both translations are grammatically possible, but it

7 Moderate Conceptualism and Spatial Representation 165

has no spatial extension. In light of this, what does it mean to say that, as contained in a single instant, a representation cannot be anything but absolute unity? And what reason does this provide for one or more of (i) through (iv)? Presumably, a representation that has absolute unity is one that lacks internal complexity. A representation that has parts and so is internally complex would then have relative unity: it is a "one" in one respect, but a "many" in another respect. By contrast, a representation that has absolute unity is not a "many" in any respect. It has no parts (of the relevant sort). If this is right, then it is clear why the mind's "distinguish[ing] the time in the succession of impressions" is a condition on a representation's being internally complex (i.e. containing a manifold in itself), especially once we take into account that the manifoldness at issue is a manifoldness of temporal parts or stages.[40] Obviously, a representation that has no temporal extension cannot contain this kind of manifold.

Kant goes on to argue as follows. The mind must distinguish the time in the succession of impressions. And to represent a succession of impressions as a relative unity—in particular, as constituting a representation that has the "*unity* of intuition" (A99)—an act Kant calls the synthesis of apprehension is required. In the terminology of the A-Deduction, this act comes in an empirical and an a priori version. Without the a priori version, "we could have *a priori* neither the representations of space nor of time" (A99). And he explains that the reason for this is that "these can be generated only through the synthesis of the manifold that sensibility provides in its original receptivity" (A99–100; trans. amended).

The claim here is twofold. First, there is the claim that our a priori representations of space and time exhibit a complex (or relative) unity: in the case of time, this is the unity that is manifest, for instance, in the idea that different temporal intervals succeed one another as parts of a single time. Second, Kant claims that this unity depends on the

---

should be clear that e.g. a point is a limitation of the intuition of space rather than the intuition of space being a limitation of a point.

[40] Note that the passage is preceded by a "general remark" on which, Kant says, "one must ground everything that follows" and which says that, qua modifications of the mind, all representations belong to inner sense and are therefore subject to the "formal condition" of inner sense, which is time (A98–9).

a priori version of the synthesis of apprehension. But, since the mind must "distinguish the time in the succession of impressions" if it is to represent as such the manifold that every intuition—including, in particular, empirical intuition—contains in itself, it follows that this kind of time-consciousness is dependent on the a priori version of the synthesis of apprehension. This, however, is just the synthesis by means of which the understanding determines sensibility a priori (as Kant puts it in the B-edition). Accordingly, this synthesis is a condition of the possibility of having an empirical intuition.[41]

These three passages, then, provide textual evidence for the contention that the actualisation of sensibility in empirical intuition depends on its actualisation in pure intuition, which Kant characterises as an act of synthesis by means of which the understanding determines sensibility with regard to its form. It is a consequence of this dependence that nothing that is given in empirical actualisations of sensibility is atomistic. Rather, as a result of this dependence every such actualisation exhibits the holistic structure possessed by the representations of space and time. So Kant is not a sense atomist, and the moderately conceptualist reading is not committed to ascribing this view to him.[42]

---

[41] Note that Kant's talk of sensibility's "original receptivity" in the passage from A99–100 quoted in the preceding paragraph might be taken as additional evidence, since it might be taken to suggest a distinction between original and derivative receptivity. Sensibility's original receptivity would be the receptiveness to its a priori determination by the understanding. Sensibility's derivative receptivity would be its receptiveness to affection by objects in empirical intuition, which presupposes the a priori determination. In terms of this distinction, the charge of sense atomism rests on confounding original and derivative receptivity.

[42] It might be thought that on the moderately conceptualist view there is no longer any robust sense in which intuition is given, since according to this view intuition depends on synthesis. But this is unwarranted. The moderate conceptualist allows for givenness in intuition at two levels, each of which is sufficiently robust. With regard to pure intuition, the character of the sensible manifold—for instance, the fact that it has three-plus-one dimensions—is independent of synthesis. The same goes for the fact that there is an "original" manifold to be synthesised, which for the moderate conceptualist amounts to saying that the character of the pure intuitions of space and time cannot be derived from the pure concepts of the understanding and is therefore not brought about by synthesis. With regard to empirical intuition, synthesis does not determine *what* is apprehended as unified; that is, what kind of object and which sensible qualities. Synthesis merely determines that these are apprehended as objects and as sensible qualities. That is, synthesis is responsible for the fact that an intuition is a representation of an object (in the sense in which the moderate conceptualist takes this phrase).

7.6 The Holistic Character of Intuition

I have been considering the claim that the moderately conceptualist interpretation of Kant's theory of intuition is supported by a number of passages in which Kant discusses the representation of determinate spaces, and I have argued that three objections to this claim that have been raised by nonconceptualists fail. However, in addition to objecting to the moderately conceptualist reading of these passages, nonconceptualists also contend that other aspects of Kant's theory of spatial representation support their own position over any conceptualist alternative. In particular, they contend that the holistic character of spatial representation counts in their favour and cannot be accommodated by conceptualist positions generally. In this section I wish to argue that this contention is false.

To say that spatial representation is holistic is to say that space is represented in such a way that there are no smallest parts of space. Any part of space is represented, in Kant's words, as a "limitation" of the whole of space. According to proponents of nonconceptualism, this doctrine is easily accommodated by a nonconceptualist reading, but presents a serious problem for conceptualist readings. On their view, any conceptualist reading is committed to construing spatial representation as a function of the understanding. But since, according to nonconceptualists, any act of the understanding exhibits a priority of part over whole, such an act cannot account for a kind of representation that is essentially holistic (see McLear 2015).

This line of thought, however, both underestimates the resources available to moderately conceptualist readings and overlooks an important aspect of Kant's position. With regard to the first point, the nonconceptualist claim relies on the implicit assumption that a representation is either an actualisation of sensibility or an actualisation of the understanding, but not both. Given this assumption, it is indeed hard to see how moderate conceptualists could accommodate the doctrine that spatial representation is holistic and maintain that it depends on exercises of spontaneity (at least when these are conceived along the lines of the nonconceptualist view). However, as I have argued elsewhere (Land 2014a), this assumption is not warranted. To see this, recall the discussion of the doctrine

168   T. Land

of the productive imagination (and the related doctrine of the a priori determination of sensibility by the understanding) above. This doctrine commits Kant to recognising a kind of exercise of spontaneity that is such as to generate *sensible* representations. Being sensible, the representations generated by this exercise of spontaneity exhibit the holistic character essential to such representations. They do so because they involve not *only* spontaneity, but sensibility as well, for they consist in actualisations of sensibility brought about by acts of spontaneity. That is, they involve the actualisation of a capacity whose very form entails that all of its actualisations exhibit the structure of a homogeneous manifold of holistic parts (and whose form, for this reason, also entails that any actualisation of sensibility in successive synthesis could in principle go on indefinitely).[43] There is, to be sure, a clear sense in which acts of the productive imagination proceed from part to whole, and so exhibit what the nonconceptualist line of thought just canvassed takes to be the defining characteristic of finite spontaneous representation in general.[44] But as I am about to show, Kant is explicit that this is perfectly compatible with the holistic character of spatial representation.

This brings me to the second point, namely, the aspect of Kant's position that is overlooked by this line of thought. Consider that Kant explicitly affirms that space and time are represented both as extensive magnitudes and as continuous magnitudes.[45] An extensive magnitude is such that the representation of the part precedes the representation of the whole. A continuous magnitude is such that no part is the smallest (hence such that the part presupposes the whole). Why does Kant not think that this presents a problem? Because he holds that representing a determinate space or time involves a kind of synthesis which ensures that, even though there are no smallest spatial (temporal) parts, the synthesis nonetheless runs through "all [the] parts" (A162/B203) of the space (or time) being represented:

---

[43] Thanks to Steve Engstrom for bringing the point in parentheses to my attention.

[44] There are, however, good reasons for thinking that as a general characterisation of finite spontaneous representation this cannot be correct. See Land (2014a).

[45] A162–3/B202–4; A169–70/B211–12. For discussion see Sutherland (2005a).

7 Moderate Conceptualism and Spatial Representation 169

> [Continuous] magnitudes … can also be called *flowing*, since the synthesis (of the productive imagination) in their generation is a progress in time, the continuity of which is customarily designated by the expression "flowing" [*fließen*] ("elapsing" [*verfließen*]). (A170/B211–12)

The point here is best brought out by means of Kant's example of representing a line. In representing a line, the synthesis of the productive imagination is an act of describing a space by means of the motion of a point.[46] Motion is itself continuous and thus guarantees that every one of the indefinitely many parts of the line is being represented. Motion is also successive and its successiveness guarantees that the representation of the whole line is possible only through the representation of all of its parts—which is just what makes the line an *extensive* magnitude.[47]

Since moderate conceptualism maintains that intuition depends on acts of a specifically sensible synthesis—in particular, on the act of the productive imagination—it is in a position to accommodate the holistic character of space and time. It is not true, therefore, that the holistic character of spatial representation speaks in favour of a nonconceptualist reading.

7.7 Conclusion

I have argued that, contrary to what is often supposed, Kant's theory of spatial representation does not lend support to a nonconceptualist reading of his theory of intuition, and that, on the contrary, it is best accommodated by a moderately conceptualist reading. Central to my argument is the contention that, for Kant, outer empirical intuition constitutively involves the representation of determinate spaces. The representation of determinate spaces, however, is dependent on the synthesis of the produc-

---

[46] Cf. the doctrine of "motion, as action of the subject" (B154–5). For discussion see Friedman (1992:74–8). We can see here one respect in which the two forms of intuition, space and time, are interdependent: spatial representing, for Kant, is necessarily extended in time.

[47] "I call an extensive magnitude that in which the representation of the parts makes possible the representation of the whole (and therefore necessarily precedes the latter). I cannot represent to myself any line, no matter how small it may be, without drawing it in thought, i.e., successively generating all its parts from one point, and thereby first sketching this intuition" (A162–3/B203).

tive imagination, that is, a synthesis that constitutes an exercise of spontaneity. This exercise of spontaneity is specifically distinct from judgement because its products exhibit the characteristics of sensible representations.

In making the case for this contention I have considered a number of objections and argued that none of these succeed. In responding to these objections, I have appealed both to the doctrine of the productive imagination and, closely related, to the doctrine of the a priori determination of sensibility by the understanding. Although the case I have made may well be found to be less than conclusive, I hope at least to have shown that these two doctrines need to be given more sustained consideration in debates over Kant's theory of intuition.

8

Getting Acquainted with Kant

Colin McLear

8.1 Introduction

Philosophers, and not just philosophers of mind, commonly speak of the "content" of a mental state. If one is comfortable talking in this manner, then a natural question to ask is what *kind* of content a mental state might have, and whether, in particular, mental states like belief have the same or a similar kind of content as an experience. My question here concerns whether Kant claims that experience has nonconceptual content, or whether, on his view, experience is essentially conceptual.[1]

---

[1] Note that my usage of the term "experience" here and throughout is *not* meant to correspond to Kant's technical term *Erfahrung* but rather to his notion of an intuition. For discussion of how Kant's technical terms line up with our contemporary notion of an experience, see McLear (2014b:771–2).

C. McLear (✉)
Department of Philosophy, University of Nebraska-Lincoln, Lincoln, Nebraska, USA
e-mail: mclear@unl.edu

© The Editor(s) (if applicable) and The Author(s) 2016
D. Schulting (ed.), *Kantian Nonconceptualism*,
DOI 10.1057/978-1-137-53517-7_8

For Kant scholars, figuring out how Kant might have answered this question has been one of central importance. Part of the reason for this stems from the relevance of Kant's account of intuition to three central and enduring issues of philosophical interest, namely, our acquisition of empirical concepts, the fixation of basic perceptual belief and the epistemic warrant we attain for such beliefs.[2] However, as I shall discuss below, there is a sense in which this debate concerning the content of intuition is ill-conceived. Part of this has to do with the terms in which the debate is set, and part to do with confusion over the connection between Kant's own views and contemporary concerns in epistemology and the philosophy of mind.

However, I think much of the substance of the debate concerning Kant's views on the content of experience can be salvaged by reframing it in terms of a debate about the dependence relations, if any, that exist between different cognitive capacities. Below, in Sect. 8.2, I clarify the notion of "content" I take to be at stake in the interpretative debate.[3] Sect. 8.3 presents reasons for thinking that intuition cannot have content in the relevant sense. I then argue, in Sect. 8.4, that the debate be reframed in terms of dependence. We should distinguish between Intellectualism, according to which all objective representation (understood in a particular way) depends on acts of synthesis by the intellect, and Sensibilism, according to which at least some forms of objective representation are independent of any such acts (or the capacity for such acts). Finally, in Sect. 8.5, I further elucidate the cognitive role of intuition. I articulate a challenge which Kant understands alethic modal considerations to present for achieving cognition, and argue that a version of Sensibilism that construes intuition as a form of acquaintance is better positioned to answer this challenge than Intellectualism.

---

[2] Examples of work which most clearly attempt to address these issues in both contemporary philosophy and the study of Kant include Lewis (1929), McDowell (1996), Sellars (1968) and Strawson (1966).

[3] In this chapter, I do not pretend to give a comprehensive survey of positions or arguments. I aim instead at discussion of some central issues. For a more thorough attempt to chronicle the extent of the debate, see McLear (2014b); cf. Grüne (2009).

8.2 What Is Content?

Contemporary philosophy typically construes the phrase "mental content" as referring to that thing which fulfils a certain functional role—namely, it is that (i) which may be the object of different cognitive states within the same subject (e.g. of belief and desire), (ii) which may be the object of the same (or a different) cognitive state in other subjects (e.g. that you and I might be able to believe the same thing and thus communicate), and (iii) which has veridicality conditions (e.g. that which you and I both believe is true).[4]

So typically, when we ask about the content of a mental state, we are asking about something which is supposed to fulfil these three roles. The traditional satisfier for this functional specification is an abstract entity— a proposition.[5] For example, I might both hope *that there is snow on Mt Washington* and desire *that there is snow on Mt Washington*. You and I may both believe *that there is snow on Mt Washington*. And the contents of our beliefs may well be true.

This notion of content also requires a conception of the thing which *has* content, namely, the "vehicle".[6] One example of a vehicle is a sentence. The English sentence "snow is white" expresses the proposition *that snow is white*. There is a set of corresponding English phonemes that

---

[4] As it turns out, these conditions are partly constitutive of our notion of conceptual content. Whether there are other kinds of mental content has been an issue of some controversy. For relevant discussion, see Beck (2012), Heck (2009) and Peacocke (1992). As I argue below, while it is plausible to think that Kant admits a notion of "content" in this sense, it is doubtful that he allows for any other kind of content. This does not, however, mean that conceptualism is correct.

[5] For some historical context for this view, see King et al. (2014), Chaps. 1–3. Once propositions are admitted, much of the debate about nonconceptual content can be transposed into a debate about the constitution and structure of propositions. For representative discussion, see Heck (2009) and Stalnaker (1998). I examine Kant's conception of propositional content below.

[6] The fact that there is a difference between vehicle and content does not mean, however, that the two are unconnected. For example, a mental state might inherit its content from features of the vehicle. If one admits the existence of sense-data, then one might take their representational properties (or some subset thereof) as inherited from features of the sense-data—e.g. a red sense-datum represents the property *red* in virtue of the sense-datum's instantiating that very property. In the end though, what I am concerned with here is specifically the content and not the vehicle. When Kant is careful he makes similar distinctions. See e.g. his discussion of sensation (*Empfindung*) and feeling (*Gefühl*) in the Third *Critique* (KU, 5:189, 203–6). It is therefore no resolution of our question to say that Kant admits the existence of nonconceptual *vehicles* (such as feelings).

when uttered together also express the relevant proposition. Finally, we might also postulate a *mental* vehicle (i.e. the psychological state or event) for content, such as the thought (an occurrent psychological state) *that snow is white*.[7]

So in asking whether Kant accepted the (possible) existence of nonconceptually contentful mental states, we first need to know whether it is even coherent to ascribe to him a notion of "content", conceptual or not (and irrespective of whether he would use the corresponding German word *Inhalt* for this notion), in the terms set out above.

It seems highly plausible that Kant did accept the existence of content as specified. This is his notion of a "judgement" (*Urteil*). The vehicles for judgement are mental states, "representations" (*Vorstellungen*). Judgements are the product of "relating" representations, in the *act* of judging, in one consciousness:

> The unification of representations in a consciousness is judgment. ... Thinking is the same as judging or as relating representations to judgments in general. (Prol, §22, 4:304; cf. Log, §17, 9:101; V-Lo/Wiener, 24:928)

What kinds of representation are related in one consciousness? Kant specifically has concepts in mind (cf. KU, 5:287; B146, B283; Log, 9:101; V-Lo/Wiener, 24:928). Judgements consist of concepts that, due to an act of the mind in which they are unified in one consciousness, are brought together to form truth-bearing contents via the process of *synthesis* (I leave open how exactly Kant thinks this is accomplished, but it must involve appeal to his notion of a "transcendental unity of apperception"). But what is grasped in the judgemental act—the judgement proper—is not itself something merely psychological (B142; Prol, 4:298–9; cf. Anderson 2001). This is why Kant can say of logic—the study of concepts, judgements and inference—that it "has no empirical principles, thus it draws nothing from psychology ..., which therefore has no influence at all on the canon of the understanding" (A54/B78).

---

[7] I leave open here what this mental vehicle is. It could be a neural state type, or something at a higher and more abstract level of specification.

In addition to serving as the content of psychological vehicles and the bearers of truth, Kant also considers judgements to be the objects of different epistemic attitudes. For example, he distinguishes between varieties of "holding for true" or "assent" (*Fürwahrhalten*) in the Canon of Pure Reason at the end of the First *Critique*:

> Assent [*Das Fürwahrhalten*] is an occurrence in our understanding that may rest upon objective grounds, but that also requires subjective causes [*Ursachen*] in the mind of *him who judges*. (A820/B848; trans. amended and emphasis added)

Kant then identifies three different kinds of assent with respect to judgement, namely, opining, believing and knowing, as well as a kind of defective form of assent that he terms "persuasion" (for discussion see Chignell 2007). Depending on one's evidence or "ground" (*Grund*) for assent (A822/B850), one might at one time opine what at a later time one knows. Hence, Kant seems to acknowledge the existence of content in the relevant sense. There is something—judgement—that is carried or expressed by psychological states, which can be the object of different epistemic attitudes, and which is the bearer of truth and falsity. Furthermore, since judgements are constituted by concepts, Kant obviously accepts that at least some mental states—acts of judging—have conceptual content.

However, one might object that Kant does not conceive of the content of an intuition or a judgement in the way that I have suggested. For example, Clinton Tolley (2013, 2014) has argued that Kant's use of "content" (*Inhalt*) concerns not our contemporary notion of a proposition, specified above, but rather something else. For example, there are a number of texts where Kant connects both the content of cognition (B79; B83; B87) and that of intuition (B67; cf. Tolley 2014:207) with a "relation to an object". Kant also partly *defines* intuitions and concepts in terms of how they relate, immediately or mediately, to objects (B93). I want to raise two points concerning Tolley's discussion.

First, based on Kant's use of "content" there is a short argument to the conclusion that intuitions do not have conceptual content (Tolley 2013:128):

176   C. McLear

1. The content of a cognition (whether intuition or concept) consists in, that is, is nothing but, a relation to an object.
2. Concepts and intuitions relate to objects in different ways, that is, mediately and immediately.
3. The content of intuition is different from the content of concepts, that is, it is nonconceptual.

This argument gives us good reason to reject the idea that intuition could have, *in Kant's sense of the term*, a concept as its "content" (*Inhalt*).[8] Indeed, Kant's notion of content does not obviously fit with the conception of content that I have been working with thus far.

Second, Tolley's analysis of Kant's use of "content" might nevertheless be compatible with the contemporary notion that I have been working with thus far. The basic idea would be that the kind of relation to an object, which constitutes Kant's use of "content", is itself determined by the kind of correctness condition, and thus "content" in our contemporary sense, of the relevant psychological state. In an empirical judgement we have a specification of some logically possible state of affairs. For Kant, thought is directed to its object by means of a condition which an object or state of affairs may or may not satisfy. As long as something satisfies it, whatever it is, then the judgement is true. In this sense a judgement only *mediately* relates to an object. It relates to it mediately because it specifies a general condition, which any number of possible objects might meet. Thus, one can have a particular object in mind only to the extent that that object satisfies the specification which is the content of one's thought.

If mediate relation to an object is understood in terms of a kind of content that specifies a condition that may or may not be satisfied, immediate relation to an object might similarly be understood in terms of a different kind of content, one that is singular rather than satisfactional, and thus could only refer to a specific thing. Singular content is not content that specifies a condition. Instead the relevant object is part of the content itself (I leave open how best to interpret "part of" here). On this way of thinking, then, the mediate/immediate relation that Kant speaks

---

[8] For opposing views see e.g. Engstrom (2006), Griffith (2012) and Willaschek (1997).

of is best understood in terms of a difference between descriptive (i.e. satisfactional) and singular content.[9]

Although this attempt at a rapprochement between the two senses of "content" (Kant's and our own) is attractive, I think it cannot ultimately work. The problem, as I discuss in the next section, is that, although Kant obviously accepts that intuitive representations have relation to an object, he does not obviously intend this as an endorsement of a notion of "contentful" experience in our contemporary sense.

8.3 Does Experience Have Content?

Our question is whether Kant endorses the claim that experience has nonconceptual content. I have argued that the standard notion of content which is presupposed by this question is that of a proposition— something which is the potential object of different epistemic attitudes in one subject, is communicable across subjects, and which is the bearer of truth and falsity. I have argued further that the correlative notion of a proposition in Kant's philosophy is that of a judgement and that his own usage of the term "content" to specify a type of relation to an object can partially be accounted for in terms of our contemporary notion of a descriptive specification of an object or state of affairs.

However, there are several hurdles that face the intelligibility of the question as to whether Kant admits that experience, that is, intuition, has nonconceptual content. The first is that if the analysis in Sect. 8.2 is correct then the claim that intuition has conceptual content is really just the claim that it has *judgemental* content, without which it could not qualify as intuition. While there have been prominent interpretations which tie intuition essentially to judgement, the view has recently been roundly criticised for a variety of reasons including the fact that it seems to conflate judgement with synthesis more generally.[10] Moreover, in a 1791 letter to

---

[9] For example, this seems to be one of the central ways in which Robert Hanna distinguishes between conceptual and nonconceptual representation. See Hanna (2005, 2008); cf. Thompson (1972).

[10] For interpretations tying judgement to intuition, see Paton (1936:285), Pippin (1982:33) and Strawson (1966:94). For extensive criticism of "judgementalist" readings of Kant, see Grüne

J. S. Beck addressing just this issue, Kant explicitly denies that "the relation of intuition to an object in general" is the work of judgement (Br, 11:311). Since concepts are, for Kant, "predicates of possible judgment" (A69/B94) and the "understanding can make no other use of [them] ... than that of judging by means of them" (A68/B93; cf. Heis 2014a), their deployment is restricted to their role in judgement. Since Kant has ruled out judgement as that which connects an intuition to its object, it seems that concepts cannot themselves be contents of intuition.

If it is not textually plausible to understand the content of an intuition in conceptual terms (at least as Kant understands the notion of a concept) then what would it mean to say that Kant endorses conceptualism with regard to experience? In keeping with our contemporary notion of a content as setting a veridicality condition for a mental state, one might be tempted by the line of thought suggested at the end of Sect. 8.2, namely, that intuition relates to its object immediately in virtue of the kind of veridicality condition ("content" in our sense) possessed by intuitive representations.

The conceptualist would then have to explain how the intuition has the kind of content that it does, namely, the possession of a veridicality condition, something that could be the object of an epistemic attitude and (potentially) communicated in an explicit judgement—without thereby construing it in terms of judgement (or even a concept). And since we have ruled out a concept's figuring, via judgement, as the *content* of an intuition, the most plausible thing a conceptualist might say is that concepts are nevertheless partly responsible for the *generation* of the intuition, as rules for synthesis enacted on (non-contentful) sensory impressions.[11]

Though the details of the view may vary, I take the heart of this version of the conceptualist interpretation as one according to which concepts play a role in the generation of intuitive representations. The conceptualist can then argue that it is at least partly in virtue of this generative role that intuitions possess veridicality conditions. These generative conditions are what serve to constitute an intuition's presentation of an object (often construed in terms of the intuition's intentionality), as well as the

---

(2009), Chap. 2.2, and Land (2015b).

[11] For examples of this kind of view, see Anderson (2015), Friedman (2015), Ginsborg (2008), Grüne (2009), Haag (2007), Land (2015a), Longuenesse (1998a) and Pereboom (1988).

intuition's relevance to other epistemic attitudes, both in the *acquisition* of empirical concepts, and in the *warrant* the intuition provides for basic perceptual beliefs. Prescinding from the details of this interpretation (or family of interpretations), it is this central claim regarding the generation of intuition that I think is mistaken, and which I take to be the primary issue of debate between so-called conceptualists and nonconceptualists.

But even this alternative way of interpreting the issue of conceptualism in Kant's theory of experience is problematic, for at least two reasons. First, a central motivation for nonconceptualist readings of Kantian intuition stems from the case of apparent perceptual experience in beings which lack the relevant concepts, such as infants and non-human animals. The animal case is especially problematic since non-human animals lack (according to Kant) even the capacity to acquire concepts. Thus the need to account for such cases remains even if a conceptualist construes their position in terms of the role concepts play in the generation of intuition rather than as its "judgemental" content. Second, the "generative" reading, which eschews positing judgements and their component concepts as the contents of intuitions, still presupposes that the relevant distinction between mere sensation and genuine intuition hinges on the possession of a correctness condition. But, as I have argued elsewhere, this presupposition is incorrect. Kant does not ascribe to correctness conditions any fundamental explanatory role in his conception of intuition. In fact, he seems to eschew ascribing correctness conditions to intuition altogether (see McLear 2016 for extensive discussion). The fact that this central assumption is mistaken threatens the coherence of a content-centred interpretative debate between conceptualists and nonconceptualists.

If the debate concerning the content of intuition has presupposed a notion of "content" that Kant rejects, then how should we understand the debate? In the next section, I argue that we should not frame the debate in terms of the presence or absence in experience of a particular kind of *content, and thus of the presence or absence of correctness conditions that could be the object of doxastic attitudes*, but rather in terms of the presence or absence of particular kinds of cognitive *ability* and the dependence relations that may or may not hold between such abilities and the occurrence or generation of experience (intuition).

180   C. McLear

8.4   Reframing the Debate

I have argued thus far that, at root, the conceptualism debate should be understood as concerned with the conditions under which intuitions are generated rather than the "content" of an intuition as a kind of correctness condition.[12] Here we can distinguish two broad camps, each of which construe these conditions differently. On the one side is Intellectualism, which construes the generation of intuition as dependent on the higher discursive activity of the intellect (i.e. understanding, judgement and reason).[13] By contrast, Sensibilism argues that at least some intuitions do not rely for their existence or generation on any activity of the intellect.

Sensibilism and Intellectualism can agree that sensing and thinking involve distinct (and distinctive) cognitive abilities. In this regard, Sensibilism is not to be confused with a crude *empiricism*. Moreover, both Sensibilism and Intellectualism explain the generation and structure of representations or mental states at least partly in terms of the relevant cognitive capacity or faculty. The key difference is that Intellectualism construes the structure of intuitive representations, and ultimately even their generation, as dependent not only on sensibility *but also on the understanding*, and possibly other "higher" cognitive faculties as well (e.g. judgement or reason). For the Intellectualist, the only representations which do not admit of this dependence are the simple sensations that are the supposed initial product of sensibility, in its interface with, or passive "affection" by, mind-independent reality.[14]

By contrast, Sensibilism argues that at least some objective sensory states, including the "pure" representations of space and time, possess structure which is not the product of the activity of the intellect. Moreover, Sensibilism construes such representations, at least in some cases, as generated without, and in principle independently of, the activity of the intellect.

---

[12] In this sense I am in agreement with the emphasis on generation of intuition in recent interpretations such as Grüne (2009), Land (2015b) and Longuenesse (1998a).

[13] Note that I use "discursive" here to denote not concepts, but the activity of the mind in the "running through, and taking together" of representations (A99).

[14] Since sensations are simple, they do not admit of structure, and thus according to Intellectualism do not depend on the activity of the intellect.

8 Getting Acquainted with Kant 181

There are at least three benefits to reframing the debate in this manner. First, we avoid any attribution to Kant of the (in my view) controversial assumption that intuition essentially has a correctness condition that could be the object of epistemic attitudes.[15] Of course, a proponent of Intellectualism might argue *to* the conclusion that intuitions essentially have correctness conditions as a result of their generation by acts of synthesis. But this would need to be shown as part of the Intellectualist's argument, rather than as an assumption thereof.

Second, and perhaps surprisingly, avoiding the content assumption and reframing things in terms of cognitive abilities actually brings Kant *closer* to aspects of the contemporary debate in the philosophy of mind. This is due to two features of the contemporary debate. The first feature I have in mind is the extraordinarily wide range of views concerning the existence and nature of concepts.[16] Hence, asking whether Kant accepts the existence of nonconceptual content in experience requires a great deal of triangulation with respect to what one might mean by "concept" or its cognates.[17] Reframing things in terms of cognitive abilities lets us sidestep much of this discussion. A second feature of contemporary debate in the philosophy of mind is that, since Gareth Evans's seminal 1982 work, *The Varieties of Reference*, many philosophers have been influenced by the idea that what we mean in talking about thought as being "conceptual" or "conceptually articulated" is best understood in terms of its having a structure that is the product of the exercise of two or more distinct abilities. Evans puts things this way:

---

[15] There are, nevertheless, various weaker senses in which an intuition might have a correctness condition. For further discussion, see McLear (2016).

[16] For a sampling of the variety, see Machery (2009) and Margolis and Laurence (2014).

[17] For example, much of the contemporary debate has been concerned with the difference between "state" views and "content" views (see Heck 2000, Speaks 2005 and Van Cleve 2012). This distinction has also exerted itself in the Kantian debate (e.g. Allais 2009, Faggion 2015, Grüne 2011 and Hanna 2011a, b). But according to e.g. the Fregean tradition of understanding conceptual content, it makes no sense to say that one could be in a state with conceptual content C without also thereby being able to grasp that content C, i.e. without also possessing the concept. Of course, one could argue that Kant should or should not be understood in terms of the Fregean tradition (cf. Tolley 2014 for a defence of the Fregean reading), but this would be a further move. It would perhaps be better if we could avoid these interpretative difficulties altogether.

If a subject can be credited with the thought that *a* is *F*, then he must have the conceptual resources for entertaining the thought that *a* is *G*, for every property of being *G* of which he has a conception. This is the condition that I call "The Generality Constraint". ... I shall speak ... of the concepts a subject has, of this or that property. And I shall allow myself to say that this or that particular thought-episode comprises such-and-such an Idea of an object, as well as such-and-such a concept. This is simply a picturesque way of rephrasing the notion that the thought is a joint exercise of two distinguishable abilities. (1982:104)

So part of what Evans means by the notion of a content's being *conceptual* is that it belongs to an episode of thinking understood as an exercise of the distinct cognitive abilities defined by the Generality Constraint. Evans also appeals to this conception of concept possession to distinguish between states that have and states that lack conceptual content (cf. Evans 1982:104n.22, 226–7).

The view that conceptual content be understood in such terms has been influential, and several of the central participants in the contemporary debate concerning the content of perception endorse it.[18] It is therefore unsurprising that those who would accept that experience might have nonconceptual content also reject the claim that all content be understood in terms of the exercise of abilities which obey the Generality Constraint (cf. Beck 2012, 2013).[19] So a benefit of reframing the Kantian debate with respect to cognitive abilities is that it intersects nicely with contemporary discussion without thereby requiring us to say anything more specific about the nature of concepts.

A third benefit is that the Intellectualist/Sensibilist distinction brings unity where we might otherwise find dissent. For example, with respect to the debate concerning whether the content of intuition should be understood in terms of judgement, or instead in terms of the exercise

---

[18] See e.g. Dummett (1993), Geach (1957), Kenny (2010), McDowell (1990, 1998) and Peacocke (1992). For criticism, see Davis (2005:144–5). For recent work implicitly or explicitly connecting Kant to this tradition, see Allais (2015), Dunlop (2012), Hanna (2005), Heis (2014b) and Longuenesse (1998a).

[19] There is, of course, the question as to whether Kant endorses the Generality Constraint as it is typically understood. Some support for thinking that he does comes in the footnote at B133–4, but more needs to be said concerning this matter. I shall pursue this issue in future work.

of a conceptually guided synthesis (cf. Land 2015b), it might seem that there is strong disagreement concerning the content of experience and the role of the understanding in cognition. However, this internecine debate hides what I take to be fundamental agreement between the two "conceptualist" camps—namely, that Kant strongly ties the exercise of intellectual cognitive capacities to the conditions governing the possibility of objective sensory experience. This position takes as central Kant's claim that

> the same function that gives unity to the different representations in *a judgment* also gives unity to the mere synthesis of different representations *in an intuition*, which, expressed generally, is called the pure concept of understanding. (A79/B104–5)

The Intellectualist reading of this passage focuses on the claim that the very same cognitive capacities are at work in judgement and in intuition. Since this claim concerns the unity of judgement and intuition it might even seem reasonable to say that the structure of each kind of representation is supposed to depend on the activity of the intellect. It would then be this activity which brings it about that the representations have objectivity in Kant's sense of "relation to an object" (B137).[20] By reframing the conceptualism debate in terms of the Intellectualist/Sensibilist divide, we can highlight the most important aspects of the dispute, while nevertheless allowing that there might be differences of interpretation within each camp regarding the precise way in which Kant adheres to one or the other side of the divide.[21]

With these points in mind we can revise our previous framing of the conceptualism debate in Sects. 8.2 and 8.3 to read it as instead resting on three distinct but interrelated claims: (i) the content of an intuition is a kind of relation to an object; (ii) the relation to an object depends on

---

[20] For an alternative reading of this passage, and the notion of a "relation to an object", see McLear (forthcoming a); cf. Allais (2015), Chap. 11.

[21] A further virtue of the capacities-based approach that I advocate here is that it helps to make sense of the way in which Kant understands that infants and non-human animals might or might not have experience of an objective world. I lack the space to discuss appropriately this issue here, but see McLear (2011) and McLear (forthcoming a) for further discussion.

the possession of a privileged set of cognitive capacities—specifically, the capacity to carry out a "synthesis" directed in accordance with concepts; (iii) synthesis in accordance with concepts sets correctness conditions for the intuition's representation of a mind-independent object.

If the conceptualism debate is thus really best reconceived as concerning the kinds of mental acts a cognitive subject is able to perform, and the role of those acts in imparting a particular kind of structure to a subject's mental states, then our original question as to whether Kant recognises the existence of nonconceptual content in experience breaks down into two more fundamental ones. First, we can ask whether the cognitive capacities necessary for the generation of an intuition themselves impart or otherwise determine a correctness condition for the intuition. Second, we can ask whether the generation of an intuition always and everywhere depends on the exercise of distinctively intellectual capacities, whether or not such an exercise would impart or otherwise determine any sort of correctness condition. I argue elsewhere that we have reason to answer both questions negatively.[22]

One might try to circumvent the Intellectualism/Sensibilism dichotomy that I have sketched by arguing that the two aspects of Intellectualism as I have articulated it—namely, the determination of correctness conditions in intuition and the dependence of intuition on an exercise of distinctively intellectual cognitive capacities—come apart. It seems possible to reject the first claim—that intuition has content determined by the exercise of intellectual capacities—but endorse the second claim—that the generation of intuition is nonetheless dependent on distinctively intellectual capacities.

For example James Messina (2014) argues for a reading of the relationship between the output of representations by sensibility and the exercise of intellectual capacities that seeks to exploit a supposed middle ground between the two kinds of dependence that I have sketched. This reading states that the unity of the pure forms of intuition—namely, the representations of space and time—metaphysically depends on, and is only possible through, the activity of the original synthetic unity of apperception. Since I take this form of dependence to be a central point

---

[22] See McLear (2015, 2016); cf. McLear (2014b).

8 Getting Acquainted with Kant 185

at issue, I would regard such a position as a form of Intellectualism. But what distinguishes Messina's position from other forms of Intellectualism is his denial that "this unity [of the representations of space and time] is the output or result of the figurative synthesis, or any other act of synthesis for that matter" (2014:23).[23]

While this view is very interesting, and coherently maps a portion of logical space, I fail to see any compelling reason for thinking that Kant would have (or should have) endorsed it. The problem is that the view seems to inherit a central fault of Intellectualism without inheriting one of its (putative) central merits. According to Messina, the objective status of a subject's sensory states depends on her possessing, and exercising, intellectual cognitive capacities. This means that Messina's interpretation inherits all of the traditional problems with respect to non-rational beings that dog more standard versions of Intellectualism. But since, on this reading, intuition does not ultimately depend for its structure on the activity of the intellect, but rather on the (unsynthesised) "pure" forms of space and time, there is no sense in which we can appeal to the structure of thought (or the capacity to think) to explain the ultimate intelligibility of spatially and temporally structured objects, as Intellectualism attempts to. Intellectualism can at least purport to offer an explanation as to why spatial and temporal objects are intelligible to thought. This is because it sees the generation of the pure intuitions of space and time as dependent upon a figurative synthesis which is itself dependent upon the possession and exercise of intellectual cognitive capacities (such as the understanding and the capacity to judge). But Messina's proposed interpretation provides no such benefit, because it denies that the intuitions of space and time are the result of a figurative synthesis, while nevertheless severely limiting the sense in which sensibility is construed by Kant as an independent faculty capable of generating its own class of objective mental states. So while I take Messina's interpretation to be logically possible,

---

[23] However, Messina (2014:13) does seem to think that the representation of determinate spaces and lines depends on synthesis, which would seem to preclude infants and non-human animals from having such representations. That would mean that they could neither represent locations in space or edges or boundaries of objects. This seems both philosophically and textually problematic. For discussion regarding Kant's views on the cognitive capabilities of non-human animals, see Allais (2009:405–8), McLear (2011), McLear (forthcoming a) and Naragon (1990).

8.5 Modality and Cognition

As I mentioned in Sect. 8.1, three issues of central and enduring philosophical interest concern the relationship that experience has to the content of our concepts (and thus what we believe and know), the fixation of basic perceptual belief, and the justification or warrant for those beliefs. It is at least partly due to interest in Kant's position regarding these enduring issues that scholars have focused so heavily on the question of his views concerning concepts and the content of experience.

It is widely acknowledged that, with respect to the first issue, Kant's conception of empirical concept acquisition via abstraction faces serious interpretative and philosophical difficulties.[25] Concerning the second, Kant says remarkably little about exactly how it is that sensory experience gives rise to empirical judgement. I shall focus, in a somewhat indirect way, on the third issue, concerning empirical warrant, and specifically on the way in which intuition puts a subject in a position to prove the real possibility of a represented object. Such proof is a necessary condition of cognition, and although cognition is different from knowledge (i.e. *Erkenntnis* is not *Wissen*), it is necessary for possessing substantive empirical knowledge (see Chignell 2014; Schafer, forthcoming). My aim here is both to clarify the role of intuition in proving the possibility of the objects of cognition, and to show that the Intellectualist position faces a significant challenge in accommodating this account, one not faced by Sensibilism as I interpret it.[26]

---

[24] Thanks to James Messina for discussion concerning these points.

[25] See Anderson (2015), Ginsborg (2006a, b), Longuenesse (1998a) and Pippin (1982).

[26] For previous discussion of intuition, content and modality, see McLear (2016). For criticism of this account, see Grüne (2014a). For ease of exposition I construe cognition as a necessary condition of empirical knowledge. However, as Chignell (2014:576–9) points out, Kant seems to allow that there are cases where the grounds of knowledge may not require cognition, such as with analytic knowledge and negative knowledge of things in themselves. These caveats are assumed throughout my discussion.

8 Getting Acquainted with Kant 187

One of the central claims of Kant's Critical philosophy is that reasoning in accordance with logical principles cannot, by itself, provide a subject with knowledge of the world. The possibility of ampliative knowledge concerning the world requires that the mind obtain its subject matter from something other than the activity of the intellect, and thus, given our cognitive constraints, via sensibility. This is one of the many ways in which our understanding differs from that of an intuitive intellect (B145–6).

A second contribution of intuition to knowledge, beyond that of obtaining a subject matter for thought, is in the satisfaction of what we can call Kant's *modal condition* on cognition and knowledge. One of Kant's main criticisms of the German rationalist tradition is that the principle of contradiction cannot provide us with positive cognition of the world. He (here in agreement with Crusius) argues that a further positive contribution is needed to separate what is merely logically possible from what is genuinely metaphysically possible.[27] In this way, Kant's Critical philosophy is a radical departure from the German rationalist tradition exemplified by Leibniz, Wolff and Baumgarten, amongst others.

Cognition, and ultimately empirical knowledge, depends on being able to show the metaphysical possibility of the concept's being instantiated—its "objective validity".[28] The point that a proof of real possibility is necessary for cognition is made explicitly by Kant in the preface to the B edition of the First *Critique*:

> To *cognize* an object, it is required that I be able to prove its possibility (whether by the testimony of experience from its actuality or *a priori* through reason). But I can *think* whatever I like, as long as I do not contradict myself, i.e., as long as my concept is a possible thought, even if I

---

[27] As L.W. Beck says, "what Kant did learn from Crusius must not be underestimated; he learned that 'the rain never follows the wind because of the law of identity'" (Beck 1978:94). Beck cites here Kant's *Negative Magnitudes* from 1763 (NG, 2:203). See also Hogan (2009) and Watkins (2005:162–5).

[28] Note that I take the notion of objective validity to be distinct from, and typically more demanding than, objective reality. As Winkler (2010:69) has helpfully noted, for Kant, a concept is objectively real if and only if its corresponding object is really possible, while a concept is objectively valid if and only if objects can be thought or experienced only by its means (A97; A89–90/B122; A93/B126; A111). It is presumably this demanding sense that is at issue in TD. At other times there is a less demanding use of "objective validity", where it seems to act more as a substitute or synonym for "objective reality" (see Bxxiv; Bxxvii; A156/B195; A311/B368; A669/B697).

cannot give any assurance whether or not there is a corresponding object somewhere within the sum total of all possibilities. But in order to ascribe objective validity to such a concept (real possibility, for the first sort of possibility was merely logical) something more is required. (Bxxvin.)

Kant's point here is that the structure of thought is governed ultimately by the rule of non-contradiction, and in this way mirrors what is logically possible. But an analysis of thought tells us nothing as to whether there really, that is, metaphysically, could be an object such as the thought specifies. Kant further distinguishes between logical and real possibility in terms of the notion of "cancellation" (*Aufhebung*). The subject matter of a thought is *logically* possible if the thought's constituent concepts may be combined in judgement without contradiction, and thus without being logically cancelled out (A151/B190; NG, 2:171–2). The subject matter of a thought is *really* possible, by contrast, if it can be shown that the subject matter to which the thought corresponds consists of properties which are mutually empirically compossible and not, in Kant's terms, "really repugnant". This is perhaps best illustrated with examples involving physical forces (e.g. opposite motions, or opposing attractive and repulsive forces; cf. A264–5/B320–1). Since real repugnance cannot solely be determined via consideration of the logical possibility of the subject as conceived, cognition requires the demonstration of the real possibility of the object through some means other than mere conception.[29] Call this condition on proof of possibility the "Modal Condition" (Chignell 2010:146). Kant indicates in the passage quoted above that real and not merely logical possibility must be provable via experience or a priori argument (e.g. a transcendental deduction) if cognition is to be possible. We can then more clearly define the modal condition on cognition as follows:

---

[29] See Chignell (2010:144–5; 2014:581–2), Warren (2001), Chap. 1, and Watkins (2005:162–5).

Modal condition:
Necessarily, S cognises an object O only if S is in a position to prove the real possibility of an object possessing the features constituting the content of the representation of O.[30]

While it is not totally obvious what proof of real possibility comes to in all cases,[31] it is clear from the quoted passage that Kant thinks that *one* way of proving the real possibility of an object is to demonstrate its *actuality* via a presentation of that object in experience. Surely then, in such a case the content of an intuition must play a decisive role in satisfying the Modal Condition, for what other kind of representation could do so in the case of experience?

Kant's modal condition on cognition thus presents a challenge: how must experience be if it is to play its stated role in satisfying the Modal Condition? As I discuss below, Intellectualism must provide a specific answer to this question, which I argue is less convincing and more problematic than the kind of answer provided by a Sensibilist interpretation.

8.5.1 Intellectualism and the Modal Condition

Recall that Intellectualism makes two claims concerning the relation between the intellect and sensibility. First, it claims that the generation of intuition by sensibility depends in part on cognitive acts carried out by the intellect. Second, it claims that these cognitive acts are necessary for imparting content (in our contemporary sense) to the intuition, in virtue of which it has relation to an object.

This conception of the generation and content of intuition puts constraints on how intuition might satisfy the modal condition. Insofar as it is the content of intuition that makes the relevant contribution to proof of real possibility, it must either come from the cognitive activity of the

---

[30] Relatedly, if O is really impossible, then S could cognise its real impossibility only if she were in a position to prove it (cf. Chignell 2014:584).

[31] For discussion of complications surrounding the articulation of the modal condition, see Chignell (2014); cf. Stang (2011, 2016).

190   C. McLear

intellect, or from the nature of intuition itself. In the former case, there can be no proof of real possibility, for intellectual acts of synthesis are discursive, and thus constrained only by the law of non-contradiction and the categories. The Intellectualist should therefore prefer the latter case, in which the (a priori) formal sensory conditions of space and time determine what is really possible. The vast extent of the logically possible would thus be understood as constrained by the nature of experience and its spatial and temporal conditions.

This view seems to accord with Kant's explanation of his notion of real possibility in the section of the First *Critique* entitled The Postulates of Empirical Thinking. There he writes:

> Whatever agrees with the formal conditions of experience (in accordance with intuition and concepts) is *possible*. (A218/B265)[32]

According to this passage, cognition of the real possibility of an object requires only that it conform to the formal conditions, both sensible and conceptual, of experience. Clearly, every object of intuition conforms to the sensible formal conditions of experience, since every object of intuition or experience must have spatial or temporal structure. Furthermore, according to Intellectualist interpretations of Kant, every object of experience or intuition conforms to the conceptual formal conditions of experience, namely the categories, because every intuition is *generated* by a synthesis that takes place in accordance with the categories.[33] Thus, every intuition, regardless of whether the object it represents exists or not, conforms to the formal conditions of experience, and is therefore the representation of an object that is really possible. Moreover, the discussion of the formal conditions of experience says nothing about real repugnance or compossibility. Hence, according to this defence of Intellectualism, there is no need to recognise a further contribution of intuition to a

---

[32] Even though, in this passage, Kant only uses the term "possibility", from the context it is clear that he is concerned with real possibility. A little bit later he equates "objective reality of the concept" with "possibility of such an object as is thought through the concept" (A220/B268). And in other passages he equates objective reality with real possibility (see e.g. FM, 20:325ff.).

[33] Exemplars of this view include Grüne (2009, 2014a), Haag (2007), Longuenesse (1998a) and Pereboom (1988).

proof of real possibility other than its contribution of spatial and temporal form.[34]

While this manner of responding to the challenge of articulating the contribution of intuition to the satisfaction of the modal condition is attractive, it also suffers from three serious problems. These are, respectively, that (i) it is too weak, (ii) it does not properly distinguish between perception and hallucination, and (iii) it does not account for Kant's appeal at Bxxiv (quoted above) to the actuality of what is presented in experience. I take these points in turn.

First, there are cases in which intuition of the actuality of an object proves its real possibility, but does so in virtue of something much richer than mere formal possibility as construed above.

Consider, for example, the discovery of the platypus. The existence of such an egg-laying, duck-billed, beaver-tailed, otter-footed mammal was surely something that was in conformity with the *formal* laws of experience (i.e. the categories plus the pure forms of intuition), but European scientists had no idea prior to the discovery of a live specimen in 1798 that the co-instantiation of such features was *really possible* in nature. The intuition that proved its real possibility, in this case via its actuality, thus did more than show just that its existence conformed with the formal conditions of experience.

Further, Kant himself mentions several cases whose real possibility does not seem to be determinable by appeal to formal conditions alone. He mentions the power to be present in a space without filling it (e.g. as a ghost) or to intuit the future (e.g. clairvoyance) and to have telepathic contact with the minds of others (A222/B270). He considers these all possibilities which are "entirely groundless" because they "cannot be grounded in experience and its known laws" (A223/B270). As other commentators have noted, it is not clear why these examples could not be grounded in the relatively weak conditions designated by the elaboration of formal possibility described above.[35] So Kant's appeal to experience

---

[34] A further avenue of objection to Intellectualism, which I do not pursue here, concerns whether it makes sense to construe spatial and temporal form as, on the Intellectualist account, sufficiently independent of the intellect and its activity to count as making a genuinely independent contribution to cognition. For relevant discussion, see McLear (2015) and Messina (2014).

[35] For discussion, see Chignell (2014:588–9).

192   C. McLear

and its known laws would suggest that he has something in mind stronger than simply formal possibility. Intellectualism, limited as it is to appealing solely to formal possibility, cannot explain what this might be.

Second, returning to the example of the platypus, Intellectualism cannot explain how seeing a platypus would be any different for proving its real possibility than hallucinating a platypus (or a mammal with platypus-like features). This is not to say that Intellectualism cannot distinguish between hallucination and perception, but rather that its basis for doing so is neutral with regard to answering the question of the contribution of intuition to the satisfaction of the Modal Condition. For the Intellectualist, the representational content contributed by an intuition in both cases will be identical.[36] But, prior to 1798, while many biologists might have believed that one could hallucinate such an animal, no one would have thought hallucination proof enough that such an animal was really a possible denizen of the natural world.[37]

A proponent of Intellectualism might respond here by pointing out that, given the reproductive nature of the imagination, all merely imaginative acts which nevertheless show the real possibility of something— e.g. of a platypus before 1798—depend on awareness of actual sensory qualities that the subject has been aware of in the past (Anth, 7:167–8).[38] So Intellectualism can allow a role for actuality in order to explain how the imagination can engage in the kinds of recombinative acts necessary to determining real possibility. The important difference is that, according to this reply, we do not need the actuality of a *particular object* to prove its real possibility, but rather only the actuality of the relevant property or properties it would instantiate so that sensation of such properties can be imagined and recombined with other (previously) sensed properties into the intuition of, for example, a (hallucinated) duck-billed platypus.[39]

---

[36] Here John McDowell's interpretation stands as an outlier for he argues both that the content of sensory experience depends on intellectual capacities and that intuition is object-dependent. See McDowell (1998) for discussion. More paradigmatic examples of Intellectualism as I am conceiving it here are Grüne (2009, 2014a), Pereboom (1988) and Stephenson (2011).

[37] This would be true even in a case of "veridical hallucination" where one, say, visually hallucinates a platypus while in the presence of a platypus matching the features so hallucinated.

[38] See McLear (forthcoming b) and Stephenson (2015b) for extensive discussion of the issue of hallucination.

[39] Thanks to Anil Gomes and Andrew Stephenson for discussion on this point.

In reply to this, it is important to note that one of the primary motives for Kant's rejection of logical possibility as an appropriate guide to metaphysical possibility lies in the fact that it is too weak to exclude arbitrary (though logically consistent) combinations of predicates (see Chignell 2010). If Kant allows that the reproductive imagination can combine any sensory property it pleases with any other, so long as they have been previously experienced, without their ever having been instantiated in one and the same object (something that seems not to be ruled out by the very wide definition of formal possibility as concerning merely the categories plus the pure forms of intuition), then sensibility might offer only slightly more demanding constraints on arbitrary combination than those put on the understanding by the law of non-contradiction. This way of construing Kant's position effectively collapses the satisfaction of the Modal Condition into the provisioning of sensory material for thought. On this view the role of sensibility is to provide the mind with raw sensory material and nothing else. All other cognitive work is done by the recombinative activity of the imagination and of thought. While I cannot entirely rule this out as an interpretation, it seems to fit poorly with Kant's conception of sensibility as providing significant cognitive constraint on the arbitrary activities of our spontaneous discursive nature.

Third, in Kant's statement of the Modal Condition on cognition in the preface to the First *Critique* he explicitly mentions the revelation of actuality in experience. Once again, in the relevant portion of that text Kant states that

> it is required that I be able to prove [the object's] possibility (whether by the testimony of experience *from its actuality* or *a priori* through reason). (Bxxvi; emphasis added)

However, Intellectualism leaves it a mystery as to why Kant would appeal to actuality in this manner. According to Intellectualism, there is no need to appeal to an actually presented object in order to prove its real possibility. Instead, all that is needed is for the representation of the object to be one whose features satisfy the formal conditions of experience. This is why, on the Intellectualist view, hallucination can suffice for proof of real possibility. But if that were true, then appeal to actuality would do no genuine work with respect to proof of real possibility. Thus, it is unclear why, on the Intellectualist interpretation, Kant would specifically mention actuality in a central statement of the nature of cognition and the contribution of experience to the satisfaction of its requirements.

If the above discussion is correct, then Intellectualism cannot construe intuition as satisfying the Modal Condition on anything other than the most general "formal" level. Intuition, according to Intellectualism, makes no further contribution to determining whether something is really possible according to the specific natural laws governing our world. This leaves it a complete mystery as to how cases of the actuality of the object, as presented in an occurrent intuition, might play any special sort of role in providing the proof necessary for cognition. This is dissatisfying both philosophically and textually.

8.5.2 Acquaintance and the Modal Condition

In contrast to Intellectualism, I suggest that we understand intuition as a cognitive route to actuality.[40] Intuition can prove the possibility of an object by relating the subject to an actuality which is the ground of the relevant possibility, thus providing its "proof". Intuition, being partly constituted by some actuality to which it relates, thereby provides an intuiting subject with access to an actuality in virtue of which, and in combination with her higher cognitive capacities of understanding and judgement, she can cognise, and perhaps come to know, the real possibility of some truth or judgement.

According to my preferred Sensibilist account, an intuition is a relation that immediately—i.e. non-inferentially and without appeal to any of the subject's background beliefs—presents its object. Since intuition

---

[40] I am specifically concerned with empirical intuition here, but I think the claim could be generalised to cover Kant's conception of intuition as a whole. For such a general framework to work, more needs to be said about how intellectual and a priori intuition fit into this framework. As I see it, intellectual, a priori and empirical intuitions are all relations to actualities. The difference is that in intellectual and empirical intuition there is causal determination, either from intellectual intuition to its object, or from object to the (subject of the) empirical intuition. A priori intuition is the most difficult case, since space and time are not existing objects in their own right (A291/B347), and so cannot straightforwardly cause or be caused by the intuition of them. I intend to address these issues in future work.

is understood to be a relation, it could not exist without the presence of its object, and it is in virtue of the object's being, in this sense, a constituent of the subject's mental state that she is in a position to appeal to it in the course of making judgements about the subject matter of her experience.[41]

Thus, on this reading, intuition is a form of non-propositional awareness, which can be thought of along the lines of "acquaintance" with one's environment. Intuition (or the psychological state thereof) need not be thought of in terms of a relation to a "content" in the contemporary sense, nor as depending on the exercise of intellectual cognitive capacities. Visual, auditory and tactile experience are perhaps the most prominent sense modalities for acquainting a subject with her environment, and do so in obviously distinctive ways. These sensory modalities (and perhaps the others) provide a form of access to the environment, that is, they make it immediately available to consciousness in a particular sensory way.[42]

The term "acquaintance" has connotations often associated with its deployment by British philosophers as an epistemically foundational mental state which must itself satisfy stringent epistemic conditions. The stringent character of these epistemic conditions, such as possessing infallible knowledge of the existence, identity and nature of what is experienced, convinced figures such as Russell that acquaintance relations cannot hold between subjects and their environment but rather only between subjects and mental items (e.g. sense-data) or universals (cf. Russell 1997:46–7; 1910).

Kant does not adopt Russell's stringent epistemological characterisation of acquaintance. In particular, he does not hold that being acquainted with some part of one's environment E, of itself, entails that one *knows* anything about E. Acquaintance is thus not to be con-

---

[41] This position raises obvious issues concerning intuition and hallucination. I articulate an account of intuition with respect to hallucination in McLear (forthcoming b).

[42] Kant specifies that three of the five senses, namely sight, touch and hearing, are forms of "objective" empirical intuition (Anth, 7:154) in virtue of being more conducive to physical object cognition than introspective cognition of the subject's own state. The other two senses, taste and smell, are "subjective" and have less to do with our perception of objects than with our "enjoyment" (*Genuss*) in the object (Anth, 7:154). It is thus possible that Kant thinks the sensory modes of taste and smell do not provide outer intuitions at all.

196   C. McLear

fused with knowledge. Neither does Kant privilege certainty concerning the character of one's subjective states over certainty concerning the character of one's environment (A370–1).[43] According to the version of Sensibilism I advocate, Kant understands acquaintance as serving a more cognitively basic epistemic function than either providing knowledge or, more generally, warranting an epistemic attitude. Instead, it is the basis of what Kant calls "cognition" (*Erkenntnis*), insofar as the term "cognition" attaches primarily to representations and not propositional attitudes.

We can see the advantages of this account when we look at the three objections I raised to Intellectualism in the previous section. Clearly, my interpretation accords with the Bxxvi textual reference to actualities that are presented via experience. My preferred interpretation also properly distinguishes between perception and hallucination. Since the intuited object is a partial constituent of the relevant sensory experience, it is the actuality of the object that grounds proof of its real possibility. In the case of hallucination, no external object is present, and so there is no corresponding ground of proof. Finally, in the case of the platypus prior to 1798—as well as Kant's own examples of telepathy, clairvoyance and ghostly matter—I take Kant to be appealing to the fact that there is no experienced or causally inferable actuality to which one might appeal in grounding the real possibility of such cases. This is clear from his point at the beginning of the next paragraph that

> I leave aside *everything the possibility of which can only be derived from actuality in experience*, and consider here only the possibility of things through concepts *a priori*, about which I proceed to assert that it can never occur by itself solely from such concepts, but always only as formal and objective conditions of an experience in general. (A223/B270–1; emphasis added)

I take Kant's point here to be that his prior appeal to "experience and its known laws" (A223/B270) was an appeal to actualities that are either presented in particular experiences or are inferable via appeal

---

[43] It is this dependency relation that Kant emphasises when he says in *Metaphysik* K2 (1790s) that "I would have no inner sense if I had no outer sense" (V-Met-K2/Heinze, 28:771). Similar points are made in the Refutation of Idealism in the *Critique*.

to causal laws (A225–6/B272–3).[44] Again, I take my interpretation to explain better his appeal to actuality than that which could be offered by Intellectualism.

8.6   Conclusion

I have argued that "content", conceived in terms of a correctness condition that can be the object of differing epistemic attitudes in and across persons, does not play an explanatorily significant role with respect to the constitution or generation of "intuition"—Kant's term for the most primitive or basic kind of perceptual experience. I then argued that the debate concerning the content of experience be reconceived along the lines of the possession of cognitive abilities and the dependence relations that may or may not hold between intellectual and sensory abilities in the generation of intuition. The resulting framework for debate, between the positions I have labelled "Sensibilism" and "Intellectualism", more fruitfully captures the central lines of contention that have implicitly or explicitly driven the conceptualism debate. I also presented several reasons why Sensibilism may be a preferable interpretation of Kant, not least because it seems best suited to make sense of a central aspect of his Critical philosophy—namely, the modal contribution of sensibility, via acquaintance, to our cognition of reality.[45]

---

[44] For a weaker reading of Kant's position in this passage, see Chignell (2014). I agree with Chignell that demonstration of empirical possibility requires showing that an object or state of affairs is not ruled out by the formal conditions of experience plus the actual obtaining empirical laws. I also agree that in many cases such demonstration may be too demanding. But I do not see that as licensing an interpretation according to which Kant is merely stating a kind of coherence condition with respect to background knowledge (Chignell 2014:591). By contrast, I concede that Kant may well be overstating his case against the possibility of telepathy, etc. However, all I need for my interpretation is that Kant appeals to something stronger than mere formal conditions of experience in determining real possibility, and that he construes experience's contribution in many cases in terms of a presentation of actuality, rather than merely appealing to conditions of formal possibility. These points I take to be amply demonstrated by the relevant passages cited above from the Postulates.

[45] Thanks to Anil Gomes, Stefanie Grüne, Dennis Schulting, Andrew Stephenson and an anonymous reviewer for helpful comments and suggestions for clarification.

9

Is There Room for Nonconceptual Content in Kant's Critical Philosophy?

Christian Onof

9.1 Introduction

This chapter aims to establish whether there is any role for nonconceptual content in Kant's Critical philosophy by focussing both on some of the many relevant statements in his texts and on the systematic coherence of his position. The implication of the question about nonconceptual content is that there is a consensus as to the role for conceptual content in these works. Sect. 9.2 will briefly explicate the role of such content in cognition. In Sect. 9.3 I consider representations with conceptual content and ask whether there is more to their content than is defined by concepts. With the question answered in the affirmative, the next task is that of investigating the possibility of representations whose content is *merely* nonconceptual (Sect. 9.4). That further step is required because the identification of nonconceptual content that is always *bound up with*

C. Onof (✉)
Department of Philosophy, Birkbeck College, London, UK
e-mail: c.onof@imperial.ac.uk

© The Editor(s) (if applicable) and The Author(s) 2016
D. Schulting (ed.), *Kantian Nonconceptualism*,
DOI 10.1057/978-1-137-53517-7_9

199

conceptual content in a representation leaves a question mark as to whether any properly nonconceptual content has been singled out at all. Further, the identification of representations with purely nonconceptual content leaves open an issue that represents a problem for standard nonconceptualism, namely that of the *interdependence between nonconceptual and conceptual content*. Sect. 9.5 addresses this question by examining what nonconceptual content is about and further characterising the functions of the limited notion of such content that the chapter identifies.

9.2   Kant's Account of Cognition and the Notion of Conceptual Content

For Kant, "the synthetic unity of apperception is the highest point to which one must affix all use of the understanding, even the whole of logic and, after it, transcendental philosophy; indeed this faculty is the understanding" (B134n.). Apperception is Kant's notion of self-consciousness which he characterises as the accompanying of one's representations with an "I think" (B131). The representations that he has in mind are those which he describes as the "manifold of intuition" (B132). That is, they are sensible representations,[1] so the question of how an "I think" is to accompany such representations is not trivial. Because the "I think" is an empty representation, no self-consciousness in Kant's sense can arise from having a single representation in consciousness.[2] Rather, it is by combining a plurality of representations that the identity of the consciousness in these representations makes it possible to accompany their synthesis with an "I think". This is what Kant means when he claims that the synthetic unity of apperception is a condition for the analytic unity thereof: the analytic identity of the subject of different representations can only be

---

[1] Whether or not these are intuitions, is an issue we shall return to below.

[2] This is a point overlooked by standard criticisms of Kant's understanding of self-consciousness as leading to the typical regress that if self-consciousness amounts to a new representation "I think" directed at the contents of consciousness, this representation itself can only be taken up in self-consciousness through a further representation "I think", and so on. This is however not Kant's theory and he can conclude that the "I think" "cannot be accompanied by any further representation" (B132).

9 Room for Nonconceptual Content? 201

represented as the unity of a synthesis of its representations. This synthesis can either involve unifying representations that are not homogeneous by identifying a common feature (dynamical synthesis of connection) or by combining homogeneous representations (mathematical synthesis of composition) (see B201–2).

As Kant's summary of the result of §19 in the B-Deduction states, "that action of the understanding ..., through which the manifold of given representations ... is brought under an apperception in general, is the logical function of judgments", which leads to the claim that "the manifold in a given intuition also necessarily stands under categories" (B143). The connection or combination carried out in the synthesis involves the use of these a priori concepts, namely, the categories. For this reason, cognising an object for Kant involves having conceptual representations that relate to the object: this defines *conceptual content*.

The latter claim leaves it unclear how, through the categories, a relation to a particular object is achieved, and what this relation is. A standard way of answering this question involves appealing to empirical concepts. As Kant writes at B137, "an object ... is that in the concept of which the manifold of a given intuition is *united*". This makes sense of the way in which the "I think" accompanies the manifold in intuition: it issues in a judgement involving a determination of an object under the categories. Thus, I might say *(I think that) this is red* or *(I think that) the bird knocked the vase*, whereby concepts of "red" and "knocking" are applied, and the role of the categories of reality and causality is made explicit.[3] Judgement amounts to a determination of a red object and is a determination of a relation between two objects previously determined as bird and vase respectively.

This, however, is not an uncontroversial issue, as some Kant scholars will want to claim that the sensible synthesis of the manifold does not require such judgements (Grüne 2009) and may only involve the

---

[3] Note that all categories are involved insofar as an object is determined, but the other categories are not apparent from the judgement. So, for instance, the bird in the above judgement is primarily determined under the category of causality, but it is also determined as some reality in the quantity of one.

202 C. Onof

categories (Land 2015b; Longuenesse 2000).[4] The systematic grounds for finding this option attractive are that it is implausible that my being related to one or more objects must involve making judgements. Taking a more extreme view, some nonconceptualist theorists claim that the manifold can define a unity that refers to one or more objects without any subsumption under any concepts whatsoever.

It is not necessary here to take a stance upon the appropriateness of the above interpretations of Kant's requirements for objective cognition. All that is needed for our purposes is to observe that there is agreement about the existence of the kind of conceptual content described above in which syntheses bring the manifold in intuition under sensible concepts (e.g. Hanna 2006:100). In the next section, I want to examine such syntheses and consider the nature of their content.

9.3 The Content of Syntheses of Sensible Concepts

In the A-Deduction, Kant famously provides a detailed account of the three syntheses that are involved in bringing a manifold in intuition under a concept. The interpretation of this account is central to many disagreements among scholars: this text has been used by both conceptualists and nonconceptualists as evidence for their views. By drawing upon the connections between the syntheses of apprehension, reproduction and recognition, conceptualists argue that, in the passages where these are discussed, Kant explains how an intuition is constituted (Grüne 2009:178–85). Nonconceptualists rather put the emphasis upon the distinctness of these three syntheses, and in particular the first two from the third, to show that it is possible to have syntheses of apprehension and reproduction without any involvement of concepts (Allais 2009:396–8).

In this section, I shall set these issues aside and revisit them in the next, to focus here upon the outcome of the third of the three syntheses, the synthesis of recognition. Kant explains that the concept used for

---

[4] There is also a view that it is only schemata that are involved, but they make indirect reference to concepts, so I shall not distinguish this option here.

9 Room for Nonconceptual Content? 203

the recognition, that is, the concept of which the manifold is recognised as instantiating it, is a consciousness that "unifies the manifold … into one representation" (A103). The outcome of the synthesis of recognition is therefore a unified representation. What kind of representation is it? Insofar as it produced by unifying sensible representations in intuition, this has to be an intuition. We therefore have an account of the genesis of a *unified intuition*.

What differentiates this from the original manifold in intuition is its having been unified by recognising it as falling under a certain concept. Kant does not say more about how the subject recognises something as falling under a concept, but he turns to this issue in the chapter on Schematism. There, Kant explains that "the empirical concept … is always related immediately to the schema of the imagination, as a rule for the determination of our intuition in accordance with a certain general concept" (B180/A141). This is where the imagination has a role to play: so, if we recognise something as a dog, the schema of dog provides a rule for bringing the manifold under the concept of dog. The schema translates into sensible form those marks which are characteristic of the concept. As a result, when we see a dog, we see an animal within a range of height and length, typically with four legs and a tail. So when perceiving something that suggests applying this concept, the transcendental synthesis of recognition unifies the manifold in intuition into a representation that has its matter drawn from the sensible inputs and organised by the imagination's schema.[5]

---

[5] This intuition, insofar as it is an intuition unified by the concept "dog", and not the concept "dog seen under this perspective", therefore has some features for which there is no perceptual input, and others for which there is. The original sensible input is in the intuition, but it is organised spatially according to the concept structuring it. This issue is not just a gestalt type point about the psychology of perception, but is the important epistemological distinction between intuitions and images, much as they are closely connected insofar as "the imagination is to bring the manifold of intuition into an *image*" (A120). So, while unifying the manifold with the concept "dog", I actually only receive perceptual inputs of parts of the dog that are visible to me, and my image of a dog results from the infilling guided by the schema. But the schema also ensures that my intuition is of a dog with completely hidden parts, insofar as it enables me to produce an intuition of the whole of the dog. The same can be said of my intuition of a line: what I construct in thought is a limited section of the line, but my intuition is of an indefinitely long line. What is *not explicitly represented* in image form in the intuition is something of which I am obscurely conscious: I am conscious of the dog as a whole, but have no clear consciousness of, for instance, the hidden side, however much I have an obscure consciousness of it (I am aware that it is not wooden, stretching out a mile, etc.).

The key step that Kant makes at this point in the A-Deduction is to claim that, by bringing the manifold under a concept, the unified representation is taken to be a representation of an object determined under this concept, that is, "an object corresponding to and therefore also distinct from the cognition" (A104). But what exactly is the content of the representation of this object? One might be inclined to say that the object is *a dog*. But actually, it is not any dog, but *the dog* that I am perceiving: there is more in the intuition than the structure generated by the dog-schema.

And indeed, when asked about what I saw, I may be probed further to give details about the colour, height, type of dog, and so on. To do that, I shall bring this representation under further concepts, such as "beagle" or "brown and white". But the matter required for these further determinations is already contained in the manifold in intuition unified through the concept "dog". Even once the manifold has been brought under conceptual unity, its manifoldness is still cognitively relevant, contributing as it does to the consciousness I have of this object, and it defines the existing spatial parts of the object.[6] As such, it amounts to content of the intuitive representation that is *nonconceptual*.[7,8]

A first objection to calling this content nonconceptual is the observation that this is simply one aspect of the content of the concept "dog" in this particular instantiation of it, so there is no reason to call it

---

[6] A conceptualist might want to object that a spatial representation inherits conceptual features (minimally, the structuring role of the categories) from the fact that space is a formal intuition. For a refutation of such claims, see Onof and Schulting (2015).

[7] Note that the notion of (non)conceptual content arises in contemporary philosophy of mind and philosophy of language when addressing the question of how a mental state represents the world as being. That is, typical mental states of belief, desire or hope are propositional attitudes; their object, a proposition, represents the world in a way which is essentially conceptual: this defines conceptual content and accounts for its central role (Toribio 2007). Asking the question of the existence of nonconceptual content in Kant's philosophy therefore requires adapting this general question to the Kantian framework, thereby (i) appealing to a different notion of concept (see Grüne 2009:35–65), and (ii) transposing it to a transcendentally idealistic framework in which representations are not simply mental occurrences, but rather fulfil a transcendental function in an account of the possibility of objects.

[8] I agree with Hanna's (2011a:354) view that the content of an intuition is essentially different from that of a concept. In terms of the contemporary debate, arguments against allowing for a distinctive sort of content that is not conceptual often resort to a distinction between the *vehicle* and the *content* of the representation. This distinction is questionable, as Crane (2013:242–3) has shown. I set this issue aside here since my concern is the dependence upon conceptual content.

nonconceptual. The problem with the objection is that it glosses over the notion of "particular instantiation": the object is a particular occupying a particular region of space and being acquainted with this is something over and above the content of the concept of the object.

A rejoinder might then involve the claim that this content is only *accidentally* nonconceptual: it is only a contingent feature of the degree to which the object has been determined that leaves out as nonconceptual the additional determinations characteristic of it as the particular that it is. Indeed, it could be argued that (i) the filling of space by the object which defines which regions of space are part of, and which are not part of, the object, and (ii) any further differentiation in the manifold (colours, textures, etc.) could be captured through further conceptual determinations.

Such an objection would, however, amount to overlooking Kant's dissociating himself from any Leibnizian notion of a fully determinate individual when it comes to empirical objects: "Every *genus* requires different *species*, and these *subspecies*, and … reason demands in its entire extension that no species be regarded as in itself the lowest" (A655/B683). For Kant, there will therefore always be a surplus of intuitive material that is not conceptually determinate in any intuition (see Onof 2011a:226–30).

Be that as it may, the conceptualist could retort with a stronger argument here: the so-called nonconceptual content which has been identified plays second fiddle to the conceptual structure of the intuition. It is only *dependent*[9] *nonconceptual content* because it is the concept which ensures that the unified intuition relates (intentionally) to an object. This is indeed the case, and it could be argued that this does not define a sufficiently strong notion of nonconceptual content to deserve the name.[10] I shall not discuss this point in this chapter, but rather move to the next task which is the identification of nonconceptual content that is not conceptually dependent in any way.

---

[9] I use this term rather than the term "relative" which Speaks (2005) uses to denote the claim that a subject's representation can have a certain content even though the subject does not possess the concepts to articulate it conceptually. The difference is that, here, the issue is just that the subject does not determine the object under the said concepts.

[10] It is however arguable that McDowell (1998) would not even accept a role for such dependent nonconceptual content.

9.4 Are Concepts Required to Have Intuitions?

In this section, I address the controversial issue of whether concepts are required in the genesis of intuitions. As indicated at the start of the previous section, the opening sections of the A-Deduction have been used by both conceptualists and nonconceptualists to shore up their case. I shall start with a presentation of the conceptualist reading of these sections (Sect. 9.4.1) and a critique of some aspects of the nonconceptualist interpretation of it (Sect. 9.4.2). Questions relating to the implementation of cognitive syntheses will however lead me to revisit this original critique. In Sect. 9.4.3 I consider to what extent the possibility of "concept-free" intuitive content has been exhibited.

9.4.1 The A-Deduction A98–110: A Conceptualist Reading

Kant announces the principle of the A-Deduction as follows: the a priori concepts "must be recognized as *a priori* conditions of the possibility of experiences (whether of the intuition that is encountered in them, or of the thinking)" (A94/B126). It would therefore seem reasonable to conclude from this that the threefold synthesis which Kant presents at A98–110 provides an account of the possibility of both intuitions and thoughts of objects of experience. He starts off with the assumption that there is a manifold in intuition (A99) before successively arguing the following. First, for a unified intuition to arise from this manifold, the *synthesis of apprehension* is necessary (A99). Second, while apprehension involves my grasping each one of the manifold representations one after another, "if I were always to lose the preceding representations … from my thoughts and not reproduce them when I proceed to the following ones, then no whole representation … could ever arise" (A102). Consequently, apprehension requires a *synthesis of reproduction*. Third, Kant argues that "without consciousness that that which we think is the very same as what we thought a moment before, all reproduction in the series of representations would be in vain". As a result, we need *recognition in* a concept which Kant defines here as "this *one* consciousness that unifies the manifold that has been successively intuited, and then also reproduced, into one representation" (A103).

This provides us with an account of the three moments of the genesis of a *unified representation*, the unified intuition of an object. Importantly, since each moment depends upon the next, the synthesis of recognition in the concept plays a key role. On the conceptualist reading, without this synthesis, we could not have intuitions. This reading is not only well grounded in the text; it is also very powerful as a tool against any attempt to identify a place for anything more than dependent nonconceptual content in Kant's account of cognition.

9.4.2 The A-Deduction A98–110: A Nonconceptualist Response

Against this, nonconceptualists may wish to focus upon the distinction between these three syntheses. Although the first two would seem to be closely related ("the synthesis of apprehension is therefore inseparably combined with the synthesis of reproduction"; A102), the third is more loosely connected (e.g. Brook 2013).[11] Without it, "all reproduction in the series of representations would be in vain" (A103); but this just means that the kind of cognition Kant is scrutinising here, that is, "a whole of compared and connected representations", requires it (A97). What is at stake here is the "possibility of experience" (A94/B126; trans. corrected). But such cognition is not the only possible type of cognition. In particular, Kant allows for weaker forms of cognition, such as perception, according to the Jäsche Logic for instance. It is worth quoting the passage in full as the several distinctions are useful to the issues discussed in this chapter:

> The *first* degree of cognition is: *to represent* something;
> The *second*: to represent something with consciousness, or *to perceive* (*percipere*);

---

[11] There is also room for a moderate conceptualist response to the position I presented in the previous section which is very close to the position I arrive at in this chapter (see Schulting 2017, Chap. 6).

The *third: to be acquainted* with something (*noscere*), or to represent something in comparison with other things, both as to *sameness* and as to *difference*;

The *fourth*: to be acquainted with something *with consciousness*, i.e., to *cognize* it (*cognoscere*). Animals are acquainted with objects too, but they do not *cognize* them.

The *fifth: to understand something* (*intelligere*), i.e., to cognize something *through the understanding by means of concepts*, or to *conceive*. ...

The *sixth*: to cognize something through reason, or *to have insight* into it (*perspicere*). (Log, 9:64–5)

Since concepts and the faculty of the understanding only first make an explicit appearance at the fifth stage of cognition,[12] it is apparently the case that perception does not require concepts. It would therefore seem that the involvement of concepts is not necessary for perception as opposed to full-blown experience of an objective world (Allais 2009:405–6). This would imply that the third synthesis is not required for such cognition (Allais 2009:396–7n.).

There is certainly more to say about the use of this evidence to support the nonconceptualist reading, and we shall return to it below. For the moment, an effective conceptualist response (e.g. Land 2015a:33) to such worries arising from the Jäsche Logic would amount to simply turning to the B-Deduction where Kant explicitly spells out the dependence of the syntheses upon the categories: "All synthesis, through which even perception itself becomes possible, stands under the categories" (B161).

With this appeal to the B-Deduction, one might ask whether this is indicative of a shift between the A and the B editions of the First *Critique* on these issues. There is little evidence for this. Just as there are conceptualist interpretations of the A-Deduction passages examined above, which maintain the necessity of treating the three syntheses as inseparably related (Grüne 2009; Schulting 2017), the nonconceptualists have drawn upon passages which are not exclusive to the A-Deduction. Indeed, some prima facie strong support for the possibility of intuitions of objects which are independent of concepts is to be found in the section "On the principles

---

[12] In fact, the fourth stage refers to a form of cognition not available to animals, and must therefore also involve the faculty of understanding.

9 Room for Nonconceptual Content? 209

of a transcendental deduction in general", where Kant introduces the task of the deduction. Using this passage, in her critique of John McDowell's conceptualist reading of Kant, Lucy Allais (2009:387) draws support for her claim that intuitions make a notionally separate contribution to the content from concepts by noting that Kant claims that "objects can indeed appear to us without necessarily having to be related to functions of the under-standing, and therefore without the understanding containing their *a priori* conditions" (A89/B122).[13] This and other statements in the aforementioned section would seem to provide strong support for such a nonconceptualist reading.

However, it is important to bear in mind the context in which such statements are made. Kant is here presenting the problem of accounting for why objects should be subject to the conditions of thought, which are the categories. Unlike the case of the conditions of sensibility, where objects are indisputably in space and time, there is no obvious connection between objects and pure concepts of thought:

> For that objects of sensible intuition must accord with the formal condi-tions of sensibility that lie in the mind *a priori* is clear from the fact that otherwise they would not be objects for us; but that they must also accord with the conditions that the understanding requires for the synthetic unity of thinking is a conclusion that is not so easily seen. (A90/B122–3)

This is because, as Béatrice Longuenesse (1998a:226) puts it, the pure concepts of the understanding, that is, the categories, are not "like space and time, intuitive representations in which appearances are *given*"; that is to say, appearances "are not given *in* a category (as 'in' an intu-ition)". It is therefore "conceivable" that these appearances should not conform to the categories. What this means is that in the statement at A89/B122, Kant is evoking a *logical* possibility of objects appearing to us "without the understanding containing their *a priori* conditions". Indeed, a bit further on, talking about the category of causality, Kant states that it is "*a priori* doubtful whether such a concept is not perhaps entirely empty and finds no object anywhere among the appearances"

---

[13] See also Hanna (2001:46–65; 2005:259–60).

210   **C. Onof**

(A90/B122). Even if one argues that these possibilities are in fact *real* as opposed to mere *logical* possibilities (see Schulting 2015b), their evocation cannot provide any support for the nonconceptualist reading since the A-Deduction precisely claims to establish that "all empirical cognition of objects is necessarily in accord with such concepts", that is, the categories (A93/B125–6).

Kant's solution to the problem he raises in these passages is to show that the reason why the a priori conditions of thought are indeed conditions of the cognition of objects, is that, without these conditions, there would not be objects of experience. Kant's Critical solution therefore rests centrally upon the doctrine of transcendental idealism according to which empirical objects are not things-in-themselves but rather appearances, not only because space and time are transcendentally ideal, but also because our objective experience is constituted by the categories through the principles of the understanding. Thus the Transcendental Deduction (TD) will establish that a priori concepts "must be recognized as *a priori* conditions of the possibility of experience"; and to this Kant adds, as if to settle the case in favour of conceptualism, "(whether of the intuition that is encountered in them or of the thinking)" (A94/B126).

While nonconceptualists can therefore not appeal to A90–1/B122–3 to support their claim, this still leaves us with the above passage from the Jäsche Logic about the different levels of cognition. This appears to contradict flatly conceptualist interpretations of the First *Critique* by allowing for perception that is not conceptual insofar as this level defines a cognition that is implicitly available to animals, and hence cannot involve the faculty of the understanding.[14] The tension can be considerably defused here by noting that the notion of perception can be taken in a subjective or an objective sense. As Kant says at the beginning of the famous passage known as the *Stufenleiter*,

> The genus is *representation* in general (*repraesentatio*). Under it stands the representation with consciousness (*perceptio*). (B376/A320)

---

[14] Additionally, in the "deduction from beneath" part of the A-Deduction, Kant talks of perceptions as prior to the syntheses of apprehension and reproduction (A120).

This is in line with the passage from the Jäsche Logic, but now Kant adds a very useful differentiation:

> A *perception* that refers to the subject as a modification of its state is a *sensation* (*sensatio*); an objective perception is a *cognition* (*cognitio*). (B376/A320)

So a perception need not be understood as objective, and therefore involving concepts. The subjective understanding of perception is appropriate for the second level of the types of cognition considered in the Jäsche Logic. And this is confirmed by the fact that in the *Stufenleiter*, objective perception corresponds rather to the fourth level of cognition of the Jäsche Logic, as this defines a proper *cognition*, in line with *cognoscere* (Log, 9:64–5). There is therefore a distinction between *mere perception*, that is, representation "with consciousness" (Log, 9:64–5) in which the consciousness need not have more than merely subjective validity, and the *Stufenleiter*'s notion of perception of an object in which it has objective validity.

9.4.3 Revisiting the A-Deduction (A98–110)

Nevertheless, there is something phenomenologically appealing about nonconceptualists separating out the act of recognition from those of apprehension and reproduction. Indeed, when Kant introduces the role of *apprehension*, he explains that "every intuition contains a manifold in itself, which however would not be represented as such if the mind did not distinguish the time in the succession of impressions on one another" (A99). So the question that is being addressed is the possibility of the manifold being represented as manifold. I understand this as the question of how the manifold can be brought to consciousness as manifold. Apprehension just is, therefore, the act of bringing to consciousness a manifold, that is, of perceiving it in its manifoldness.

While *apprehension* ensures a consciousness of the manifoldness of what is given in intuition (A99), Kant views this activity as "inseparably combined" with that of *reproduction*, through which I "reproduce [the parts of the manifold] … when I proceed to the following ones"

(A102). By describing these activities as "inseparably combined", Kant is indicating that, if we are to have the manifoldness of intuitions in our consciousness, the partial representations (parts of the manifold) which have been apprehended must not disappear from consciousness as we move to the next partial representation. Reproduction is therefore a condition for having a manifold combined in consciousness. This combination is a step-by-step process that generates a representation by reproducing previous partial representations (through association), while apprehending new ones. If no *recognition* is involved in these acts of apprehension and reproduction, there is no grasp of the constructed representation *as a whole*, that is, this representation is not grasped *as a unity*. Rather, as Kant indicates, we would have "a new representation in our current state" (A103). Such a constructive process is in effect blind to its nature as a construction. But it has two important features:

(i) Insofar as this process involves reproducing previously apprehended parts, there is a partial representation of something that is the same as what was previously represented;
(ii) Insofar as this process involves combining this reproduced partial representation with a newly apprehended partial representation, there is a partial representation of something different from what was previously represented.

We therefore find that this constructive process enables what Kant calls acquaintance (*noscere*), that is, the third stage of the Jäsche Logic scale. While we noted earlier that concepts are not necessary for stage 2 of the Jäsche Logic scale insofar as perception can be subjective, they are not involved in stage 3 if the sameness and differences that are represented are not grasped as such (i.e. stage 4 does not obtain). This latter is what happens when there is, at no stage in the construction, a consciousness of the constructed representations *as the product of the parts they combine.*

As indicated above, the text of the Jäsche Logic implies that both stages 2 and 3 of the scale of cognition it presents are available to animals (Log, 9:64–5). If the interpretations I have just given are correct, this suggests that apprehension and reproduction are similarly available to animals and

9 Room for Nonconceptual Content?   213

do not require conceptual activity.[15] Now, against this, we saw above how conceptualists might object to an attempt to separate out the syntheses of apprehension and reproduction from that of recognition. They would insist that such a separation ignores the fact that Kant is actually presenting one synthesis which he is breaking down into three moments (cf. A97–8). Dennis Schulting (2015b) shows that such a separation leads to a problematic regress. I would argue that the very use of the term "synthesis" indicates that such a separation is not possible: while synthesis is "the mere effect of the imagination, of a blind though indispensable function of the soul" (A78/B103), it has a unity which is provided by the understanding (A78/B103–4). This unity, which is provided by the faculty of concepts, must therefore guide the imagination's syntheses of apprehension and reproduction, and it is the same as that of the synthesis of recognition: it is the content of the concept that guides which representations are to be gathered to be unified under this concept.[16]

But while we may reserve the term "synthesis" for such conceptually guided activity, the cursory analysis of apprehension and reproduction (i.e. not the syntheses thereof) above suggests that this need not be conceptually guided. Although Kant writes that "without consciousness that that which we think is the same as what we thought a moment before, all reproduction in the series of representations would be in vain" (A103), thereby showing the necessity of "the synthesis of recognition in the concept" (A103; heading), this "in vain" refers to the aim of objective cognition, and the necessity is therefore conditional upon this being the aim of these activities. But if that is not the kind of cognition at stake, apprehension and reproduction could take place without recognition in the concept, that is, without any cognition (*cognoscere* as opposed to *noscere*), and (i) apprehension would be guided by the contingency of the temporal occurrences of the partial representations in inner sense, which defines "the time in the succession of impressions on one another" (A99), while

---

[15] I am only considering the empirical acts of apprehension and reproduction here. Certainly, the pure synthesis of apprehension involves a role for the productive imagination, which means that the spontaneity of the understanding has a part to play here (A119).

[16] The issue of finding an appropriate concept for a manifold in intuition is another problem, that of empirical judgement, and this is not addressed in the *Critique of Pure Reason*.

214   C. Onof

(ii) reproduction would be guided by the associations that define the "law of reproduction" (A100).

When we turn to the "deduction from below" that Kant carries out further in the A-Deduction, we find an unequivocal statement about the "subjective and *empirical* ground" of reproduction in "the *association* of representations" (A121). This is followed by his claim that the only way that objective cognition is possible is if such associations have an objective ground.[17] But there is no implication that, if such objective cognition is not the goal, there should necessarily be a synthesis of recognition at work here. The very absence of the mention of such a synthesis confirms that it is not necessary for apprehension and reproduction.[18] Rather, it is the association of representations that provides the ground for reproduction. It is also noteworthy that, in the "deduction from below" (A120–1), Kant refers to apprehension and reproduction, rather than the *synthesis* thereof.

Moreover, although without recognition in a concept such activities are not unified in any objective sense, Kant does recognise the existence of the "subjective unity of consciousness" (B139) that comes about in connection with associations in inner sense.[19] This would enable us to say that we have a consciousness of the intuition resulting from these acts of apprehension and reproduction, although this is not a consciousness of them *as wholes* because the unity of the manifold is merely subjective. The intuition is thus subjectively unified but does not define a whole of which I am conscious as such.[20]

---

[17] Note that such a ground would also be an objective ground for the temporal sequence of the representations which are apprehended.

[18] Kant is concerned with the objective ground of our associations here, which he identifies as "original apperception" (A122). The distinction between this section and the presentation of the threefold synthesis (A98–110) is that the latter presents us with an account of the generation of intuitions of which we are conscious as a whole, i.e. of objectively *unified intuitions*, which is Kant's stronger notion of intuition. These require conceptualisation. If it were impossible to have any other type of intuition, the deduction would be complete at the end of A110. What Kant has to show afterwards is that for any intuitions of which we are conscious there must be an objective ground for their being connected, even if only associatively.

[19] In referring to the B-Deduction here, I am avoiding getting into the detail of the differences between the two versions of TD on the issue of how the manifold arises. In particular, note that there is no mention of synopsis in the B-Deduction.

[20] To illustrate this in contradistinction from Kant's example of addition to illustrate the synthesis of recognition (A103–4), consider the act of counting to 50 when it is carried out mechanically,

9 Room for Nonconceptual Content?   215

Such a unification of the manifold in intuition which is not conceptual, and therefore not objective,[21] nevertheless produces an intuition in a weaker sense of the word than its use for the unified intuition which results from the threefold synthesis. That is, Kant is arguably operating with more than one notion of intuition, only one of which is the product of the threefold synthesis, while the other involves only sensibility and the imagination. On this latter understanding of the word "intuition", we would therefore have to give a negative reply to the question at stake here: *concepts are not required to have intuitions.*

To understand the role of concepts, we need to see what is required for our acts of apprehension and reproduction to refer to an object. As already indicated, the additional ingredient is the recognition in the concept (A103). As Kant puts it, such recognition enables us to be conscious of the identity of what is represented now and was previously. In other words, with this recognition, we move to stage 4 of the Jäsche Logic scale, in that we do not only represent differences, but we are also conscious of what is identical (and what is different). But what characterises this unity as opposed to the subjective unity guiding the mere acts of apprehension and reproduction? Kant says that, without recognition, "the manifold would never constitute a whole" (A103). From his subsequent example, he would appear to be claiming that there would be no consciousness of the manifold in intuition as a whole. That is, while apprehension and reproduction provide a notion of intuition which is subjectively unified, the synthesis of recognition ensures that the intuition is unified in such a way that I grasp its unity. In the rest of the chapter, I reserve the term "unified intuition" for objectively unified intuitions.

---

e.g. when doing one's morning exercises. There is a unity in the sequence that is defined by the associations between each number and its successor which guide our ability to count without reflecting. But this is distinct from the unity of the objective synthesis of all the units which determines their sum as 50. The first case does not feature a grasp of 50 *as sum* of so many units, which characterises the second case, so that only the second case involves the cognition of a number.

[21] While this unity is not objective, the A-Deduction purports to show that it is nevertheless grounded in an objective unity (A121–2): this is the "transcendental affinity of which the empirical affinity is the mere consequence" (A114). Nevertheless, the empirical associations we make have a subjective dimension beyond this objectivity, as Kant explains in the B-Deduction: "The empirical unity of apperception ... which is ... derived only from the former [i.e. the original unity of consciousness], under given conditions *in concreto*, has merely subjective validity" (B140).

216   C. Onof

That the consciousness of the unity of the intuition can only be brought about by a concept is an interesting issue that has been examined in depth by Stefanie Grüne (2009). There is no space to discuss her well-argued proposal in detail, but the important claim she makes is that obscure (unclear) concepts are the kind of concepts involved in the synthesis of recognition.[22] This enables her to defend the genetic primacy of intuitions with respect to clear concepts, while upholding their dependence upon obscure concepts. While I would not follow Grüne in all the detail of her account of the nature of obscure concepts,[23] for the purpose of this chapter I endorse her conclusion that intuitions, understood as unified intuitions, are generated by the threefold synthesis and do not define nonconceptual content. What the synthesis of recognition adds to apprehension and reproduction is the relation to an object because the concept, "however imperfect or obscure it may be", is "something that serves as a rule" (A106). The necessity of this rule, which Kant shows to be grounded in the transcendental unity of apperception (hereafter TUA), is what ensures the relation to the object. The necessary agreement of representations with one another is a condition for their relating to an object that is distinct from them (A104).

---

[22] I cannot follow Grüne (2009:227–32) in the role she assigns to the categories as obscure concepts. Concepts guiding the sensible synthesis must be sensible, I would argue, and it is their schemata that are all that is actually involved in sensible synthesis without judgement, but there is no space to argue for this here.

[23] The notion of obscure concept is a difficult one to pin down in Kant's writings, for the simple reason that in A103 Kant defines a concept as "this *one* consciousness that unifies the manifold that has been successively intuited, and then also reproduced, into one representation", while clear concepts are "concepts of which we are conscious" (V-Lo/Busolt, 24:617). It would therefore seem that obscure concepts are both a form of consciousness and something of which we are not conscious. Grüne (2009:85) draws the conclusion that clear concepts imply the ability to apperceive, which she spells out as the ability to judge that the object does indeed fall under the concept in question. This seems correct, but if an obscure concept were not to involve this ability, then, according to Kant's famous claim at B131–2, such a concept "would either be impossible or else at least would be nothing for me". I think rather that recognition in the case of the involvement of a clear concept involves an *actual* apperception. This need not, however, involve the formulation of an explicit judgement, but an implicit judgement is involved, such that I take the object in question to be determined in certain ways, which is how I understand Kant's conception of an "I think" that "accompan[ies] all my representations" (B131). In this way, the act of apperception corresponds to full clarity of a concept, and anything less implies that no actual apperceptive act is involved. This is, arguably, also in line with Schulting's (2015a:28) characterisation of the distinction obscure/ clear as one pertaining to the intensity of the consciousness, if, unlike Schulting, apperception is taken to be a type of consciousness that has maximal intensity.

We must now ask whether the decoupling I argued for between apprehension/reproduction and recognition creates the space for content which involves no role for concepts in its genesis. It may seem that the answer to this question has already been given as a "yes" insofar as I have claimed that concepts are not necessary for intuitions *tout court*. However, the cognition that non-(objectively) unified intuitions, that is, that of the third level of the Jäsche Logic classification, is characterised by Kant as not being proper cognition, but merely acquaintance (*noscere*). The question therefore is whether such representations really have a content, that is: are they about something?

9.5 Locating Nonconceptual Content

9.5.1 Have We Identified Nonconceptual Content?

The interpretation I have just given chimes with claims made by nonconceptualists insofar as it operates a distinction between the synthesis of recognition in the concept and the roles of apprehension and reproduction. As we saw earlier, nonconceptualists would then want to make use of this to identify a form of nonconceptual cognition. But what exactly is the nature of the cognition at stake here, that is, acquaintance?

The move that Allais (2009:405–6) makes is to view this as cognition of objects that are not full objects of experience, that is, a form of cognition that would also be available to animals. This view recognises that the cognition that Kant focusses upon in the *Critique of Pure Reason* is that of an objective world under the categories, and therefore governed by the principles of the pure understanding. Nevertheless, the objects in this world can be cognised in a weaker sense, that is, not as these full objects of experience, but just as particulars. Here Allais (2009:384) draws upon P. F. Strawson's (1959:15) notion of particular, taking these to be "spatially continuous and unified individuals existing outside the subject and located in space" (Allais 2009:405).

The weakening move is an interesting one, but I do not think that it is the right one. What nonconceptualists are in effect doing is implicitly relying upon the fact that objects of experience are in place to consider some

218   **C. Onof**

other way of accessing *these same objects*. Such a move could be justified on an interpretation of Kant's metaphysics which ignores the central Critical move according to which fully determinate objects are not available to be picked out, but cognition of objects involves their being determined in conformity with the transcendental conditions of experience. The Kantian response to this Strawsonian interpretation is that it leaves unexplained how a subjective mental representation can acquire the status of representation of an object.

But nonconceptualists do not want to revert to such a transcendental realist position. Rather they accept that a priori conditions are required for objects of experience to be possible, but then consider a weaker form of cognition *of the same objects*. So, to simplify, as I understand it, Allais's move involves (i) accepting that, when I perceive, the manifold in intuition *could* be brought under TUA and therefore I know that there are indeterminate objects out there, but (ii) considering some other access to *these same objects* that does not determine them under any empirical concept, but, for instance, identifies them as distinct, or identifies their spatiotemporal relations. And the justification for the possibility of (ii) lies in the distinction between intuition and concept: "It is intuition alone that enables our mental representations to latch on to individual things" (Allais 2009:391). So the justification for talk of perception of mere particulars is that (i) there is a domain of objectivity guaranteed by TUA and the categories, and (ii) objects can be picked out in this domain without necessarily determining them objectively because of the distinction between intuition and concept: with intuition alone, they are identified in terms of what makes them *particulars*, that is, distinguishable from one another, in certain relations in space-time and so on.

So if we accept a sense of "intuition" which is independent of any conceptual contribution, as I have argued for above, it would seem that we should accept this nonconceptualist proposal. There is, however, a problem in (ii), which I have highlighted in italics above: Nonconceptualists need to be able to refer to *the same objects* as could be identified through full cognition. That is doubly problematic: (a) because these objects are left completely indeterminate unless there is an act of apperception, through which *I take them as* having certain properties; (b) because, should nonconceptualists want to appeal to the possibility of such determination

9 Room for Nonconceptual Content?   **219**

as sufficient for their purpose, why would the particulars that are picked out through intuition be items that would be cognised as objects? In support of (b), nonconceptualists might want to appeal to the fact that perceptual associations are objectively grounded: this "*affinity* of the manifold" (A113) rests upon TUA through which "all appearances ... stand in a thoroughgoing connection according to necessary laws" (A113–14). But that is not sufficient to ensure the things we determine in space-time as objects are also those we pick out as particulars: *the objectivity of these particulars has not been established.* We can easily see this by considering how associations can be used to define particulars: if I associate the smell of burning wood with the taste of certain foods (assumed odourless for simplicity), it is open to me to take as particular an item that has that smell and that taste. This is clearly not what nonconceptualists have in mind as particular, but that is because they are relying upon determinate objects being available to "latch on to" (Allais 2009:391) perceptually. However, unless nonconceptualists are relying upon a residual Strawsonian realism, they have to accept that an object determined as φ is only available to me insofar as I have brought the manifold in intuition under the concept of predicate φ. It is not possible for me to have a mere perception of such an object without this determination. In the absence of any conceptual involvement, while this perceptual cognition involves acquaintance with some features of that which affects our senses, it is not a form of cognition that is accessible to apperceptive self-consciousness. It thus only plays a role that can be described, in relation to my cognitive self, as *subpersonal.*

Although particulars are not therefore objects in the sense of *transcendental logic* (that which defines the objective world of appearances), that is, determined under TUA, they are items in my perceptual experience that are objects in the sense of *general logic*,[24] which, as nonconceptualists indicate, are individuated by being distinguished from one another. The term "particular" certainly captures this, but its realist connotations are too strong: they are not grasped *as* objects and are therefore subjective features of the content of my intuitions (this is clarified below). It is just in philosophical reflection upon the content of the nonconceptual

---

[24] This is the sense of "object" Kant uses in the Jäsche Logic classification, e.g. when describing level 4: "Animals are acquainted with objects too, but they do not *cognize* them" (Log, 9:64–5).

220   **C. Onof**

aspects of my experience that the term "object" (general logic) can be used insofar as I am thinking about distinctions within this experience.[25] I shall take what Kant describes as the third level in the Jäsche Logic classification, that is, "represent[ing] something in comparison with other things, both as to *sameness* and as to *difference*" (Log, 9:64–5), as defining a coherent notion of the *perceptual cognition of things* (PCT),[26] whereby the things in question are features of my subjective experience.

9.5.2 PCT and Nonconceptual Content

My proposal here is that, through the acts of apprehension and recognition, we are conscious of particulars defined through patterns of sameness and difference in space, without being conscious of them *as* distinct (which would require the involvement of a more or less clear concept), and therefore without treating them as objects. This is not cognition as Kant analyses it in the *Critique of Pure Reason*, but would amount to a lower form of cognising according to the Jäsche Logic, and insofar as it is completely independent of concepts, therefore defines *nonconceptual content.*

This proposal would have the advantage that it provides a direct answer to the conceptualist's complaint that nonconceptualists fall foul of TD's claim that, as Land puts it succinctly, "all objects of which we can in principle have empirical knowledge instantiate the categories" (Land 2015a:30). The possibility of some particulars that are not identified as

---

[25] Nothing plays the function of transcendental object in relation to these merely logical "objects". *Pace* Allais (2009:412), *there is thus no intentional relation of the subject of knowledge to these "objects"* (since these representations are not within the purview of transcendental apperception).

[26] In terms of the content of the subject's intuitive representations, there is little that distinguishes PCT from content that is brought under an obscure concept through the synthesis of recognition (see Grüne 2009 and note 23 above). The reason is that, since the concept is obscure, there is no clarity as to what the objective determination in question actually is. But the important difference is that, even when the concept involved is obscure, that which I perceive is grasped *as* an instantiation of a general concept, i.e. of a certain type. This means that it is available for further clarification and further determination: the "I think" must be able to accompany the representations that are thereby synthesised. By contrast, in PCT, what is differentiated is not considered in this way: it is not available for further clarification within PCT, or further determination within PCT. It is only through a further cognitive act of synthesis that it could be made accessible to apperception.

objects being cognised—through a form of cognition that is distinct from empirical knowledge—does not directly impinge upon the business of TD.[27]

Nevertheless, a worry now arises, which is that of how PCT stands with respect to the empirical knowledge of objects. A first aspect of this worry, that is, its theoretical form, can be substantiated by referring to Kant's claim in the B-Deduction that all synthesis of apprehension stands under the categories (B160). This claim from the B-Deduction can however immediately be seen as irrelevant to PCT, because there is no synthesis here: as explained above, there is apprehension and reproduction, but these processes are driven by the contingencies of temporal contiguity and associative properties.

A second aspect of this worry is the residual concern that there appear to be two distinct types of entity in my conscious experience: empirical objects and the things that constitute the objects of PCT. Although the latter are objects in a merely logical sense, so that we do not face the problem of "rogue objects" (Hanna 2011b:408), we need to clarify how they are related to the objective empirical domain. For much as these things are subjective because of the subjective nature of the associations that give rise to them, these associative properties are grounded in objective relations between objects. So these things will have properties that derive from objectively determinable properties of objects, but combined with additional subjective features. As indicated above, the smell of burning wood and the taste of certain foods may characterise such a thing in my perceptual experience. I can analyse this by bringing the perceptual experience in question under more or less clear concepts of burning wood, types of food, and so on, that is, by re-apprehending and reproducing the intuitive material I am presented with, but this time with the understanding steering these processes through the synthesis of

---

[27] I am therefore not self-conscious (in Kant's apperceptive sense) in having these representations, and could not be. That does not mean that I am not conscious, however. As such the representations in question are *clear* representations, i.e. representation with consciousness (level 2 of the Jäsche Logic classification). Moreover, there is room for them to be *distinct* on Kant's understanding of "distinctness", that is, for the parts of the representation to be clear (Grüne 2009:81), so that one is thereby aware of what is identical and what is distinct in the representation (level 3 of the Jäsche Logic classification), although this is not necessarily the case for all the parts of the representation, as Kant's famous example of the Milky Way shows (Log, 9:35).

recognition. This ensures that the "objects" of PCT are indeed anchored in what can be determined as empirical objects, although they have no objective features themselves.

This notion of PCT would seem particularly useful to describe how, on a Kantian account, animal perception operates. In a letter to Marcus Herz, Kant in effect describes how representations might be "connected according to empirical laws of association" so that "I am even conscious of each individual representation, but not of their relation to the unity of representation of their object, by means of the synthetic unity of their apperception" (Br, 11:52).[28] Although Kant clearly indicates that we would never "represent objects" (ibid., trans. amended), this leaves room for animal consciousness (McLear 2011), and also infant and some forms of adult consciousness (see Schulting 2015a:113), and thereby awareness of identities and differences in their environment, which is characteristic of PCT. But there is also a role for PCT in specifically human practice that I want to examine briefly in the next section.

9.5.3 The Practical Role of Nonconceptual Content

I want to draw attention to the practical importance of nonconceptual content by briefly outlining how PCT accounts for the development of inclinations which play a key role in our human practice. As Kant indicates, the imagination's role in representing that which is not present is, in particular, at work in bringing about transitions from one representation to another through *association*. By *reproduction* of the previously apprehended representations, one is conscious of a representation of what one is actually presented with, *together* with representations of what is not there. The sensations which constitute the matter of these representations have a subjective dimension which Kant refers to as "feeling" (KU, 5:206). Depending upon whether the associated states of affairs thereby feel more or less pleasant than the actual state of affairs, this *juxtaposition of representations will define inclinations towards or away from* the

---

[28] Cf. McLear (2011:8) and Schulting (2012a:268n.34).

(currently absent) associated states of affairs. This can be seen as important both to moral and phenomenological aspects of our agency.

Starting with the moral aspects, it is well known that Kant's account of agency is dualistic in that it separates a deterministic empirical description of agency guided by inclinations from an intelligible account of free agency in terms of the choice between incentives of duty and inclination (Allison 1990:108). While Kant explains that the agent's behaviour could be fully explained in terms of a set of subjective maxims characterising her empirical character, this does not necessarily imply that the agent is herself aware of such subjective maxims, as we shall see below. This does not, however, take anything away from the agent's ability to act freely as it is established practically in the *Critique of Practical Reason*. All that is required is that, at the intelligible level, the agent be able to choose between acting on inclinations and acting out of duty (see Onof 2011b).

This intelligible choice is however not temporal, and there is therefore no representation in inner sense of how we choose. This can be viewed as a ground for Kant's scepticism about our ability to know what incentive we are actually acting upon (GMS, 4:406–7). Against Kant's scepticism in this matter, one might however argue that inclinations are experienced through the pull they exert upon us. Our tendencies to act upon certain inclinations define the subjective maxims that characterise our empirical character, which forms the centrepiece of Kant's empirical account of agency (A549–50/B577–8). Insofar as these inclinations are experienced by us, one could argue that, when one can eliminate as possible grounds for one's action all the inclinations one is aware of being active, one must therefore be acting from duty (given Kant's motivational dualism).

This is where the inclinations arising in PCT are important because we have no clear consciousness of them *as inclinations*, for the very same reason that, in PCT, we are not conscious of distinctions in our intuitive representations *as distinctions*.[29] As a result, it is not because we can discount any inclination that we are aware of influencing our action that we are not still acting upon other inclinations of which we are not aware.

---

[29] This does not absolve us from full responsibility for our actions because we ought to be actively seeking to do our duty, whatever inclinations we might be aware of or not.

This means that we cannot, after all, know with certainty if we are acting on an inclination or out of duty. So the proposed outline of how inclinations arise in PCT enables us to uphold Kant's scepticism about our real motivations for action.

The phenomenological dimension of agency is at the core of important aspects of the McDowell–Dreyfus debate about how to account for the type of agency characterised by "in-the-flow" behaviour. In this debate, the nature of which is complex in that it involves both descriptive and normative aspects, Hubert Dreyfus claims that "in-the-flow" behaviour, that is, the way in which we operate when we carry out actions that do not require any explicit deliberation, does not involve any role for conceptual representations.[30] PCT, together with the account of how inclinations arise from it, can form the basis of a type of behaviour that would seem to match what Dreyfus understands as "in-the-flow" action: there is no role for concepts, and the inclinations based upon associative properties define a nexus of guides to action that enable the agent to cope with certain tasks without reflection being involved in any way. This connection between PCT and the theme of the McDowell–Dreyfus debate enables us to offer some observations on this debate from a Kantian position, as I interpret it.[31] First, this leads us to concur with Sebastian Gardner's (2013:134) conclusion that, since PCT essentially defines behaviour that is subpersonal with respect to the theoretical subject of experience, it is largely irrelevant to McDowell's concern with the normative dimension of experience.

Second, it is relevant here to note that perception governed by the synthesis of recognition in an obscure concept does not differ much in its experiential dimension from PCT.[32] This observation helps to explain

---

[30] This characterisation of the debate is highly simplified. First, it is unclear exactly what counts as action "in-the-flow", as Dreyfus and McDowell disagree on how specific examples of behaviour should be classified (see McDowell 2013:49). Second, the notion of concept employed in the contemporary debate is broader than Kant's (it includes demonstratives for instance). Third, there is a sense in which these authors are not engaged in the same discussion: whereas McDowell's concerns are ultimately normative, Dreyfus's are about the nature of mental content (see Gardner 2013:110–11).

[31] There are appeals to Kant on both sides of the debate, but mostly in support of McDowell's views (e.g. Pippin 2013:102).

[32] See note 26 above.

why a number of examples discussed by Dreyfus and McDowell are not uncontentiously classifiable under either of the two broad species of action type: concept-involving or not.

These two observations indicate that a mere description of the phenomenology of a type of behaviour is not sufficient to draw conclusions about its conceptual content or whether it involves reference to a subject. While the possibility remains that we should deal with the particular without resorting to the universal has been illustrated with PCT, it is easy to understand how much of our behaviour is likely to involve a reference to the universal insofar as a grasp of how particular things are similar (which would seem essential to the possibility of "in-the-flow" behaviour) can be obtained through a grasp of how these things belong to the same universal species.[33]

9.6   Conclusion

In this chapter, I have examined where, and in what sense, Kant's account of cognition can be said to leave room for nonconceptual content, that is, for mental representations whose genesis features no role for concepts of any kind, although we have some consciousness of them. The main conclusion that emerged from this investigation is that there is no role for any such separable nonconceptual content in the cognition of objects as Kant accounts for it in his Critical period. But Kant's view of the genesis of intuitions does not require that the synthesis of recognition in a concept always be involved, and he clearly emphasises the role of associations in connecting representations in intuition. From this, as well as his contrast between the subjective and objective unities of consciousness, we can infer the possibility of a type of perception (PCT) that does not provide any cognition of objects, but has some nonconceptual content enabling distinctions to be made in one's perceptual experience, so that it can be described as an acquaintance with things in our subjective experience.

---

[33] Such a grasp does not require adopting any detached perspective as Dreyfus (2013:34) claims, since actual apperception is not required here. As Grüne shows (see note 23 above), sensible synthesis under obscure concepts enables such a grasp, for instance through the use of schemata.

A brief examination of the practical implications of the proposed interpretation has shown that Kant's theoretical framework does leave room for "nonconceptual behaviour", that is, behaviour that does not involve any role for a subject of knowledge but is nevertheless relevant to an account of human agency, because of the part played by the inclinations that characterise it. But this should not detract from the conclusion that Kant's theory of cognition's primary focus is the importance of our experience of objects, which is where the normativity of TUA plays a defining role.[34]

---

[34] Dennis Schulting's insightful comments on an earlier draft of this chapter are gratefully acknowledged.

10

On an Older Dispute: Hegel, Pippin and the Separability of Concept and Intuition in Kant

Dennis Schulting

10.1 Introduction

If by conceptualism is roughly understood the thesis that all that can be represented is amenable to being brought under concepts and thus susceptible to judgemental or rational organisation for it to have any normative meaning, there is little doubt that Hegel can be called the quintessential conceptualist since, for Hegel, it can be held, anything that is representable is in principle intelligible—or, "there is nothing in principle unintelligible" (Pippin 2015a:168). The traditional picture that most contemporary philosophers have of Hegel is certainly that of an extreme conceptual or even an ontological *idealist*, who believes, respectively, that everything that is real *must* be able to be thought or is just constituted by what can be thought; or put more radically, that everything in the world is just a product of mental states or acts, or even more implausibly and

---

D. Schulting (✉)
Independent Scholar, Germany
e-mail: ds196901@gmail.com

© The Editor(s) (if applicable) and The Author(s) 2016
D. Schulting (ed.), *Kantian Nonconceptualism*,
DOI 10.1057/978-1-137-53517-7_10

227

mysteriously, that everything simply emanated from some cosmic mind. Scores of text passages in Hegel's corpus could be quoted that, out of context, at least appear to show Hegel's strong conceptualism about the possibility of representational content, or even about the very possibility of having sensations, which, if only inchoately, contain already a rational capacity or the seeds for their being understood rationally (e.g. in the famous chapter on Sense Certainty in the *Phenomenology of Spirit*).

A crucial aspect of Hegel's conceptualism—and one that I shall concentrate on here—is that he also explicitly says, both in early work such as *Faith and Knowledge* and in his magnum opus the *Science of Logic*, that it is inspired by Kant's form of conceptualism, particularly its emphasis on the central constitutive role of subjectivity. This would seem to mean that, if we take Hegel at his word when he says that, in a certain respect, he builds on Kant, and assuming Hegel's strong conceptualism (in its more plausible variant), it is prima facie ruled out that Kant himself can be read as a nonconceptualist, if by the latter is meant the thesis that, at least, not all that can be represented *must* be brought under concepts,[1] or put in the terms that Kant uses, that not all intuitions must be brought under concepts, in order for representations or intuitions *to be* what they are (whatever they are or represent). Or, of course, Kant is indeed a nonconceptualist and Hegel is fundamentally mistaken about Kant's conceptualism. In reality, the contrasts are not as stark as this disjunction suggests. Hegel's relation to Kant is rather complex. This is already indicated by Hegel's frequent qualifications of his Kantianism, that is, that in his view Kant's conceptualism or idealism is not yet the right kind of, or is an inadequate, conceptualism or idealism and must be amended. And the caricatures of Hegel that I mentioned at the outset are of course just that: Hegel's own positive story is much more nuanced and complicated, and also philosophically valuable, than the traditional view of it has us believe. But to keep my account here relatively straightforward, I shall focus on Hegelian criticisms of Kant, specifically those advanced by Robert Pippin since his seminal book *Hegel's Idealism* (Pippin 1989), and examine to what extent these criticisms are, at least to some extent, misguided or misleading, and shall leave a more favourable delinea-

---

[1] This is not the same as saying that no nonconceptual content *could* be brought under concepts.

tion of Hegel's revisionist Kantianism for another occasion.[2] I shall also here largely leave out issues of idealism, so as not to complicate matters, although of course Hegel's form of conceptualism is very much intertwined with his so-called absolute idealism.

In this chapter, I am specifically interested in how, following Hegel's critique of Kant in the aforementioned works, recent Hegelians have read Kant's claims in the Transcendental Deduction of the categories (TD), in particular the claim that there is a synthetic a priori connection between the intuition of objects and their conceptualisation; or, to put it in the famous words of Kant, that intuition and concepts must be conjoined to enable knowledge, otherwise intuitions remain blind and concepts empty (A51–2/B75–6). Hegelians think that in TD Kant effectively "compromise[s]" (Sedgwick 1993:275)[3] the distinction he stipulates at A51/B75, that he "waver[s] on the strict separability of concept and intuition" (Pippin 2015b:74). For if the argument of TD, in particular in its B-version, is that the categories are not only the necessary conditions under which I *think* objects, by virtue of applying concepts, but also the necessary conditions under which *anything is first given in sensibility*, the fixed separation of concepts and intuitions seems incompatible with the very aim and conclusion of TD. The way this argument is framed is based on a phrase that Kant uses in the important introductory section of the so-called "second step" of the B-Deduction (§21), where he says that in

> the sequel … it will be shown *from the way in which the empirical intuition is given in sensibility* that its unity can be none other than the one the category prescribes to the manifold of a given intuition in general according to the preceding §20. (B144–5; emphasis added)

Pippin, as one of the most prominent Hegelians who has written extensively on Hegel's Kantianism, takes this phrase as an indication

---

[2] In a planned work on Hegel's *Science of Logic*, I expand on the positive story of Kant's influence on Hegel. A more detailed interpretation of the early Hegel's critique of Kant in *Faith and Knowledge*, in particular, is given in Schulting (2017), Chap. 8.

[3] Sedgwick (1993) comes very much to the defence of Kant, but in other work (Sedgwick 1992, 1997, 2000, 2001, 2004, 2005, 2012) she defends Hegel's reading of Kant (and also that by Hegelians such as McDowell). See Schulting (2016).

that Kant's separation of intuition and concept, when read in the context of the argument of TD, is not as strict as it seems. Similarly, the distinction between receptivity, as the form of sensibility, and spontaneity is rendered problematic, if it is the case that Kant argues that the spontaneity of the understanding "determine[s] sensibility inwardly" (Pippin 1989:28–9).

In the following, I want to examine these charges by looking more closely at Pippin's reading of TD. Pippin believes the orthodox Kant cannot be retained, if we want to extract something of philosophical value from TD; he wants to focus on "the Kant that can speak to us"[4] (Pippin 2015b:75). Heeding Hegel's so-called immanent criticism of Kant (Sedgwick 1993:273) shows us a Kantianism beyond the strictures of the orthodox Kant: a Kantian conceptualism shorn of the remaining nonconceptualist tendencies, which are in fact antithetical to the spirit of the Critical revolution. I believe, however, that we must retain the orthodox Kant, including its nonconceptualist tendencies, in order not to succumb to an intemperate conceptualism, the sort of which, rightly or wrongly, solicited the caricatures of Hegel I mentioned at the beginning.

In Sects. 10.2 and 10.3, I address some more general issues relating to the separability of concept and intuition. Subsequently, in Sect. 10.4, I bring the problems underlying Pippin's conceptualist reading of separability to bear on a key section (§26) in the second half of the B-Deduction, where, in a notorious but pivotal footnote, it seems that Pippin thinks Kant is wavering most clearly on the strict separability of concept and intuition, as well as on the distinction between spontaneity and receptivity. I think that the textual and philosophical evidence rather points to the necessity of a nonconceptualist remainder that is compatible with Kant's overall conceptualist aims.

---

[4] I am not sure if such tendentious, ahistorical validations are a good start in helping us *understand* Kant's position, as it runs the risk of begging his question or at least missing (some of) its essential elements. Philosophical evaluation is dependent on faithful interpretative work. In reality, however, Pippin's reading is much more heedful of strictly interpretative issues than his statement suggests.

10.2 Distinguishability and Inseparability

Pippin wants to exorcise a picture of Kant's argument about the cooperation between the capacities for intuitions and concepts that takes that cooperation to consist in an application of concepts *to* an already given manifold in intuition, so that the received intuition is exogenous to the conceptual activity, or that any judgement is based on what was first a mere nonconceptual representation. Secondly, Pippin argues that the relation to objects is not "'secured' *by* receptivity, by the deliverances of sensibility, *alone*" (2015a:168). Only the conjoining of concepts and intuitions fixes the relation to objects; hence, concepts and intuitions are inseparable, insofar as the relation to an object is concerned. The nonconceptualist thesis that intuitions have a separable role to play in establishing knowledge might indeed be seen as entertaining the idea that concepts are applied to intuitions exogenously, namely, to already more or less determinate given particulars (see e.g. Allais 2009:391). Moreover, nonconceptualists might indeed appear to be committed to the view that intuition already "secures" a relation to the object, even before categorially governed determination, in an actual judgement, further determines the given object *as* having certain properties (see e.g. Allais 2009:384). Kant does of course argue that an intuition *gives* us the object immediately (A320/B377; Prol, 4:281; A68/B93), but at the same time, according to Kant, the "relation ... to an object" (B137), which is a "determinate relation", is solely a function of judging,[5] so what secures the relation to an object in the strict sense, *in addition* to the (equally) necessary *immediate* relation provided by the intuition (which is a relation in the weaker, non-explicit or indeterminate sense),[6] is a judging. Securing the connection with the object is therefore achieved by virtue of the act of judging, not through receptivity (intuition). This is what Pippin says is expressed by the Hegelian claim that "it is only because our uptake of the sensory world is already conceptually articulated that these deliverances [of sensibility] can assume a justificatory

---

[5] See Schulting (2017), Chaps. 3–4.

[6] Cf. A19/B33. As Kant says here, the relation that an intuition has to the object is an immediate one, consistent with the definition of an intuition as designating immediacy. But this relation (*Beziehung*) is only "secured" as a relation proper, a *determined* relation, by the functions of the understanding.

232   D. Schulting

role", and thus that "thought's relation to ... objects cannot be secured or *even intuitionally* pinned down, by the deliverances of sensibility alone" (Pippin 2015a:168; emphasis added).[7]

The nonconceptualist reading of intuition as separably providing the relation to an object is also problematic in the sense that on that reading it is difficult to fathom how Kant can be taken to have established a synthetic *a priori connection between* concepts, more precisely, the categories, and intuitions. A post hoc application of categories to pre-given intuitions is not a priori, but simply a posteriori—quite the contrary of what Kant is aiming for in his analysis of the possibility of knowledge of objects.[8] The nonconceptualist reading cannot explain the way in which the understanding and sensibility *do cooperate* so that knowledge arises out of this combined effort. We would not be able to explain how the categories are in fact not just the necessary (and sufficient) conditions of our thought of an object, but also the necessary conditions of the intuition of objects. In this light, Pippin seems right to stress the *inseparability* of conceptuality and intuitions. The inseparability of conceptuality and intuitions is most clearly shown by Kant's *Leitfaden*, which says that

> the same function that gives unity to the different representations *in a judgment* also gives unity to the mere synthesis of different representations *in an intuition*, which, expressed generally, is called the pure concept of understanding. The same understanding, therefore, and indeed by means of the very same actions through which it brings the logical form of a judgment

---

[7] I agree with Pippin here, insofar as nonconceptualists tend to see, wrongly, intuition as functioning wholly separately from a priori concepts in securing reference to particulars. The relation that intuitions have to objects, as Kant indeed suggests they do (A19/B33), is an immediate one, where the relata, object and intuition, are entirely undifferentiated; this relation is only first determined *as* a relation in the strict sense (the way that Kant uses the term *Beziehung* at B137, as a "determinate relation"), namely, a relation between two *differentiable* items, a subject of intuition and the object of intuition, by the determining act of the understanding.

[8] Cf. Pippin (1989:85). Hegel in fact accuses Kant himself of subverting his own idea of a productive imagination as an original a priori synthesis by regarding it in the end as just an act of the understanding, which Hegel regards as a derivative, a posteriori, act in comparison to the imagination (for details, see Schulting 2017, Chap. 8). This putatively shows that Kant sees the relation between concept and intuition purely as a "mechanical relation of a unity of self-consciousness which stands *in antithesis to* the empirical manifold, either determining it or reflecting on it" (GuW, 4:343; emphasis added), thus seeing the relation not as genuinely a priori and as an organic unity holding opposites together (cf. WL, 12:22–3).

10 Separability of Concept and Intuition 233

into concepts by means of the analytical unity, also brings a transcendental content into its representations by means of the synthetic unity of the manifold in intuition in general, on account of which they are called pure concepts of the understanding that pertain to objects *a priori*. (A79/B104–5)

As Kant writes here, it is not only that representations are united so as to form concepts, serviceable in judgements, by a unifying function of the understanding, that is, by certain "actions" of the understanding, but these same "actions" also unify manifolds of representations in *intuition*, and hence are called categories that pertain to objects given in sensibility in an a priori manner. These "actions" connect concepts and intuition at the fundamental level. It is one and the same set of actions that *originally and simultaneously* form concepts that serve as predicates in judgement *and* unite intuitional representations that are the correlate of perceived objects. In this way, Kant here, in the run-up to TD, indicates a guiding thread to finding the *synthetic a priori* connection between intuitions of objects and concepts, whose function or set of functions (the same "actions") *ex hypothesi* cannot be shared out *between* concepts and intuitions: the synthetic a priori connection, provided by a unifying action of the understanding, is rather the original intermediary or "third thing", as Kant calls it elsewhere (A155/B194), which binds concept and intuition. Thus, the roles that concept and intuition play *in* this synthetic a priori connection that is due to *one* function (or *one* set of functions, i.e. the combined categorial forms of synthesis) cannot be *separated* into distinct "components that belong severally to sensibility and understanding" (McDowell 2009:124), on pain of inviting an infinite regress that would ensue as a result of asking which even more originary function would bind the separate components.

However, notwithstanding the valid reasons for not allowing room for a notion of nonconceptual content that is separably contributory to knowledge, there are some apparent problems with Pippin's belief that the "strict *putative* separability between the sensory deliverance of a manifold of appearances and the conceptual conditions of unity really is *not* a possibility". He sees showing this impossibility as "the goal of the deduction" (Pippin 2015b:71), and at the same time this goal, namely, the ultimate inseparability of intuition and concept, is incompatible with Kant's

234   D. Schulting

own "fixed", a priori formal separation between the two components. In a typical Hegelian move, Pippin thus urges Kant's readers to go beyond Kant's own formulations, whilst heeding the innermost principles of his thought, be mindful of the "spirit" of Kant, and not be bound by the letter. Pippin writes:

> If it turns out, as it begins to seem in the second-edition deduction, to be impossible to consider the intuited manifold "purely" and as a separable component of any knowledge claim, if "what presents themselves to the senses" must be considered always already conceptually articulated and that conceptual articulation cannot be considered an immediately *given* aspect of the manifold as such, then *any a priori claim about the fixed, necessary conditions of receptivity and thereby strong objectivity in experience … cannot be made in the terms originally proposed by Kant.* In Hegelian terms, this means there cannot be a fixed, a priori determinable separation between the subject of experience on one side and some formal consideration of all possible deliverances of sensibility on the other; or, more familiarly, the subject and the object side of this equation are far too intertwined to allow one to say that what the subject side requires from the object side can never be contravened by any deliverances from the object side. (Pippin 2015b:72–3; emphasis added)[9]

Pippin here refers to the conclusion of the B-Deduction, namely §26, specifically the notorious note to B160, where indeed it seems that, as Pippin puts it, the categories "determine sensibility inwardly" (1989:28), seemingly undermining the strictness of the separability of at least spontaneity and receptivity, because it is here that they appear to intertwine inextricably. It would appear though that seeing the goal of TD the way Pippin does conflates two different kinds of enabling condition, which Kant keeps clearly separate even in that difficult footnote, that is, the conditions for "merely" intuiting something in space (the conditions of sensibility) and the conditions of *representing* something *determinate* in space,

---

[9] Sedgwick (2012) likewise argues that Hegel takes Kant to task for the fixation of the separability of form and content, which in Hegel's view is unsustainable, if one is to take seriously the Kantian invention of a truly original-synthetic unity of form and content, spontaneity of the understanding and receptivity of sensibility. I briefly discuss the unresolved contradictions in Sedgwick's Hegelian reading of Kant in Schulting (2016).

10 Separability of Concept and Intuition   235

respectively, and relatedly, two different ways of construing the argument of the conclusion—the latter concerns the modality of Kant's argument. I briefly discuss the footnote, and the conclusion of the B-Deduction, in Sect. 10.4.

However, less ambivalently, Kant does appear to insist quite explicitly on the separability (or distinguishability[10]) of concept and intuition in a famous passage at A51/B75. This is a crucial passage that conceptualists and nonconceptualists alike cite as evidence for their respective readings:

> Neither of these properties [sensibility and understanding] is to be preferred to the other. Without sensibility no object would be given to us, and without understanding none would be thought. Thoughts without content are empty, intuitions without concepts are blind. It is thus just as necessary to make the mind's concepts sensible (i.e., to add an object to them in intuition) as it is to make its intuitions understandable (i.e., to bring them under concepts). Further, these two faculties or capacities cannot exchange their functions. The understanding is not capable of intuiting anything, and the senses are not capable of thinking anything. Only from their unification can cognition arise. But on this account one must not mix up their roles, rather one has great cause to separate [*abzusondern*] them carefully from each other and distinguish [*unterscheiden*] them. (A51–2/B75–6)

Pippin says the passage has "a dialectical and somewhat unstable form", for "*both* distinctness *and* necessary intertwining (inseparability in any claim to knowledge) are emphasized" (2005:25). At any rate, according to Pippin, Kant does not mean to say here "that we are first subject to blind intuitions which can be said to become 'informing' and 'guiding' intuitions 'after' concepts are applied to them" (2013:102). The argument about the possibility of objective experience as grounded in the cooperation between intuition and concepts should not be understood as if there

---

[10] Pippin differentiates distinguishability (or "notional separability"; 2015b:67) from separability (see Pippin 2005; also 2013:162): formally, concept and intuition are of course "distinguishable", but in actual fact, in experience, they are never separable. Or so Pippin argues. It is important to note, in light of criticism by some nonconceptualists (Allais 2009), that by inseparability Pippin (and also McDowell 1996:9, *et passim*) does not mean that intuition does not have a distinctive and distinct role to play in cognition, but rather that the distinctive role it plays is inseparable from the role concepts play; they play their roles together.

were "a move or transition of any sort *from* a perceptual uptake [construed as being in a state with nonconceptual content] *to* a judgmental state of conceptual content [understood as a result of a separable cognitive function]" (Pippin 2005:29).[11] That would indeed be contrary to Kant's aim to explain the possibility of synthetic *a priori* knowledge. The idea of nonconceptual content that informs our cognition, and *becomes* specifically intentional, or comes to have objective purport, *after* concepts have been applied to it, has the appearance of being a posteriori, rather than a priori, as noted earlier. Thus, "there are no blind intuitions, waiting to be conceptualized". "Kant means to be rejecting the idea of nonconceptual content, not specifying its initial blindness. Blind intuitions are no more determinate intuitions than dead eyes are eyes", says Pippin (2013:102). For this reason, Pippin points out the "'blurring' of the strictness of the distinct roles [concept and intuition] should play in cognition … not … its elimination" (2005:30). The issue is to refute a "strict *separation* claim", not indistinguishability per se, according to Pippin.[12]

But it is unclear to me what the difference between separability and distinguishability is supposed to suggest, the more so because Kant seems to identify "separating" (*absondern*) with "distinguishing" (*unterscheiden*) concept and intuition. What does it mean to say that Kant cannot uphold a "strict separation claim" concerning concept and intuition? Kant clearly says that they must be differentiated, cannot be confused, that is, cannot exchange their functions, *whilst* they must also be conjoined for cognition to arise. It is unclear what is meant by strictness and what the problem with it amounts to. Does it mean that, although concept and intuition are formally distinguishable—since, of course, an intuition is a singular representation, whereas a concept is always a general or universal representation, and so by definition they are irreducible to each other (A320/B376–7)—they are not really distinct or separate, because in reality, that is, in cognition, the understanding as the conceptual capacity and sensibility as the capacity for having intuitions *must* always cooperate?

---

[11] This is in direct contrast to how Gareth Evans pictures the relation between sense content and conceptualisation (see Evans 1982:227).

[12] Pippin says that Hegel's critique is concerned with the "strictness" of the distinction (2005:30n.19), not with the distinction per se.

10 Separability of Concept and Intuition 237

Pippin's reading suggests that, notwithstanding their irreducible defining characteristics, there is a necessary entailment between intuition and concept, that is, that intuitions *always* entail conceptualisation. However, the reciprocality between the manifold in intuition and conceptuality—the activity of the apperceiving "I"—holds only *insofar as* this "I" indeed apperceives (for herself) the manifold that is before her. To this extent and this extent only, intuition and concept are indeed inseparable. This, I contend, is indicated by an implicit conditional contained in Kant's remark that "only from their unification can cognition arise", that is, the conditional that if there should be cognition, then concept and intuition are unified. The cooperation of which Kant speaks does not obtain because conceptuality is always already, as it turns out, necessarily contained in intuition, but because of the biconditional claim that *if and only if* intuition should yield cognition, then it is necessarily connected with concepts. This connection happens, just because the subject *takes* the manifold in intuition as her own (this is often also stressed by Pippin). This shows that intuition is not *necessarily* conjoined with concepts *simpliciter*, that is, absolutely. Kant does not deviate from the strict separation of concept and intuition, as both have very distinct and distinctive roles to play in their cooperation to yield knowledge, and because intuitions *need* not be unified with concepts in all cases (cf. A90–1/B123). Intuitions are not intrinsically disposed to being brought under concepts; this is why in fact Kant needs a deduction to show that, despite their irreducible natures, they must be considered conjoined in the specific case of objective knowledge. But there is no "blurring", no "lessening" or "weakening" of the strictness of the separability (or distinguishability), and the strictness of the separability of concept and intuition is not incompatible with their necessary cooperation in the case of knowledge.

There is also a problem with Pippin's admission that there is indeed a "notional separability between intuitional and conceptual elements in experience—albeit one entertained in order to be denied" (Pippin 2015b:67, also 71, 73), referring to an oft-discussed passage in §14 of TD at A89–91/B122–3, where Kant suggests the possibility of separability, which conceptualists argue is eventually, when we reach the conclusion of TD, ruled out. Pippin does not think reference to this passage by nonconceptualists is warranted, as it does not settle the issue of whether it is possible to intuit *an object* independently of concepts. In Pippin's view, Kant is not here endorsing the viewpoint that there could be nonconceptual content, but talks "rather only about the nonconceptual, *formal* aspects of any *relation* to an object", and these intuitional features can of course not "be attributed to the results of the understanding's determination" (Pippin 2015a:165). Notwithstanding Pippin's rightful observation that, at A89–91/B122–3, there is no suggestion about the possibility of "a *cognitively* significant pre-conceptual experience of an *object*" (2015a:165; emphasis added), I think that he misses Kant's conclusion that, independently of concepts, "appearances would nonetheless offer objects to our intuition"(A91/B123), even if this would only yield a "blind play of representations" (A112) with no objective validity. In earlier work (Schulting 2015b), I have argued in detail why the strongly conceptualist reading of this passage must be dismissed on textual grounds alone.

There is an implicit conceptualist bias in Pippin's analysis, both of A51/B75 and A89–91/B122–3, in the very manner that he analyses the relation between intuition and concept: namely, intuition presumably can only be relevantly considered from a conceptualising perspective, so must already be conceptual in some sense, and can therefore not really be considered, formally, in separation from concepts—but this just begs the question against Kant's strict separation between intuition and concepts.

10.3 The Short Argument Towards Inseparability

One of the reasons why Pippin thinks that the strict separability cannot be upheld harks back to an argument that Hegel adopts from Fichte, and which is often employed by Hegelians to refute Kant's restriction thesis, that is, the idealist thesis that we cannot know things in themselves (see e.g. Sedgwick 1993:276–8). In relation to the argument of TD and abstracting from issues concerning idealism, the idea is that the categories are not just

10 Separability of Concept and Intuition   239

mere subjective requirements of thought imposed on the "matter" of sensible intuition because the very possibility of *determinate conceptual content* at all, even in the intuitional presence of the world to consciousness, requires both categorical and intuitional conditions. (Pippin 2015b:71; emphasis added)

Apart from an ambiguity here in the italicised phrase (which I address later, in Sect. 10.4, in relation to the conclusion of the B-Deduction), Pippin means to say that there could not be intuitional content that has any cognitive relevance, if it were not already conceptually laden. This is made clearer by what he asserts next:

There could be "nothing" contrary to these conditions because such a putative exception could not even be a content of thought; it would be "less than a dream". (Pippin 2015b:71)

In a footnote, he adds that such "a putative exception could *not* be, ultimately, a content of thought, because it could not be self-ascribable by an apperceptive subject continuous in all its experiences" (Pippin 2015b:71n.25). The implication is that Kant insufficiently appreciates the intertwinement of concept and content, where in a discursive logic such as that of Kant concepts as mere forms of unity (analytic universals) rely on exogenous material content for their objective validity. But his own argument in TD, presumably, shows that whereas concepts that have objective validity do indeed rely on externally, independently given content, that content must in its turn be apprehended and conceptually recognised *by an apperceptive subject* as that content; so external content can only count as external content from the perspective of the subject apprehending it as a necessary complement in her act of cognition. In other words, the externally, independently given content only counts as such *just because* a subject apprehends it as her own. *Outside* the perspective of the apprehending subject, the external content fulfils no cognitive role, and could in fact be said to come down to nothing, at any rate "less than a dream". With that last phrase, Pippin refers to a passage in the A-Deduction, where significantly, it says:

The possibility, even the necessity of these categories rests on the relation that the entire sensibility, and with it also all possible appearances, have to the original apperception, in which everything is necessarily in agreement with the conditions of the thoroughgoing unity of self-consciousness, i.e., must stand under universal functions of synthesis, namely of the synthesis in accordance with concepts, as that in which alone apperception can demonstrate *a priori* its thoroughgoing and necessary identity. Thus the concept of a cause is nothing other than a synthesis ... *in accordance with concepts*; and without that sort of unity, which has its rule *a priori*, and which subjects the appearances to itself, thoroughgoing and universal, hence necessary unity of consciousness would not be encountered in the manifold perceptions. But these would then belong to no experience, and would consequently be without an object, and would be nothing but a blind play of representations, i.e., less than a dream. (A111–12)

Kant's argument here is—and we shall have cause to return briefly to this passage in Sect. 10.4, when we come to discuss B160—that without the categories no necessary unity would be encountered in the manifold of appearances, which would then not amount to *experience*, and would be without a relation to an object. Without the categories, grounded in the identity of the apperceiving subject, representations would thus have no objective representational content; they would be just a "blind play of representations".

The Fichtean heritage of the above Hegelian reasoning regarding inseparability, which is a short-argument version of Kant's longer argument leaving out the categories as the constitutive elements of the objective content, is nicely put by Sally Sedgwick:

Any content taken to be independently given is in fact no more than a product of the "I think's" act of self-limitation—of positing in addition to the "I", the "not-I". *Any* content for thought is the product of the self's a priori determinations, even if that content is supposed to represent what is external to or independent of the self. (Sedgwick 1993:276)

The Fichtean point is that, however much there is something that is not the self, namely sense content, even if independently given (Sedgwick 2012), such content does not have cognitive relevance except by way of the self's knowing

10 Separability of Concept and Intuition 241

or determining it as *her* content, by way of the self's self-determination (where determination must *also* be taken literally as a negation).[13] Thus, as Sedgwick says, "there can be no thought-content for us which is independent of [formal] determinations" (1993:276), indeed, "all content available to consciousness is necessarily subject to the determinations of form, and … therefore [we] have no access—not even in *thought*— to what may lie outside those determinations" (1992:158).[14] Pippin takes this to imply that the a priori identity between subject and object—an identity that lies at the heart of Kant's thought of the original-synthetic unity of apperception as a principle, not just of *representation* of objects, but also of the *objects* themselves, a claim most clearly advanced at B138 (cf. Pippin 2015b:71; 2005:32)[15]—must be more radically interpreted than Kant himself seems to allow. That is to say, in Pippin's view the fixed separation between concepts and intuition is incompatible with Kant's truest insight into the original identity of the subject and object of thought. Hence, the Hegelian overtures of shifting the separability of concept and intuition to *within* the domain of the conceptual: any difference is only determinable within identity, and so is *relative* rather than *absolute* or *fixed*, or, in Hegel's original terms, Kant's original-synthetic unity

---

[13] What Fichte says is actually more radical than this. In his *Versuch zu einer neuen Darstellung zur Wissenschaftslehre* from 1797/98, Fichte has explicit recourse to Kant in support of refuting the at the time widely held belief that his *Wissenschaftslehre* is not authentically Kantian, and offers his own interpretation of Kantian themes, which are relevant to the present topic. With reference to B136, where Kant says that "all the manifold of intuition stand under conditions of the original synthetic unity of apperception", Fichte writes the following: "That something intuited is *thought* is only possible under the condition that the possibility of the original unity of apperception can exist thereby, and, I infer further—since according to Kant the intuition is also only possible by being thought and understood, while according to him <u>intuition without concept is blind</u>, <u>that is</u>, <u>is nothing at all</u>—therefore the intuition itself stands under the conditions of the possibility of thinking, not only thought in an immediate fashion, but by virtue of the latter also the intuiting conditioned by it, hence *all consciousness*, stands under the conditions of the original unity of apperception" (W, I,4:227–8; trans. mine, my underlining). For a critical assessment of the Fichtean legacy of reading Kant's principle of apperception, see Ameriks (2000), esp. Chap. 5.

[14] I discuss Sedgwick's own, more recent, take on these issues concerning the relation between Kant and Hegel in my review of her book (Sedgwick 2012) in Schulting (2016).

[15] I agree with Pippin's radically literal interpretation here, where most Kantians attempt to explain away any constitutive talk here. Kant's account in TD is not about a "subjective unavoidability" but constitutes a "strong objectivity claim". That is, "Kant will try to establish such objectivity by insisting that the categories *constitute* what any possible relation to an object could be, and so what any object in possible relation to us could be" (2005:32). This indeed goes beyond, as Pippin says (2005:32), the claim that for objects to be *knowable* to us, they must conform to our forms of knowledge. See my own account, also in relation to Pippin, in Schulting (2017), Chaps. 3–4.

is an "identity of identity and difference";[16] this means that the difference or distinction between concept and intuition comes only to the fore within the theoretical *a priori* perspective, from the conceptual point of view.

But I think that this conclusion is too hasty—not least because it seems to be saying that, contradictorily and question-beggingly, the position of nonconceptualism is only first possible if one assumes the truth of conceptualism! The Fichtean line of reasoning is at least ambiguous about the precise kind of conditions we are talking about in the claim that there is an entailment relation between sense content and the self's conceptual determinations. Two different arguments can be discerned, namely, arguing that

(A) Any (sensible) content for thought is a product of thought's self-limitation or determination;

and that

(B) Any (sensible) content is a product of thought's self-limitation or determination.

Fichte, and following him Hegel and the Hegelians, seems to slide from "any content *for thought*" to "any content". Argument A contains a claim about what is epistemologically necessary for any content to be a thought content, namely, that it should be a product of the self's own determination (in good Kantian: that it should be "apperceivable" by a self). In argument B, there is an implicit claim about the constitutive condition of content *tout court*, namely, that it only *exists* as a product of thought's self-determination.[17] Where self-determination is understood as saying that sensible content is determined as the not-self, or what is other than thought, it is trivially true—from a Critical perspective, at least—that any content that is *for thought* is the product of thought's self-determination, namely, insofar as the content is *thought about as*

---

[16] I expand on the details of Hegel's reading in Schulting (2017), Chap. 8.

[17] And this is in fact what Fichte believes. See the quotation from the 1797 *Wissenschaftslehre* in note 13.

10 Separability of Concept and Intuition 243

not-being-thought, or being other-than-thought. This should be understood in the sense that, as Pippin says, "the distinction between what we take to be the case and what is the case is *one we make*, in response to what we learn about the world, not an intrusion from outside that happens to us, whatever that could mean" (2015a:164). In other words, any content *for us*, that is, relevant to us, is a content *we* make relevant for ourselves. There is of course no question of us, as rational agents, literally producing our own sense content—rather, the *distinction* between the content and ourselves, and so *its* relevance to us, is one we make, not the content *an sich*. But it is of course not trivially true that just any content is the product of thought's self-determination, if such content is not content *for thought*, for it is trivially true that content that is *not thought about* is not a product of thought's self-determination.[18]

Pippin obviously realises that there could, in principle at least, as a possibility entertained, be content ("putative content") that is not the product of thought, but, as we saw earlier, such content would, according to Pippin, be "less than a dream", since it would "not be self-ascribable by an apperceptive subject continuous in all its experiences" (2015b:71n.25).[19] I agree to the extent that such content would not be relevant to us, and so *ex hypothesi* it would not be content determined by us. But I think we should be careful not to infer from the unthinkability of "putative content" that contravenes the conditions under which that content is thought, which, again, is a trivial truth, that *that* content could not *exist* (in some mind, albeit not *for a self aware of her mind's contents*), regardless of strict epistemic relevance.[20]

---

[18] Cf. Schulting (2015b:570).

[19] I agree with Pippin that reference to animal "experience" is not going to help here. In Pippin (2013), he explicates what he sees as a fundamental difference between the way human beings and animals perceive. See e.g. Pippin's interesting reference to his non-apperceiving dog Molly in Pippin (2013:101–2). Cf. McDowell (1996:64, 182–3).

[20] Notice that I am of course not here charging Pippin with conflating the existence of a particular intuition X with the condition of X being conceptualised. Indeed, Pippin argues that "X cannot be representationally significant except as Y'ed" does not imply "There are no X's; there is only Y'ing" (2005:27n.8). This points to his insistence that inseparability does not mean indistinguishability, to avoid any neo-Leibnizian style reductive conceptualism. That intuitions must be conceptualised in order for knowledge to arise does of course not mean that intuitions are just confused concepts,

244   D. Schulting

I think that Pippin's qualification that neither Hegel nor Fichte aim to "*eliminate* the idea of a 'not-self'" and that "in Fichte there is always a 'shock' delivered *to* the I's self-positing" is a welcome one. But his emphasis on the fact that "*what comes to count as* a determinate not-self, experienced as such for the self, is always a matter of conceptual determination" and that "the distinction between self and not-self is ... one always resulting from a theoretical view of the self-world relation" (1993:291; emphasis added)[21] might appear to downplay the essential distinction between epistemological and existential type claims, that

---

that intuitions and concepts cannot really be distinguished. But by employing the terminology "representationally significant", Pippin fudges the difference between representing by means of an intuition, as one species of representation, and representing by means of a concept, as another species of representation (cf. the *Stufenleiter* at A320/B376–7), whilst thus suggesting that *any* representing entails conceptualisation. A lot hinges on what "representationally significant" is supposed to convey. If it means that a brute, say, cannot have a representation, in *any* significant sense (to him, even if in a very limited way), of an object that is a house without employing the concept "house"—an object which anyone familiar with houses would normally recognise as "a dwelling established for men" (Log, 9:33)—then the requirement that "X cannot be representationally significant except as Y'ed" seems too strong, where by Y we understand "conceptualised". For clearly Kant suggests (in the passage at issue in the Jäsche Logic) that there are two real possibilities: either one represents the house by way of intuition *only* (*bloße Anschauung*), as the brute does, or one represents the house by way of *both* intuition and concept (*Anschauung und Begriff zugleich*) (Log, 9:33). The brute's seeing (intuiting) the house without knowing that he sees a house because he is not acquainted with the concept "house" is not "representationally" *insignificant* in the sense that he does not represent at all—in fact, Kant calls the brute's seeing a form of cognition (*Erkenntniß*). His seeing the house by means of intuition alone would only not be "representationally" significant in the sense of seeing the house by way of *both* intuition and concept inseparably (*zugleich*), namely, "determinately". The distinction between these two ways of being "representationally significant" is fudged by the Hegelian. Of course, Pippin could rejoin that the example of the brute does not at all provide a convincing ground for denying the inseparability thesis, for the brute could very well be incapable of assigning the right property or *empirical* concept ("house") to what he intuits, while nonetheless the view can be endorsed that the brute's intuitional representations must at any rate be taken to instantiate *pure* concepts, the categories, in order even to be able to intuit the object that he sees. This would then still suggest that intuition and *pure* concepts (which is what Kant effectively means at A51–2/B75–6, not empirical concepts) are inseparable, and that thus *anything* that is "representationally significant" presupposes conceptualisation in the specific Kantian sense of being subsumed under the categories. But I think that the Jäsche example at any rate shows that a kind of representation (intuiting) is possible that does not require an occurrent conceptualisation (in the sense of applying empirical concepts).

[21] See also Pippin (1989:31): "We are here shifting from an account of thought's relation to the pure manifold of intuition to thought's 'self-determination'. ...This does not at all eliminate the role of the given in knowledge, but it will radically relativize to 'thought' the ways in which the given *can be taken to be given*" (emphasis added).

10 Separability of Concept and Intuition   245

is, the difference between claims A and B explicated above, or at least to silently sanction a slide from the one claim to the other.[22] And, as we shall see in the next section, it appears that Pippin does need the stronger (implicitly) existential claim B, when considering Kant's central claim in §26 of TD, that the very "way in which the empirical intuition is given in sensibility" (B144) is necessarily in accord with categorial determination—a lot here is dependent on how one interprets "empirical intuition".[23] I take it Pippin does not want to read this claim as amounting to the triviality of A, but wants a stronger claim which encompasses "anything given in sensibility", not just "any objects given in sensibility", precisely because so much hangs on the fact that the apperception principle is, as Pippin rightly emphasises, not just a subjective principle of representability or analytic thought, but an objective, constitutive principle that *first establishes* what it is to conceive of an "object" and thereby fixes the relation to an object (see e.g. Pippin 1993:293; 2015b:71–2)—so objects cannot just be assumed to be *already given in sensibility*, so that the categories are subsequently *merely* applied to these. But we must tread carefully here. I address this important issue in the next section, when discussing Kant's foremost important argument in TD, namely, the apparent conclusion that the categories "determine sensibility inwardly" (Pippin 1989:28).

---

[22] Fichte, it should be noted, quite explicitly conflates epistemological and existential conditions. For Fichte—in his interpretation of Kant—receptivity or sensibility is something we ascribe to ourselves purely through thought: "'The capacity to acquire representations by the way in which we are affected by objects'*—what is it? Since we only think the affection, we undoubtedly only think the common [*Gemeinsame*] of it; it is a mere thought. When one posits an object while thinking it has affected one, one thinks of oneself as being *affected in this particular case*; and when one thinks that this happens with *all* objects of one's perception, one thinks of oneself as *being capable of being affected in general* [*affizierbar überhaupt*], or in other words: *through this thinking* [*durch dieses dein Denken*], one ascribes receptivity or sensibility to oneself. Thus the object as given is *merely thought*. … Naturally, all our knowledge starts with *an affection*; but not *through an object*" (W, I,4:241; trans. mine and my underlining; *Fichte paraphrases A19/B33).

[23] And of course one should note the following "its unity" in the subordinate clause of that sentence (B145).

10.4 Inseparability and the Conclusion of the B-Deduction, Specifically, the B160 Note

Pippin argues that Hegel concurs with Kant that there is a necessary cooperation between the capacities for intuitions and concepts, and also that there *are* such distinguishable aspects of cognition,[24] but also that

> he is objecting to a "mechanical" opposition in favor of an "organic" role for the imagination in understanding the relation between intuition and concept, and that he is enthusiastically applauding those passages in the second-edition deduction where Kant, by Hegel's lights, follows the logic of his own argument and begins to understand that the concept–intuition distinction is not strictly congruent with the distinction between spontaneity and receptivity, that there is an "active" and even conceptual element in the sensible uptake of the world (a claim which, again, hardly disputes that there is any such uptake). (2005:28)

As Pippin says, "Hegel wishes to stress *more*, make more out of, the organic unity or organic inseparability of such elements than Kant" (2005:28).[25] The cooperation between intuition and concept happens by means of the productive imagination—as Kant argues in §24 of the B-Deduction—which is the "effect of the understanding on sensibility" (B152). The imagination is the faculty which enables sensibility to be conceptually determined by the understanding by means of the categories. Hegel understands this in such a way that the imagination is in fact the mediating factor between intuition and concept, such that intuition and concept, or sensibility and the understanding, can only retroactively, from a formal "understanding" perspective, be considered separately. Hegel accuses Kant of hypostatising this formal "understanding"

---

[24] Of course, Hegelians want to stress that Hegel does not, like the rationalists, want to reduce perceptions to confused ideas or concepts (Pippin 1993:291), and also that we are dependent on a content we do not make—because we are discursive thinkers, rather than noetic or intuitive intellects (cf. Pippin 1993:292; Sedgwick 2012). Pippin says: "Hegel clearly has no interest in returning to some neo-Leibnizian position as a result of his dissatisfaction with Kant's concept–intuition distinction in the Deduction" (1993:295).

[25] See also Sedgwick (2012), in particular Chaps. 2 and 4. Cf. Sedgwick (2004).

10 Separability of Concept and Intuition 247

perspective, which makes the synthetic a priori, original unity look like a mechanical opposition between intuition and concept. Their apparent separateness is in fact merely an *abstraction from* their original "organic" unity that Hegel says they have in the imagination.[26] Hence Pippin's claim that concept and intuition are formally "distinguishable", namely, as formal elements in what is "organically" united, but not in fact separable.

This original "organic" unity of the imagination plays a significant role in the conclusion (the "second step") of Kant's argument in the B-Deduction, where he labels it the *synthesis speciosa* (B151), to distinguish it from the intellectual synthesis, which merely concerns the organisation of representations on the conceptual level. *Synthesis speciosa* is veritably concerned with sensible images of objects, which have a direct connection, via empirical intuition, to actual spatiotemporal objects in experience. Already in the A-Deduction, Kant indicates that the imagination's "action exercised immediately upon perceptions" is apprehension, but in the B-Deduction it is even more clearly stated that the productive imagination as active in sensibility itself is the synthesis of apprehension (B160–1). Crucially, Hegel interprets the productive imagination therefore as the very "principle of … sensibility" itself (GuW, 4:327). This might seem confirmed by Kant's own argument in the earlier quoted passage at A111–12, where he says that "the entire sensibility, and with it also *all possible* appearances" (emphasis added), is bound by the categories, which are the "universal functions of synthesis". It is therefore not unreasonable to claim that the imagination, which is the synthesis at issue here, and instantiates the categories in sensibility, is indeed the very "principle" of sensibility. Pippin writes that, for Kant,

> "from the side of givenness, sensibility" as it were, … there could not be such deliverances not subject to the unity made possible by categories. We have a way of representing the domain of the immediately, sensibly given as such (because it has a pure form accessible as a pure intuition, a distinct representation) and so … [1] the categories not only prescribe the unity required for objective purport at all *to* any manifold, but also [2] that any

---

[26] See note 8 above. For more details, see Schulting (2017), Chap. 8.

248   D. Schulting

manifold, given especially its temporal aspects, *requires* categorical unity <u>if it is to provide any possible content for thought</u>. (2005:33; my underlining)

Pippin means the second clause [2] to be an additional claim, but really, the condition contained at the end of the clause makes the second clause just repeat what was said in [1]: the categories are required for any manifold that has objective purport or objectively valid representational content. The categories are not required for a manifold just to be that manifold, in contrast to what in earlier work Pippin did explicitly assert, namely, that "nothing given *in* intuition can fail to be subject to the categories" (1989:29), "there can be no intuitions not subject to the categories" (1989:30) and, most emphatically, "the content of any intuited manifold must be subject to the categories just to *be* an element of a spatiotemporal manifold in the first place" (1989:31).[27] Unlike what Pippin seems to be suggesting in these passages, the categories are not required for an intuition *to be* an intuition. Pippin can on this basis therefore not claim that "there could not be such deliverances not subject to the unity made possible by categories" (2005:33). He could rejoin to this that Kant might be thought to say as much, when he writes that "all synthesis, through which *even perception itself becomes possible*, stands under the categories" (B161; emphasis added), quoted by Pippin (2005:33). Or in an earlier passage, at B160, also quoted by Pippin (1989:28), where Kant writes that "everything that may ever come before our senses must stand under the laws that arise *a priori* from the understanding alone". But this must be seen in the context of the claim made earlier in the same paragraph, which says that what "is to be explained" in §26 is

the possibility of cognizing *a priori through categories* whatever <u>objects *may come before our senses*</u>, <u>not as far as the form of their intuition but rather as far as the laws of their combination are concerned</u>. (B159; my underlining)

---

[27] See also Sedgwick's (1993:279–80) critique of Pippin on this point.

10 Separability of Concept and Intuition   249

The passage at B161 is indeed a more ambivalent one, but it depends on how one reads Kant's notion of "perception".[28] From the context of the "second step" of the B-Deduction, it should be clear that what is at issue is the unity or combination in intuition that is due to the determination by virtue of *synthesis speciosa*. This is also already made clear in the above-quoted passage in §21, where Kant says that "in the sequel (§26), it will be shown from the way in which the empirical intuition is given in sensibility that *its unity* can be none other than the one the category prescribes to the manifold of a given intuition in general" (B144–5; emphasis added). So the *unity* of empirical intuition is concerned, and not just intuition or mere sensibility.

But Pippin refers to the notorious footnote to B160 as more evidence for a Hegelian alteration of Kant's official thoughts about the separability of concept and intuition "towards a version more in keeping with Kant's spirit" (2005:34). It is here that he believes

> that thought is not merely presented with[,] and then applied to and restricted by, a thoroughly nonconceptual sensory manifold. The manifold is already conceptually articulated; concepts are engaged in our "sensory uptake" of the world, and the separation claim *and* the strategy it grounds *and* the mind-world picture it assumes must now all be qualified, even re-thought. (Pippin 2005:34; my underlining)

The reason for this belief is that Kant seems to be saying that what previously—in the Aesthetic (TAe)—was considered sensibility's own *sui generis* unity turns out to be the result of the understanding's determination of sensibility. Pippin believes that the crucial claim in the footnote is that "the issue for [Kant] is not only … how intuitions, as given, are conceptualized", but also "that conforming to the *intuitional* constraints

---

[28] In the *Stufenleiter* (A320/B376–7), Kant appears to define "perception" as either a sensation (the modification of a subject's inner state) or a cognition, which can in its turn be either an intuition or a concept. This seems to indicate that by "perception" any representation in sensibility, subjective or objective, can be meant (see also A115; A120; B207; A192–3/B237–8; B275). Perception as such is not *experience*, since experience is "perception according to rules" (Refl, 2740, 16:494; trans. mine), or "cognition through *connected* perceptions" (B161; emphasis added; cf. Prol, 4:298 [§19], 305; FM, 20:276). Experience is contrasted with "mere perception—whose validity is merely subjective" (Prol, 4:304).

of sensibility itself requires a minimal conceptualization" (1989:30). This "minimal conceptualization" concerns the unity of spatiotemporal manifolds, without which we could not even *receive* these manifolds. This is reason for Hegel (and Pippin) to say that the strict distinction between the understanding's spontaneity and sensibility's receptivity, and a fortiori the strict distinction between the form of intuition (namely, its unity) and conceptuality as that which provides this unity, can no longer be upheld (cf. GuW, 4:327ff.).

But if we read the note carefully (and Christian Onof and I have done this *in extenso* in Onof and Schulting 2015), then it becomes clear that the separation between intuition and concepts remains as it is—this is reflected by Kant's distinction, in the footnote, between "form of intuition", which "merely gives the manifold", and "formal intuition", which "gives unity of the representation", under guidance of the imagination, by means of an act of the understanding that determines sensibility. While imagination *determines* the manifold in sensibility, it is not suddenly the principle of sensibility *simpliciter*, as Hegel alleges, nor is the imagination the common denominator of sensibility and understanding, where supposedly the imagination is the higher principle in comparison to the *discursive* principle of the understanding, or an "organic unity" that holds understanding and sensibility together. It would mean that imagination is the principle of space and time; but there are a series of problems with such a reading that go against the core of Kant's doctrine in TAe, which are addressed in Onof and Schulting (2015) but which I have no space here to rehearse.[29] It is clear that Hegel wants to read it the way he does,

---

[29] Briefly, in our nonconceptualist reading of the unity of space in Onof and Schulting (2015), we argue for a distinction between, on the one hand, the *sui generis* unity of space, which we call the unicity of space, and is as such independent of the unity of apperception (categorial unity) and thus independent of the synthesis of the imagination, and, on the other hand, the unity of a determinate space (or determinate spaces), which *is* due to the unity of apperception, by virtue of the synthesis of the imagination. The *sui generis* unity of space defines the essential characteristics of space as the form of intuition (singularity, infinity, mereological inversion), which cannot be reduced to conceptual unity by virtue of the unity of apperception (and thus neither to the synthesis of imagination). This, we argue, refutes conceptualist interpretations of the unity of space (such as Pippin's). Nevertheless, our reading allows for the conceptual grasp of the *sui generis* unicity of space *as* a unity for the understanding, and thus accommodates Kant's claim in the footnote that the understanding determines the spatial manifold "inwardly" by means of the synthesis of the imagination. See also Tolley, Chap. 11, and Land, Chap. 7, in this volume for a nonconceptualist and a conceptualist reading, respectively, of the unity of space.

10 Separability of Concept and Intuition 251

but his claim (and Pippin's endorsement thereof) that his reading is an immanent one that is in keeping with the spirit of Kant's thoughts can hardly be vindicated.[30] Kant's "formal intuition" is an intuited object as determined by the understanding, so indeed not any longer *merely* an intuition (an indeterminate appearance) but a determinate object, that is, the result of a conceptual determination of the mere intuitional manifold (by means of the categories). This does not, however, sublate the *strictness* of the distinction between intuition and concept—a *mere* manifold is still just an intuition—nor does it imply that intuitions per se *must* be conceptually determined.

Pippin seems to play "dualistically inclined" interpretations of Kant's distinction between intuition and concept, endorsed by nonconceptualists, off against "holistically inclined" readings, such as his own. Dualists think that intuitions by themselves already refer to objects and constitute intentionality, while holists emphasise the fact that "representationally significant intuited content at all" (Pippin 2005:36n.27) is solely due to the unifying function of the understanding (as demonstrated by the *Leitfaden* passage). Pippin is right to criticise the nonconceptualists on this score. But it is important to acknowledge, based on Kant's own clear distinction in the footnote between "form of intuition", *giving the mere manifold*, and "formal intuition", that, on the one hand, *determinate* intuitions are indeed not separable from the unifying function of the understanding, and that intuitions by themselves have no *cognitively significant* content, if by that is meant a content that represents the object of intuition *as* object, but also that, on the other hand, *mere* intuitions are perfectly separable from concepts and a fortiori from judgements, since not being cognitively relevant they do not presuppose categories nor do they have an inbuilt tendency toward judgement.

Only insofar as intuitions (or perceptions) are to be seen as determinate (unified) intuitions (or perceptions), as an indispensable and

---

[30] It is also unclear how Pippin can acknowledge that "orientation in space is in some sense pre-conceptual" (1993:291). How is this possible if he denies that there are pure intuitions? For pre-conceptual orientation in space requires a pre-conceptual form of such orientation, which is the pure form of intuition, space. But if Kant's distinction between form of intuition and formal intuition is blurred, as Hegel and Pippin argue, then it seems hard to visualise a *pre-conceptual* form for spatial orientation, given that, on the Hegelian reading, its unitary form is provided by the understanding via the synthesis of imagination.

252   D. Schulting

inseparable part of a determinate cognition of objects, *must* intuitions (or perceptions) themselves be taken to be affected[31] by the understanding. This means that it is not true to say that the conclusion of TD is that, *necessarily*, intuitions or perceptions are conceptualised or are susceptible to conceptual or categorial determination, or judgemental organisation. There is nothing in intuitions or perceptions that makes them susceptible to conceptual or categorial determination such that they are or become perceptions of external (or internal) objects. Kant's argument does not show this, but it would also be odd if it did, since it would mean that he could have spared himself all the effort of the second half of the B-Deduction and rested content with the principle of apperception explicated in the first half, if interpreted (wrongly, as it happens) as a principle of sheer representation, which holds that every representation is subject to the principle of being *thought*. (In actuality, as we saw earlier, Pippin himself does not believe that the "first step" of TD is sufficient to prove that objects actually instantiate the subjective forms of thought, but his apparent belief that in the "second step" Kant proves that *any* representational content is subject to the categories stands in tension with this.)[32] Such an argument—that perceptions show a susceptibility to being affected by the understanding—also could not explain why Kant would worry about how to differentiate genuine objectively valid representations from merely subjectively valid representations.

We should keep in mind that the intimate connection between perceptions (intuitions) and the understanding in the case of genuine empirical knowledge is seen *from the perspective of the understanding*, of the cognising subject, which is a transcendental or sideways-on perspective. The transcendental perspective does not allow us to locate the internal ground of the connection in the perceptions themselves, as if they showed some inner disposition to being conceptualised or had an inbuilt tendency towards judgement, a conation to being determined

---

[31] I employ Longuenesse's (1998a:243) phrasing here (cf. B152).

[32] This not only affects Pippin's reading. Ever since Dieter Henrich's (1969) proposal of a two-step proof structure for the B-Deduction, also many Kantians believe that the "second step" is meant to prove that any sense content is subject to the categories. For a different reading, see Schulting (2017), Chap. 7.

10 Separability of Concept and Intuition   253

categorially, as Béatrice Longuenesse (1998a) argues.[33] The determination of perceptions—and this was clearly and rightly seen by Fichte, and later Hegel—is of course a determination that is wholly due to the understanding, and also wholly internal to the understanding, that is, the self-conscious "I". But Fichte's mistake was thereby to reduce the very givenness of perceptions, of what is external to thought, to merely being an aspect of thought's self-determination, one of the formal *relata* in the conceptual differentiations of self-determining reason.[34]

10.5 Concluding Remarks

Hegelian conceptualists are wont to relativise the immediacy and absolute externality of sense content. They do not deny that it is required, and they do not deny that it is, in some sense, irreducible to thought; they are not neo-Leibnizians. The "in some sense" is the operative issue here. Of course, the absolute distinction between sense content and thought that Kant emphasises is not such that it poses a problem for, as it were, bridging the gap between them. The solution for bridging the apparent gap between them, which Kant proposes in TD, is not a solution aimed at *relativising* the absolute distinction (let alone collapsing it), thus in fact *denying* that there is any gap to be bridged (cf. Pippin 2015b:72). Rather, the solution is provided in terms of offering a unique and irreducible perspective from the side of the cognising subject; that is, insofar as the goal is to explain the possibility of knowledge, which is the premise of the analysis in TD, and insofar as *mere* conceptuality cannot of itself provide the modal constraint for such knowledge—namely, the connection with *real, existing* objects—the apperceiving subject of understanding must be seen as *taking up sensible content as a cognitively relevant constraint on our conceptuality.* To this extent and to this extent only is sensible content to be seen as a content that is not itself given *in* thought but still determined *by thought* as a content given to it, and so it is only relatively distinct

---

[33] See Longuenesse (1998a:196). Cf. Pippin's reflections on Longuenesse's interpretation in Pippin (1997:322–3).

[34] See again note 22.

from thought or conceptuality—"relatively", because external content is defined as external only to the extent that the apperceiving subject of understanding takes up such content *as her own*, that is, *internalises* it, and in this way "determines sensibility inwardly", as Pippin puts it. This does not in the least relativise the absolute distinction between sensibility and conceptuality as such; it only relativises that distinction insofar as from the cooperation between sensibility and understanding knowledge should arise, which is guaranteed by the subjective act of apperception.

Hegelians and Kantians can agree on these core issues to the extent that the possibility of knowledge is concerned. But it appears that the Hegelians want to deny that this leaves Kant's strict distinction between sensibility and the understanding intact. They do not see any warrant for keeping this distinction as an absolute one (see especially the reasoning in Pippin 2015b:72–4). The problem with this failure to understand Kant's distinction is, as I see it, twofold.

First, it confuses the epistemic and constitutive levels: sense content is *intelligible* only on condition that it is grasped or determined by an act of understanding, but it is not *constituted* by such an act. This becomes clear when we look at the way in which the understanding determines space, and how the unity of space is said by Kant to presuppose a synthesis (B160n.). This latter requirement does not reduce space, or indeed its *sui generis* unity, to a function of the synthesis of the understanding, by way of the imagination, as (some) Kantian as well as Hegelian conceptualists would like to believe. Space and time are not products of the understanding. Only determinate spaces and determinate times or time intervals are products of the understanding, by way of the imagination.

Second, it ignores the counterfactual possibility of cognitive failure or indeed the real possibility (for human beings) of subcognitive intuitional coping with one's environment.[35] Kant allows for this possibility, even though it is not the focus of his argument in TD. But the correlation between, on the one hand, the intimate epistemological relation between sense content and conceptuality and, on the other, the fact that sense content is intelligible only by means of conceptuality should have given

---

[35] See the essays on the McDowell–Dreyfus debate in Schear (2013), and Pippin's own essay in that volume (Pippin 2013). See also Onof, Chap. 9, in this volume.

10 Separability of Concept and Intuition 255

pause to Kantian as well as Hegelian conceptualists: if it is the case that sense content is *intelligible only* within the perspective of conceptuality, the perspective of the apperceiving subject, then this does not entail that there could not *be* sensible content that is not made intelligible within that perspective. Surely there is the real possibility of sensible or representational content that is not (although it could be) taken up by some apperceiving subject of understanding, for example, the sensible content that some non-apperceiving representer X, Kant's brute, say, has when he sees the house without knowing (apperceiving) what he sees,[36] or, the sensible content that a properly functioning apperception-equipped adult human being, but one with a penchant for dark moods, has when (and only when), for example, he is staring wearily out the window after having read about Levinas's *il y a*.[37]

---

[36] See note 20.

[37] I would like to thank Christian Onof for his useful comments on an earlier draft, as always. I also thank Kees Jan Brons, Robert Hanna, Dietmar Heidemann and Marcel Quarfood for their helpful remarks.

11

The Difference Between Original, Metaphysical and Geometrical Representations of Space

Clinton Tolley

11.1 Introduction: Separating the Metaphysical From the "Original" (Intuitive) and the Geometrical

Despite substantial strides in recent research into a number of different dimensions of Kant's views on space,[1] we are still in need of a more adequate taxonomy than has been previously provided of the distinctions at work in Kant's Critical account of space. Having such a taxonomy ready to hand would help head off the not uncommon assumptions that Kant thinks there is only *one* object that merits the name "space"—the space of outer appearances—and only *one* possible kind of representation of

---

[1] See Carson (1997), Heis (2014b), Messina (2015), Onof and Schulting (2015), Patton (2011), Shabel (2004), Sutherland (2005b), and especially Friedman (2000, 2012, 2015).

C. Tolley (✉)
Department of Philosophy, University of California San Diego,
San Diego, CA, USA
e-mail: ctolley@ucsd.edu

© The Editor(s) (if applicable) and The Author(s) 2016
D. Schulting (ed.), *Kantian Nonconceptualism*,
DOI 10.1057/978-1-137-53517-7_11

257

that space—the intuition of space. A closer look at the *Critique of Pure Reason* and other Critical-period writings reveals that Kant holds there to be both a *plurality* of kinds or species of space—and so a variety of *objects* besides the immediate object of pure intuition of space, which merit the name "space"—and a *plurality* of the kinds (species) of *representation* of these spaces, besides the pure intuition of the space of outer appearances.

One of the most important and most often-neglected distinctions that Kant works with concerning *objects* which each merit the name "space" is that between (a) the space which is "given" a priori in a pure "original" *intuition*, which is under discussion in the Transcendental Aesthetic (TAe), and in which *sensations* are ordered to yield an outer appearance, a space which might be called "*appearance* space", and (b) the space which is given only a posteriori in *experience*, which is under discussion in the Analytic's treatment of the "dynamical" principles and then again in the *Metaphysical Foundations of Natural Science*, and in which *substances* are ordered to yield nature, which might be called "*physical* space" (cf. MAN, 4:481). In future work, I hope to be able to clarify better the nature of this distinction between spaces, and in particular its significance for a proper understanding of the related distinction Kant introduces in the Analytic between the *mathematical* and *dynamical* categories and principles (cf. B110–11; B199–200; B220–1; B557–8).[2] Getting clear on this pair of distinctions is, in turn, absolutely crucial for understanding the scope and consequence of Kant's transcendental idealism, insofar as it is first and foremost a thesis about the metaphysical standing of *appearances* and their form, and not a

---

[2] *Mathematical* categories and principles are distinguished precisely as applying directly and "constitutively" to "objects of intuition (pure as well as empirical)" (B110), i.e. to appearance space as well as to the relations of sensations (*appearances*) within this space, whereas *dynamical* categories and principles "do *not* concern appearances" (B220; emphasis added) but rather "the *existence*" that is related to appearances (B110; emphasis added; cf. A160/B199, A178/B221)—i.e. the really existent *substances* which are responsible for bringing about appearances—and the relations (of causality, community) among these existents.

11 Representations of Space 259

thesis about the ideality of the *existence* (substance) which appears through these appearances (cf. Prol, 4:292–3; A92/B125).[3]

Yet even if we restrict our focus—as I shall in what follows—to (a) the space of appearances, as the object given a priori in pure original intuition,[4] careful attention to Kant's texts will show that he is working with a further, equally important and equally often-overlooked, distinction between a variety of kinds of a priori *representation* we possess of this space. Laying out and clarifying the nature of these distinctions among representations of the space of appearances will be the main focus of the present chapter. More specifically, I shall argue that, throughout the Critical period, Kant is working with a threefold distinction among kinds of representation of the space of appearances: (i) the primitive "original" pure *intuition* of this space, (ii) the philosophical or "metaphysical" representation of this space by way of a (pure) *concept*, and (iii) the mathematical or specifically "geometrical" representation of this space, by way of the *construction* of a concept of a delimited part within the original intuition of this space (the representation of "*a* space" within space). My analysis will focus first on how this threefold distinction can be seen in Kant's account of representations of space in TAe (Sect. 11.2), before showing its presence in the discussion of representations of space in his 1790s' remarks on the work of Abraham Kästner (Sect. 11.3), and then demonstrating its manifestation at key points in the Analytic as well (Sect. 11.4).

I then turn (in Sect. 11.5) to the second main goal of the chapter, namely, that of showing how more careful attention to this threefold distinction opens up a fairly straightforward way to avoid a recent revisionary line of interpretation of certain remarks Kant makes about representations of space in the Transcendental Deduction (TD).

---

[3] I explore these distinctions, and their role in Kant's idealism, at length in Tolley (MS a), and more briefly in Tolley (MS c).

[4] Here and throughout, unless otherwise noted, I use the term "object" in the very broad sense of a subject of true predication in judgement, such that even e.g. that which is non-existent, or non-substantial—i.e. that which is (in some sense) *nothing*—counts as an object, since it can be the subject of true predications. At the end of the Amphiboly, Kant himself uses the term "object in general" (*Gegenstand überhaupt*) to range over both that which is "something" (*Etwas*) and that which is "nothing" (*Nichts*) (B346), and explicitly to comprise both noumena and also pure space as the form of intuition (which are also, incidentally, both classified as forms of *ens* rather than *nihil*).

This interpretation argues that, although in TAe Kant might have seemed to accord to intuitions an independence from concepts and acts of synthesis by the understanding, both as to the occurrence of intuitions and their content, by the time of the Analytic, and especially by the end of TD, Kant indicates that this independence was a mere semblance, since intuition in general, and the pure original intuition of space in particular, does depend both for its occurrence (as an act) and for its content upon the understanding.[5] I shall argue, to the contrary, that the relevant remarks have a perfectly nonconceptualist, non-intellectualist interpretation available—one, therefore, which integrates quite naturally with the traditional, and prima facie quite plausible, reading of Kant's account of the intuition of space in TAe. Once we have the threefold distinction between kinds of representation of space in view, we shall be more alert to contextual cues Kant gives as to which of these representations is under discussion, and also more sensitive to the fact that a claim about the dependence that *one* of these representation of appearance space bears on concepts, acts of synthesis or the understanding in no way implies such dependence for *all* of these representations of space.

In this I am in sympathy with several recent, helpful, nonconceptualist discussions of TD in light of the remarks on Kästner,[6] over and against the very fruitful, though broadly conceptualist, or at least "intellectualist", readings recently offered by Longuenesse and Friedman.[7] My analysis here will go further than previous nonconceptualist/non-intellectualist accounts, however, in more sharply drawing apart the *metaphysical-conceptual* representation of space from both the original intuition of space as well as the geometrical construction of concepts of spaces in intuition. I also show

---

[5] For the stronger "conceptualist" interpretation of intuition, according to which the original intuition of space requires the involvement of concepts (categories), see McDowell (2009). For the weaker, merely "intellectualist" interpretation, according to which only an act of understanding is necessary for the original intuition of space, though no concept or specifically conceptual synthesis (instead: something "pre-discursive"), see Friedman (2012, 2015), Longuenesse (1998b), Messina (2014) and Grüne, Chap. 4, in this volume. (I am borrowing the "conceptualist"/"intellectualist" contrast from McLear 2015.)

[6] Compare especially Fichant (1998) and Onof and Schulting (2014, 2015). For broadly sympathetic nonconceptualist and non-intellectualist interpretations of the original representation of space on grounds besides the Kästner remarks, see Allais (2009) and McLear (2015).

[7] See Friedman (2000, 2012, 2015) and Longuenesse (1998a, b).

how the metaphysical/geometrical distinction closely tracks the philosophical/mathematical distinction that Kant draws later in the Doctrine of Method (among other places), insofar as the metaphysical representation of space (and its features) takes place through *concepts alone*, whereas the geometrical representation of space (and its parts) occurs only through the "construction" of concepts *in pure intuition* (cf. B741–2).

11.2 Intuitive, Metaphysical and Geometrical Representations of Space in the Transcendental Aesthetic

One of the best-known *results* of TAe is that we possess a pure a priori *intuition* of space. Yet to establish this result, Kant *begins* his analysis, not with this intuition of this object, but instead with a *concept* that we possess of an object we call "space". More specifically, Kant begins with what he calls the "exposition" of a concept we have of a specific aspect of our "outer sense", as comes out in the following introductory sentences:

> By means of outer sense (a property of our mind) we represent to ourselves objects as outside us, and all as *in space*. *In this*, their shape [*Gestalt*], magnitude [*Größe*], and relation to one another is determined [*bestimmt*], or determinable [*bestimmbar*]. (A22/B37; emphasis added)

Now, Kant thinks that the "exposition" of the concept of this space will show that it has certain distinctive things that "belong to" it (B38), namely, that its content represents space as possessing certain features. Most importantly, Kant thinks that the exposition of the concept of space shows (1) that we conceive (think) of space as something whose representation "must ... ground [*zum Grunde liegen*]" the possibility of representing *sensations* as being not just different but as "in different places" (A23/B38); (2) that we thereby think of space as something whose representation "grounds", and serves as a "condition of the possibility" of, all *appearances* in outer sense (A24/B39), where these are understood as composites of a "matter" (provided by the manifold of different sensations) ordered in a "form", and also of outer *empirical intuitions* (A24/B38), that is, those intuitions which are "related to … object[s] through sensations" and which have these appearances as their ("undetermined") objects (A20/B34); (3) that we think of space as having a compositional structure that prohibits it from being had by the mind first as the content of a "discursive or … general *concept*", but must rather be first had in an intuition, albeit (in light of the previous thesis) a non-empirical, pure a priori one (A25/B39; emphasis added); and finally (4) that it is a part of the concept of space that we think of space as "an infinite *given* magnitude", in the sense of space itself being "thought" in this concept "as if it contained an infinite set of representations *within itself*", since "all the parts of space, even to infinity, are simultaneous" (B39–40; emphasis added). From the results of this exposition of how the concept we have of space represents space as being, Kant takes it to follow that the "*original* representation" of space itself must not be a discursive or universal concept *at all* (whether pure or empirical), but rather *an intuition* we have a priori and which is "pure" of all sensation (B40; emphasis added).[8]

Now, because this exposition successfully "exhibits" the fact that it also "belongs to a concept" (i.e. the concept of space) that it can be "*given* a priori"—since this concept (along with empirical intuitions and appearances) has been shown to be "grounded" in an a priori intuition—Kant calls this exposition "metaphysical" (B38). It is "metaphysical" in much the same way that the later metaphysical deduction of the pure concepts (categories) of understanding is "metaphysical", insofar as this exposition, too, shows how we can trace back the concept of space to an a priori "birthplace" (A66/B90) or "origin" (B159). What is of more interest for our analysis, however, is an even simpler and more straightforward corollary of Kant's proceedings here: the Metaphysical Exposition gives clear indication that Kant holds us to possess at least *two* distinct representations of the space of outer appearances—namely, the initial *concept* of space, now known to be pure and of a priori origin itself,[9] and then the pure a priori *intuition* which serves as the ground of both this concept

---

[8] For further discussion of Kant's argument in this exposition, see Messina (2015) and Shabel (2010).

[9] For other references to the *concept* of space at issue in TAe in terms of its purity and apriority, compare B118–21, B195 and B207 (see also the discussion below in Section 11.4).

11 Representations of Space 263

and all other outer intuitions, and also is ultimately that representation through which "outer *experience* is itself first possible" (A23/B38).

While this twofold distinction among a priori representations of space has not gone unnoticed, what has been less emphasised is the fact that TAe's multiplication of representations of this object (the space of outer appearances) does not end here. For we see Kant making use of a *third* sort of representation of this same space already implicitly in the Metaphysical Exposition itself, but even more explicitly in the very next section, which he distinguishes as the specifically "*transcendental* exposition" of the concept of space (B40). For in addition to (i) the "original representation" (B40) of space in a priori *intuition*, and (ii) the a priori *concept* of space which has just been metaphysically expounded and whose possession is shown to be grounded on this original intuition, in the third part of the Metaphysical Exposition Kant also refers to (iii) representations of the "limitation" of this space, representations which he suggests can occur simply by *thinking* such limitations "*in*" the space originally intuited (B39; emphasis added). Kant argues that these acts of thinking limitations in space are what lead us to acquire the representation of a "manifold" *in* space, which is then what enables us to form "the general concept of *spaces*" (B39; emphasis added)—rather than being stuck only with the initial intuition of space per se, or with the very abstract concept of the indeterminate as-of-yet undelimited object of this intuition. But then, while the pure intuition of space is that "from [*aus*; i.e. *out of*] which" such further delimitative representations are "derived", and that which "grounds" these representations (B39), these further representations cannot themselves be identical to the original intuition itself. Rather, "the general concept of *spaces* in general" and the more specific "concepts" of kinds of delimited space (e.g. line, triangle) both "rest … on" not just the original intuition of space but also on these further acts of delimitation in thought (B39; emphasis added).

Yet it is equally crucial to note that, though these "derivative" geometrical concepts depend on acts of thinking and yield conceptual representations of space and its parts and their interrelations, they cannot be identical to the aforementioned a priori *concept* of space that is metaphysically expounded in TAe. Nor can geometrical concepts (and basic propositions [*Grundsätze*]) be derived from the mere analysis of this a priori concept of space alone—say, by thinking more clearly about what is contained "in" this concept. This is because they contain the further conceptual addition of delimitation in its various species, and hence arise only through thinking delimitations "in" the original *intuition* of space, and in this way "deriving" geometrical representations (propositions, concepts) specifically "from the intuition" (B39).

The distinctness of (iii) geometrical representations of space from both (i) the original intuition and (ii) the metaphysical concept of space is confirmed in the subsequent *transcendental* exposition of the concept of space (B40–1). Here Kant's stated topic is to identify certain representations which "*flow from* the given concept" (B40; emphasis added), that is, from (ii) the concept of space given a priori, the concept now known to be possessed on the basis of (i) the original intuition of space. As with the previous talk of "derivative", the language of "flowing from" further suggests that Kant means to be referring to a separate sort of representation, one which cannot be identical to either the a priori concept of space (since it "flows from" it) or the original intuition which grounds this concept.[10]

As in the Metaphysical Exposition, here too the main examples Kant gives of representations that we can see "flow from" this concept of space a priori are specifically *geometrical* representations. Geometry itself is characterised as the "science that determines the properties of space ... *a priori*" (B40). Yet Kant quickly makes it clear that the particular "determination" involved in geometrical representations must involve *more* than the mere concept of space, and more than any analysis or exposition of the content already "thought *in it*" (B39; cf. A7/B11). Geometrical determination is said here to "*go beyond* the concept" of space (B41; emphasis added), and so engage in a determination of space itself by way of a "synthetic" addition or amplification to the given concept of space (B40). Yet while it is clear that Kant means to imply that this "addition" to the a priori concept of space happens by way of intuition, it is equally clear that merely *having* the original intuition of space will not be sufficient. As we have already seen, further acts of thinking (delimiting, determining)

---

[10] In fact, it should follow from the Metaphysical Exposition that this "original" intuition, if it is truly original, cannot itself "flow from" *any* concept, or any other representation.

what is given in this intuition are required. Crucially, then, geometrical representation involves acts which therefore "go beyond" *both* the original intuition of space *and* the metaphysical-conceptual representation of space.

Now, if we had our eyes on charting out a more complete taxonomy of spatial representations, we would need to look more closely at the three *empirical* (sensation-involving) representations involving outer appearances (and hence the space of outer appearances) that Kant also describes in TAe as being "grounded on" the original pure a priori intuition of space, namely, outer empirical *intuition, perception (Wahrnehmung)* and outer *experience.*[11] For now, however, it is enough that we have uncovered a threefold differentiation in the kinds of representation of the space of outer appearances in TAe:

(i) The original a priori *intuition* of this space;

(ii) An a priori *concept* of this space per se, which is shown through *metaphysical* exposition (analysis) to be grounded on the original intuition;

and finally,

(iii) Further (a priori) representations of "determinations" of space through *delimitation* of spaces (as its parts), which are "derived" ("flow") from the previous two representations, by way of a *synthetic* determination of certain properties of space through "thinking" delimitations "in" the intuition of space, and which belong to the science of *geometry*.

---

[11] I provide a brief sketch of the account of the difference between these mental acts (intuiting, perceiving, experiencing) in Tolley (2013), and more fully in Tolley (MS a). I also argue there that keeping track of these distinctions is of utmost importance for understanding Kant's account of "cognition" (*Erkenntnis*). In Tolley (MS c), I take up the further and difficult question of how the space of the objects of outer intuition (outer *appearances*) relates to the space of the objects of outer experience (corporeal *substances*), drawing on Sellars's (1968) analysis of counterpart-relations.

266   C. Tolley

11.3 Intuitive, Metaphysical and Geometrical Representations of Space in the Kästner Remarks

Before moving on to the key passages about the representations of space from the Analytic and especially TD, I want to further solidify a broadened sense of the conceptual background in play in these passages, by looking first at some of Kant's remarks from 1790, written for Johann Friedrich Schultz, concerning the views on mathematics presented in Kästner's treatises.[12] Towards the end of these remarks, Kant takes up the question of the differences in "the use of the concept of the infinite" in the sciences of geometry and metaphysics, respectively (OKT, 20:418), and in the course of addressing this question he also takes up the topic of how the two sciences treat space and its representations (OKT, 20:419–20). What I want to bring out in this section is the extent to which these remarks also make use of the same threefold differentiation among representations of the space of outer appearances: original-intuitive, metaphysical-conceptual and geometrical-delimitative.

Here Kant claims that metaphysics has the task of "show[ing] how one can *have* the representation of space" in the first place (OKT, 20:419). In particular, in metaphysics "space is considered in the way it is *given, before* all determination of it in conformity with a certain concept of object" (OKT, 20:419; emphasis added). Metaphysics therefore considers the space that is "*original*" (*ursprünglich*), and aims to uncover "the basic representation" (*Grundvorstellung*) of space which makes possible whatever other spatial representations might be made (OKT, 20:419). As in TAe's Metaphysical Exposition, Kant again claims that this "basic representation" of space is an "a priori *intuition*" (OKT, 20:421; emphasis added).

Geometry, by contrast, is the science which treats this space, not as to its original representation per se, but rather as to what can be *further* represented "in" it: geometry "teaches how one can *describe* [*beschreiben*]

---

[12] For more background context-setting about the occasion for writing, see Friedman (2000) and Onof and Schulting (2014). I have also consulted the recent translation of these remarks by Onof and Schulting (in Kant 2014) in the course of providing translations for the quotations below. However, I have departed from their renderings without comment where it seemed appropriate.

11 Representations of Space 267

a space, viz., exhibit [*darstellen*] it in the representation *a priori*" (OKT, 20:419). In geometry "a space is *made* [*gemacht*]", in the sense that "(many) *spaces*" can be "*derived*" from "the basic representation of space" by being "thought [*gedacht*] as parts of the unitary original space" (OKT, 20:419; emphasis added). Kant then characterises this process of "thinking" parts "in" space, which TAe had referred to as "delimitation", by a term mentioned in TAe (cf. B39, A48/B65) but not actually explained until much later in the *Critique*, namely, "construction". As Kant defines it in the *Critique*, to construct is "to give ... an object ... *a priori*" (A223/B271); more specifically, it is "to display [*darzulegen*] the object that corresponds to [a concept] in intuition" (A240/B299), to "exhibit [*darstellen*] *a priori* the intuition corresponding to [a concept]" (A713/B741).

By providing that initial, infinite, not yet determined or delimited object "in" which the relevant geometrical description (determination) is to be "given", the original a priori intuition of space thus also "contains the *ground* of the *construction* of all possible geometrical concepts" (OKT, 20:420; emphasis added). Nevertheless, here again Kant indicates that neither the original intuition itself, nor the metaphysical representation of its content or its standing, is sufficient for the construction of a space in space. Rather, a further act of thinking, of description or partition, is required. To "give" a space to the mind through a priori construction is thus to have an intuition of space itself in which certain delimitations are "added" in thought.

Even so, Kant continues to claim that both metaphysical and geometrical treatments of space "derive" from one and the same "basic representation" (pure a priori intuition) of space. What is more, he also here emphasises perhaps more directly that, despite further differences that emerge as to how they go on to represent this space, both metaphysics and geometry begin not only by representing the same object (space) first given in original intuition, but also by representing it as to several of the same properties, including its infinity and givenness: "The geometer, as well as the metaphysician, represents the original space as infinite, in fact as infinitely given" (OKT, 20:419).

But despite representing this same object and some of its same basic properties, Kant here perhaps even more sharply distinguishes the *way* in which metaphysics and geometry each represent this space, especially as to its infinity. The geometer's "task" is ultimately that of describing "a space"

268   C. Tolley

out of space, and is therefore one that is understood to go on "to infinity", since, given the infinity of space itself, it is possible for the geometer to "increase" the description of space beyond any already described part of it (OKT, 20:420). This *possibility* of the increase of geometrical descriptions "to infinity", however, is itself something that is grounded on the *actual* infinity of the space in which all such descriptions will occur, that is, the actual infinity of the space already given in pure intuition: "The geometer grounds the possibility of his task of increasing *a space* (of which there are many) to infinity on the original representation of a unitary, infinite, *subjectively given space*" (OKT, 20:420; emphasis added). Hence, while "the *mathematician* is always only concerned with an *infinito potentiali*" in relation to his construction projects, an "*actu infinitum*" nevertheless already "*is given* … on the side of *the thinker*" (OKT, 20:421; emphasis added), as that wherein any such construction will occur. The *actual* infinity that is *already* in "what is metaphysically-given [*das Metaphysisch gegebene*]" is therefore what "grounds [*zum Grunde liegt*] the infinitely progressing constructions of geometrical concepts" (OKT, 20:421), even as to their *possibility* (OKT, 20:420).

However, what must be emphasised at this point—and has not yet been sufficiently appreciated, but which the review of TAe has put us in a position to notice more clearly—is that this implies that Kant here also is assuming there to be a distinct *metaphysical* representation of this space, which *itself* represents this space "as infinite" (OKT, 20:419). This is the representation that factors into the *science* of metaphysics and is possessed by "the metaphysician": "The geometer, *as well as the metaphysician*, represents the original space as infinite, in fact as infinitely given" (OKT, 20:419; emphasis added). This metaphysical representation represents space, however, neither by itself being an *intuition* of this space, nor by engaging in a geometrical *description* or construction in intuition of some part of this space. Rather, it does so by representing this space *conceptually*, that is, through a *concept* that discursively characterises its object as something "unitary" (*einig*), "infinite", "given" and a "magnitude" (OKT, 20:420). Which is to say: "the metaphysician" therefore makes use of the very concept which was itself being (metaphysically) expounded in TAe as also characterising space as possessing just these same features ("unitary", B39; "infinite *given* magnitude", B39–40).

11 Representations of Space   269

Hence, in the remarks on Kästner, too, we find Kant again making use of the threefold division among representations of intuitive space:

(i) The original a priori *intuition* of infinite space;

(ii) The representation of this space and some of its properties through a concept by "the *metaphysician*";

and

(iii) the *geometrical* representation of this space as to its determinations (delimitations, parts) through the "description" or "construction" of "*a* space" (or spaces/figures, e.g. lines, triangles) in this space.

What is more, we now have further evidence that all three represent some of the same features of this space (infinite, given, unitary, magnitude), albeit in different ways: (i) by simply *giving* them, (ii) by representing them in *thought* through a concept, and (iii) by (progressively) *constructing* concepts pertaining to these features "in" intuition.

Now, it is true that Kant here goes on to say that "the geometrically and objectively given space is always *finite*", on account of "its being given only because it is *made*", whereas "the metaphysically, i.e. originally, nonetheless merely subjectively given space" is "*infinite*" (OKT, 20:420). Taken out of context, Kant might here seem to be differentiating the two spaces.[13] Yet once we recall that each "geometrically given" space in question is "a space in space", and is given by being "made" out of a "determination" or "description" of the "originally metaphysically given" space, then we can see that the geometrical "giving" of a space in construction is ultimately a "giving" of *one and the same space*, albeit now with further determination, through partition, "thought" into it.[14]

---

[13] For interpretations which can seem to slide from noting distinctions among representations of space into talking as if there were distinctions in kinds of space ("metaphysical space" over against "geometrical space", with geometrical space seemingly identified only with a "subset" of metaphysical space), see Friedman (2000, 2012, 2015) and Patton (2011).

[14] Here I mean to emphasise the fact that the original intuition of infinite space is itself not only presupposed by, but actually contained in, every act of construction (description, delimitation),

270   **C. Tolley**

Before moving on to the remarks on space in the Analytic, we should bring to the fore one further point of clarification that Kant gives in the Kästner remarks, one which also helps to bring out further the systematic significance of these terminological distinctions. As was touched upon above, Kant here makes the striking claim that the space which is "originally given" in the "basic representation" of space is first given only "*subjectively*" (OKT, 20:419–20). What the immediate context suggests he would seem to mean by this is that, in the original *intuition* of space, considered all on its own, space is merely *had* in mind, prior to being thought[15] of in any way, under any *concept*, as to *its* being an object in its own right, or as to any of the *properties* it bears or any of the potential *parts* that might later be delimited within it. In Kant's words, space is merely "subjectively" given in the original intuition because it is given prior to "all determination of it in conformity with a certain *concept of object*" (OKT, 20:419; emphasis added).[16]

This way of taking the classification is further supported by how Kant characterises the transition to representations in which space is instead "*objectively* given" (OKT, 20:420). This transition occurs by representing this *same* space, which is initially *merely* given (present "in" the mind, in "the subject"), now in thought, by way of concepts *of objects* (parts, determinate quantities, figures, etc.)—that is, first representing (thinking of) space itself *as an object*, and then representing its features (*as* a unity, given, infinite) and its parts (spaces) also *as objects*. These further forms

---

such that every geometrical representation of space not only depends (abstractly) on the presence of the original intuition of space but actually takes place "in" this intuition, as its infinite backdrop. A space delimited "in" space is always finite relative to the space in which it is delimited—i.e. the infinite space of original intuition—and so it is right to say that there is something finite "given" in each construction. At the same time, however, there is *also* an infinity "given" in each construction as well—and *also* (for that matter) an infinity given in each empirical intuition (as its form). The co-givenness of infinite space in geometrical construction and empirical intuition is obscured in Friedman's insistence, for example, on the finitude of every visual or perceptual field (cf. Friedman 2000), to try to help account for the difference he recognises Kant is marking between metaphysical and geometrical representations of space.

[15] Compare: "That representation that can be given prior to all thinking is called *intuition*" (B132).

[16] This in no way implies that Kant means to deny that the space given in original intuition *is* an object, or that it *can* be represented under the concept of an object, or that it *has* properties which can be represented conceptually. As we have seen, Kant is quite clear throughout that the space of original intuition *is* the object of the metaphysically expounded concept of space, and that this space is already infinite, unitary, a magnitude and given in intuition.

11 Representations of Space 271

of "givenness" to mind (to thought, in conscious relation to concepts) contrast with merely "having" something in mind which does in fact represent space and its features per se, though not yet *as* anything.[17]

The main example Kant gives here of space as "objectively given" is how space is represented in *geometry*, referring to "the geometrically and objectively given space" that is only "given" if and when it is actually "made" (OKT, 20:420), in the sense of being the outcome of a description in thought of some part of space, such that "a" space is constructed or delimited within space itself. It would seem, however, that the *metaphysician*, too, represents space "objectively", in the sense of representing space explicitly as an object of a concept, in order to represent it in thought "as infinite", "as infinitely given" (OKT, 20:419), and indeed as *"subjectively given"* (OKT, 20:420). The original intuition merely gives space to the mind ("in the subject"). Both the metaphysician and the geometer take up this space (as it is given in its original representation) objectively, as an object of concepts and thought.[18]

---

[17] Compare Allais (2009) for further discussion of the importance of the contrast between space simply being given (in mere intuition) and space being given "as" something (even: as an object).

[18] Although this distinction is not front and centre in TAe, it does contain several terminological markers that suggest a parallel understanding of the subjective/objective contrast. Kant there claims that the originary "outer intuition" must "inhabit [*beiwohnen*] the mind" in a way that "precedes the *objects* themselves", and therefore "has its seat merely *in the subject* [*im Subjecte*], as its formal constitution for being affected by objects and thereby acquiring *immediate representation*, i.e., *intuition*, of them" (B41; emphasis added). This kind of "subjective" givenness is also touched upon in the *Prolegomena*, §9: "There is therefore only one way possible for my intuition to precede the actuality of the object and occur as an a priori cognition, *namely if it contains* [*enthält*] *nothing else except the form of sensibility, which* <u>*in me as subject*</u> *precedes all actual impressions through which I am affected by objects*" (Prol, 4:282; my underlining). To be sure, here Kant's concern is primarily to emphasise that space is given prior to external affection—that is, prior to further objects being given to the mind through the sensations they produce, and in fact given prior to even the sensations themselves being given—rather than its priority to thinking (whether conceptualisation or construction). In TAe, however, this point about space already being given and present "in the subject" is made precisely at the end of the Transcendental Exposition that aims to show a priori (as we can now emphasise), not just that certain *representations* "flow from" the concept of space, but rather that certain *cognitions* (*Erkenntnisse*)—i.e. certain representations "with consciousness" *of objects* (A320/B376–7)—can "flow from" this concept (combined with the original intuition). And the cognitions of objects that are shown to "flow from" the concept (plus intuition) in this way are none other than geometrical cognitions. In any case, this also should allay any concern that Kant's differentiation here between subjective and objective forms of givenness could require a corresponding differentiation in whatever *objects* are given in these manners. This would be so only if

11.4 Metaphysical (Transcendental, Philosophical) vs Geometrical (Mathematical) Representations of Space in the Analytic (and Beyond)

With this context in mind, we are now finally ready to turn to the Analytic and TD in particular. In this section, I present the case for thinking that in the Analytic, too, Kant makes use of this same threefold distinction of intuitive, metaphysical and geometrical representations of the space of outer appearances. I also show how these distinctions are at work in the concluding Doctrine of Method, by looking at its discussion of the difference between philosophical and mathematical cognition. This recognition will allow us, in the next section (Sect. 11.5), to formulate a fairly straightforward nonconceptualist, non-intellectualist alternative to recent conceptualist interpretations of some of Kant's remarks in the Analytic, and especially TD, about the dependence of certain representations of space upon the understanding.

Already in the Introduction to the Logic, Kant distinguishes *space* itself (or as the context suggests, its original representation via *intuition*), on the one hand, from both the a priori *geometrical* determinations of it, and also what he there calls the "*transcendental* representation" of space, on the other (A56/B80–1). The specifically "transcendental" representation of space refers to "the *cognition*" that these other representations—i.e. the intuition and the geometrical determinations of space—"are not of empirical origin at all, and the possibility that they can nevertheless be related *a priori* to objects of experience" (A56/B81; emphasis added). Now, because it is a "cognition" of something *about* the intuition and geometrical representations of space, rather than the mere intuition or the geometrical representations themselves, this transcendental representation of space cannot be identical to either one of them. Moreover, the specific features cognised in this transcendental representation about these other representations are, first, that they are of "pure" origin (and so

---

one and the same thing were not able to be first given in one manner and then in the other. But not only is this not in any way conceptually prohibited, it is exactly what Kant seems to have in mind in this particular case. Space is first given "in" the subject in pure intuition, and then given "objectively" in consciousness to thought, as the correlate of a concept.

11 Representations of Space   273

able to be given a priori), and second, that they relate to objects a priori. This sounds quite close to the cognition of the concept of space gained in TAe's metaphysical and transcendental expositions, respectively.

What is more, in the lead-up to TD, Kant explicitly refers to the *concept* of space as something that "relate[s] to objects completely *a priori*" (A85/B118), and also as itself "a priori" (A89/B121), and does so in contradistinction to both the "pure *intuition*" of space itself (A89/B121–2; emphasis added) and the equally a priori cognitions of space in *geometry*, which are said to arise in part from "its basic concept" (*Grundbegriff*) and in part to be "grounded on intuition *a priori*" (A87/B120; trans. amended).

In the introductory sections of the Principles (*Grundsätze*, basic propositions), Kant continues to fill out this distinction, noting that there are two different kinds of pure basic propositions a priori, one set which goes "*from concepts* to intuition", and another that goes "*from the intuition* to concepts" (A160/B199). The latter are the basic propositions of mathematics, whereas the former actually function as "a principle" (*Principium*) for the mathematical propositions, a principle "on which is grounded a priori the possibility and objective validity" of mathematical propositions (A160/B199; trans. amended). So, while *mathematical* basic propositions are "derived from ... pure *intuitions* (although by means of the understanding)", the mathematics-*grounding* a priori basic propositions are instead "derived from pure *concepts*" (A159–60/B198–9; emphasis added). What is more, it is *only* the latter, mathematics-grounding propositions, *rather than* the specifically mathematical ones, which Kant says here are to be included in the Transcendental Analytic's "systematic representation" (A159/B197) of the basic propositions of pure understanding. Here again, then, Kant is distinguishing between what sort of representation of space pertains to geometry (mathematics) and what pertains to (transcendental) philosophy, and also again ordering the latter as the ground or principle of the former—all the while, however, presupposing TAe's account of the ultimate origin of the concept of space used in philosophy in original intuition.

This distinction is revisited and further clarified in the important discussion of the difference between philosophical and mathematical cognition in the Doctrine of Method. Here Kant makes two points that are

274 C. Tolley

especially relevant for our purposes. First, he claims that while mathematical cognition is a priori cognition "from the *construction* of concepts", philosophical cognition, by contrast, is simply cognition "from *concepts*" (A713/B741). More specifically, Kant claims that philosophical cognition "confines itself ... to general *concepts*", whereas mathematical cognition "cannot do anything with the mere concepts but hurries immediately to *intuition*" (A715/B743; emphasis added). The philosopher can only "*reflect on*" concepts, can "analyze" them and "make" them "distinct", whereas the mathematician, that is, the geometer, can "*construct*" concepts a priori (A716/B744; emphasis added), by using "imagination" to "exhibit *a priori* the intuition corresponding to [the concept]" (A713/B741).

In fact, the closest the philosopher gets to intuition is with *concepts* of kinds of *synthesis* of intuitions, which Kant explicitly distinguishes from any intuitions themselves (cf. A722/B750). "Pure philosophy", Kant writes, "fumbles around in nature with discursive *a priori* concepts without being able to make their reality intuitive *a priori* and by that means confirm it", whereas mathematicians can "determine an intuition a priori in space (shape)" (A725/B753). Crucially, this situation obtains even with respect to the synthetic a priori basic propositions (principles) of the Analytic, insofar as, for example, the Second Analogy does not actually contain, or refer to, any intuition, but merely judges about "time-conditions in general": here the philosopher "proceed[s] [therefore] merely in accordance with concepts, and cannot proceed through construction of concepts" (A722/B750n.). The same is true, Kant insists, of all the other basic propositions (cf. A724/B752), even the ones entitled "Axioms of Intuition": each of these, too, is a basic proposition "*from concepts*'" (A733/B761; emphasis added). It is a short step from here to conclude that even in TAe, Kant really means for the philosopher ("the metaphysician"; OKT, 20:419) to be dealing directly only with the *concept* of space, and providing an argument based on the exposition (analysis) of its content, rather than directly engaging with (let alone constructing concepts in) any intuition, even the original intuition itself.

Second, Kant here again claims that this difference in cognition ultimately consists in a difference in the "form" of the cognition of the relevant object (e.g. space), not a difference in the "matter" or in the "objects" of the cognition (A714/B742). In particular, Kant claims that "philosophy as well as mathematics does deal with magnitudes, e.g. with totality, infinity, etc." (A715/B743). This nicely complements the point made in the Kästner remarks (cf. Sect. 11.3 above), namely, that the metaphysician and the geometer both represent space, and also both represent it "as infinite" (OKT, 20:419), although, as Kant noted there, they represent this infinity in two different ways: by giving something actually infinite (space) to the mind, in contrast to giving something only potentially infinite (an increase in space) to the mind.[19]

11.5 Using the Threefold Distinction to Clarify TD's Remarks about the Relation between the Understanding and Certain Representations of Space

In the foregoing, we have seen Kant consistently identify the most originary representation of the space of outer appearances with a pure a priori *intuition* that is "given" or "had" in the mind. This intuition is both contrasted with, but also placed at the "ground" of, two other a priori representations of the space of appearances (as the "condition" of their possibility): the metaphysical concept of space and the geometrical construction of concepts of spaces in the intuition of space. While these latter concept-involving representations are said to be "derived" from the original intuition of space, the original intuition of space itself, as "an originally acquired representation" of "the form of outer objects in general", is something whose presence in the mind "long precedes the determinate *concepts* of things that are in accordance with this form" (ÜE, 8:222).

---

[19] In the Dialectic, Kant notes a further difference even in relation to the *progressus* that has otherwise been the focus of the foregoing remarks on the mathematical representation of infinity: whereas mathematicians are happy to speak of this *progressus* going *in infinitum*, philosophers restrict themselves to speaking of a *progressus in indefinitum* (A510–11/B538–9)—which is in further accord with the general distinction above, between the metaphysical though indeterminate representation of space as infinite and given, and the geometrical "determination" of space as to its parts "to infinity".

276   C. Tolley

What I want to show in this section is that, contrary to recent interpretive trends, this consistently stated, widely repeated priority and independence of the original intuition of space, over and against not just these (and all other) *conceptual* representations of space (and spaces), but also over and against any activity of the *understanding*, is something which Kant in fact maintains throughout TD. In other words, I argue against those who hold that certain passages from TD require ascribing to Kant either a conceptualist or an intellectualist view of the original intuition of space, according to which this intuition ultimately requires the involvement of an act of understanding (synthesis) for its occurrence, or even involves concepts in its content.[20]

The remarks that have seemed to suggest either the conceptualist or intellectualist account of the intuition of space occur in a small handful of dense passages in TD, including several footnotes, with the most often-discussed passage being the footnote at B160–1.[21] Despite such determined efforts in this direction, I shall now show why the traditional interpretation of the original intuition of space remains open, why the relevant passages about the representation of space from TD give us no clear or decisive reason to believe that Kant ever meant to give up on the priority and independence of intuition itself, in relation to both concepts and acts of understanding, and, finally, why we can maintain, to the contrary, that Kant consistently rejects the idea that the understanding, its acts or its representations (concepts) in any way stand as a condition for intuitions (whether pure or empirical) to be what they are.

The priority of sensibility (and the "a priori representations" that it "contains" and thereby "gives" to the mind) over and against the understanding (and its representations) is itself announced fairly clearly already in the Introduction of the First *Critique*:

> The transcendental doctrine of the senses will have to belong to the *first* part of the science of elements, since the conditions under which alone the

---

[20] See note 5 for references to conceptualist and intellectualist interpreters.

[21] For an overview of the variety of interpretations of this footnote, see Onof and Schulting (2015). For a survey of some of the key passages in TD and elsewhere for the broader debate about the nonconceptuality of the content of intuitions, see Allais (2015), Schulting (2015b) and Tolley (2013). See also Allais, Chap. 1, in this volume.

11 Representations of Space · 277

objects of human cognition are *given* precede those under which those objects are *thought*. (A15–16/B30; emphasis added)

The same sort of priority of sensibility to understanding is repeated at the outset of the Logic itself, early in the Analytic. There, Kant reminds us, first, that TAe has established that "only by means of such pure forms of *sensibility*" can "an object ... *appear* to us ... i.e., be an object of *empirical intuition*", which implies that space itself (along with time) is a pure intuition "that contain[s] *a priori* the conditions of the possibility of objects as *appearances*" (B121–2; emphasis added). This is then immediately contrasted with how things stand with the *understanding*, the a priori representations that *it* contains (i.e. the "pure *concepts*" or "categories" of understanding), and the forms ("functions") of *thinking* which make these concepts (categories) themselves possible:

> The categories of the understanding, on the contrary, *do not* represent to us the conditions under which objects are given in intuition *at all*, hence objects can indeed appear to us without necessarily having to be related to functions of the understanding, and therefore without the understanding containing their *a priori* conditions. ... Intuition by no means requires the functions of thinking. (B122–3; emphasis added)

Hence, not only is the pure intuition of space *reaffirmed* at the outset of TD as an autonomous condition on outer appearances and outer intuitions (and all of the further representations that these make possible: perception, experience), the understanding is itself clearly *rejected* as a condition of the same sort: neither the pure concepts of understanding nor the forms of its activity add any further conditions to appearances and intuitions.[22]

The attention to the foregoing threefold distinction in representations of space can now allow us to appreciate better that Kant continues to accord the same autonomy to sensibility in general, and to the originary pure intuition of space in particular, throughout TD.

---

[22] Indeed, as Kant says just a bit later in the Analytic: "That representation that can be given prior to [*vor*] *all* thinking is called intuition" (B132; emphasis added). For more discussion of these and similar passages, see Allais (2009).

In the A-Deduction, for example, Kant begins by highlighting a fact already established in TAe, namely, that "sense" *by itself* is responsible for a certain a priori ordering of the "manifold" given in sensation, an ordering that he here calls the "*synopsis*" of sense (A94/B127). Synopsis of the manifold is something he "ascribe[s] to sense" alone, although he means to show that there are syntheses by the imagination and understanding which can and do "correspond" to this synopsis (A97). Indeed, *before* he introduces the first act of synthesis in the A-Deduction, Kant emphasises both that "every intuition contains a *manifold* in itself" and that "*as contained in an instant*, each representation can *be* nothing other than an absolute *unity*" (A99; trans. amended and emphasis added). Presumably, this unity is something achieved by the synopsis of sense before any synthesis of understanding; synopsis therefore appears to be that which is responsible for bringing about an empirical intuition by ordering sensations into spatial form.

To be sure, Kant admits that an intuition "would not be *represented as*" containing a manifold "if the mind did not *distinguish* the time in the succession of impressions on another" (A99; emphasis added). Note, however, that this further act of distinguishing by the mind is only required for the *further representation* of the unity of the manifold which the intuition itself already possesses "absolutely" on its own, in the moment—and not for this (absolute) unity of the intuition itself. For the *representation* of the unity that an intuition already *has*—and so *not* for the intuition to "have" the unity in the first place—Kant thinks that "first the running-through [*das Durchlaufen*] of the manifold is necessary, and then a taking-together [*Zusammennehmung*]" (A99; trans. amended); it is *this* act which is "aimed directly at the intuition" (and *not constitutive of* the intuition in the first place) that he calls "the synthesis of apprehension" (A99). The result of this act of running-through, distinguishing and taking-together is thus a *representation* of the unity of the manifold contained in an intuition, rather than the intuition itself.

Now, to be fair, if read either out of the immediate context, or even just without a sense of the broader context following TAe, there are sentences in this same passage which might suggest that Kant means to be making a stronger claim, that the intuition itself first *comes to have* its unity *only* after the synthesis of apprehension has been directed at it. Kant

11 Representations of Space 279

writes, for example, that this synthesis is necessary "for *unity* of intuition to come out of this manifold" (A99; trans. amended). Even more strikingly, Kant goes on to remark that, without synthesis, we also "could have *a priori* neither the representations of space nor of time, since these can be generated [*erzeugt*] *only* through the synthesis of the manifold that sensibility in its original receptivity provides" (A99–100; emphasis added). Again, out of context, this can seem to contradict directly what Kant has been claiming about sensibility and the original intuition of space (and time) in the previous hundred or so pages.[23]

Once recontextualised, however, we can see that this sort of "synthesis-dependent" reading of original intuition is not at all forced on us by this passage. For one thing, as we have just seen, Kant's target of explanation at this step in TD is not how *intuition* per se comes about in the first place, but rather what is required for the *representation* of intuition via an act of mind which is "directed" at it. This itself fits well with the broader context of the Analytic of our capacity for *understanding*, insofar as the Analytic has already identified the fundamental act of understanding with combining or synthesising representations in *judgement* (A69), and has already characterised judging itself as "the representation *of a representation* of [an object]" (A68/B93; emphasis added).

Our understanding therefore has an essentially "reflective" relation to the representations given in sensibility, as is suggested by the *Prolegomena*: "All our intuition happens only by means of the senses; the understanding intuits nothing, but only *reflects*" (Prol, 4:288), that is, reflects on the intuitions afforded by the senses.[24] As the part of the *Prolegomena* corresponding to TD further clarifies, this reflection first takes the form of a *judgement of perception*, which expresses the reflective "consciousness of my state" (Prol, 4:300). It then continues on to a *judgement of experience*, which "express[es] not *merely* a relation of a perception to a subject", that is, the initial reflection in perception upon what is given and

---

[23] Cf. Grüne, Chap. 4, in this volume.

[24] For a very instructive analysis of the more general role of reflection in Kant's conception of understanding and concepts, compare Longuenesse (1998a), although she at times seems to wish to downplay the "subjective" standing that Kant accords to the initial targets of reflection in perception (sensations, "my state"; Prol, 4:300) and too quickly wishes to identify these items with the ultimate "objective" objects of judgements of experience.

280   **C. Tolley**

present in my mind in intuition, but rather "a property *of an object*", that is, something "objective" and distinct from what is contained in my own intuition (Prol, 4:298; emphasis added).

What I want to suggest is that just this shift of perspective—from intuition as representation, to the reflected, conscious *representation of* intuition—is at work in the aforementioned remarks from the A-Deduction about "the representation of space" as well (cf. A99–100). What is at issue here, and what is being "generated" through the synthesis, is not (i) the *original* representation of space, that is, the pure *intuition* of space (metaphysically) given prior to all acts of thinking and so on, but rather those other a priori *representations of this intuition* that were mentioned both in TAe and in the Kästner remarks—that is, (ii) the a priori *concept* of this space (i.e. the concept which represents this space) which is *metaphysically* expounded in TAe, along with (iii) the a priori *concepts* of spaces (objects) formed ("constructed") through *geometrical* "description".

This focus on the a priori *concepts* by means of which we represent space—that is, by means of which we *represent* the original intuition in which space is first given—rather than on the a priori *intuition* per se, is further confirmed just a few pages later. There, Kant claims that "the purest and first basic representations of space and time" (A102; trans. amended) enjoy a strict dependence upon the synthesis of understanding (in apprehension as well as association and reproduction). In isolation, this passage itself should surely suggest that what Kant means to assert is the dependence of original pure *intuition* of space on such synthesis, since we have seen him using just this phrase ("basic representation") in TAe to pick out the original intuition. Nevertheless, once we read on, we find that Kant ends up classifying the basic representations at issue *here* as certain "previously mentioned *thoughts*" (A102; emphasis added). Indeed, by A107, he makes it quite explicit that what he really means to be talking about, first and foremost, are "the *a priori concepts* (space and time)" (emphasis added), claiming only that *these concepts*—rather than space itself, or its original intuition—require a relation to our understanding (synthesis, apperception) in order to be possible. Hence, although it is possible to read Kant as claiming in these passages that, without a certain act of understanding responsible for "apprehension",

11 Representations of Space   281

we could not even *have* a priori "the representation of space" (A99), it would seem equally possible, and much more charitable, to read him as really referring to the conditions for the a priori *concept* of space, given as well how this particular representation was already in focus in the lead-up to TD itself (cf. A84–9).

We can also see the very same shift of perspective, from intuition per se, to the conceptual *representation of* intuition, in the B-Deduction. This can be easily missed, since, as in the A-Deduction, Kant at times compresses his expression in a way that, when read out of context, might not always wear this shift on its sleeves. Nevertheless, he does eventually give indications which show that his main focus is on those acts of understanding which are conditions for our *representing* (becoming conscious of) certain representations (intuitions)—first, their being perceived (in "empirical *consciousness*" of them; B160; emphasis added), and then, their contributing to experience (empirical "*cognition*" of objects "through connected perceptions"; B161). Similarly, the "representation of space" which is claimed only to be possible under such acts is once again the *concept* of space, not the original intuition.

At the outset of the B-Deduction, Kant again reminds us of key findings from TAe: that "the *manifold* of representations can be *given* in one intuition that is merely sensible, i.e., is nothing but receptivity", and also that "the *form* of this intuition"—that is, that in which the manifold that the (empirical) intuition contains is ordered through the synopsis of sense—"can *lie a priori in* our faculty of representation" (B129; emphasis added). What the senses are not able to contribute on their own, Kant then claims, is the *representation of* combination in the object: "We can *represent* nothing *as combined* in the object without having previously combined it ourselves", by means of a "*synthesis*" which is "an action of the understanding" (B130; emphasis added). Once again, if taken out of context, this (and nearby sentences) might make it sound like Kant thinks there could not *be* any unity of a plurality present anywhere, if an act of the understanding did not first make it so unified. Nevertheless, once contextualised, we can see that things need not be read in this manner, since we have already seen Kant in general shifting his target from what is constitutive of a *representation* (intuition) per se to what is required for the *representation of* (certain features of) *a representation*.

282   C. Tolley

A similar point should be made about Kant's claim in §20 of the B-Deduction that the "manifold that is given in a sensible intuition necessarily belongs under the original synthetic unity of apperception, since through this alone is the *unity of the intuition* possible (§17)" (B143; emphasis added). As the reference back to §17 indicates, the "*unity* of the intuition" that is under discussion is not the unity primitively had by a single intuition (or the absolute unity conferred on the manifold by being *given* "in a moment"; A99), but rather the unity the intuition must possess if it is to be "capable of being *combined in one consciousness*" (B136–7; emphasis added), that is, the unity that would pertain to the consciousness (representation) *of* the intuition, rather than the intuition per se. As he himself emphasises in this section, Kant is concerned with the conditions "under which every intuition must stand *in order to become an object for me*" (B138)—that is, for the intuition itself to be represented by me in a consciousness of an object—and not the conditions under which every intuition must stand in order to simply *be* an intuition "in" me in the first place.

The same sort of shift, finally, can also be tracked in what is surely now the most well-known footnote in the entire B-Deduction, and what would seem to be the most important single text for conceptualist and intellectualist interpreters of Kant's views on the intuition of space. This passage is even more compressed than the previous ones, and perhaps for this reason there are many different directions that this text has been taken. Here I shall limit myself to simply charting out a reading which is consistent with the text but which does not in any way require any conceptualist or intellectualist revisions to the doctrine of the autonomy, independence and priority of the original intuition of space as it has been articulated above.[25]

What has suggested such a revision to some of Kant's readers is, once again, a claim Kant makes here about a certain "unity" in relation to the intuition of space, to the effect that, while in TAe he "had ascribed this unity merely to sensibility", he now admits that it "presupposes a synthesis, which does not belong to the senses" (B160–1n.). However, being on

---

[25] For a careful and much more thorough analysis of this footnote that is broadly in line with the nonconceptualist reading I am defending here, see Onof and Schulting (2015).

11 Representations of Space 283

guard, as we now are, about a variety of unities which might be in question, and the variety of *representations* of space which might have such unities, we must try to discern which unity and which representation he means to be referring to. Tellingly, Kant begins by talking, not about the originary *intuition* of space and its unity, but rather about "space, *represented as object* (as is really required in *geometry*)" (B160n.; emphasis added), and the unity of *this* representation of space. This representation, we are told, "contains more than the mere form of intuition, namely the *comprehension* [*Zusammenfassung*; i.e. a grasping-together] of the manifold, given in accordance with the form of sensibility, into an *intuitive* representation [*anschauliche Vorstellung*]" (B160n.; trans. amended and my underlining). It is *this* "intuitive representation" of space, then—the intuition-involving representation of space as it occurs "in geometry", and not the original intuition of space—which is said to "contain" a "grasping-together" and whose unity is therefore said to "presuppose a synthesis, which does not belong to the senses". (As Kant says later, synthesis is necessary for any *apprehension* whatsoever; B206.) But then, the claim here pertains only to the *representations of* intuitions "*as intuitions*": synthesis is here claimed to be necessary only for the intuitions themselves to be first "*given as* intuitions" (B161n.; my underlining), as objects of concepts (of consciousness).

All of these added features of the description of the particular representation of space in question, then, allow this footnote to be read as claiming merely that a synthesis by the understanding is "presupposed" by *some* representation of space that was discussed in TAe. As we have seen, however, this is in no way sufficient to entail that it is specifically the originary *intuition* of space from the Metaphysical Exposition which "presupposes" such synthesis, since Kant could very well be talking instead about one of the two other *conceptual* representations of space which are "derivative" of this representation: the a priori metaphysical concept of space or, more likely, the geometrical concepts of kinds of delimited space (figures) in space. The latter is more likely, given Kant's explicit mention here of the involvement of an "intuitive representation", since (as we saw above) the metaphysical (philosophical) representation of space proceeds according to concepts (and conceptual analysis) *alone*,

284   **C. Tolley**

whereas the geometrical (mathematical) representation of space involves the construction of concepts "in" intuition.[26]

Sure enough, a review of TAe confirms that Kant did not take the opportunity in either the Metaphysical or the Transcendental Expositions to place any explicit emphasis on the role of the *understanding* in the acts of delimitation "in thought", construction, and so on, as a further condition for the possibility of distinctively geometrical representation. Indeed, *this* dependency only becomes highlighted in TD itself, and is more fully articulated only much later in the Analytic (cf. A160/B199). Note, however, that even after highlighting *this* dependence, Kant continues to reaffirm both the nonconceptuality of the content of intuitions and the independence of intuition and appearances from acts of understanding.[27]

11.6 Conclusion

I have argued, first, that in the Critical period, Kant is working with a threefold distinction between a priori representations of the space of outer appearances: (i) the originary intuition of this space; (ii) the conceptual

---

[26] Friedman rejects the idea that Kant is here discussing explicitly geometrical representations (representations constructed in the science of geometry), because he thinks Kant must be talking about a more primitive representation presupposed by all geometrical representation (cf. Friedman 2015). This may be so, since Kant does say here that it "precedes all concepts"—presumably, all concepts of spaces (cf. Longuenesse 1998b). Yet as we have seen above in the discussion of the Kästner remarks, there are still further representations of space intermediate (as it were) between the original intuition and its geometrical representation, all of which are still "derivative" of the "originary" intuition—most notably, the a priori concept of space which is "expounded" in transcendental philosophy. Furthermore, Friedman has not made the case that the metaphysically "given" *concept* of space itself will need to incorporate the specifically "kinematic" activity (or kinematic unification of perspectives thanks to apperception) into its content that Friedman's reading of the representation at issue in B160n. presupposes (cf. Friedman 2012 and 2015). This itself leaves open the possibility that *both* the original intuition of space *and* the metaphysical concept of space lack consciousness of the kinematic perspective-structure that Friedman sees as a condition for the possibility of the *geometrical* representation of space, and that this content is only represented distinctly subsequent to geometry itself, rather than in the original intuition or metaphysical concept of space.

[27] At the outset of the Schematism, for example, Kant writes that "no one would say that the *category*, e.g., causality, could also be intuited through the senses and is contained in the appearance" (A137–8/B176–7; emphasis added). And again, at the beginning of the Dialectic, Kant claims that "a representation of sense ... contains no *judgment* at all" (A294/B350; emphasis added). And in the chapter on Phenomena and Noumena, Kant describes the situation that obtains "if I take all *thinking* (through *categories*) away from an empirical cognition" as leaving in place "mere [*bloße*] intuition" (A253/B309; emphasis added).

metaphysical representation of this space as object, and as to some of its features; and (iii) the at once conceptual and "intuitive" representation of this space in geometrical construction. I have then argued, secondly, that attention to this threefold distinction allows us to retain a traditional nonconceptualist, non-intellectualist interpretation of Kant's position on the original intuition of space throughout the *Critique*, according to which, even in the course of (and after) TD, Kant upholds the autonomy of this intuition over and against the understanding and its acts. To be sure, bringing to light the more complete consistency of the traditional reading does not itself suffice to refute the revisionary readings. Nevertheless, I hope the foregoing has at least helped open up a path for the traditionalist to follow through some of the more notoriously dense thickets of the Analytic of Concepts, as well as brought to light further nuances in Kant's Critical account of space.[28]

---

[28] I would like to thank Lucy Allais, Karl Ameriks, Rosalind Chaplin, Dennis Schulting, the UCSD German Philosophy Research Group, an anonymous referee and especially Eric Watkins for helpful discussion and feedback on earlier drafts of this material.

Bibliography

Abela, P. 2002. *Kant's Empirical Realism*. Oxford: Clarendon Press.

Allais, Lucy. 2009. Kant, Nonconceptual Content and the Representation of Space. *Journal of the History of Philosophy* 47(3): 383–413.

——— 2010. Kant's Argument for Transcendental Idealism in the Transcendental Aesthetic. *Proceedings of the Aristotelian Society* 110(1), Part 1: 47–75.

——— 2011a. Idealism Enough: Response to Roche. *Kantian Review* 16(3): 375–398.

——— 2011b. Transcendental Idealism and the Transcendental Deduction. In *Kant's Idealism. New Interpretations of a Controversial Doctrine*, eds. D. Schulting and J. Verburgt, 91–107. Dordrecht: Springer.

——— 2012. Perceiving Distinct Particulars. In *Kantian Metaphysics Today: New Essays on Time and Space*, eds. R. Baiasu et al., 41–66. Basingstoke and New York: Palgrave Macmillan.

——— 2015. *Manifest Reality: Kant's Idealism and His Realism*. Oxford: Oxford University Press.

——— forthcoming a. Synthesis and Binding. In *Kant and the Philosophy of Mind*, eds. A. Gomes and A. Stephenson. Oxford: Oxford University Press.

© The Editor(s) (if applicable) and The Author(s) 2016
D. Schulting (ed.), *Kantian Nonconceptualism*,
DOI 10.1057/978-1-137-53517-7

288 Bibliography

———— forthcoming b. Transcendental Idealism and the Transcendental Aesthetic: Reading the *Critique of Pure Reason* Forwards. In *Kant's Critique of Pure Reason: A Critical Guide*, ed. J. O'Shea. Cambridge: Cambridge University Press.

Allison, H. 1990. *Kant's Theory of Freedom*. Cambridge: Cambridge University Press.

———— 1996. *Idealism and Freedom. Essays on Kant's Theoretical and Practical Philosophy*. Cambridge: Cambridge University Press.

———— 2001. *Kant's Theory of Taste: A Reading of the Critique of Aesthetic Judgment*. Cambridge: Cambridge University Press.

———— 2004. *Kant's Transcendental Idealism. An Interpretation and Defense*. New Haven: Yale University Press.

Ameriks, K. 2000. *Kant and the Fate of Autonomy. Problems in the Appropriation of the Critical Philosophy*. Cambridge: Cambridge University Press.

———— 2003a. *Interpreting Kant's Critiques*. Oxford: Oxford University Press.

———— 2003b. New Views on Kant's Judgment of Taste. In K. Ameriks, *Interpreting Kant's Critiques*, 307–323. Oxford: Oxford University Press.

———— 2003c. Taste, Conceptuality, and Objectivity. In K. Ameriks, *Interpreting Kant's Critiques*, 324–343. Oxford: Oxford University Press.

Anderson, L. 2001. Synthesis, Cognitive Normativity, and the Meaning of Kant's Question, "How Are Synthetic Cognitions A Priori Possible?". *European Journal of Philosophy* 9(3): 275–305.

———— 2015. *The Poverty of Conceptual Truth: Kant's Analytic/Synthetic Distinction and the Limits of Metaphysics*. Oxford: Oxford University Press.

Aquila, R. 1983. *Representational Mind. A Study of Kant's Theory of Knowledge*. Bloomington: Indiana University Press.

Bauer, N. 2010. Kant's Subjective Deduction. *British Journal for the History of Philosophy* 18(3): 433–460.

———— 2012. A Peculiar Intuition: Kant's Conceptualist Account of Perception. *Inquiry* 55(3): 215–237.

Beck, J. 2012. The Generality Constraint and the Structure of Thought. *Mind* 121(483): 563–600.

———— 2013. Why We Can't Say What Animals Think. *Philosophical Psychology* 26(4): 520–546.

Beck, L.W. 1978. Did the Sage of Königsberg Have No Dreams? In L.W. Beck, *Essays on Kant and Hume*, 38–60. New Haven: Yale University Press.

Bermúdez, J., and A. Cahen. 2015. Nonconceptual Mental Content. In *Stanford Encyclopedia of Philosophy*, ed. E. Zalta, http://plato.stanford.edu/archives/fall2015/entries/content-nonconceptual/.

Bibliography   289

Bowman, B. 2011. A Conceptualist Reply to Hanna's Kantian Nonconceptualism. *International Journal of Philosophical Studies* 19(3): 417–446.

Brewer, B. 2005. Perceptual Experience Has Conceptual Content. In *Contemporary Debates in Epistemology*, eds. M. Steup and E. Sosa, 217–230. Malden, MA and Oxford: Blackwell.

Brook, A. 2013. Kant's View of the Mind and Consciousness of Self. In *Stanford Encyclopaedia of Philosophy*, ed. E. Zalta, http://plato.stanford.edu/archives/fall2013/entries/kant-mind/.

Burge, T. 2010. *Origins of Objectivity*. Oxford: Oxford University Press.

Buroker, J. 2006. *Kant's 'Critique of Pure Reason': An Introduction*. Cambridge: Cambridge University Press.

Byrne, A. 2005. Perception and Conceptual Content. In *Contemporary Debates in Epistemology*, eds. M. Steup and E. Sosa, 231–250. Malden, MA and Oxford: Blackwell.

Carson, E. 1997. Kant on Intuition in Geometry. *Canadian Journal of Philosophy* 27(4): 489–512.

Cassam, Q. 1987. Transcendental Arguments, Transcendental Synthesis and Transcendental Idealism. *Philosophical Quarterly* 37(149): 355–378.

——— 1993. Inner Sense, Body Sense, and Kant's "Refutation of Idealism". *European Journal of Philosophy* 1(2): 111–127.

Chignell, A. 2007. Kant's Concepts of Justification. *Noûs* 41(1): 33–63.

——— 2010. Real Repugnance and Our Ignorance of Things-in-Themselves: A Lockean Problem in Kant and Hegel. *Internationales Jahrbuch des Deutschen Idealismus/International Yearbook of German Idealism* 7(2009): 135–159.

——— 2014. Modal Motivations for Noumenal Ignorance: Knowledge, Cognition, and Coherence. *Kant-Studien* 105(4): 573–597.

Connolly, K. 2014. Which Kantian Conceptualism (or Nonconceptualism)? *Southern Journal of Philosophy* 52(3): 316–337.

Crane, T. 2013. The Given. In *Mind, Reason and Being-in-the-World. The McDowell-Dreyfus Debate*, ed. J. Schear, 229–249. London: Routledge.

Davis, W. 2005. Concept Individuation, Possession Conditions, and Propositional Attitudes. *Noûs* 39(1): 140–166.

Dreyfus, H. 2013. The Myth of the Pervasiveness of the Mental. In *Mind, Reason and Being-in-the-World. The McDowell-Dreyfus Debate*, ed. J. Schear, 15–40. London: Routledge.

Dummett, M. 1993. *The Seas of Language*. Oxford: Oxford University Press.

Dunlop, K. 2012. Kant and Strawson on the Content of Geometrical Concepts. *Noûs* 46(1): 86–126.

290 Bibliography

Engelhard, K. 2007. Hegel über Kant. Die Einwände gegen den transzendentalen Idealismus. In *Hegel und die Geschichte der Philosophie*, eds. D. Heidemann and C. Krijnen, 150–170. Darmstadt: Wissenschaftliche Buchgesellschaft.

Engstrom, S. 2006. Understanding and Sensibility. *Inquiry* 49(1): 2–25.

Evans, G. 1982. *The Varieties of Reference*, ed. J. McDowell. Oxford: Clarendon Press.

Faggion, A. 2015. Can Mere Intuitions Represent Objects? In *Kant's Lectures*, eds. B. Dörflinger et al., 91–103. Berlin and New York: de Gruyter.

Falkenstein, L. 2006. Kant's Transcendental Aesthetic. In *A Companion to Kant*, ed. G. Bird, 140–153. Oxford: Blackwell.

Fichant, M. 1997. "L'espace est représenté comme une grandeur infinie donnée": La radicalité de l'Esthétique. *Philosophie* 56: 20–48.

Frege, G. 1960. *The Foundations of Arithmetic*. New York: Harper.

Friedman, M. 1992. *Kant and the Exact Sciences*. Cambridge, MA: Harvard University Press.

——— 2000. Geometry, Construction, and Intuition in Kant and his Successors. In *Between Logic and Intuition*, eds. G. Sher and R. Tieszen, 186–218. Cambridge: Cambridge University Press.

——— 2012. Kant on Geometry and Spatial Intuition. *Synthese* 186(1): 231–255.

——— 2015. Kant on Geometry and Experience. In *Mathematizing Space*, ed. V. De Risi, 275–309. Dordrecht: Springer.

Gardner, S. 2013. Transcendental Philosophy and the Possibility of the Given. In *Mind, Reason and Being-in-the-World. The McDowell-Dreyfus Debate*, ed. J. Schear, 110–142. London: Routledge.

Geach, P. 1957. *Mental Acts: Their Content and Their Objects*. London: Routledge and Kegan Paul.

——— 1969. What Do We Think With? In P. Geach, *God and the Soul*, 30–41. New York: Schocken.

Ginsborg, H. 1990. *The Role of Taste in Kant's Theory of Cognition*. New York and London: Garland.

——— 2006a. Empirical Concepts and the Content of Experience. *European Journal of Philosophy* 14(3): 349–372.

——— 2006b. Kant and the Problem of Experience. *Philosophical Topics* 34(1): 56–106.

——— 2006c. Aesthetic Judgment and Perceptual Normativity. *Inquiry* 49(5): 403–437.

————— 2008. Was Kant a Nonconceptualist? *Philosophical Studies* 137(1): 65–77.

Godlove, T. 2011. Hanna, Kantian Nonconceptualism, and Benacerraf's Dilemma. *International Journal of Philosophical Studies* 19(3): 447–464.

Golob, S. 2014. Kant on Intentionality, Magnitude, and the Unity of Perception. *European Journal of Philosophy* 22(4): 505–528.

————— forthcoming a. Kant as Both Conceptualist and Nonconceptualist. *Kantian Review*.

————— forthcoming b. What Do Animals See? Intentionality, Objects and Kantian Nonconceptualism. In *Kant and Animals*, eds. L. Allais and J. Callanan. Oxford: Oxford University Press.

Gomes, A. 2010. Is Kant's Transcendental Deduction of the Categories Fit For Purpose? *Kantian Review* 15(2): 118–137.

————— 2014. Kant on Perception: Naive Realism, Nonconceptualism, and the B-Deduction. *Philosophical Quarterly* 64(2014): 1–19.

————— forthcoming. Naive Realism in Kantian Phrase. *Mind*.

Griffith, A. 2012. Perception and the Categories: A Conceptualist Reading of Kant's Critique of Pure Reason. *European Journal of Philosophy* 20(2): 193–222.

Grimm, J., and W. Grimm. 1854/1961. *Deutsches Wörterbuch von Jacob und Wilhelm Grimm*. Leipzig: Hirzel.

Grüne, S. 2008. Begriffe als Regeln der Wahrnehmung. In *Recht und Frieden in der Philosophie Kants: Akten des X. Internationalen Kant-Kongresses*, vol 2, eds. V. Rohden et al., 267–277. Berlin and New York: de Gruyter.

————— 2009. *Blinde Anschauung. Die Rolle von Begriffen in Kants Theorie sinnlicher Synthesis*. Frankfurt a/M: Klostermann.

————— 2011. Is There a Gap in Kant's B Deduction? *International Journal of Philosophical Studies* 19(3): 465–490.

————— 2014a. Reply to Colin McLear. *Critique*, https://virtualcritique.wordpress.com/2014/08/20/reply-to-colin-mclear/.

————— 2014b. Reply to Thomas Land. *Critique*, https://virtualcritique.wordpress.com/2014/08/22/reply-to-thomas-land/.

————— forthcoming. Are Kantian Intuitions Object-Dependent? In *Kant and the Philosophy of Mind*, eds. A. Gomes and A. Stephenson. Oxford: Oxford University Press.

Gunkel, A. 2015. *Autonomie—Metaphysik—Endlichkeit. Die Endlichkeit des menschlichen Denkens bei Kant*, unpublished Ph.D. dissertation, University of Luxembourg.

Bibliography

Guyer, P. 2009. The Harmony of the Faculties in Recent Books on the *Critique of the Power of Judgment*. *Journal of Aesthetics and Art Criticism* 67(2): 201–221.

Haag, J. 2007. *Erfahrung und Gegenstand. Das Verhältnis von Sinnlichkeit und Verstand.* Frankfurt a/M: Klostermann.

Hanna, R. 2001. *Kant and the Foundations of Analytic Philosophy.* Oxford: Clarendon Press.

——— 2005. Kant and Nonconceptual Content. *European Journal of Philosophy* 13(2): 247–290.

——— 2006. *Kant, Science, and Human Nature.* Oxford: Clarendon Press.

——— 2008. Kantian Nonconceptualism. *Philosophical Studies* 137(1): 41–64.

——— 2011a. Beyond the Myth of the Myth: A Kantian Theory of Nonconceptual Content. *International Journal of Philosophical Studies* 19(3): 323–398.

——— 2011b. Kant's Nonconceptualism, Rogue Objects, and the Gap in the B Deduction. *International Journal of Philosophical Studies* 19(3): 399–415.

——— 2013a. Kant, Hegel, and the Fate of Nonconceptual Content. *Hegel Bulletin* 34(1): 1–32.

——— 2013b. The Togetherness Principle, Kant's Conceptualism, and Kant's Nonconceptualism. In *Stanford Encyclopedia of Philosophy*, ed. E. Zalta, http://plato.stanford.edu/archives/fall2013/entries/kant-judgment/supplement1.html.

——— 2015. *Cognition, Content, and the A Priori.* Oxford: Oxford University Press.

——— 2016. Kantian Madness: Blind Intuitions, Essentially Rogue Objects, Nomological Deviance, and Categorial Anarchy. *Contemporary Studies in Kantian Philosophy* 1:44–64.

——— MS. *Kant, Humanity, and Nature.*

Hanna, R., and M. Chadha. 2011. Nonconceptualism and the Problem of Perceptual Self-Knowledge. *European Journal of Philosophy* 19(2): 184–223.

Heck, R. 2000. Nonconceptual Content and the "Space of Reasons". *Philosophical Review* 109(4): 483–523.

——— 2009. Are There Different Kinds of Content? In *Contemporary Debates in Philosophy of Mind*, eds. B. McLaughlin and J. Cohen, 117–138. Malden, MA: Wiley.

Heidegger, M. 1997. *Kant and the Problem of Metaphysics.* Bloomington: Indiana University Press.

Heidemann, D. 1998. *Kant und das Problem des metaphysischen Idealismus.* Berlin and New York: de Gruyter.

Bibliography   293

———— 2002. Anschauung und Begriff. Ein Begründungsversuch des Stämme-Dualismus in Kants Erkenntnistheorie. In *Aufklärungen. Festschrift für Klaus Düsing zum 60. Geburtstag*, ed. K. Engelhard, 65–90. Berlin: Duncker & Humblot.

———— 2012. The "I think" Must Be Able to Accompany All My Representations. Unconscious Representations and Self-Consciousness in Kant. In *Kant's Philosophy of the Unconscious*, eds. P. Giordanetti et al., 37–59. Berlin and Boston: de Gruyter.

————, ed. 2013a. *Kant and Nonconceptual Content*. London and New York: Routledge.

———— 2013b. Kant and Nonconceptual Content: The Origin of the Problem. In *Kant and Nonconceptual Content*, ed. D. Heidemann, 1–10. London and New York: Routledge.

———— forthcoming. Diskursivität und Einheit des Selbstbewusstseins. In *Immanuel Kant: Die Einheit des Bewusstseins*, eds. G. Motta and U. Thiel. Berlin and New York: de Gruyter.

Heis, J. 2014a. The Priority Principle from Kant to Frege. *Noûs* 48(2): 268–297.

———— 2014b. Kant (vs. Leibniz, Wolff, and Lambert) on Real Definitions in Geometry. *Canadian Journal of Philosophy* 44(5/6): 605–630.

Henrich, D. 1969. The Proof-Structure of Kant's Transcendental Deduction. *Review of Metaphysics* 22(4): 640–659.

Hintikka, J. 1969. On Kant's Notion of an Intuition (*Anschauung*). In *The First Critique*, eds. T. Penelhum and J. MacIntosh, 38–53. Belmont: Wadsworth.

Hogan, D. 2009. Three Kinds of Rationalism and the Non-Spatiality of Things in Themselves. *Journal of the History of Philosophy* 47(3): 355–382.

Howell, R. 1973. Intuition, Synthesis, and Individuation in the *Critique of Pure Reason*. *Noûs* 7(3): 207–232.

Hughes, F. 2007. *Kant's Aesthetic Epistemology*. Edinburgh: Edinburgh University Press.

Hume, D. 1978. *Treatise of Human Nature*, ed. L. Selby-Bigge, second edition rev. P. Nidditch. Oxford: Clarendon Press.

Kalar, B. 2006. *The Demands of Taste in Kant's Aesthetics*. London and New York: Continuum.

Kant, I. 2014. On Kästner's Treatises, trans. and eds. C. Onof and D. Schulting. *Kantian Review* 19(2): 305–313.

Kenny, A. 2010. Concepts, Brains, and Behaviour. *Grazer Philosophische Studien* 81(1): 105–313.

King, J., S. Soames, and J. Speaks. 2014. *New Thinking About Propositions*. Oxford: Oxford University Press.

294 Bibliography

Kirwan, J. 2004. *The Aesthetic in Kant. A Critique.* London and New York: Continuum.

Kreis, G. 2015. The Varieties of Perception. Nonconceptual Content in Kant, Cassirer, and McDowell. In *The Philosophy of Ernst Cassirer*, eds. T. Friedman and S. Luft, 313–338. Berlin and New York: de Gruyter.

Kukla, R., ed. 2006. *Aesthetics and Cognition in Kant's Critical Philosophy.* Cambridge: Cambridge University Press.

Laiho, H. 2012. *Perception in Kant's Model of Experience*, Ph.D. dissertation, University of Turku.

Land, T. 2011. Kantian Conceptualism. In *Rethinking Epistemology*, eds. G. Abel et al., 197–239. Berlin: de Gruyter.

———— 2014a. Spatial Representation, Magnitude and the Two Stems of Cognition. *Canadian Journal of Philosophy* 44(5/6): 524–550.

———— 2014b. Thomas Land on Stefanie Grüne's *Blinde Anschauung. Critique*, https://virtualcritique.wordpress.com/2014/08/21/thomas-land-on-stefanie-grunes-blinde-anschauung/.

———— 2015a. Nonconceptualist Readings of Kant and the Transcendental Deduction. *Kantian Review* 20(1): 25–51.

———— 2015b. No Other Use Than in Judgment? Kant on Concepts and Sensible Synthesis. *Journal of the History of Philosophy* 53(3): 461–484.

———— forthcoming. Conceptualism and the Objection from Animals. In *Akten des 12. Internationalen Kant-Kongresses.* Berlin and New York: de Gruyter.

La Rocca, C. 2013. La formazione dei concetti in Kant. Su un'interpretazione recente. *Studi kantiani* XXVI: 137–146.

Laywine, A. 2001. Kant in Reply to Lambert on the Ancestry of Metaphysical Concepts. *Kantian Review* 5: 1–48.

Lear, J. 1984. The Disappearing "We". *Proceedings of the Aristotelian Society* 58: 219–242.

Lewis, C.I. 1929. *Mind and the World-Order: Outline of a Theory of Knowledge.* New York: Dover.

Longuenesse, B. 1998a. *Kant and the Capacity to Judge.* Princeton: Princeton University Press.

———— 1998b. Synthèse et donation. *Philosophie* 60: 79–91 [translated in Longuenesse (2005), 64–78].

———— 2000. Kant's Categories and the Capacity to Judge: Responses to Henry Allison and Sally Sedgwick. *Inquiry* 43(1): 91–110.

———— 2005. *Kant and the Human Standpoint.* Cambridge: Cambridge University Press.

Bibliography 295

Machery, E. 2009. *Doing Without Concepts*. New York: Oxford University Press.

Makkreel, R. 2006. Reflection, Reflective Judgment, and Aesthetic Exemplarity. In *Aesthetics and Cognition in Kant's Critical Philosophy*, ed. R. Kukla, 223–44. Cambridge: Cambridge University Press.

Manning, R. 2006. The Necessity of Receptivity: Exploring a Unified Account of Kantian Sensibility and Understanding. In *Aesthetic and Cognition in Kant's Critical Philosophy*, ed. R. Kukla, 61–84. Cambridge: Cambridge University Press.

Margolis, E. and S. Laurence. 2014. Concepts. In *Stanford Encyclopedia of Philosophy*, ed. E. Zalta, http://plato.stanford.edu/archives/spr2014/entries/concepts/.

Matherne, S. 2015. Images and Kant's Theory of Perception. *Ergo* 2: 737–777.

McDowell, J. 1990. Peacocke and Evans on Demonstrative Content. *Mind* 99(394): 255–266.

——— 1994. *Mind and World*. Cambridge, MA: Harvard University Press.

——— 1996. *Mind and World*, 2nd edn. Cambridge, MA: Harvard University Press.

——— 1998. Having the World in View: Sellars, Kant and Intentionality [The Woodbridge Lectures]. *Journal of Philosophy* 95(9): 431–491.

——— 2009. *Having the World in View: Essays on Kant, Hegel, and Sellars*. Cambridge, MA: Harvard University Press.

——— 2013. The Myth of the Mind as Detached. In *Mind, Reason and Being-in-the-World. The McDowell-Dreyfus Debate*, ed. J. Schear, 41–58. London: Routledge.

McLear, C. 2011. Kant on Animal Consciousness. *Philosophers' Imprint* 11(15): 1–16.

——— 2013. *Essays on Kant on Perception and Cognition*, unpublished Ph.D. dissertation, Cornell University.

——— 2014a. Colin McLear on Stefanie Grüne's *Blinde Anschauung. Critique*, https://virtualcritique.wordpress.com/2014/08/19/colin-mclear-on-stefanie-grunes-blinde-anschauung/.

——— 2014b. The Kantian (Non)conceptualism Debate. *Philosophy Compass* 9(11): 769–790.

——— 2015. Two Kinds of Unity in the *Critique of Pure Reason. Journal of the History of Philosophy* 53(1): 79–110.

——— 2016. Kant on Perceptual Content. *Mind* 125(497): 95–144.

——— forthcoming a. Animals and Objectivity. In *Kant on Animals*, eds. L. Allais and J. Callanan. Oxford: Oxford University Press.

Bibliography

———— forthcoming b. Intuition and Presence. In *Kant and the Philosophy of Mind*, eds. A. Gomes and A. Stephenson. Oxford: Oxford University Press.

Messina, J. 2014. Kant on the Unity of Space and the Synthetic Unity of Apperception. *Kant-Studien* 105(1): 5–40.

———— 2015. Conceptual Analysis and the Essence of Space. *Archiv für Geschichte der Philosophie* 97(4): 416–457.

Moore, A. 2012. *The Evolution of Modern Metaphysics*. Cambridge: Cambridge University Press.

Nagel, T. 1991. What Is It Like to Be a Bat? In T. Nagel, *Mortal Questions*, 165–180. Cambridge: Cambridge University Press.

Naragon, S. 1990. Kant on Descartes and the Brutes. *Kant-Studien* 81(1): 1–23.

Natorp, P. 1910. *Die Logischen Grundlagen der exakten Wissenschaften*. Leipzig: Tübner.

Newton, A. 2016. Nonconceptualism and Knowledge in Lucy Allais's *Manifest Reality*. *Kantian Review* 21(2): 273–282.

Onof, C. 2011a. Thinking the In-Itself and Its Relation to Appearances. In *Kant's Idealism. New Interpretations of a Controversial Doctrine*, eds. D. Schulting and J. Verburgt, 211–235. Dordrecht: Springer.

———— 2011b. Moral Worth and Inclinations in Kantian Ethics. *Kant Studies Online*: 116–61.

Onof, C., and D. Schulting. 2014. Kant, Kästner and the Distinction between Metaphysical and Geometric Space. *Kantian Review* 19(2): 285–304.

———— 2015. Space as Form of Intuition and as Formal Intuition: On the Note to B160 in Kant's *Critique of Pure Reason*. *Philosophical Review* 124(1): 1–58.

Parsons, C. 1992. The Transcendental Aesthetic. In *The Cambridge Companion to Kant*, ed. P. Guyer, 62–100. Cambridge: Cambridge University Press.

Paton, H. 1936. *Kant's Metaphysic of Experience*. London: Allen and Unwin.

Patton, L. 2011. The Paradox of Infinite Given Magnitude: Why Kantian Epistemology Needs Metaphysical Space. *Kant-Studien* 102(3): 273–289.

Peacocke, C. 1992. *A Study of Concepts*. Cambridge, MA: MIT Press.

Pendlebury, M. 1995. Making Sense of Kant's Schematism. *Philosophy and Phenomenological Research* 55(4): 777–797.

Pereboom, D. 1988. Kant on Intentionality. *Synthese* 77(3): 321–352.

Pereira, R. de Sá. 2013. What is Nonconceptualism in Kant's Philosophy?. *Philosophical Studies* 164(1): 233–254.

Pippin, R. 1982. *Kant's Theory of Form: An Essay on the 'Critique of Pure Reason'*. New Haven: Yale University Press.

———— 1989. *Hegel's Idealism. The Satisfactions of Self-Consciousness*. Cambridge: Cambridge University Press.

———— 1993. Hegel's Original Insight. *International Philosophical Quarterly* 33(3): 285–295.

———— 1997. Review of Béatrice Longuenesse *Kant et le pouvoir de juger* (PUF, 1993). *Journal of Philosophy* 94(6): 318–324.

———— 2005. Concept and Intuition. On Distinguishability and Separability. *Hegel-Studien* 39/40: 25–39.

———— 2013. What is "Conceptual Activity"? In *Mind, Reason and Being-in-the-World. The McDowell-Dreyfus Debate*, ed. J. Schear, 91–109. London: Routledge.

———— 2015a. Finite and Absolute Idealism. The Transcendental and the Metaphysical Hegel. In *The Transcendental Turn*, eds. S. Gardner and M. Grist, 159–172. Oxford: Oxford University Press.

———— 2015b. John McDowell's Germans. In R. Pippin, *Interanimations. Receiving Modern German Philosophy*, 63–90. Chicago: University of Chicago Press.

Prauss, G. 1971. *Erscheinung bei Kant. Ein Problem der 'Kritik der reinen Vernunft'*. Berlin: de Gruyter.

Roche, A. 2011. Allais on Transcendental Idealism. *Kantian Review* 16(3): 351–374.

Rohs, P. 2001. Bezieht sich nach Kant die Anschauung unmittelbar auf Gegenstände? In *Akten des 9. Internationalen Kant-Kongresses. Bd. II*, eds. R.-P. Horstmann et al., 214–228. Berlin and New York: de Gruyter.

Russell, B. 1910. Knowledge by Acquaintance and Knowledge by Description. *Proceedings of the Aristotelian Society* 11: 108–128.

———— 1997. *The Problems of Philosophy*. Oxford: Oxford University Press.

Schafer, K. forthcoming. Kant's Conception of Cognition and Our Knowledge of Things-in-Themselves. In *The Sensible and Intelligible Worlds: New Essays on Kant's Metaphysics and Epistemology*, eds. K. Schafer and N. Stang. Oxford: Oxford University Press.

Schlicht, T. 2011. Nonconceptual Content and the Subjectivity of Consciousness. *International Journal of Philosophical Studies* 19(3): 491–520.

Schulting, D. 2010. Kant, nonconceptuele inhoud en synthese. *Tijdschrift voor Filosofie* 72(4): 679–715.

———— 2012a. *Kant's Deduction and Apperception. Explaining the Categories*. Basingstoke and New York: Palgrave Macmillan.

———— 2012b. Kant, Nonconceptual Content, and the "Second Step" of the B-Deduction. *Kant Studies Online*: 51–92.

Bibliography

—— 2012c. Non-Apperceptive Consciousness. In *Kant's Philosophy of the Unconscious*, eds. P. Giordanetti et al., 271–303. Berlin and New York: de Gruyter.

—— 2015a. Transcendental Apperception and Consciousness in Kant's Lectures on Metaphysics. In *Reading Kant's Lectures*, ed. R. Clewis, 89–113. Berlin and New York: de Gruyter.

—— 2015b. Probleme des "kantianischen" Nonkonzeptualismus im Hinblick auf die B-Deduktion. *Kant-Studien* 106(4): 561–580.

—— 2016. Review of Sally Sedgwick *Hegel's Critique of Kant* (OUP, 2012), *Kant-Studien* 107(2): 414–419.

—— 2017. *Kant's Radical Subjectivism: Perspectives on the Transcendental Deduction*. London and New York: Palgrave Macmillan.

Sedgwick, S. 1992. Hegel's Treatment of Transcendental Apperception in Kant. *Owl of Minerva* 23(2): 151–163.

—— 1993. Pippin on Hegel's Critique of Kant. *International Philosophical Quarterly* xxxiii(3): 273–283.

—— 1997. McDowell's Hegelianism. *European Journal of Philosophy* 5(1): 21–38.

—— 2000. Hegel, McDowell, and Recent Defenses of Kant. *Journal of the British Society for Phenomenology* 31(3): 229–247.

—— 2001. "Genuine" versus "Subjective" Idealism in Hegel's *Jenaer Schriften*. In *Idealismus als Theorie der Repräsentation?*, ed. R. Schumacher, 233–245. Paderborn: mentis.

—— 2004. Hegel on Kant's Idea of Organic Unity: The Jenaer Schriften. In *Metaphysik und Kritik*, eds. S. Doyé et al., 285–298. Berlin and New York: de Gruyter.

—— 2005. The Emptiness of the "I": Kant's Transcendental Deduction in *Glauben und Wissen*. In *Hegel-Jahrbuch 2005. Glauben und Wissen. Dritter Teil*, eds. A. Arndt et al., 171–175. Berlin: Akademie Verlag.

—— 2012. *Hegel's Critique of Kant*. Oxford: Oxford University Press.

Sellars, W. 1963. Empiricism and the Philosophy of Mind. In W. Sellars, *Science, Perception, and Reality*, 127–196. New York: Humanities Press.

—— 1967. Some Remarks on Kant's Theory of Experience. *Journal of Philosophy* 64(20): 633–647.

—— 1968. *Science and Metaphysics: Variations on Kantian Themes*. London: Routledge and Kegan Paul.

Bibliography 299

——— 1976. Kant's Transcendental Idealism. In W. Sellars, *Kant's Transcendental Metaphysics*, ed. J. Sicha, 403–417. Atascadero: Ridgeview.

——— 1978. The Role of Imagination in Kant's Theory of Experience. In *Categories: A Colloquium*, ed. H. Johnstone, 231–245. University Park, PA: Penn State University Press.

——— 1997. *Empiricism and the Philosophy of Mind*. Cambridge, MA: Harvard University Press.

Setiya, K. 2004. Transcendental Idealism in the Aesthetic. *Philosophy and Phenomenological Research* 68(1): 63–88.

Shabel, L. 2004. Kant's "Argument From Geometry". *Journal of the History of Philosophy* 42(2): 195–215.

——— 2010. The Transcendental Aesthetic. In *The Cambridge Companion to Kant and Modern Philosophy*, ed. P. Guyer, 93–117. Cambridge: Cambridge University Press.

Speaks, J. 2005. Is There a Problem About Nonconceptual Content? *Philosophical Review* 114(3): 359–398.

Stalnaker, R. 1998. What Might Nonconceptual Content Be? In *Concepts*, ed. E. Villanueva, 339–352. Atascadero: Ridgeview.

Stang, N. 2011. Did Kant Conflate the Necessary and the A Priori? *Noûs* 45(3): 443–471.

——— 2012. Kant on Complete Determination and Infinite Judgement. *British Journal for the History of Philosophy* 20(6): 1117–1139.

——— 2016. *Kant's Modal Metaphysics*. Oxford: Oxford University Press.

Stephenson, A. 2011. Kant on Non-Veridical Experience. *Kant Yearbook* 3: 1–22.

——— 2015a. Kant, the Paradox of Knowability, and the Meaning of "Experience". *Philosophers' Imprint* 15(27): 1–19.

——— 2015b. Kant on the Object-Dependence of Intuition and Hallucination. *Philosophical Quarterly* 65(260): 486–508.

——— forthcoming. Imagination and Inner Intuition. In *Kant and the Philosophy of Mind*, eds. A. Gomes and A. Stephenson. Oxford: Oxford University Press.

——— MS. Kant and A Priori Knowability.

Strawson, P.F. 1959. *Individuals*. London: Methuen.

——— 1966. *The Bounds of Sense*. London: Methuen.

300 Bibliography

Sutherland, D. 2005a. The Point of Kant's Axioms of Intuition. *Pacific Philosophical Quarterly* 86(1): 135–159.

———— 2005b. Kant on Fundamental Geometrical Relations. *Archiv für Geschichte der Philosophie* 87(2): 117–158.

Tennant, N. 2000. Anti-Realist Aporias. *Mind* 109(436): 825–854.

Thompson, M. 1972. Singular Terms and Intuitions in Kant's Epistemology. *Review of Metaphysics* 26(2): 314–343.

Tolley, C. 2013. The Nonconceptuality of the Content of Intuitions: A New Approach. *Kantian Review* 18(1): 107–136.

———— 2014. Kant on the Content of Cognition. *European Journal of Philosophy* 22(2): 200–228.

———— MS a. Kant on the Place of Cognition in the Progression of Representations.

———— MS b. Kant on the Distinction between Perception and Experience.

———— MS c. *Kant's Doctrine of Appearances: Transcendental Idealism as a Theory of Intentionality.*

Tomaszewska, A. 2014. *The Contents of Perceptual Experience: A Kantian Perspective.* Warsaw and Berlin: de Gruyter.

Toribio, J. 2007. Nonconceptual Content. *Philosophy Compass* 2/3: 445–460.

Vaihinger, H. 1892. *Commentar zu Kants Kritik der reinen Vernunft*, vol. 2. Stuttgart: Union deutsche Verlagsgesellschaft.

Van Cleve, J. 1999. *Problems from Kant.* New York: Oxford University Press.

———— 2012. Defining and Defending Nonconceptual Contents and States. *Philosophical Perspectives* 26(1): 411–430.

Vanzo, A. 2012. *Kant e la formazione dei concetti.* Trento: Verifiche.

———— 2013. Kant e la formazione dei concetti. Risposta a Claudio La Rocca. *Studi kantiani* XXVI: 147–151.

———— 2014. Review of Stefanie Grüne *Blinde Anschauung. Die Rolle von Begriffen in Kants Theorie sinnlicher Synthesis* (Klostermann, 2009). *Studi kantiani* XXVII: 163–166.

Warren, D. 1998. Kant and the Apriority of Space. *Philosophical Review* 107(2): 179–224.

———— 2001. *Reality and Impenetrability in Kant's Philosophy of Nature.* New York and London: Routledge.

Watkins, E. 2005. *Kant and the Metaphysics of Causality.* Cambridge: Cambridge University Press.

———— 2008. Kant and the Myth of the Given. *Inquiry* 51(5): 512–531.

————, ed. 2009. *Kant's Critique of Pure Reason: Background Source Materials.* Cambridge: Cambridge University Press.

—— 2012. Kant, Sellars, and the Myth of the Given. *The Philosophical Forum* 43(3): 311–326.

Watkins, E. and M. Willaschek. forthcoming. Kant's Account of Cognition. *Journal of the History of Philosophy*.

Wenzel, C. 2005. Spielen nach Kant die Kategorien schon bei der Wahrnehmung eine Rolle? Peter Rohs und John McDowell. *Kant-Studien* 96(4): 407–426.

Willaschek, M. 1997. Der transzendentale Idealismus und die Idealität von Raum und Zeit. *Zeitschrift für philosophische Forschung* 51(4): 537–564.

Williams, J. 2012. How Conceptually-Guided are Kantian Intuitions? *History of Philosophy Quarterly* 29(1): 57–78.

Wilson, K. 1975. Kant on Intuition. *Philosophical Quarterly* 25(100): 247–265.

Winkler, K. 2010. Kant, the Empiricists, and the Enterprise of Deduction. In *The Cambridge Companion to Kant's 'Critique of Pure Reason'*, ed. P. Guyer, 41–72. Cambridge: Cambridge University Press.

Wright, C. 2001. On Being in a Quandary: Relativism, Vagueness, Logical Revisionism. *Mind* 110(437): 45–98.

Index[1]

A

Abela, Paul, 57n2
abstraction, 37n6, 160n32, 186, 247
accuracy condition(s), 30
acquaintance, x, 8, 14, 22, 56, 64,
172, 194–7, 205, 208, 212,
217, 219, 225, 244n20
direct, x, 14, 56
action, 12, 17, 103, 122, 163n36,
169n46, 201, 223–5,
224n30, 232, 233, 247, 281
actuality, 67, 70, 74, 76, 79, 91,
91n6, 161, 187, 189,
191–4, 194n40, 196, 197,
197n44, 271n18
A-Deduction, the, xi, 18, 164, 165,
202, 204, 206–8, 210, 211,

214, 215n21, 239, 247,
278, 280, 281
aesthetic idea, xvi, 119n5, 126,
139–43
aesthetics, xvi, 117–44
affection, affective, 53, 93, 94,
101, 102, 124, 128,
129, 142, 152, 157,
159, 159n31, 160–2,
166n41, 180, 219,
245n22, 252, 271n18
affinity, 215n21, 219
agency, 103, 223, 224
cognitive, 103
free, 223
practical, 103, 223, 224, 226
agreeable, the, 130, 134, 135

---

[1] Note: Page number followed by n denotes Footnote.

© The Editor(s) (if applicable) and The Author(s) 2016
D. Schulting (ed.), *Kantian Nonconceptualism*,
DOI 10.1057/978-1-137-53517-7

304 Index

Allais, Lucy, xi, xiii–xv, 1–25, 27, 29, 29n2, 33, 33n4, 36–8, 36n5, 37n6, 41n9, 43, 46, 47, 48n13, 56, 56n1, 58n4, 64n12, 82, 103n7, 145, 146n2, 154, 155, 156n22, 158, 162, 181n17, 182n18, 183n20, 185n23, 202, 208, 209, 217–19, 220n25, 231, 235n10, 260n6, 271n17, 276n21, 277n22

Allison, Henry, 35, 124n9, 126n13, 154n20, 156n23, 223

Ameriks, Karl, 120n5, 241n13

Analogies, the, 39, 42
  Second Analogy, the, 38, 43, 274

Anderson, Lanier, 174, 178n11, 186n25

animals, viii, xv, 8, 9, 29–31, 30n3, 34, 41, 45, 46n12, 47–51, 101, 108, 114, 179, 192, 203, 208, 210, 212, 217, 219n24, 222, 243n19
  non-human, 108, 146n2, 179, 183n21, 185n23

anthropology, 102

appearance, xi, xviii, 6–8, 20, 40, 59, 97, 98, 106n9, 107, 110, 113, 114, 152, 153, 155, 158, 209, 210, 219, 233, 238, 240, 247, 251, 257–63, 265, 266, 272, 275, 277, 284
  nonconformity of …s with the categories (forms of understanding/thinking), xi, 7, 8, 20, 114, 190, 209, 247, 284

merely formal (logical or epistemic) possibility of, xi, 7, 233

real (metaphysical) possibility of, xi, xviii, 7

apperception, 11, 12, 45n11, 47, 102, 128, 132n18, 151, 161, 201, 216n23, 218, 220n25, 220n26, 225n33, 240, 245, 250n29, 254, 255
  empirical, 215n21
  original synthetic unity of, 11n15, 128, 161, 184, 200, 214n18, 222, 241, 241n13, 282
  (transcendental) unity of (TUA), 47, 132n18, 174, 216, 218, 219, 226

apprehension. *See* synthesis

Aquila, Richard, 57

artwork, 127, 139–41

assent (*Fürwahrhalten*), 63, 65, 66, 136, 138n22, 175

association, associative, 39, 40, 48, 131, 149, 212, 214, 215n20, 215n21, 219, 221, 222, 224, 225, 280. *See also* imagination

attitude
  epistemic, 175, 177–9, 181, 196, 197
  propositional, 196, 204n7

Axioms of Intuition, the, 39, 42, 48n14, 97, 109, 152, 154–8, 163, 274

B

Bauer, Nathan, xiii, 11n15, 12n17, 12n20, 13, 17n29, 18n30, 19, 21, 103n6

Index

Baumgarten, A.G., 187
B-Deduction, the, 18, 33, 34, 37, 47, 113, 114, 153, 160, 162, 201, 208, 214n19, 215n21, 221, 229, 230, 234, 235, 239, 246, 247, 249, 252, 281, 282
Beck, Jacob, 173n4, 182
Beck, J.S., 178
Beck, L.W., 78n18, 187n27
behaviour, 9, 149, 223, 226
    "in-the-flow", 224, 224n30, 225
belief, v, vi, 13, 63, 102, 122, 135, 149, 171, 173, 194, 204n7
    basic perceptual, 143, 144, 172, 179, 186
    justified true, 62
Berkeley, George, 36
Bermudez, José, 101n3, 121n6, 127n14
Bowman, Brady, xiii, xiiin7, 7, 12n19, 24, 33, 34, 49, 103n6
Brewer, Bill, viiin1
Brook, Andrew, 207
Burge, Tyler, 28, 64n13
Buroker, Jill Vance, 57n2
Byrne, Alex, viiin1

C

Carson, Emily, xiv, 257n1
Cassam, Quassim, 44, 57n2
categories (functions of thought/ understanding), *passim*.
    See also concept(s)
    as a priori concepts, ix, x, 36, 38, 74, 113, 123n8, 201, 206, 209, 210

as conditions of empirical concept use, 36–8, 40, 44, 48n13, 229
dynamical, 40, 41, 51, 258, 258n2
justification / justified
    employment of, 35, 38, 41
mathematical, 40, 41, 51, 258, 258n2
objective validity of, xii, 18, 23, 33, 34, 49, 74–8, 150, 187
as rules of (guiding) synthesis, 17, 18, 240
causal, causality, vi, 25, 42–4, 49, 50, 56, 105, 121, 137, 194n40, 196, 197, 201, 201n3, 209, 258n2
    laws, 37, 43, 49, 50, 197
    relation(s), vi, 37, 56, 258n2
characteristic, 43, 59, 105, 109, 110, 132, 168, 170, 237, 250n29
Chignell, Andrew, 175, 186, 186n26, 188, 188n29, 189n30, 191n35, 193, 197n44
choice (*Willkür*), 102, 223
clairvoyance, 191, 196
cognition, *passim*. *See also* knowledge
    conditions on 12, 36, 50, 54, 59, 61–5, 61n8, 67–71, 75, 77, 123, 155, 187–91, 193–5, 210, 218, 237, 239, 281
    modal condition on, xv, xvii, 54, 67–74, 77, 187–9, 191–5, 197
    object-dependent views of, 64–6, 71, 73, 76, 78
    relation of ... to knowledge, 62, 63, 63n10, 64n11, 65, 71, 78, 186, 186n26, 196, 221, 244n20

306   Index

cognitive faculty/ies, viii, xvii, 24,
30n3, 58, 81, 94, 122, 124,
126, 126n13, 128, 136–8,
141, 142, 180, 185, 200,
235, 246, 281. *See also*
imagination; intellect;
sensibility; understanding
combination, 6, 12, 18, 43, 46, 149,
162, 192, 193, 200, 201,
212, 248, 249, 279, 281,
282. *See also* connection;
synthesis
  of the manifold, 12, 43, 152,
162, 163n36, 201, 212,
248, 249, 281
  necessary, 43
complexity, 20, 21, 44, 88, 150,
164, 165
composition, composite, 39, 41,
84, 85, 131, 132, 136,
152, 153, 201, 261, 262
compossibility, compossible, 188,
190
conatus, conation, 252
concept(s), *passim*. *See also* categories;
conceptuality
  application of ... in judgement,
132, 155, 158
  a priori, ix, x, 35, 36, 38, 39, 74,
123n8, 201, 206, 210,
232n7, 263–5, 274, 280,
281, 283, 284n26
  (*see also* categories)
  clear, 216, 216n23, 220, 221
  conceptual laden(ness), xiii, 239
  distinct, x, 220, 221n27, 223, 274
  empirical, 36–8, 43, 44, 48n13,
119n3, 119n5, 172, 179,
186, 201, 203, 218, 244n20

  empty, v, 7, 11, 60, 72, 107, 209,
229, 235 (*see also* intuition
(blind))
  obscure, xiii, 216, 216n22, 216n23,
220n26, 224, 225n33
conceptual content. *See* content
conceptualism, conceptualist, *passim*
  about intuition, vi, ix, xii, xiii, xv,
4, 6, 11, 17, 21, 22, 30, *et*
passim
  about perception, 2, 4–6, 30, *et*
passim
  Hegel's, xiv, xvii, 118n1, 227–55
  McDowell's, v–ix, xiv, 12, 13, 34,
56, 57, 192n36, 209, 224,
224n30, 233
  moderate or weak, xvi, xvii,
10, 101, 103, 113, 145–70,
207n11, 260n5
  Pippin's, ix, xiv–xviii, 227–55
  strong, 48, 101, 103, 147, 148,
150, 151n17, 228, 260n5
conceptuality, conceptualisation, v,
vii, ix, x, xv, 3, 9, 19–22,
25, 214n18, 229, 232,
236n11, 237, 244n20, 250,
253–5, 271n18
connection, connectedness,
  of (the manifold of)
representations, xvi, 21,
46, 47, 50, 51, 132, 201,
214n18, 219, 222, 229,
232, 233, 237, 249n28,
252, 281
Connolly, Kevin, xiii, 11n15
Consciousness, *passim*. *See also*
self-consciousness
  animal, 51, 222
  empirical, 6, 152, 281

Index 307

obscure, 203n5, 216n23
phenomenological, 4, 51, 129
subjective unity of, 214, 215
transcendental (*see* apperception)
(analytic) unity of, 174, 200,
203, 240, 282
construction, xviii, 90, 109, 158,
203n5, 212, 259–61,
267–9, 269–70n14, 271,
271n18, 274, 280, 284,
285. *See also* geometry;
space; synthesis of the
imagination
content, *passim. See also* mental
content; nonconceptual
content
conceptual, v, vii, xii, xiii, xvii,
57, 101, 101n3, 103,
121n6, 127n14, 141,
173n4, 174–7, 181n17,
182, 199–202, 204n7,
204n8, 225, 236, 239
experiential, vii, viii, 9, 177–9
judgemental, 177, 179
perceptual, vii, 3, 6, 25,
57, 122, 135
phenomenal, 88n4,
129, 134, 143
representational, vi, viii, 4, 5, 11,
11n15, 18, 33, 56, 57, 101,
103, 121n6, 129, 143, 192,
228, 240, 248, 252, 255
for thought, 239–43,
248, 253, 254
contiguity
spatial, 154
temporal, 154, 221
contingency, contingent,
49, 100, 205, 213, 221

continuity, 97, 164n39, 169, 217,
239, 243. *See also*
magnitude; *quanta continua*
correctness condition(s), vi, viii, 130,
176, 179, 181, 181n15,
184, 197
Crane, Tim, 204n8
Critical philosophy, the, x, xvii, 119,
187, 197, 199–226
the Critical revolution, xviii, 230
Critique of the Power of Judgement,
xvi, 118, 123–5, 130, 137,
173n6, *et passim*
Critique of Practical Reason,
71, 125, 223
Critique of Pure Reason
(First *Critique*), *passim*
Crusius, Christian, 187, 187n27

D

Davis, Wayne, 182n18
Descartes, René, 9
Dialectic, the. *See* Transcendental
Dialectic
Directions in Space, xi, xvi, 99–115
discursivity, 41n9, 57, 59n6, 84,
109, 119, 122, 139, 142,
180, 180n13, 190, 193,
239, 246n24, 250, 260n5,
262, 268, 274. *See also*
concept(s); conceptuality;
spontaneity; understanding
drawing, of a line, 40, 41, 153, 157,
158, 169, 169n47. *See also*
construction; synthesis of
the imagination
Dreyfus, Hubert, 224, 224n30, 225,
225n33, 254n35

308 Index

Dummett, Michael, 73n15, 182n18
Dunlop, Katherine, 182n18

E

egocentric centring. *See* space
empiricism, 13, 42, 44, 49, 180
Engelhard, Kristina, 118n1
Engstrom, Stephen, 32, 151n15,
   159n31, 176n8
Evans, Gareth, vii–ix, 57, 64n12,
   101n3, 127n14, 181, 182,
   236n11
   and the Generality Constraint, 182
   on nonconceptualism, vii–ix,
      101n3, 127n14, 181, 182
existence, xv, 14, 24, 54–8, 69, 76–9,
   100, 111, 125, 130, 173n6,
   174, 175, 180, 181, 184,
   191, 195, 202, 204n7, 214
   243n20, 258n2, 259
experience, *passim*
   aesthetic, xvi, 118, 134,
      135, 137, 142
   categorial, 35, 38, 50, *et passim*
   the formal conditions/laws of,
      69, 71, 190, 191, 193, 196,
      197n44
   the normative dimension of,
      119n3, 224
   outer, 263, 265, 265n11
   perceptual, vii, viii, ix, 9, 14, 34,
      56, 179, 197, 219, 221, 225
   the possibility of, 50, 69, 74, 190,
      206, 207, 210, 218
   possible, 22
   the sensible conditions of, 190
   transcendental conditions of,
      44, 51, 218

F

Faggion, Andrea, xiii, 181n17
Faith and Knowledge, 228, 229n2,
   232n8, 247, 250
Falkenstein, Lorne, 10n14, 27
feeling, 102, 107, 110, 120, 123–6,
   125n10, 128–31, 136–8,
   136n21, 138n23, 143,
   173n6, 222
Fichant, Michel, 260n6
Fichte, J.G., 238, 240, 241n13, 242,
   242n17, 244, 245n22, 253
finite, 16, 83–93, 87n3, 95–8, 97n9,
   140, 141, 168, 168n44,
   269, 270n14. *See also*
   geometry; space; time
finitude, 50, 270n14
free play, of the imagination and
   understanding, 124, 136, 137
Frege, Gottlob, 63, 181n17
Friedman, Michael, xiv, 169n46,
   178n11, 257n1, 260,
   260n5, 260n7, 266n12,
   269n13, 270n14, 284n26

G

Gardner, Sebastian, xiiin7, 224,
   224n30
Geach, Peter, 148n11, 182n18
geometry, xviii, 10, 41n10, 90, 91,
   109, 111, 152, 155,
   157n24, 257–85
   argument from, 41n10
   Euclidean, 104
   topology, 104, 105, 108
Ginsborg, Hannah, xiii, xiiin7, xv,
   15n26, 17n29, 18, 23, 30,
   33–5, 45, 45n11, 103n6,

119n3, 119n4, 145,
147n5, 148, 148n8,
178n11, 186n25
given, givenness, x, xi, xv, xviii, 7, 10,
11, 22–5, 47, 49, 53,
59–61, 72, 75, 76, 79, 83,
84, 90, 91, 107, 153, 155,
161, 166, 166n42, 201,
209, 211, 229, 234, 239,
240, 245, 247–9, 253,
266–71, 277–83, *et passim*.
See also receptivity; space
given magnitude, 16, 85, 93, 262,
268, 270n16
Myth of the Given, v, 12, 13
Godlove, Terry, xiii, xiiin7
Golob, Sacha, xv, 4n5, 6n9, 27–52
Gomes, Anil, xiii, xv, 7, 14n24, 18,
22, 29, 30, 35, 37, 38,
46–8, 48n13, 53–79
Griffith, Aaron, xiii, 3n3, 6n10, 18,
19, 21, 22n37, 27, 30, 34,
35, 45, 103n6, 145, 147n5,
176n8
ground, 9, 47, 51, 62, 70, 90, 92–4,
102, 106, 110, 125n10,
128–35, 132n19, 133n20,
136n21, 137–40, 138n23,
152, 153, 157n24, 165n40,
175, 186n26, 191, 194,
196, 214, 214n17, 214n18,
215n21, 216, 219, 221,
223, 235, 240, 252, 261–5,
267, 268, 273, 275
*Groundwork of the Metaphysics of
Morals* (GMS), 223
Grüne, Stefanie, xiii–xvi, xiiin7,
xivn8, 7, 18–19, 25, 34, 57,
58, 58n3, 81–98, 103n6,

147n5, 148, 148n8, 172n3,
177n10, 178n11, 180n12,
181n17, 186n26, 190n33,
192n36, 201, 202, 204n7,
208, 216, 216n22, 216n23,
220n26, 221n27, 225n33,
260n5, 279n23
guiding thread, the (*Leitfaden*),
232–3, 251
Guyer, Paul, 60, 136n21

H

Haag, Johannes, xiiin7,
178n11, 190n33
hallucination, 65, 69, 70,
191–3, 195n41, 196.
See also illusion
relation of … to cognition,
64, 69, 70
Hanna, Robert, vii–x, ixn2, xii–xiv,
xiiin7, xvi, 9n13, 18, 19,
21, 24, 29, 32, 34, 50,
57n2, 58n4, 82, 99–115,
146n2, 177n9, 181n17,
182n18, 202, 204n8,
209n13, 221
Heck, Richard, viii, 30, 101n3,
173n4, 173n5, 181n17
Hegel, G.W.F., xiv, xvii, 50, 118n1,
227–55
Heidegger, Martin, 28
Heidemann, Dietmar, xiii, xiiin7,
xvi, 117–44
Heis, Jeremy, 178, 182n18, 257n1
Henrich, Dieter, 252n32
Herz, Marcus, 79, 79n20, 112, 222
Hintikka, Jaakko, 58n3
Hogan, Desmond, 187n27

310 Index

holism, 142, 146, 162, 251
    holistic character of intuition,
        151, 167–9
    holistic structure of space and
        time, 166
homogeneity
    the homogeneous manifold,
        152–3, 168
    homogeneous parts, 153, 201
Howell, Robert, 58n3
Hughes, Fiona, 119n4
Hume, David, xv, 35–8, 41,
        42, 49, 52, 133n20
    Hume's Problem, 78, 79
        (*see also* scepticism)

idealism
    absolute, 229
    conceptual, 227
    Kant's, xvi, 32, 33, 37, 41, 44,
        50, 55, 71, 99–115, 118,
        143n25, 210, 228, 229,
        238, 258, 259n3
    ontological, 227
    phenomenalist interpretation /
        reading of, 50
    Refutation of, 78, 196n43
    transcendental, xvi, 32, 33, 55,
        99–115, 118, 143n25,
        204n7, 210, 258
illusion, 30, 65, 69. *See also*
    hallucination
    relation of ... to cognition, 65, 69
imagination
    and association, 48, 215, 215n20,
        215n21, 222

    productive, xvi, 142, 147, 148,
        148n9, 156–9, 161, 162,
        168–70, 193, 213n15,
        232n8, 246, 247
    recombinative activity of the, 193
    relation of ... to cognition, 123,
        124, 126, 128–30, 135–7,
        140, 141, 158, 203, 213,
        215, 246, 274
    relation of ... to understanding, xii,
        21, 123, 128–30, 135–40,
        142, 157, 162, 163n36, 213,
        232n8, 246, 250, 250n29,
        251n30, 254, 278
    and space, xi, xvi, 90, 148n9, 156–9,
        169, 250, 250n29, 254
    synthesis of (the), xi, xii, xiii, 18, 19,
        48, 250n29, 251n30, 254
    as synthesis of apprehension,
        213, 247
immediacy of intuition, x, 3–5, 9,
        14, 53, 54, 59, 91, 122,
        146, 175, 194, 231, 231n6,
        232n7, 271n18. *See also*
        intuition(s)
immediate. *See* concept(s);
    intuition(s); object
impression(s), sensory, ix, 18, 33, 58,
        94, 119, 164–6, 178, 211,
        213, 271n17, 278
Inaugural Dissertation, the, xi, 35, 79,
        100, 106n9, 109, 111, 112
inclination, 222–4, 226
    incentives of, 223
incongruent counterparts,
        9, 25, 105, 108, 114.
        See also space
individual, viii, 16, 217, 218

(fully) determinate, 205, 218
infants, 30n3, 108, 179, 183n21,
    185n23, 222
infinite, infinity (infinitude).
    See also space; time
    actual, 91, 91n6, 268
    space as, 16, 83–93, 95–8, 262,
        267–71, 275, 275n19
    time as, 86–93, 95, 97n9
inner sense, 107, 129, 138,
    148n11, 161, 162,
    163n36, 165n40,
    196n43, 213, 214, 223
intellect, xvii, 16, 59n6, 97n9,
    148n11, 172, 180, 180n14,
    183, 185, 187, 189,
    191n34. *See also*
    understanding
Intellectualism, xvii, 82, 84–9, 96,
    102n4, 172, 180, 180n14,
    181, 184, 185, 189–94,
    196, 197
    intellectualist, xvii, 102, 103,
        180, 182, 183, 186, 190,
        191n34, 192–4, 260,
        260n5, 276, 282
intentionality, 28, 30, 32, 34, 45n11,
    57, 121, 122, 178, 251
introspection
    introspective cognition, 195n42
intuition(s)
    a priori, 10, 16, 90, 93, 95, 96,
        194, 261–3, 265–7, 269,
        275, 280
    blind, v, 11, 11n15, 60, 229, 235,
        236, 241n13
    a brute's, 244n20
    dependence of ... on existence on
        objects, xv, 54–7, 76–9

empirical, x, 7, 18, 19, 23, 31,
    37n6, 44, 46, 47, 51, 56,
    61, 75, 76, 86–9, 94–6, 98,
    107, 108, 114, 148, 148n9,
    150, 153–6, 156n23,
    158–63, 159n31, 160n32,
    163n35, 166, 169, 194n40,
    195n42, 229, 245, 247,
    249, 262, 265, 279n14,
    277, 278, 281
formal, 10, 94, 102, 161, 162,
    162n34, 204n6, 250, 251,
    251n30
form of, x, xi, 10, 15, 107, 108,
    110, 148n9, 153, 155, 162,
    162n34, 163, 169n46, 184,
    191, 193, 195n42, 248,
    250, 250n29, 251, 251n30,
    259n4, 281, 283
the generation of, xi, xiii, xv, 18,
    88, 89, 157, 178–80, 184,
    185, 189, 190, 197, 214n18
as giving us objects, 3, 59, 72, 78
having (an), 30, 46, 49, 52, 85,
    95, 98, 140, 156, 157n25,
    158, 166, 236, 264
immediacy of, x, 3, 4, 14, 19, 20,
    53, 54, 56, 58, 59, 91, 122,
    146, 175, 176, 194, 231,
    231n6, 232n7, 271n18
as independent of understanding/
    thought/categories/
    concepts, 2, 4, 5, 7, 17, 21,
    22, 25, 27, 82–6, 107, 146,
    208, 218, 238
inner, 78n17, 108, 141, 151n16
justificatory role of ... in
    cognition, vi, 12,
    13, 125, 231–2

312 Index

intuition(s) (*Cont.*)

as modal constraint, xv, 67–74, 77, 172, 186–97, 253

object-dependence of, 54–60, 66, 76, 77, 192n36

object-independence of, 54, 55, 57, 66, 75

organic unity of concept and, 232n8, 246, 247, 250

outer, 78n17, 107, 110, 148n9, 151, 156, 169, 195n42, 263, 265n11, 271n18, 277

as presenting us with particulars, 9, 17, 19, 21, 218, 219

as product of sensible synthesis, 82, 84–9, 95–8, 148, 151, 154, 169

as product of the (synthesis of) imagination, xi, xiii, 18, 141, 147, 157, 215, 250

pure, 7, 82n1, 83–7, 92–6, 97n9, 106n9, 107, 109, 112, 114, 152, 158, 163, 166, 166n42, 185, 247, 251n30, 258–63, 267, 268, 272n18, 273, 277, 280

pure … of space (time), 83, 84, 86, 87, 93–7, 97n9, 106n9, 108, 112, 166n42, 258–61, 263, 265, 267, 273, 277, 280

(in)separability of … and concept, 227–55

separable contribution of … to cognition, 225, 231, 233–6, 251

singularity of, x, 3–5, 14, 16, 17, 19, 20, 59, 68, 91, 106n9, 146, 236, 250n29

spatiotemporal, 27, 29–31, 38, 45n11, 46, 247

as subject to the categories / functions of thought, xii, 22, 248, 252

synthesis as the generation of, xi, xiii, xv, 18, 40, 88, 89, 98, 152, 157, 158, 165, 184, 185, 190, 214n18, 216, 279, 280

unsynthesised, 19, 185

J

Jäsche Logic, the, 106n9, 132, 207, 208, 210–12, 215, 217, 219–21, 244n20

judgement, *passim*

aesthetic, 119, 120, 128, 134, 138n22

of taste, xvi, 118, 119n3, 119n5, 121–39, 143, 144

reflective, 119, 124, 131

justification, v, vi, 14, 61n8, 62, 63, 149, 186, 218

justified true belief, 62. *See also* belief

justifier, 13. *See also* reason

K

Kästner, A.G., 259, 266

remarks on (*see On Kästner's Treatises*)

Kenny, Anthony, 182n18

knowledge. v, x–xiii, xv, 13, 60, 62–6, 71, 78, 100, 112, 117–19, 142, 186, 187, 195, 196, 197n44, 220, 221, 226, 229, 231–7, 241n15, 244n21, 245n22, 252–4. *See also* cognition

a priori, 63, 100, 112, 187, 236

empirical, x, xii, 186, 186n26, 187, 220, 221, 252
Kreis, Guido, xiii
Kukla, Rebecca, 119

L

Land, Thomas, xiin5, xiii, xiv, xivn8, xivn9, xvi, xvii, 7, 13, 18, 18n30, 19n31, 23n38, 103n6, 145–70, 178n10, 178n11, 180n12, 183, 202, 208, 220, 250n29
La Rocca, Claudio, xiiin7
laws, 192, 196, 222, 248
a priori, 17, 191
causal, 37, 43, 49, 50, 197
natural, 71, 74, 194
necessary, 219
Laywine, Alison, 79n19
Lear, Jonathan, 50
Leibniz, Gottfried, 105, 187
Leibnizian, 104, 105, 205, 243n20, 246n24, 253
Leibnizian-Wolffian, 112
Lewis, C.I., 172n2
limitation, 84, 92, 164, 165n39, 263, 264, 284. *See also* space
of infinite space, 87, 87n3, 167, 263–5, 267, 269
logic
general, 219, 220
transcendental, 58, 219
logical functions of thought, xi, 7, 8, 107, 123, 124, 277
Longuenesse, Béatrice, 147n5, 148n8, 152n18, 159n31, 178n11, 180n12, 182n18, 186n25, 190n33, 202, 209,

252n31, 253, 253n33, 260, 260n5, 260n7, 279n24, 284n26

M

Machery, Edouard, 181n16
magnitude
continuous, 96–8, 168, 169 (*see also quanta continua*)
extensive, 40, 97, 98, 152, 155, 158n29, 168, 169
infinite, 16, 85, 93, 262, 268
intensive, 97
Makkreel, Rudolf, 119, 119–20n5, 120
manifold. *See also* combination; connection; representation
in intuition, 12, 17, 20, 23, 47, 48, 61, 74–5, 123, 148n9, 152, 153, 161, 162, 164, 166, 200–4, 206, 211, 213n16, 215, 218, 219, 229, 231, 233, 237, 241n13, 249, 278, 281, 282
running-through of, 278
mathematics, mathematical knowledge, xiv, 100, 112, 157n24, 266, 272–5
Matherne, Samantha, 6n8
McDowell, John, v–ix, xiv, 12, 12n21, 13, 21, 32, 34, 56, 57, 101n2, 102n5, 103n6, 118n1, 119, 147n5, 151n15, 160n32, 172n2, 182n18, 192n36, 205n10, 209, 224, 224n30, 224n31, 225, 229n3, 233, 235n10, 243n19, 254n35, 260n5

McLear, Colin, xiin5, xiii–xvii, 3n2, 4, 5n7, 6n8, 8, 9n11, 14n23, 15, 16, 56, 58, 64n12, 78n17, 82–7, 89, 90n5, 96, 97n9, 103n7, 103n8, 108n10, 145, 146n2, 154, 155n21, 156n22, 167, 171–97, 222, 260n5, 260n6

mediacy of concept, x, 3, 14. *See also* concept(s)

mediate. *See* concept(s); intuition(s); object

mental content, 1–4, 129, 130, 135, 141–4, 173, 224n30. *See also* content; representation

mereological, mereology, 15, 16, 40–2, 45, 82–7, 96–8, 155, 159, 167–9

mereological relation(s), 15, 16, 39–42, 49, 82–7, 96–8, 110, 150, 155, 156, 167–9, 212, 250n29

parts dependent on whole, 83–7, 96, 110, 155, 156

whole dependent on parts, 39, 41, 83–7, 97, 98, 158n29, 167

Messina, James, xiin5, xivn9, 184, 185, 185n23, 191n34, 257n1, 260n5, 262n8

Metaphysical Exposition, the. *See* space

Metaphysical Foundations of Natural Science, 68, 258

metaphysics, 11, 49, 99, 102, 104, 114, 115, 218, 266–8

mind, *passim. See also* cognitive faculties, intellect; understanding

Moore, Adrian, 53

motion, 141, 148n9, 157, 169, 188

N

Nagel, Thomas, 134

Naragon, Steve, 185n23

Natorp, Paul, 28

necessity
objective, 138n22
subjective, 38, 46, 138n22

neo-Kantianism, 28

Newton, Alexandra, xiii

Newton, Isaac, 50, 104, 105, 111

nonconceptual content, *passim*
dependent, 205, 207
essential, 57, 101, 104–13

nonconceptualism, *passim*
essential, or, absolute, 29, 101–4
Fichte and, 242
Hegel and, 242
relative, xi, xiii, 29, 31

nonconceptual mental content, xvi, 1, 2, 141, 143, 144. *See also* nonconceptual content

nonconceptual reading of intuition, 2, 232, *et passim. See also* intuition(s)

noumenal, 100, 105, 112

O

object. *See also* particular
"an object for me", 11n15, 12, 20, 209
-directed(ness), 19, 64–7, 76, 176
as mind-independent, vi, 184
as particular, 17, 19, 21, 29, 30, 32, 36, 46, 192, 201, 205, 217–20, 225, 231, 232n7
presence of, 14, 56, 76, 195, 275

relation to an, vi, ix, x, 11n15, 43,
56, 68, 91, 147, 175–7, 183,
189, 201, 216, 220n25,
231, 231n6, 232, 232n7,
238, 240, 241n15, 245
securing, ix, 68, 231, 232n7
rogue, 24, 50, 114, 221
spatiotemporal, ix, 24, 29, 30, 37,
37n6, 46, 50, 154, 185, 247
as unity of representations, 15,
43, 128, 152, 153, 216, 222
object-dependent, 54–8, 64–7, 68–71,
73, 74, 76–9, 192n36
object-independent, 54–8, 64–6,
68–70, 74–6, 78, 79
objective purport, 21, 64–7, 70, 75,
146–8, 151, 159n31, 236,
247, 248
objective validity. *See* validity
objectivity, 21, 28, 29, 43, 125, 218,
219, 234, 241n15
obscurity. *See* concept(s);
consciousness
On a Discovery, 93–5, 156n23, 275
On Kästner's Treatises, xxv, 90–2, 260,
266–71, 274, 275, 280,
284n26. *See also* Kästner,
A.G.
Onof, Christian, xii–xiv, xivn8,
xivn9, xvii, 10, 10n14,
16, 23, 24, 103n7, 145n1,
162n34, 199–226, 250,
250n29, 254n35, 257n1,
260n6, 266n12, 276n21,
282n25
ontology, ontological, 50, 139, 227
orientation (spatial), 109, 251n30
outer sense, 107, 108, 110, 196n43,
261. *See also* experience,
outer; sensibility

P

Parsons, Charles, xiv, 58n3
Patton, Lydia, xiv, 257n1, 269n13
Peacocke, Christopher, 173n4,
182n18
Pendlebury, Michael, 14n25
perception, *passim*
adult human, 51
animal, 8, 9, 30, 30n3, 34,
41, 47, 50, 108, 208,
210, 212, 222
by infants, 30n3, 108, 179,
183n21, 185n23, 222
mere, 27, 40, 45, 97, 211, 219,
249n28
sense, x, 22n37, 101, 102,
108, 121
perceptual content. *See* content;
perception
Pereboom, Derk, 57, 58, 178n11,
190n33, 192n36
Pereira, Robert, de Sá, xiii
phenomenal, 49, 50, 88–90, 92, 93,
95, 100, 107, 108, 112,
113, 117, 121, 122, 129,
134, 138, 142, 143
phenomenalism, 50
phenomenology, 28, 49, 51
Phenomenology of Spirit, 228
Physical Monadology, 105
Pippin, Robert, ix, ixn3, xiii,
xiiin7, xiv, xvii, xviii,
19n31, 103n6,
147n5, 177n10,
186n25, 224n31
on inseparability of concept
and intuition, xvii, xviii,
227–55
pleasure, displeasure, 123–5,
128–31, 133n20, 135–8

316 Index

possibility
    formal, 7, 69, 70, 72–7, 79,
        191–3, 197n44
    logical, 7, 67, 68, 176, 187, 188,
        190, 193, 209, 210
    metaphysical, 7, 187, 193
    proof of real, 71, 77, 186, 187,
        189–91, 193, 194, 196
    real, 7, 54, 67–79, 100, 186–94,
        196, 197n44, 210, 254, 255
Postulates of Empirical Thinking,
    the, 69, 190, 197n44
Prauss, Gerold, 57
presence, present. *See also* object
    of object(s), 14, 76, 195
    phenomenal, 89–95
Principles (of experience), the, 29,
    39n8, 40, 41, 43, 44, 273.
    See also Analogies, the
Prize Essay, the, 39, 190n32, 249n28
Prolegomena, the, 9, 28n1, 51,
    59, 78, 109, 110, 118,
    123n8, 156n23, 174, 231,
    249n28, 259, 271n18,
    279, 279n24, 280
psychological state(s), 174–6, 195
purposiveness, 124, 137, 138,
    141, 142

Q

quanta continua, 97, 164n39. *See also*
    continuity; magnitude
    flowing magnitude(s), 169
quantity, categories of, 39, 42, 51,
    131, 153, 158
quantum, 152
quid juris, the, 33, 37, 46, 48, 49

R

Raphson, Joseph, 90, 91
rationalism, x, xiii, 35, 187, 246n24
reason, *passim*
receptivity, vi, 33, 58, 93, 94,
    161, 165, 166n41, 230,
    231, 234, 245n22, 246,
    250, 279, 281
recognition, conceptual, 202, 203,
    206, 207, 211–17, 220,
    220n26, 221, 224, 225. *See*
    also imagination; synthesis
reference, viii, 9, 38, 46, 47, 56, 60,
    106n9, 110, 117, 122, 124,
    125, 129, 130n17, 132,
    144, 176, 181, 211, 215,
    225, 232n7, 251
representation
    clear, 221n27
    conceptual, 138, 201, 224, 260,
        263, 265, 276, 281, 283
    conscious, 280
    distinct, 61, 247
    first-order, 39, 40
    general (universal), 122, 236
    geometrical ... of space, 257–85
    immediate, 3–5, 14, 17, 19,
        20, 271n18
    intuitive, 10, 30, 48, 98, 152,
        157, 159, 177, 178,
        180, 204, 209, 220n26,
        223, 283, 285
    manifold of, xiii, 281
    mediate, 3
    mental, 3, 4, 121, 141, 174,
        180, 218, 225
    obscure (*see* concept;
        consciousness)

partial, 16, 212, 213
singular, 3–5, 14, 15, 17, 19,
  20, 91, 106n9, 117, 123,
  146, 236
of space (*see* space)
unconscious, 39
of a/the whole, 16, 82–6, 97, 98,
  150, 158n29, 168, 169n47,
  203n5, 207, 212
representational capacity, 42
representational content. *See* content
representationalism, 28, 30
Roche, Andrew, 58n3, 58n4
Rohs, Peter, xiiin7, 103n7
Russell, Bertrand, 64n12, 195

S

satisfaction, 118, 127, 130–3, 138n22
sceptic, sceptical, scepticism, xii, 38,
  41, 41n10, 42, 46, 78, 79,
  100, 223, 224
  anti-sceptical, 41, 41n10, 49
  Humean scepticism, 35, 38, 41,
    42, 78, 79 (*see also* Hume
    Problem, the)
Schafer, Karl, 62n9, 64n12, 186
Schematism, the, 203
Schlicht, Tobias, xiii, xiin7
Schulting, Dennis, xi–xiv, xin4,
  xiin6, xiiin7, xivn8, xivn9,
  9n12, 10, 10n14, 16,
  19n33, 19n34, 23, 24, 32,
  35, 48, 103n7, 114n14,
  118n1, 144n26, 145n1,
  147n7, 162n34, 204n6,
  207n11, 208, 210, 213,
  216n23, 222, 222n28,
  227–55, 257n1, 260n6,
  266n12, 276n21, 282n25

Science of Logic, 228, 229n2
Sedgwick, Sally, xiiin7, 229, 229n3,
  230, 234n9, 238, 240, 241,
  241n14, 246n24, 246n25,
  248n27
self-activity, 148n11.
  See also spontaneity
self-consciousness, 40, 46n12, 102,
  149, 150, 200, 200n2, 219,
  232n8, 240, 253. *See also*
  apperception
  (transcendental) unity of,
    232n8, 240
self-determination, 241–3,
  244n21, 253
self-positing, 244
self, the, not-self, 240–2, 244, 253
Sellars, Wilfrid, vi, 13, 57, 101n2,
  119, 147n5, 148n8,
  154n20, 172n2, 265n11
sensation, vi, xvi, 2, 3, 13, 19–21, 28,
  30, 33, 60, 61, 81, 93, 94,
  97, 109, 132, 133, 137, 155,
  160–2, 160n32, 161n33,
  173n6, 179, 180, 180n14,
  192, 211, 222, 228, 249n28,
  258, 258n2, 261, 262, 265,
  271, 278, 279n24
sense atomism, 155, 159–66
sense-data (sense-datum),
  13, 173n6, 195
Sensibilism, Sensibilist, xvii, 82,
  84–7, 172, 180, 182–4,
  186, 189, 194, 196, 197
sensibility, *passim*
  as delivering intuitions,
    19, 81, 82
  as delivering sensations, 81
Setiya, Kieran, 57n2
Shabel, Lisa, 257n1, 262n8

318   Index

singularity of intuition, 14, 16, 59, 250n29. *See also* intuition(s)

space
absolute, 105, 111
the argument from the infinite divisibility of, 96–8
concept of, xviii, 10, 84, 89, 93, 106n9, 109, 259–65, 268, 270n16, 271, 271n18, 273–6, 280, 281, 283, 284n26
construction in intuition of, xviii, 90, 158, 259–61, 263–5, 267–9, 270n14, 271, 271n18, 274, 280, 284, 284n26, 285
describing, 90, 109, 110, 148n9, 157, 169, 266–9, 271, 280, 283
determinate, xii, 146, 152–6, 158, 167–9, 185n23, 250n29, 254
determination of, 110, 264–70, 272, 275n19
egocentrally centred, orientable, 32, 46n12, 105, 108, 111
Euclidean, 104
exposition of the concept of, 261, 262, 264, 265, 274
as extensive magnitude, 97, 98, 152, 155, 168, 169
as finite spatial region, 83–7, 89, 93, 95
generation of, 152, 185, 280
geometrical-delimitative representation of, 259, 261–72, 284, 284n26
global, 104, 105, 111
as infinite, 16, 85–93, 95, 250n29, 267–71, 275

as infinite given magnitude, 16, 85, 93, 262, 268
infinitely large, 83, 90
as infinite magnitude, 16, 85, 93, 96–8, 262, 268, 269, 270n16, 275
intuitive, 269
(de)limitation(s) of, 84, 87, 164n39, 165n39, 167, 263–5, 267, 269
metaphysical, 91, 269, 269n13
metaphysical-conceptual representation of, 260, 265, 266
the Metaphysical Exposition of, xvi, 16, 82, 84, 85, 87, 89, 92, 93, 97n9, 262–4, 266, 273, 283, 284
Newton on, 104, 105, 111
as non-discursive, 142
noumenal, 111
as object, 10, 91–5, 257–9, 261, 263, 267, 268, 270, 270n16, 271, 271n17, 274, 280, 283, 285
as objectively given, 90, 91, 269–71
original acquisition of the pure intuition of, 93–5
original (pure) intuition of, 258–60, 260n5, 263–5, 267, 269–71, 269n14, 270n14, 270n16, 275, 276, 279, 280, 282, 283, 284n26, 285
original-intuitive representation of, 266
as originally given, 269, 270
parts of, 16, 42, 83–7, 87n3, 96–8, 104, 110, 153, 155, 158,

164n39, 167, 168, 261–3, 265, 267–71, 275n19
physical, 105, 106, 108, 258
as product of a priori synthesis, xi
as product of sensible synthesis, 82, 84–7, 96, 97
properties of, 105, 108, 264, 265, 267, 269, 270
pure intuition of, 7, 83–7, 93–6, 97n9, 106n9, 109, 112, 158, 166n42, 185, 258–60, 263, 267, 273, 277, 280
representation of, xvi, xviii, 10, 16, 23–5, 85, 90, 91, 97n9, 100, 106n9, 108, 109, 111–13, 146, 152–5, 165, 166, 169, 180, 184, 185, 257–62, 264–70, 272, 275–7, 279–81, 283, 284
single all-encompassing, 84, 85, 95, 97n9
space in, 267, 269
as subjectively given, 90, 91, 268–71
the Transcendental Exposition of, 263, 264, 271n18, 273, 284
transcendental representation of, 272
unicity of, 24, 250n29
uniqueness of, 84
unity of, xii, xiv, 47, 153, 154, 165, 185, 250n29, 254, 282, 283
as a whole, 15, 16, 42, 44, 83–7, 97, 97n9, 98, 110, 155, 167–9
spaces
determinate, 146, 152–6, 167, 169, 185n23, 250n29, 254
geometrical, 269, 275
space-time, 44, 50, 218, 219

Speaks, Jeff, viii, xi, 29, 181n17, 205n9
spontaneity, vi, 23, 59, 146–50, 153, 155, 156, 159, 161, 162, 167, 168, 170, 193, 213n15, 230, 234n9, 246, 250
Stalnaker, Robert, 173n5
Stang, Nicholas, 68n14, 161n33, 189n31
Stephenson, Andrew, xiiin7, xv, 5n7, 14n24, 53–79, 192n36, 192n38
Strawson, P.F., 29n2, 78n17, 172n2, 177n10, 217–19
Stufenleiter, the, 60, 61, 210, 211, 244n20, 249n28
subject, apperceptive, 221n27, 239, 243
subjective, subjectivity, 37, 38, 41, 43, 44, 46, 47, 49, 60, 89–91, 93, 94, 110, 117, 124–6, 126n13, 128–32, 134–8, 142–4, 160n32, 175, 195n42, 196, 210–12, 214, 215, 215n21, 218–23, 225, 228, 239, 241n15, 245, 249n28, 252, 254, 268–71, 271n18, 279n24
Sutherland, Daniel, 152n18, 168n45, 257n1
synopsis, 214n19, 278, 281
synthesis. *See also* combination; connection
a priori, xi, 17, 232
of apprehension, 40, 97, 153, 155, 159, 159n30, 163, 163n35, 165, 166, 202, 206, 207, 213, 213n15, 221, 247, 278

320 Index

synthesis (*Cont.*)

  categorial / categorially governed,
19, 21, 24, 38, 39, 41, 43, 48

  categories as rules for guiding,
17, 18

  conceptually governed, 15, 19, 20

  dynamical, 201

  figurative, 48, 157n26, 162,
163n36, 185

  of the (productive) imagination,
xi, xii, xiii, 18, 19, 21, 48,
156–8, 162, 163n36, 169,
170, 213, 232n8, 247,
250n29, 251 (*see also*
imagination)

  intellectual, xvi, 247

  mathematical, 201

  of recognition in a concept,
202, 203, 206, 207,
213–16, 214n20,
220n26, 224, 225

  rules of, 17–19, 178

  sensible, 18, 81–98, 146–51, 154,
169, 201, 216n22

  successive, 39, 40, 97, 98,
148, 155, 157, 157n24,
158, 168

  synthesis speciosa, 144n26,
247, 249

  the threefold, xi, 206, 214n18,
215, 216

synthetic, synthetic a priori

  connection, 11n15, 12, 16,
21, 23, 49, 82, 128, 152–4,
159, 161, 163, 163n36,
184, 200, 209, 222, 229,
232, 233, 234n9, 236, 241,
241n13, 247, 264, 265,
274, 282

telepathy, 196, 197n44.

  See also clairvoyance

Tennant, Neil, 73n15

thing in itself, 91, 110, 112,
186n26, 210, 238

Thompson, Manley, 57n2, 177n9

time, x–xii, 7, 10, 15, 16, 22–5, 42,
44, 47, 49, 50, 69, 83,
86–97, 100, 106n9, 107,
112, 137, 148, 148n9, 149,
149n11, 152, 153, 155,
157, 160n32, 162–6,
164n39, 165n40, 168,
169, 169n46, 175, 180,
184, 185, 209–11, 213,
218, 219, 250, 254, 274,
277–80. *See also* intuition(s)

  as finite temporal interval, 83, 86,
87, 89, 92, 93, 165

  as infinite given magnitude, 92

  as pure (form of) intuition, x, xi,
7, 83, 86, 87, 93, 94,
106n9, 107, 112, 162, 163,
166n42, 184, 185, 277

  temporal relation(s),
38, 39, 41, 46, 218

Tolley, Clinton, xiii, xiv, xviii, 3n2,
4n5, 6n8, 15, 24, 56, 60n7,
103n7, 145n1, 146n2,
155n21, 164n37, 175, 176,
181n17, 250n29, 257–85

Tomaszewska, Anna, xiii, 143n25

Toribio, Josefa, 204n7

Transcendental Aesthetic, the (TAe),
x, xii, xvi, xviii, 10, 15–17,
21–3, 25, 28, 47, 54, 58,
82, 94, 95, 106n9, 111,
112, 152, 153, 249, 250,

258–68, 271n18, 273, 274, 277, 278, 280–4. *See also* space

Transcendental Analytic, the, 28, 258–60, 266, 270, 273, 274, 277, 279, 284, 285

transcendental apperception. *See* apperception

Transcendental Deduction of the categories, the (TD), *passim. See also* A-Deduction; B-Deduction

the first step of, 252

the second step of, 229, 247, 249, 252, 252n32

Transcendental Dialectic, the, 65, 275n19, 284n27

Transcendental Exposition, the. *See* space

transcendental idealism. *See* idealism

truth, vi, 61n8, 64, 84, 119n3, 130, 174, 175, 177, 194

U

understanding (intellect), *passim. See also* cognitive faculty/ies

cooperation of ... and sensibility, x, xvi, 155, 232, 236, 254

"determines sensibility inwardly", 230, 234, 245, 250n29, 254

unity, *passim*

absolute, 164, 165, 278, 282

analytic, 200, 233

conceptual, 15, 16, 20n36, 136, 204, 239, 250n29

of apperception (*see* apperception)

of consciousness (*see* consciousness)

of the homogeneous manifold in intuition (*see* homogeneity)

intuitional, 15, 16, 19–21

objective, 13, 18, 128, 215n21

original, 215n21, 241n13, 247

of space (*see* space)

subjective, 214, 215

synthetic, 11n15, 12, 23, 128, 152–4, 159, 161, 163, 184, 200, 209, 222, 233, 234n9, 241, 247, 282

synthetic ... of consciousness, 12, 200, 241

universal(s), 109, 118, 125–8, 131, 132, 135, 136, 138, 195, 225, 236, 239, 240, 247, 262

universality, x, 125, 126, 126n13, 131, 132, 132n18, 132n19, 135, 136, 144

V

Vaihinger, Hans, 57

validity

objective, ix, xii, 7, 18, 22, 33, 67, 72, 74–8, 91, 107, 150, 160n32, 187, 187n28, 188, 211, 238, 239, 248, 252, 273

subjective, 91, 160n32, 211, 215n21, 249n28, 252

Van Cleve, James, 40, 50, 79n18, 181n17

Vanzo, Alberto, xiiin7, xiv

veridicality condition(s), 173, 178

W

warrant, 45, 172, 179, 186, 196

322 Index

Warren, Daniel, 57n2, 188n29
Watkins, Eric, xiiin7, 13, 56,
    187n27, 188n29
Wenzel, Christian, xiii, 103n6
*What Does it Mean to Orient Oneself
    in Thinking?*, 109, 110
whole
    representational, 83, 150,
        158n29, 169n47, 206,
        207, 212, 214, 215
    space as a, 16, 83–7, 96–8,
        110, 167, 168

spatial, 42, 84, 85, 87
spatiotemporal, 44
whole-part structure / relation.
    See mereology
Willaschek, Marcus,
    56, 57n2, 176n8
Williams, Jessica, xiii, 11n16,
    12n21, 18, 21, 103n6
Wilson, Kirk, 58n3
Winkler, Kenneth, 187n28
Wolff, Christian, 187
Wright, Crispin, 73n15

CPSIA information can be obtained
at www.ICGtesting.com
Printed in the USA
LVHW081822120519
617555LV00012B/228/P